TRANSLINGUAL GLOBALIZED APPROACHES TO THE TEACHING OF WRITING

TO MY
DEAR FRIEND
RHEA
I ♡ YOU
ALWAYS!

Juliet
Rosenman

INTERNATIONAL EXCHANGES ON THE STUDY OF WRITING

Series Editors, Terry Myers Zawacki, Magnus Gustafsson, Joan Mullin, and Federico Navarro

The International Exchanges on the Study of Writing Series publishes book-length manuscripts that address worldwide perspectives on writing, writers, teaching with writing, and scholarly writing practices, specifically those that draw on scholarship across national and disciplinary borders to challenge parochial understandings of all of the above. The series aims to examine writing activities in 21st-century contexts, particularly how they are informed by globalization, national identity, social networking, and increased cross-cultural communication and awareness. As such, the series strives to investigate how both the local and the international inform writing research and the facilitation of writing development.

The WAC Clearinghouse, Colorado State University Open Press, and University Press of Colorado are collaborating so that these books will be widely available through free digital distribution and low-cost print editions. The publishers and the series editors are committed to the principle that knowledge should freely circulate. We see the opportunities that new technologies have for further democratizing knowledge. And we see that to share the power of writing is to share the means for all to articulate their needs, interest, and learning into the great experiment of literacy.

RECENT BOOKS IN THE SERIES

Charles Bazerman, Blanca Yaneth González Pinzón, David Russell, Paul Rogers, Luis Bernardo Peña, Elizabeth Narváez, Paula Carlino, Montserrat Castelló & Mónica Tapia-Ladino (Eds.), *Knowing Writing: Writing Research across Borders* (2019)

Sylvie Plane, Charles Bazerman, Fabienne Rondelli, Christiane Donahue, Arthur N. Applebee, Catherine Boré, Paula Carlino, Martine Marquilló Larruy, Paul Rogers & David Russell (Eds.), *Research on Writing: Multiple Perspectives* (2017)

Lisa R. Arnold, Anne Nebel & Lynne Ronesi (Eds.), *Emerging Writing Research from the Middle East-North Africa Region* (2017)

Theresa Lillis, Kathy Harrington, Mary R. Lea & Sally Mitchell (Eds.), *Working with Academic Literacies: Case Studies Towards Transformative Practice* (2015)

TRANSLINGUAL DISPOSITIONS: GLOBALIZED APPROACHES TO THE TEACHING OF WRITING

Edited by Alanna Frost, Julia Kiernan, and Suzanne Blum Malley

The WAC Clearinghouse
wac.colostate.edu
Fort Collins, Colorado

University Press of Colorado
upcolorado.com
Louisville, Colorado

The WAC Clearinghouse, Fort Collins, Colorado 80523

University Press of Colorado, Louisville, Colorado 80027

ISBN 978-1-64215-043-8 (PDF) | 978-1-64215-100-8 (ePub) | 978-1-64642-103-9 (pbk.)

DOI 10.37514/INT-B.2020.0438

Produced in the United States of America

Library of Congress Cataloging-in-Publication Data

Names: Frost, Alanna, 1969– editor. | Kiernan, Julia, 1980– editor. | Blum-Malley, Suzanne, 1966- editor.
Title: Translingual dispositions : globalized approaches to the teaching of writing / edited by Alanna Frost, Julia Kiernan, Suzanne Blum-Malley.
Description: Fort Collins, Colorado : The WAC Clearinghouse ; Louisville, Colorado : University Press of Colorado, 2020. | Series: International exchanges on the study of writing | Includes bibliographical references.
Identifiers: LCCN 2020022859 (print) | LCCN 2020022860 (ebook) | ISBN 9781646421039 (paperback) | ISBN 9781642150438 (pdf) | ISBN 9781642151008 (epub)
Subjects: LCSH: English language—Rhetoric—Study and teaching (Higher) | English language—Study and teaching (Higher)—Foreign speakers. | Academic writing—Study and teaching (Higher)—Social aspects. | Translanguaging (Linguistics) | Multilingualism.
Classification: LCC PE1404 .T763 2020 (print) | LCC PE1404 (ebook) | DDC 808/.042071—dc23
LC record available at https://lccn.loc.gov/2020022859
LC ebook record available at https://lccn.loc.gov/2020022860

Copyeditor: Don Donahue
Design and Production: Mike Palmquist
Cover Photo: Mike Palmquist
Series Editors: Terry Myers Zawacki, Magnus Gustafsson, Joan Mullin, and Federico Navarro
Series Associate Editors: Ana M. Cortés Lagos, Anna S. Habib, and Matthew Overstreet

The WAC Clearinghouse supports teachers of writing across the disciplines. Hosted by Colorado State University, and supported by the Colorado State University Open Press, it brings together scholarly journals and book series as well as resources for teachers who use writing in their courses. This book is available in digital formats for free download at wac.colostate.edu.

Founded in 1965, the University Press of Colorado is a nonprofit cooperative publishing enterprise supported, in part, by Adams State University, Colorado State University, Fort Lewis College, Metropolitan State University of Denver, University of Colorado, University of Northern Colorado, University of Wyoming, Utah State University, and Western Colorado University. For more information, visit upcolorado.com.

In memory of Juheina Fakhreddine.

Contents

PART 3: TRANSLANGUAGING PRACTICES

TRANSLINGUAL DISPOSITIONS: GLOBALIZED APPROACHES TO THE TEACHING OF WRITING

Introduction

Alanna Frost
UNIVERSITY OF ALABAMA HUNTSVILLE

Julia Kiernan
KETTERING UNIVERSITY

Suzanne Blum Malley
METHODIST UNIVERSITY

[T]here is the challenge that the ideology of monolingualism inheres not merely in our discourse but in the academic and institutional structures of programs and curricula as pedagogies and placement and existing assessment technologies and daily practice.

—Horner & Tetreault, 2017, p. 7

This [translingual] disposition allows individuals to move beyond preconceived, limited notions of standardness and correctness, and it therefore facilitates interactions involving different Englishes. Considering the historical marginalization of "nonstandard" varieties and dialects of English in various social and institutional contexts, translingual dispositions are essential for all users of English in a globalized society, regardless of whether they are "native" or "nonnative" speakers of English.

—Lee & Jenks, 2016, p. 319

The construct of translanguaging has taken hold in the research and pedagogies of post-secondary writing instructors. Teachers of writing have long been troubled by the implications of promoting the Standard Written English (SWE) that is imagined to be necessary for educational advancement, global business, and educated citizenship. Forces of globalization, in general, and the global movement of multilingual students and scholars through new physical and digital spaces, in particular, have demanded that we engage in reflexive critique of the monolingual and colonial assumptions that undergird our approach to writing instruction. The capital afforded by English coupled with a desire for linguistic social justice[1] for students and teachers increas-

---

1   Writing studies as a field has been articulating the political tenets of language and languaging since the ubiquitously cited 1974 *Students' Right to their Own Language* https://secure.ncte.org/library/NCTEFiles/Groups/CCCC/NewSRTOL.pdf.

DOI: https://doi.org/10.37514/INT-B.2020.0438.1.3

ingly drives exploration of what to do with "language difference" (Horner & Tetrault, 2017) in writing classrooms.

In response to the exigencies listed above, a translingual understanding of language use clearly resonates with scholars working in English-medium writing programs. The response to the initial call for contributions to this collection was so enthusiastic that we, as editors, were able curate a second collection, *Translingual Pedagogical Perspectives: Engaging Domestic and International Students in the Composition Classroom,* focusing on describing classroom assignments informed by an understanding of translanguaging as practice. Contributors to both collections include those who have experienced the movement of U.S.-program philosophies into non-U.S. institutions, those who teach in increasingly linguistically diverse classrooms in the US, and those who appreciate that a pedagogy that approaches language difference as a deficit is not in our students' best educational interests. While use of the term translanguaging has evolved over the course of the past several years and has intersected with numerous other descriptive labels,[2] a shared, central tenet has emerged that reconceptualizes language use in terms of "fluid and dynamic practices that transcend the boundaries between named languages and other semiotic systems" (Li, 2017, p. 9). The term remains contested, but by focusing on the utility of the translanguaging construct to counter monolingual constructs, the scholars in this collection offer the results of their search for ways to open our theory and praxis to wider and more informed understandings of

---

2   It is important to acknowledge that any exploration of the impact of translingual dispositions on English-medium writing classrooms is influenced by the many scholarly understandings of linguistic negotiation of meaning that have surfaced recently across research disciplines, including a variety of naming conventions for the perspectives that challenge deeply held political, social, and cognitive beliefs about language use, including: "symbolic competence" (Kramsch & Whiteside, 2008), "superdiversity" (Arnaut, 2015; Blommaert, 2013; Rampton & Spotti, 2015), "heteroglossia" (Blackledge & Creese, 2014—via Bakhtin), "translanguaging" (Garcia & Leiva, 2014; Garcia & Wei, 2014), "translingual approach" (Horner et al., 2011), "translingual model" (Horner et al., 2011), "translingual literacy" (Canagarajah, 2013; Lu & Horner, 2007), "translingual practice; negotiated literacies" (Canagarajah, 2013); "tricotissage" (Dompmartin-Normand, 2011), "rhetorical attunement" (Lorimer Leonard, 2014), "metrolingualism" (Otsuji & Pennycook, 2015), and "lingua franca English" (Canagarajah, 2013; Firth & Wagner, 1997). This robust list of neologisms created to address our collective, and increasingly nuanced, complex, and trans, approaches to languaging is by no means comprehensive, particularly in terms of international orientations towards linguistic and social negotiation of meaning, but it serves as a reminder that we are in the early stages of theory-and-practice-building in relation to translingual dispositions toward languages and literacies.

translanguaging. Indeed, those who adhere to explorations of the possibilities for translingual dispositions in purportedly "English" institutions, embrace such dispositions as a means of ethically attending to the increasing number of global citizens requiring English-medium writing instruction in university classrooms nationally and internationally.

Contributors to this collection are invested in the multiple disciplinary perspectives and representations of language ideology that fuel considerations of the *trans-* aspects of language and languaging and in the ways in which a focus on language practices can transform the writing classroom. A focus on the social action of *trans-* further emphasizes a move away from *multi-* understandings of language and culture (e.g., multilingual, multicultural, etc.), namely the fact that the prefix *multi-* defends linguistic systems as discrete and compartmentalized. Therefore, we intentionally invited our contributors to explore their work in English-medium writing classrooms and contexts through the frame of a *translingual disposition*, which responds to the proclivity of the prefix *trans-* for characterizing language as fluid and actional across social contexts, and to the intellectual orientation(s) that such an approach to language and language practices requires.

That writing instructors adopt a translingual disposition was first suggested by Horner et al. (2011) as part of an appeal for writing instructors to employ a "disposition of openness and inquiry that people take toward language and language differences" (p. 311). Since that appeal, and in the midst of continuing research in applied linguistics, sociolinguistics, education, and writing studies, scholars have negotiated the value of translanguaging in the writing classroom and have engaged in what Li Wei (2017) describes as a "perpetual cycle of practice-theory-practice" that constructs knowledge through "descriptive adequacy" (p. 3). This descriptive cycle has allowed for a proliferation of applications of translingualism to English-medium writing classrooms, which has generated much debate and limited consensus.

In this context, the act of pulling together an entirely coherent collection of the elements of a translingual disposition is no easy task. Nor does the effort result in descriptions of shared practices that constellate around a single, united, central definition. In short, we do not yet have enough representations of the ways a translingual disposition can manifest in the myriad ways English-medium writing programs are facilitated. In the afterword to this collection, Bruce Horner takes up the dissonance created by the competing and uneven descriptions of practice attached to translanguaging, noting:

> But such dissonance is the inevitable accompaniment to another "trans" term: transition. It is both a sign of change

and a sign of the friction necessarily accompanying such change . . . A translingual disposition attuned to that dissonance is what globalized approaches to the teaching of writing may require, and afford.

To that end, this collection directly engages the need for nuanced explorations of how a translingual disposition might be facilitated in English-medium postsecondary writing classrooms and programs. As the global reach of English, with its attendant monolingual-ideologies, increases, so too does the need for range of investigation and reflection offered here.

Contributors to this collection diverge in their approaches to translanguaging in diverse classrooms, but they collectively battle the monolingual monolith that undergirds the narrative of English-medium writing classroom curricula. Further, they share their experiences of what it means to facilitate a translingual disposition, through which they strive to respect the diversity of students seeking English-medium education and the diversity of the Englishes students employ. Notably, one aspect of consensus around working with and through a translingual disposition is evident throughout the collection: that there is limited visibility of translingual processes in final written products. Contributors subscribe to Paul Matsuda's argument that: "Restricting the scope of translingual writing to the end result can obscure more subtle manifestations of the negotiation as well as situations where writers make rhetorical choices not to deviate from the dominant practices" (2014, p. 481). A translingual disposition, then, necessarily involves a writing curriculum that invites linguistic choice and fosters linguistic awareness, but also necessitates attention to students' development of a "rhetorical sensibility that reflects a critical awareness of language as contingent and emergent" (Guerra, 2016, p. 228).

Overall, chapter authors interrogate the implications of work that recognizes translanguaging in national and international, English-medium, educational settings where monolingual ideologies remain entrenched. Included are writing scholars from an array of teaching and learning contexts with a corresponding range of institutional, disciplinary, and pedagogical expectations and pressures. For example, one contributor is a multilingual, U.S.-based scholar who designed a curriculum with a Hungarian counterpart and asked students in the US and Hungary to share English-medium blog posts; while another contributor, also U.S.-based and multilingual, designed a writing group that was guided by the use of Korean-only in order to engage students to a translingual perspective through monolingual writing. Yet another multilingual scholar investigated multilingual students' experiences in an explicitly monolingual, first-year-writing course in Lebanon, while a fourth contributor, a monolingual English speaker, engaged his largely monolingual students with the literacy practices of a student who purposefully immersed herself in learning Japanese.

The collection is divided into three thematic sections. *Part I: Multilingual Students' Experiences in English-Medium Classrooms* includes chapters that offer analyses of the ways multilingual students encounter monolingual writing curricula and theorize what those encounters mean in terms of a translingual disposition. Nancy Bou Ayash (Chapter 1), Shireen Campbell, Rebeca Fernandez, and Kyosung Koo (Chapter 2), Lilian Mina and Tony Cimasko (Chapter 3), and Yuki Kang (Chapter 4) productively illuminate the curriculum of programs that we think of as familiar, those which deal in the teaching of academic writing to multilingual student populations, but whose tacit and entrenched monolingual English policies and practices clearly problematize considerations of any translingual pedagogical choices. Each of these chapters carefully investigates the possibilities of translingual pedagogy through analyses of participants' experiences, perceptions, and texts.

Further, the studies in this section—one chapter is situated in Lebanon, with the remainder situated in the US—consider students' in-and-out-of-school languaging experiences as implicated in classroom outcomes. For Bou Ayash, this means framing her study of three students' classroom writing experiences with a clear description of the linguistically diverse socio-political climate of Lebanon and the national language policy landscape. Both Chapter 2, authored by Campbell, Fernandez, and Koo, as well as Chapter 3, authored by Mina and Cimasko, pay similar attention to students' language experiences, but in these U.S.-based studies, the terms of students' expectations for the English-medium classrooms are the central foci rather than their out of school literacy practices. Campbell, Fernandez, and Koo use participants' voices and experiences to explore how multilingual student needs and desires can complicate monolithic applications of translingual approaches. Their data demonstrates that while participants showed significant improvement in clarity and accuracy, and increased confidence as writers, they also reported a loss or atrophying of L1 skills and slight discomfort with the perceived rigidity of disciplinary expectations and practices. Mina and Cimasko similarly report on a study of international student experiences and expectations in an English as a Second Language (ESL) composition program. Their explication of student experiences and expectations speaks to the ways the enactment of a translingualism disposition can challenge socially constructed norms and expectations of ESL writing programs that uphold SWE conventions. In Chapter Four, Kang explores her students' experiences in a "single language writing group," in which students explore academic English production through their Korean home-language. Kang demonstrates how this learning environment empowers and enables students to not only draw upon multiple languages, but to challenge the ubiquity of immersive language philosophies

Part II: Investigations of Deliberately Translingual Pedagogy includes chapters that describe pedagogical practices that explore students' rich, varied, and complex communicative practices. These chapters focus on the exigencies for pedagogy and program design, dependent on the "translingual character of their [students] uses of language" (Roozen, Chapter 6, this collection); thus, chapter authors Thomas Lavelle and Maria Ågren (Chapter 5), Kevin Roozen (Chapter 6), Marylou Gramm (Chapter 7), and Santosh Khadka (Chapter 8) describe pedagogical practice crafted for students' immersed in literacies which clearly evince a translingual disposition.

Thomas Lavelle and Maria Ågren describe a Swedish graduate course, created to meet the English-production needs of thesis-writing students, and designed to attend to those students' multilingual realities. As they assert, their pedagogical decisions, importantly entail

> commitments to a de-essentialized conception of language and languages (i.e., it foregrounds language as performance and backgrounds language as system), to a recognition that this performative representation of language, like all others, operates ideologically, and finally to an acknowledgment of individual language users' strong individual agency in carrying out this performance.

Kevin Roozen (Chapter 6) describes a pedagogy that asks students to map their literate activities and reveals that translingual activity is the purview of both mono- and multilingual speakers. Focusing on one writer's literate mappings—her engagement with language and culture across a variety of textual activities and borders—enables Roozen to make transparent how translingual literacies continually re-use languages, images, texts, and textual practices across literate engagements. Roozen argues that for teachers especially, such engagements with linguistic mapping is crucial for understanding the richly literate lives their students lead both in and out of school. Marylou Gramm (Chapter 7) establishes the importance of conferencing in encouraging a translingual disposition in the writing process. Specifically, Gramm describes strategies of the translingual student-teacher conference as a means of facilitating her ESL students' exploitation of rich grammatical deviations that engender innovative ideas. Santosh Khadka (Chapter 8) similarly engages with translingualism via a multiliteracies approach, presenting findings from a qualitative study that examines how diverse students in a sophomore level writing class at a large U.S. research university responded to a curriculum and pedagogical approach framed around multiliterate development.

Part III: Translanguaging Practices includes chapters that examine the affordances of a translingual disposition in graduate classrooms, in online classrooms, in writing centers, and for transnational scholars. Central to this section is the awareness that translingualism and translanguaging practices are not confined to undergraduate, traditional, US-based classroom work—despite the fact that this is where much of the current research happens, due to the prevalence of freshman composition both nationally and internationally—and that, for growing populations of students and faculty, this research is developing as the norm across all levels of academic communicative practice. Zsuzanna Palmer (Chapter 9), Rula Baalbaki, Juheina Fakhreddine, Malaki Khoury, and Souha Riman (Chapter 10), Sarah Summers (Chapter 11), and Ligia Mihut (Chapter 12) engage the translanguaging reality of linguistic diversity and report on student and public texts produced in these environments.

Zsuzsanna Palmer (Chapter 9) presents an analysis of textual and multimodal representations of both monolingual ideology and translingual practice observed in an online blog writing project between U.S. and Hungarian students. Palmer finds that employing a cosmopolitan approach, one that asks for respect of diverse cultures and languages, offered the students in this program a productive means of practicing a translingual disposition. Rula Baalbaki, Juheina Fakhreddine, Malaki Khoury, and Souha Riman (Chapter 10) offer the results of their investigation of the texts students produce when invited to translate literature, written in their first languages, for the "English" papers they write in their composition class. Their findings suggest that multilingual students who are encouraged to analyze writing in multiple languages are better able to negotiate meanings, more skilled at constructing knowledge, and capable of producing meaningful connections in writing across language and cultural differences.

Sarah Summers (Chapter 11) focuses her study on a two under-represented aspects of translingual research: graduate students and graduate writing centers. Using transcripts of graduate writing center (GWC) tutorials with multilingual graduate writers Summers describes tutoring experiences as being pulled between two poles: the need to help navigate academic writing and the desire to help challenge linguistic norms. Of specific interest in Summers' work is the way she characterizes translingual principles as tied to patience, respect, and inquiry, as well as how tutoring based within these principles is often focused on confidence building. Finally, Ligia Mihut (Chapter 12) reports on an understudied population in translingual writing scholarship: transnational, multilingual scholars. Using the frame of linguistic justice, which she explains "offers students discursive frames and critical knowledge to understand and develop local, translocal, and intercultural communication" (Chapter 12, this collection), Mihut critically examines the politics of language difference performed in the public texts of nine transnational, multilingual writing scholars. Mihut's chapter is especially telling as much of the current work being accomplished by both U.S. and international writing scholars is (as this collection illustrates) intimately connected to their own linguistic identities. Consequently, this chapter illustrates that in order to garner a comprehensive understanding of the nuances of a translingual disposition there is an inherent need to examine the influences and pedagogical approaches of transnational, multilingual scholars because these scholars are able to shape pedagogies of language difference in a particular way.

Overall, the work of these chapters offers readers cases of translingual dispositions that do the following: (1) consider both the personal, pedagogical, and institutional challenges associated with the adoption of a translingual disposition; and (2) interrogate academic translingual practices in both U.S. and international English-medium settings. What we gain from these considerations is an increasing weight of scholarship focused on challenging the assumptions of monolingual education, which are able to describe a wide range of approaches to fostering a translingual disposition in writing classrooms. As such, this collection contributes to the "descriptive adequacy" (Wei, 2017, p. 3) necessary to continue to deepen our understanding of languaging in the writing classroom.

References

Guerra, J. C. (2016). Cultivating a rhetorical sensibility in the translingual writing classroom. *College English, 78*(3), 228–233.

Horner, B., Lu, M. Z., Royster, J. J. & Trimbur, J. (2011). Opinion: Language difference in writing: toward a translingual approach. *College English, 73*(3), 303–321.

Horner, B. & Tetreault, L. (2017). "Introduction." *Crossing divides: Exploring translingual writing pedagogies and programs* (pp. 3–16). Utah State University Press.

Lee, J. W. & Jenks, C. (2016). Doing translingual dispositions. *College Composition and Communication, 68*(2), 317–344.

Matsuda, P. (2014). The lure of translingual writing. *PMLA. 129*(3), 478–483.

Wei, L. (2017). Translanguaging as a practical theory of language. *Applied Linguistics, 39*(1), 1–23.

Part 1: Multilingual Students' Experiences in English-Medium Classrooms

1 Developing Translingual Language Representations: Implications for Writing Pedagogy

Nancy Bou Ayash
UNIVERSITY OF WASHINGTON

This chapter explores how three FYW students in Beirut, Lebanon reconcile perduring institutional monolingual and conventional multilingual ideologies and representations of language guiding academic writing instruction and curriculum design, on one hand, with their personal translingual orientation toward fluidly moving across multiple language and semiotic resources in various academic situations on another hand. Drawing on interview and textual data, this study demonstrates that the conflicting nature of such institutional and non-institutional language representations complicate student participants' abilities to capitalize on their translingual academic literacies at all times. As I demonstrate in this chapter, participants in this study are forced to come to terms with coexisting yet competing monolingual, multilingual, and translingual ideological orientations and representations of language and language relations in literacy education. With an eye toward these participants' felt tensions in their workings with language in academic literacies, I argue that our current and future disciplinary efforts to imagine the design and principles of translingual writing pedagogies require attention not only to writers' immediate language and meaning-making practices but also their representations of these, which play an influential role in complicating, often hindering, their paths toward sustained translingual academic literacies.

Keywords: Translingualism; monolingualism; multilingualism; language representations; language-ideological tensions; academic literacies

A translingual orientation with a social practice-based conceptualization of language(s) and literacy/ies is beginning to gain prominence in U.S. college composition studies. This orientation was first put forward in relation to the global enterprise of English language teaching by critical applied linguist Alastair Pennycook (2008b), was taken up and applied to mainstream writing instruction in Horner et al.'s (2011) *College English* opinion statement, and has been further extended in both Suresh Canagarajah's (2013a, 2013b) monograph and edited collection. An incipient translingual approach, which this collection builds on and develops, contests a dominant monolingual English-only ideology, which propagates problematic representations and treatments of language as stable, internally uniform, and having status outside and beyond the cultural, political, economic, and ideological forces that bring about its practice. As Canagarajah (2013b) argues, viewing language along traditional monolingual lines as a "self-standing product," pre-existing its performances, and isolated from other vibrant semiotic resources—cultural icons, visuals, typographic designs, etc.—"distorts meaning-making practices" and disrupts their "ecological embeddedness and interconnection" (p. 7). Central to this translingual rethinking of language is a move away from a long-standing monolingualist tradition of constructing language, specifically the standard variety, as a clearly demarcated and tightly sealed system to be used, taught, and learned only in its own presence and in isolation from the bodies, identities, contexts, power relations, and histories which have shaped and reshaped it and continue to do so. Stretching the limits of such myopic views of language, a translingual orientation to language foregrounds the mutable, performed, and emergent nature of language and insists on the agency of its users and learners.

In its ongoing critique of hegemonic ideology of monolingualism, a translingual language ideology has also cast suspicion on the ways in which language(s) and language relations have been described and treated under forms of conventional multilingualism[1] proposed as alternatives to the homogenizing effects of monolingualism. Though multilingual orientations to language and language use have some degree of distance from monolingualist views of language, they do not automatically carry critical or altering potential in so far as they project a quantitative rather than a qualitative understanding of language and its diversity. Despite accounting for and promoting the actual heterogeneity and hybridity of languages, particularly English(es), this sense of multilingualism reproduces precisely the same monolingual epistemolog-

---

[1]   This notion of multilingualism conflicts with what Horner & Lu (2007) in earlier work term as "multilingual" approaches to language difference in student writing, Canagarajah (2006) refers to as a "multilingual rhetorical orientation," and Horner et al. (2011) call "translingual multilingualism."

ical framework of language it seeks to disrupt and escape. That is to say, conventional multilingualism still sustains residual monolingualist assumptions about language and language relations through approaching the wide array of learners' language resources as separate, uniform, and autonomous entities, that can be possessed, named, classified, and counted (along with their users'/learners' social identity), hence becoming at best "little more than a pluralization" of monolingualism (Pennycook, 2010, p. 132).

Alongside a growing translingual-affiliated movement in language and literacy scholarship,[2] a monolingual mindset with its disguised multilingual variation still persists to this day and largely prevails in writing instruction in the U.S. and elsewhere (Horner & Trimbur, 2002; Horner & Lu, 2007) despite its emergence from the context of eighteenth century European-based thinking about language (Canagarajah, 2013b, pp. 19–20; Yildiz, 2012, pp. 6–7), and its failure to attend to drastic changes in the sociocultural realities and linguistic constellations of the twenty-first century. As I demonstrate in this chapter, student participants in the geographic location of Lebanon and the specific institution I study here are caught in a tug-of-war between these coexisting yet competing ideological orientations and representations of language and language relations in literacy education: the "mono-," the "multi-," and the "trans." With an eye toward these participants' felt tensions in their workings with language in academic literacies, I argue that our current and future disciplinary efforts to imagine the design and principles of translingual writing pedagogies require attention not only to writers' immediate language and meaning-making practices but also the descriptive and analytical terms in which they think and talk about these practices, i.e., the language representations that complicate, and often hinder, their paths toward sustained translingual academic literacies.

My own scholarly interest in vexed issues of language difference in writing, translingual literacies, and language ideologies in literacy education—issues which lie at the heart of explorations in this chapter and other contributions to this collection—has grown out of a sense of personal and professional responsibility. Being a U.S.-based scholar who enjoys membership in Lebanese society and who continuously writes, teaches, and researches within and across colloquial Lebanese Arabic, Modern Standard Arabic, English, and French affords me a strong sense of the need for the field of writing studies

---

2   To name a few in critical applied linguistics (Canagarajah, 2013a, 2013b; Hawkins & Mori, 2018; Kramsch, 2006; Makoni & Pennycook, 2007; Pennycook 2005, 2008a, 2008b, 2010); new literacy studies (Ellis et al., 2007; Leung & Street, 2012); and writing studies (Bawarshi et al., 2016; Fraiberg et al., 2017).

to productively cross borders of language, nation, and culture, a growing need that this chapter as well as the entire collection aims to address. Like my student participants, given the effectuality of monolingualism in global academic knowledge production, consumption, and reception, I am constantly grappling with the simultaneity of fluidity and fixity in language use and I am forced to continually weigh the risks and rewards of the kinds of language choices and negotiations I deliberately make in my own writing and scholarly practices. These ongoing felt tensions, which can have detrimental material effects on various language and literacy laborers, myself included, are a powerful reminder that this chapter's overarching theme of language negotiations amid complex and conflicting ideological orientations and representational practices deserves more of our scholarly and pedagogical attention.

Tensions between "Mono-," "Multi-," and "Trans-" Lingual Ideologies and Representations in Lebanon

The particular case of Lebanon I present in this chapter brings to light complex language-ideological tensions in a linguistically and culturally diverse context, one which is ostensibly more conducive to a translingual orientation to language endorsed in national language policy and sociolinguistic landscapes, but that is simultaneously pervaded with monolingualist representations in educational landscapes. Boasting strong ties to other Arab countries and its ex-colonizer, France, while still participating in the worldwide globalization movement, Lebanon has witnessed the vibrant spread of Arabic, English, and French. In fact, popular views of the normalcy and indispensability of this linguistic mélange circulate in Lebanese society, and the fluidity and dexterity of language users in daily interactions is widely accepted and expected. The country's iconic greeting of Hi, Kifak? Ça va?, in which all three language resources are meshed together, is illustrative of such engagement with translingual language practices in Lebanese sociolinguistic landscapes.[3] As I have discussed elsewhere, this "mixed-and matched" greeting is a strong

---

3   This collection deliberately chooses to not follow APA guidelines that require "foreign words" be italicized. Traditionally, this APA practice marks words that may be unfamiliar to readers; however, as this collection is seated in ideologies of a translingual disposition, which value linguistic difference as the norm, we feel this practice of italicizing counters the spirit of translingualism. By choosing not to italicize, this collection works to recognize writers' agentive and productive communicative resources across languages as equally important, and not as a point of difference marked by font. Translingual practice serves to recognize speakers agentive and productive communicative resources as equally important.

marker of its users' "Lebaneseness" and playfulness, demonstrating owner-ship of and agency over daily language resources and practices and valued socio-cultural meanings that the English-only greeting "Hi," Arabic-only "Kifak?," or French-only "Ça va?," separately fail to reflect (Bou Ayash, 2013, p. 98). It is, therefore, safe to say that my student participants encounter and experience a translingual understanding and treatment of language and lan-guage diversity as a lived sociolinguistic reality in Lebanon outside of school (see also Baalbaki, Fakhreddine, Khoury & Riman, this collection).

Acknowledging the use value of these language resources in lived realities, the state has strengthened existing linguistic attachments and affiliations in Lebanese culture through advocating Arabic-English-French trilingualism in national language and educational policies[4] (Bou Ayash, 2015, pp. 119–120). This has given rise to two dominant types of private and public schools: English-medium schools where English is the main medium of instruction for major subject areas (e.g., Mathematics, Natural Sciences, Philosophy, Computer Literacy, etc.) from primary through secondary education and French is formally taught starting from lower primary levels; and French-medium schools, where French is the language of instruction and English is first introduced as a foreign language in grades one to four. Both types of schools offer classes in Arabic language and/or literature and teach social studies in the native Arabic language.[5]

Though part of this culture, where language heterogeneity is clearly the statistical societal norm, the Anglophone university under study is typical for its tacit English-only policy, which has ultimately influenced the writ-ing program where the key to successful language and literacy learning is perfect mastery of Standard Written English (SWE) rules and conventions, and utilization of diverse language resources is generally not tolerated. The first-year writing (FYW) classroom has become a site of complex ideological stances and negotiations where teachers in this particular locale (as in many other parts of the world) are increasingly forced into an unenviable position of maneuvering the mismatch between translingual language representations and practices in students' lived realities, on one hand, and institutionalized monolingualist representations of language and language practices in academic

---

4   See Bou Ayash (2015) for a more detailed analysis of past and contemporary language-in-education policies and practices in Lebanon.

5   This is not to dismiss salient differences in the way public and private school systems are structured in the country and in the availability of qualified teachers and instructional materials and resources, which could either facilitate or hinder effective instruction in the mother tongue or both foreign languages.

literacy situations on the other. Though not the main focus of this chapter, a brief description of the prevailing pedagogy of the FYW program is central to a nuanced understanding of the representations of language and language difference in writing, which my student participants are regularly subjected to and, thus, might be maintaining, reproducing, or tinkering with in their academic written work (for more details, see Bou Ayash, 2016).

Semi-structured interviews I conducted with my participants' writing teachers afforded a closer look into some of the local pedagogical decisions taken in response to the inescapable ideological conditions and tensions within which they and their students live and work. For example, one group of teachers I interviewed echoed strong positions toward the stability and immunity of SWE in the face of dynamic translingual language practices that circulate widely in Lebanese sociolinguistic landscapes. A monolingualist ideology manifested itself in their writing instruction through an obsession with native-like attainment of SWE as a fortified, reified entity unto itself, attendant with belief in the inherent power of opening up economic and academic opportunities once accessed and mastered fluently. Voicing adherence to an idealized native-English speaker norm, one writing teacher characterized good quality student writing as "something a native speaker can understand." Such an ideological position—which projects practices with language as an abstract, fixed set of pre-given norms and rules, the internalization of which is deemed responsible and sufficient for well-formed language production and its regularity—is justified by references to the commodification of English and the varying instrumental and symbolic values attached to its high-level proficiency by the global linguistic market. As one teacher put it, "you need to have your good language skills to make it."

Under such writing pedagogies guided by a monolingual mode of understanding language and language practices, any traces of socio-linguistically legitimate language practices that deviate from the rules and conventions of SWE are relegated to the status of incompetency, error, and linguistic deficiency and are treated as grave problems to be fixed and wholly obliterated. This pedagogical practice of conveniently refusing to tolerate "nonstandard or broken English" in student writing, as another teacher explained, is a pragmatic choice reflective of the kind of ostensibly strict gatekeeping that "they're [students] going to face in the outside business world unless the world changes."

Unsure about how to properly handle and respond to language differences in student writing, another group of writing teachers felt torn between preparing students for the universal SWE demands and conventions of academic literacy and allowing students to maintain and develop the creativity and authenticity that their diverse language practices and resources in their repertoires granted them. These teachers chose to create textual spaces for alternative language practices though FYW instruction and curriculum design. These more responsive pedagogies, adopted by a handful of writing teachers, encouraged students to discuss the fluid, hybrid character of English usage evident in assigned readings authored by writers identified with particular sociocultural identities, but prohibited student use of similarly diverse language resources in their own writings. Affiliated with a conventional multilingual take on language, these writing pedagogies, which merely incorporate code-meshed reading texts into their curricula, end up increasing the number of languages and language practices explored in the writing classroom while still maintaining a monolingualist view of the superiority and appropriateness of SWE in all communicative situations and its putative immunity toward any interactive influx with other languages and language practices.

Within such friction-laden teaching and learning conditions, the representations of language and language learning that my FYW student participants carried with them in their daily personal, civic, and academic work and lives were not unitary or homogeneous. The micro- and macro- contexts of their literate lives extensively shaped—in ways of which they had been unaware—how they thought about, conceived, and represented the nature of language, their relation to it, and ultimately their use of language. We will witness in the following sections, how these language representations fluctuated and interacted with the divergent ideas about and treatments of language they were exposed to in their immediate family environments, the academic institution they attended, and the larger society in which they lived.

Studying Language Representations

The data reported in this chapter emerged from transcripts of semi-structured interviews with forty-one participants and sessions of focused "talk around texts" with eight participants chosen through a process of theoretical sampling. Unlike statistical sampling, which is aimed toward achieving a representative sample, theoretical sampling is a complex technique adopted in grounded theory studies to further refine and develop core categories, their properties, and the interrelationships that might occur in the evolving theory (for a full description, see Charmaz, 2006; Clarke, 2005). The one- to two-hour long interviews addressed participants' language and literacy history and current practices through prompting them to share memories and experiences of language and literacy learning at home and at school. "Talk around texts" is a key methodological tool adopted and further extended in various academic literacy/ies studies (see in particular Ivanič, 1998; Lillis, 2009; Lillis & Curry, 2010; Martin-Jones et al., 2009) to generate discussion between the researcher and participant about wide-ranging contextual and text-focused issues. In this study, my focus was on establishing what was significant about student participants' representations of language use and language difference in their academic writing from their own analytic lens and in relation to the specificity of their sociocultural and historical writing trajectories. Such writer-centered talk invited an exploration of participants' representations of their varied relations with English and other language resources rooted in their "take" on material locality and the specific experiences, investments, affiliations, and allegiances they brought into acts of reading and writing.

I analyzed data transcripts following the principles and procedures of constructionist grounded theory (Charmaz, 2006; Clarke, 2005). After establishing some firm analytic directions through my initial word-by-word, line-by-line, and segment-by-segment coding, I began separating, sorting, and synthesizing data through more focused coding such as, "investing (materially and/or psychologically) in English as a pre-given commodity," "taking linguistic action against English-only imperatives," "laboring with translation," "grappling with foreign language source-use practices," etc. I specifically chose gerunds with material process codes to capture a sense of fluidity and flow in my participants' ongoing "doing" of and with English specifically, and language more generally, and in their individual and/or collective thinking that shapes such doing. As I aimed toward an investigation of participants' representations in connections with specific contexts of language use and learning, I supplemented basic grounded theory practices of coding and successive memoing with situation-centered maps (see Clarke, 2005), which offered insights into how such representations were shaped by wider cultural and ideological structures of the teaching and learning of writing.

Negotiating Conflicting Language Representations

The present chapter presents three brief accounts of FYW students from Lebanon as they attempt to reconcile in their academic work the influence of monolingual representations and treatments of language with a translingual understanding of language, which offers them the opportunity to use the fluidity and porousness of language in ways they perceive as most valuable to their personal, professional, and intellectual development. For the purposes of this chapter, I selected these three participants, identified in this chapter by their chosen pseudonyms, because they best illuminate how competing institutional and non-institutional language representations complicate students' abilities to capitalize on their translingual academic literacies. As such they serve as telling cases foregrounding how the language representations that FYW students are exposed to and bring with them to their academic literacies work are inherently multiple and contradictory. I specifically showcase below the stories of participants that best accentuate the experience and practice of negotiating conflicting language representations in the FYW classroom: Naser, who echoed dominant monolingual and residual multilingual representations, which idealize English as a monolithic, hermetic system, ultimately put English first, thereby experiencing familiar ambivalence and frustration from imposed English-only imperatives guiding writing instruction; and Diva and KAPPA whose non-institutionalized translingual representations of English—as indelibly involving and tied to complex relations of hybridity, heterogeneity, and translation—allowed them to destabilize and reconfigure dominant language relations in their academic literacies work in sharp contrast with dominant monolingual English-only demands, which impeded their ability to fully and confidently exercise their writerly agency.

Language(s) as Fortress(es)

A sophomore graphic design student, Naser described a home-life immersed in advanced Arabic academic literacies, thanks to his father, a professor of Arabic language and literature. As his father piqued his interest in developing his Arabic language abilities, Naser started viewing academic writing as "a reflection of the self and others, the discovery of meaning and value." While Naser was passionate about writing in Arabic and viewed it as a means for developing and maintaining meaningful and authentic relations "not only with the self but the rest of the world," he hid this passion in the English writing classroom, where he felt compelled to blindly abide by SWE rules and practices, and thereby "separate and isolate" his personal voice and expressiveness. As Naser asserted, "through English, we can't go back to my previous definition of writing as autobiography, reflection, creativity, and authenticity." Influenced by a dominant monolingual valuation of native-like correctness and efficiency in the reproduction of standardized usages and conventions, Naser explained that language use in the academic English writing classroom resembled a fixed "set of skills we have to learn for the use of it."

What disappointed Naser the most was that he found no room for his growing Arabic linguistic and literary expertise in the FYW classroom, which he considered critical not only to his sense of self but also his professional aspirations. When working in his discipline, Naser was constantly encouraged to weave his expertise in Arabic calligraphy and typography into various projects, such as designing book covers and working with packaging and label designs for new products. He was particularly fond of two projects where his Graphic Design professor created spaces for students to mobilize their expertise in various languages and modalities. Combining his growing disciplinary knowledge of graphic communication arts and design with his Arabic expertise, Naser composed in Arabic a travel narrative describing through watercolor drawings his adventures in the cityscapes of Beirut, and an autobiography about his experiences in the department, which juxtaposed Arabic text with minimalist black and white images.

Presented with opportunities to imagine and experience the dynamics and fluidities of languages and modalities in disciplinary literacies, Naser was able to treat language (and modality) as malleable, involving and requiring design for aesthetic effects, and thereby enact the situated practice of meshing linguistic and graphic resources in disciplinary discourse to his own advantage. The kind of reading and writing that Nasser experienced in Graphic Design in ways that were productively networked across his home, university, and future work life sharply contrasted with his view of the static and fixed character of language use in his English writing course. His experiences in the FYW classroom, tainted by an illusion of linguistic rigidity and fortification, have led to his construction of English as a "narrow space" that isolated meaningful and authentic aspects of his relation to self, others, and the world. Institutionalized monolingual representations of English as a pre-given, autonomous, and immobile entity in Naser's FYW classroom counter his developing view of and engagement with the actual fluidity and flow of his linguistic and graphic resources in his discipline. While Naser realized that the available resources and practices in his repertoire could and did serve as avenues for originality and active meaning-making in Graphic Design, he was unable to make the same connections on his own and purposefully call on and cultivate these resources in his academic literacy practices, the way the next two participants, Diva and KAPPA, did.

Seeing both language and graphic design as unique forms of "communication arts," Naser lamented that instead of placing premium on making "creative," "catchy," and strategic choices in getting a particular message across to diverse audiences "in any language you prefer," his English teachers constantly emphasized the need to "follow the restrictions and right things to say in English." Because he and some of his classmates are constantly "exploring the world through Arabic," the only solution Naser is able to imagine for his dilemma of constantly writing about complex local issues, like "violence against women," "that don't happen in English" only in Lebanese society is through adding Arabic to "complement" existing instruction in English writing. Echoing "multi-"lingual representations of languages and language relations, he sees the act of simply granting students their language rights by introducing languages other than English into written work as in and of itself carrying liberatory power. However, he doesn't realize that under such a view, languages, in this case Arabic and English, are still perceived in monolingualist terms, as monolithic, fixed, enumerable, and identifiable possessions of literate individuals, or, as Pennycook aptly puts it, "language fortresses," stripped of any interaction with each other and the world (2008a, p. 38). With FYW pedagogy not affording him the same facilitating contextual possibilities for developing favorable representations as the responsive learning environment in Graphic Design, Naser does not consider the possibility of reworking both Arabic and English, with agency, to achieve specific ends and does not recognize the inevitability of leakage and traffic across seemingly tightened linguistic boundaries in each occasion of reading and writing.

Language(s) as Hybridity

Born and raised in Greece, Diva, a freshman Business student, views English as the link that glues her linguistically and culturally diverse family members together. The Greek language gives Diva a sense of uniqueness and "privacy" with her sister and Greek-speaking mother, which English alone cannot give as "almost everyone nowadays knows English." Representing "the Arab" side in her, Arabic strongly attaches Diva to her Lebanese father, her relatives, and her new circle of friends and acquaintances in her current home in Beirut.

Acknowledging the dynamic and evolving character of English in the social and educational domains of her life, Diva rejects monolingualist representations that reinforce the very "*one-ness* of English" (Pennycook, 2010, p. 80; emphasis added) as a neutral global commodity with a stable core that can be stripped of any local cultural influences. Instead, she affirms its flexibility, hybridity, and rootedness in changing local ecologies. As Diva explains, "our English is different from the English that other universities in other countries in the world teach. We have different ideas, we come from different worlds, we live in different language worlds."

Unlike Naser who views the language resources he has at his disposal as discrete, closely guarded fortresses immune to external intrusions, Diva describes how she sees and treats the full multiplicity of her language resources in her communicative repertoire as constantly and inevitably intertwined and co-dependent for her meaning-making even in the FYW classroom: "I cannot communicate in English only. Nor can I communicate in Greek and Arabic alone . . . Right now, I live, think, and write in all: Greek,

Arabic and English." Representing her language resources as feeding into and out of each other, Diva utilizes them as such in her writings. More specifically, she manages to deliberately shift and intervene with English-only norms by actively seeking to engage in a form of translingual practice, in this case code-meshing, in her academic written work, though at her own peril.

In a short reflection assignment for her FYW class asking her to explore the connections between her linguistic and cultural identity, Diva adopts a transformative negotiation strategy of what Canagarajah describes as "resisting [SWE conventions and expectations] from within" (2013b, p. 113) through demonstrating fluent mastery of SWE norms while simultaneously embedding code-meshing practices in her text for voice and agency: "I could feel detached, ma ile jledit hada, kai den thelo na kano tipota. For I don't want to do anything." As she introduces non-English codes into the rest of her text in SWE, Diva deliberately provides rhetorical cues to assist her non-Arabic and non-Greek speaking readers. Showing signs of actively accommodating her readers' lack of knowledge of Arabic or Greek and assisting their co-construction of meaning, Diva makes sure that her English text, "For I don't want to do anything," serves as a loose translation of the transliterated Lebanese Arabic phrase ma ile jledit hada (ام يلا ةدالج ادح) "I'm not in the mood for anything" and the transliterated Greek phrase kai den thelo na kano tipota (και δεν θελω να κανω τιποτα) "I don't want to do anything."

Embracing the plurality and hybridity of language and claiming ownership over her language use in literate institutionalized contexts, Diva succeeds in finding ways to nimbly work between the cracks of English-only imperatives by creating spaces for her personal voice in low-stakes writing genres. A tacit policy of English-only dominating academic writing pedagogies and practices, according to Diva, is clearly at odds with the heterogeneity of her and her classmates' linguistic realities and lived experiences:

> It's really important to write in this style. We shouldn't be limited by what we should say and how we should say it. We're in an American university but it's all based in Lebanon. yi'ni [the fact is that] we've based our knowledge in Arabic. This is how we live; in both languages, English *and* Arabic (emphasis in transcript).

While Diva seems quite adamant about the legitimacy and meaningfulness of her and her classmates' diverse translingual literacy practices, she also realizes that the stakes are high, since such counterhegemonic practices have not entirely gained favorable academic uptake in formal literate situations and genres. While she was more prepared to mobilize and personally get behind her language resources in the descriptive-type essay she composed early on in the semester, Diva felt there was no more room for individual negotiation and maneuver when working on her end of the course research paper assignment as in her mind, English-only, author-evacuated prose was a defining feature of successful argumentative writing. Forced to negotiate her translingual representations of the porous and constructed nature of language with the dominant monolingualist assumptions of language fixity guiding curricular and pedagogical designs in her FYW course, Diva's engagement with translingual literacy practices were largely shaped by the possibilities and constraints of the writing environment. Consequently, she felt compelled to isolate, disqualify, suppress, and mask her language resources when composing her final research paper on anti-domestic violence laws in Lebanon, which constituted a large percentage of her final course grade, using SWE wholesale. As she explained, "I'm doing this for my grade," so "there's no room for taking risks" anymore.

Language(s) as Translation

Prior to residing in his mother's native country, Lebanon, to pursue a degree in Landscape Design, KAPPA lived his whole life in his father's hometown Trieste, a prosperous seaport in northeastern Italy, where he started studying Law. Besides his fluency in the local Triestine dialect and his working knowledge of colloquial Lebanese Arabic, KAPPA takes great pride in his ability to "analyze and understand the various works of renowned authors" in Latin, Italian, English, and French.

KAPPA sees his English academic work in the FYW classroom as always in relation to the rich tapestry of these language resources in his repertoire, which he has come to call his "modo di dire" or his unique "way of saying" things, thereby going against dominant English-only imperatives and the negation of students' meaningful engagements with the actual complexity and dynamism of language(s). As KAPPA explains, "I feel my English writing is enclosed in rigid structures and sometimes it's nice to break the structure through this modo di dire." In illustrating how and why he actively draws on and mobilizes his modo di dire, KAPPA describes how translating and incorporating various primary and secondary Italian academic sources into his English writing across the university has become a sustained meaning-making practice.

Viewing his modo di dire as critical not only to his identity and sociocultural conditions but also the advancement of his academic literacies, KAPPA rejects common monolingualist assumptions that language difference in writing is a hindrance to successful language and literacy learning and development: "I can't accuse this *modo di dire* of being a problem in my writing. I cannot blame it." Despite the daunting and time-consuming task of translating foreign texts across different linguistic, cultural, and ideological worlds, KAPPA argues that this intellectually challenging process makes him "feel original and authentic" and "enriches" the complexity and depth of his writing and argumentation.

KAPPA's path toward translingual academic literacies, however, is not completely without tension. In preparation for his research paper assignment, KAPPA used several academic and popular Italian sources to aid in his close examination of the Mafia's linguistic and behavioral codes both within and outside the complex principle of silence and secrecy, known as Omertà. Uncovering some of the uncertainties and messiness involved in strategically selecting, reading, interpreting, and translating passages and selections from these foreign sources for his research paper and much of his other writing assignments and projects, KAPPA voiced several concerns about his lack of training in responsibly working with non-English texts in his FYW classroom, where it is a given that, as KAPPA puts it, "all sources have to be in English." As he grappled with the process of translating various Italian academic sources, he moved beyond questions of whether particular words or phrases in Italian had literal equivalents in English to broader rhetorical concerns about readability and reader response. Kappa showed concern that his teacher's and classmates' lack of knowledge of Italian might "disrupt the rhythm and reading flow" and that they might decide to skip non-English excerpts. "I am not sure if it's okay to include sentences in Italian in my English writing," and "How do I work with these sources properly?" were among some of the anxieties he echoed. The fact that KAPPA felt unguided and unprepared to pursue his dynamic and evolving engagement with cross-language relations in his academic written work and that he felt he could not do so confidently and comfortably demonstrates the degree to which a global monolingualist valuation of English-only academic knowledge production had placed powerful constraints on his sustained relationship with English, as a language always dependent on translation for the dynamic construction of meaning.

Moving Toward Translingual Language Representations in Writing Pedagogy

Dominant monolingual and residual multilingual ideologies of languages as segregated, countable, and impermeable entities and the metalanguages used to talk about and describe them, as Makoni and Pennycook (2007) remind us, are all social, cultural, and political "inventions" and abstractions, but their direct material effects on literate individuals in various subject positionalities and subsequently on their concrete language labor are "very real" (also see Calvet, 2006). The case of Lebanon is of particular interest here in bringing to light the ongoing effects of complex ideological tensions in a linguistically and culturally diverse context ostensibly more conducive to a translingual orientation to language endorsed in national language policy and socio-linguistic landscapes, but pervaded with monolingualist representations in educational landscapes. Together, these three portraits of participants' experiences of negotiating conflicting language ideologies and representations in academic writing point toward these students' shared concerns that insistence on English-only instruction does not allow them to sustain and expand complex relations with diverse language resources critical to their language and literacy learning experiences both within and outside the FYW classroom. For instance, monolingual ideologies stand as barriers to Naser's need to learn English in a way that enables him to mobilize and mesh his advanced Arabic literacy and graphic resources; to Diva's hope for pedagogical opportunities to continuously rework English in light of the specificity of her critical cultural and language resources; and to KAPPA's need for more guidance in effectively incorporating and referencing non-English medium scholarly texts in order to maximize the kind of intellectual profundity that pursuing cross-language relations might grant his academic written work.

In his ecological theory of language and language relations in the world, Calvet (2006) argues that "our representations determine our practices" (p. 3) and have an influence on the way we come to particular language accommodations and negotiations in various communicative situations, but are also "capable of modifying them" significantly (p. 131). In this sense, these writers' mediation between the translingual representations experienced in sociolinguistic landscapes and officially inscribed in national language policy and the monolingualist representations of the academy and its institutions is shaped by the nature of their language representations. Most prominently, guided by their views of the mobility, multiplicity, and hybridity of language, both Diva and KAPPA deliberately destabilize and reconfigure dominant language relations under restrictive writing pedagogies, sometimes at their personal risk. Contrastingly, weighed down by the representations of language and language resources as uniform, isolatable, and identifiable entities reinforced and propagated by FYW pedagogy, Naser is not able to entertain possibilities of bringing his language and semiotic resources into being as hybrid and plural the way he does in Graphic Design.

In a multiple-case study investigating changes in first-year college student's representations of English learning, Peng (2011) argues that language representations are responsive to pedagogical affordances, which can either facilitating favorable representations and perceptions or hinder their development. Writing pedagogy can indeed be one possible site for critically intervening in the kind of local tensions at the level of language representations that my chapter brings to light. While our first-year writing pedagogies most often contribute to the construction of language representations as discrete, bounded, enumerable objects having presence outside and beyond the local ecologies of their practice, they can at the same time challenge, considerably transform, and reconstruct such mythical representations. Interestingly, the pedagogical opportunities Naser's Graphic Design professors offered for mobilizing his linguistic and semiotic resources, for example, gave rise to the emergence of translingual representations of language as heterogeneous and multimodal and treatments of his language resources as meaningful and accessible in academic contexts, thereby serving to fuel his affirmative thinking about his language and graphic abilities and agency in the creation of meaning in his discipline.

As accounts from Lebanon demonstrate, there is a need to revise and rethink the ideas and images our students have about language and language relations in their academic written work. We cannot continue propagating myths about the nature of languages in our own pedagogical practices as existing in and of themselves in separation from our students' localities and from each other; instead, we need to provide plenty of opportunities for all students to start seeing and experiencing language generally, and English particularly, as "reinvented, renewed and transformed" (Calvet, 2006, p. 7) in all literate interactions and communications. We need to start "teaching with the flow," movement, and fluidity (Pennycook, 2005, p. 39) of language, semiotic, and cultural resources in the FYW classroom in order to develop more dynamic relations among these resources for all our students' translingual participation in the continued fashioning and refashioning of these, their identities, and ultimately their social futures. In doing so, however, we need to keep in mind that it is an intellectual slippage to assume that a translingual orientation toward language operates under the principle that merely requiring or requesting students to utilize languages other than English is sufficient (Pennycook, 2008a).[6] In fact, without attending to the particular ways

---

6   It is worth pointing out here that the same logic also applies to orientations toward multiple modes and modalities (see Horner, Selfe & Lockridge, 2016; Pennycook, 2007).

of conceiving language and language relations at the core of the problem, we run the danger of unintentionally reproducing the same representations of language territorialization, fortification, and singularity that we are seeking to challenge and rewrite.

Rather than forcing students to search for back-door ways to counter monolingualist English-only representations and sidestep the restrictions these place on students' practices, the way Diva and KAPPA do, tensions between local representations and treatments of language need to be made available for ongoing scrutiny in every reading and writing situations. One way forward would be to open up marginalized, concealed, or forgotten layers of difference and boundary transgression with a focus on translation across and within languages in all its complexities, possibilities, and challenges. Renewing and reinvigorating students' attention to the fuzzy and constructed character of language and its boundaries that they constantly witness and experience in local, translocal, and transnational sociolinguistic landscapes entails making translation a "fundamental player" in our writing pedagogies not only when working with different languages as traditionally perceived but also with the same language against asymmetrical relations of difference and power (Pennycook, 2008a). Far more progress can be made if we and our students took more seriously the productive messiness inherent in the constant and inevitable practices of translating and (re)creating language(s), oneself, and one's written texts. It is precisely the kind of critical explorations I initiated with students like Naser, Diva, and KAPPA in order to unpack the complexity and contestation of their language representations and subsequent practices that are a necessary first step for our pedagogies to serve as avenues for harnessing and developing translingual language representations guided by favorable dispositions of deliberative inquiry, intellectual curiosity, dialogue, and openness to difference and friction.

It is my hope that the recommendations I offer here are not viewed as prescriptions for a specific set of unified and stabilized practices with language as traditionally valued under a monolingual paradigm or even quick fixes to a life-long pursuit of developing translingual representations in educational landscapes. Instead, they constitute what Martin-Jones et al. (2009) call "warrantable understandings" that might conceivably spark more critical pedagogical reflections and inventions requiring the co-collaboration and co-learning of all those laboring across language and cultural difference, i.e., writing students, teachers, administrators, and scholars alike. This is not to suggest that changing local understandings and subsequent doings of language is a simple task or that I can claim to have the final say on how to best do so, but that we can start by first taking representations of language and language relations more seriously in our continued understandings of translingualism and, second, by introducing changes into our current and existing institutional representational practices in increments in ways that are within the scope of our own power and material conditions. If we are to imagine new ways of challenging and reinventing the dominant ways in which language has been construed and pursued in our scholarship, teacher-training and professional development programs, classrooms, and societies, it is necessary to start by exploring our as well as our students' local knowledge about language, the kind of knowledge which underpins institutional, programmatic, and individual policies, pedagogies, and practices.

References

Bou Ayash, N. (2013). Hi-*ein*, Hi نيو or نيو Hi? Translingual practices from Lebanon and mainstream literacy education. In S. Canagarajah (Ed.), *Literacy as translingual practice: Between communities and classrooms* (pp. 96–103). Routledge.

Bou Ayash, N. (2015). (Re-)situating translingual work for writing program administration in cross-national and cross-language perspectives from Lebanon and Singapore. In D. Martins (Ed.), *Transnational writing program administration* (pp. 226–242). Utah State University Press.

Bou Ayash, N. (2016). Conditions of (im)possibility: Postmonolingual language representations in academic literacies. *College English, 78*(6), 555–577.

Calvet, L. J. (2006). *Towards an ecology of world languages*. Polity.

Canagarajah, S. (2006). Toward a writing pedagogy of shuttling between languages: Learning from multilingual writers. *College English, 68*(6), 589–604.

Canagarajah, S. (Ed.). (2013a). *Literacy as translingual practice: Between communities and classrooms*. Routledge.

Canagarajah, S. (2013b). *Translingual practice: Global Englishes and cosmopolitan relations*. Routledge.

Charmaz, K. (2006). *Constructing grounded theory: A practical guide through qualitative analysis*. Sage.

Clarke, A. (2005). *Situational analysis: Grounded theory after the postmodern turn*. Sage.

Ellis, V., Fox, C. & Street, B. V. (Eds.). (2007). *Rethinking English in schools: Towards a new and constructive stage*. Continuum.

Fraiberg, S., Wang, X. & You, X. (2017). *Inventing the world grant university: Chinese international students' mobilities, literacies & identities*. Utah State.

Hawkins, M. R. & Mori, J. (2018). Considering 'trans-' perspectives in language theories and practices [Special Issue]. *Applied Linguistics, 39*(1), 1–8.

Horner, B. & Lu, M. (2007). Resisting monolingualism in 'English': Reading and writing the politics of language. In V. Ellis, C. Fox & B. V. Street (Eds.), *Rethinking English in schools: A new and constructive stage* (pp. 141–57). Continuum.

Horner, B., Lu, M., Royster, J. & Trimbur, J. (2011). Language difference: Toward a translingual approach. *College English, 73*(3), 299–317.

Horner, B., NeCamp, S. & Donahue C. (2011) Toward a multilingual composition scholarship: From English only to a translingual norm. *College Composition and Communication, 63*(2), 269–300.

Horner, B, Selfe, C. & Lockridge, T. (2016). "Translinguality, transmodality, and difference: Exploring dispositions and change in language and learning." *Enculturation Intermezzo, 01.* http://intermezzo.enculturation.net/01/ttd-horner-selfe-lockridge/index.htm.

Horner, B. & Trimbur, J. (2002). English only and U.S. college composition. *College Composition and Communication, 53*(4), 594–630.

Ivanič, Roz. (1998). *Writing and identity: The discoursal construction of identity in academic writing.* John Benjamins.

Kramsch, C. (2006). The traffic in meaning. *Asia Pacific Journal of Education, 26*(1), 99–104.

Lillis, T. M. (2009). Bringing writers' voices to writing research: Talk around texts. In A. Carter, T. M. Lillis & S. Parkin (Eds.) *Why writing matters: Issues of access and identity in writing research and pedagogy* (pp. 169–189). John Benjamins.

Lillis, T. M. & Curry, M. J. (2010). *Academic writing in a global context: The politics and practices of publishing in English.* Routledge.

Lu, M. & Horner, B. (2013). Translingual literacy, language difference, and matters of agency. *College English, 75*(6), 586–611.

Makoni, S. & Pennycook, A. (Eds.) (2007). *Disinventing and reconstituting languages.* Buffalo University Press.

Martin-Jones, M., Barton, D., Edwards, R., Ivanic, R., Fowler, Z., Hughes, B., . . . & Smith, J. (2009). *Improving learning in college: Rethinking literacies across the curriculum.* Routledge.

Peng, J.-E. (2011). Changes in language learning beliefs during a transition to tertiary study. *System, 39*(3), 314–324.

Pennycook, A. (2005). Teaching with the flow: Fixity and fluidity in education. *Asia Pacific Journal of Education, 25*(1), 29–43.

Pennycook, A. (2007). *Global Englishes and transcultural flows.* Routledge.

Pennycook, A. (2008a). English as a language always in translation. *European Journal of English Studies, 12*(1), 33–47.

Pennycook, A. (2008b). Translingual English. *Australian Review of Applied Linguistics, 31*(3), 30.1–30.9.

Pennycook, A. (2010). *Language as a local practice.* Routledge.

Yildiz, Y. (2012). *Beyond the mother tongue: The postmonolingual condition.* Fordham University Press.

2 Artifacts and their Agents: Translingual Perspectives on Composing Processes and Outputs

Shireen Campbell
DAVIDSON COLLEGE

Rebeca Fernandez
DAVIDSON COLLEGE

Kyosung Koo
UNIVERSITY OF TEXAS AT SAN ANTONIO

This chapter describes a longitudinal study of nine Chinese international students. Drawing on writing samples and interview data, we sought to understand how their writing changed over time as well as how they perceived these changes at the end of their junior year. Over six semesters, English L2 writers learned to navigate and succeed in disciplinary contexts characterized by both hegemonic and negotiated pedagogies. Analysis of their writing reveals statistically significant improvement in clarity and accuracy. During interviews, participants attributed their growth as writers to the self-confidence they gained with increased familiarity of disciplinary practices and strategic use of campus resources. They did not report, however, feeling discouraged or disempowered by what some believed to be a reduction of their L1 skills or the perceived rigidity of disciplinary expectations and practices. Driven to excel academically and as writers, they learned to use writing resources strategically and gained control of their writing processes. The study suggests that context as well as L2 student priorities and desires complicate any monolithic application of translingual approaches.

Keywords: translingual approaches, agency, accuracy, clarity, syntactic complexity, L2 writing, longitudinal research

Over the past two decades, changing student demographics in higher education in the United States have increased pressure on institutions to support multilingual student learners. Such is the case at our traditional liberal arts institution,

DOI: https://doi.org/10.37514/INT-B.2020.0438.2.02

which has experienced changes in enrollment, specifically, shifting countries of origin for international students. Previous college efforts to address language needs of students learning English as an additional language (EAL) through special sections of first-year writing met resistance from international students, who, like other multilinguals (Ortmeier-Hooper, 2008; Matsuda & Silva, 1999), were concerned about the rigor and stigma of a separate course. In response, the college discontinued offering any separate EAL sections and instituted a mainstreaming model in 2007 in which all students select from and enroll in first-year writing courses with varied topics, taught by faculty across disciplines. When they desire support, multilingual students can meet with their professors, schedule peer tutoring in the Writing Center, and/or opt to work with the campus language specialist, whose services are available to any student seeking individualized writing instruction. In general, this range of student services is primarily exploited by international multilingual students. Although domestic multilingual students comprise a small but growing population, they rarely identify as such or seek out writing support beyond peer tutoring.

Shifting to a mainstreaming model, accompanied by an institutional increase in enrollment of Chinese international students, exacerbated faculty anxiety about working with writers whose first language is not English. Situated at a highly selective institution that privileges academic standard written English (SWE), many faculty did not have experience with non-English-dominant academic writers or, for that matter, a translingual disposition that respects the multiple linguistic traditions and repertoires of students and empowers them to draw on these resources (Bailey, 2012; Canagarajah, 2006, 2011; Garcia, 2009; Horner et al., 2011; Lape, 2013; Matsuda et al., 2003; Olson, 2013). With our positions situated in whole or part in the campus Center for Teaching and Learning (the umbrella organization that supports both faculty and students), we set out to facilitate what Horner refers to as "a post-monolingual condition," in this collection, through research on best practices to support our growing multilingual population and diversely trained colleagues. However, given that the extant writing research on international and multilingual students at U.S. colleges has primarily focused on EAL classrooms at large, cosmopolitan universities, we could not find sufficient models that resonated in the context of our small, highly selective liberal arts college.

Recognizing the complexities of language learning and use, as well as writing development, we were eager to promote a translingual disposition when working with such students. L2 as well as translingual scholars continue to explore how to create conditions in which students can resist static linguistic norms and to provide examples of these practices in action (Atkinson et al., 2015; Blau & Hall, 2002; Bruce & Rafoth, 2009; Garcia, 2009; Grimm, 1999; Lape, 2013; Lu &

Horner, 2013; Olson, 2013). At the same time, wholesale adoption of translingual approaches without considering how local conditions and experience impact the affordances—the *possibilities*—of translanguaging could be problematic. After all, affordances may be false (seemingly possible but not really possible) or hidden to the student actor, which can lead to misunderstanding and challenge (Gaver, 1991). For us, clarifying best pedagogic practices required study of how one particular group of students translanguage, drawing on linguistic features and modes of more than one language, throughout college as well as how they experience and describe the linguistic complexities and contexts they negotiate.

In this chapter, we report on the results of a longitudinal study of nine students who have finished three full years of college and have declared majors (as well as double majors or minors in some cases). We include writing samples and interview data from all students, including four who were studying at universities in Great Britain during their junior year. Our study is unique for its length, its focus on an under-studied population—top-tier Chinese international students attending a highly-selective and writing-intensive liberal arts college—and our analysis of writing samples produced in classes from multiple disciplines. In addition to common performance descriptors (accuracy, syntactic complexity) in second-language writing, our analysis includes another key variable—clarity—that our experiences suggest matters more to faculty than superficial correctness. Further, participant interviews provide insights on student experience and highlight the imperative to work with individuals and honor their agency.

We excluded domestic multilingual students and native English speakers, not out of lack of interest, but because Chinese international students were a relatively new and under-researched student population at the time. We were attracted to notions of translinguality and translingual dispositions; however, we also needed to develop evidence-based instructional approaches, grounded in L2 writing research (Leki et al., 2008) and our students' unique characteristics in order to prepare them to navigate the writing demands of our specific institutional and political context. Research at large, urban universities in the United States or within heteroglossic communities in nations such as India, Sri Lanka, and Lebanon elsewhere in this collection did not resonate because of the small size of our non-English-dominant population and the stridently monoglossic ideologies of our region (Banes et al., 2016).

Yet beyond our specific population and institution, our research may reveal the affordances of a translingual orientation (Canagarajah, 2013) within traditional institutions and societal contexts with deeply entrenched monoglossic language ideologies, which "[value] only monolingualism, [ignore] bilingualism," and "[see] language as an autonomous skill that functions independently from the context in which it is used" (Garcia & Torres-Guevara, 2010, p. 182). In such settings, students and faculty are more likely to resist efforts at normalizing linguistic heterogeneity (Matsuda, 2006) for philosophical or practical reasons (whether real or imagined), including perceptions that translanguaging may indicate "incomplete mastery" of SWE (Ray, 2015, p. 88) and/or adversely impact students' long-term economic prospects (Neeley, 2012).

Researcher Positionality

Similar to our institution's students, we have divergent linguistic and educational backgrounds. An English L1 speaker with a doctorate in Modern Literature and Rhetoric and Composition, Shireen founded the campus Writing Center in 1995, rotates as director with a colleague, and works closely with the first-year writing program. Rebeca holds a doctorate in Language and Literacy, teaches first-year writing and second language acquisition courses, and currently provides individualized writing support to multilingual students at our college. A generation 1.5 speaker of English, her formal Spanish language education ended in third grade when she and her family immigrated to the United States. Kyosung is an L2 speaker of English with a doctorate in Second Language Acquisition and, during the project, managedthe implementation of technologies for instructional use on our campus. He began studying English in middle school and moved to the US from Korea to attend graduate school.

Research Methodology

Student-centered, longitudinal studies have a robust history in composition (Carroll, 2002; Herrington & Curtis, 2000; Sternglass, 1997), with recent research including large numbers of students, varied types of data collection and methodology (Fishman et al., 2005; Sommers, 2004, 2008). Despite acknowledging great variability in writing processes and products between subjects, most longitudinal studies in composition have a majority of English L1 participants and a relatively monolingual focus. Limited longitudinal research has been conducted on L2 writing development in immersive higher educational environments among adult learners of intermediate or higher proficiency. In such studies, a range of performance descriptors of L2 writing proficiency have been applied to student writing samples collected before, during, and after either a specific course or length of time (e.g., Larsen-Freeman, 2006; Tsang & Wong, 2000). Few studies have explored L2 writing development for longer than a semester (Yang & Sun, 2015). Also, unlike studies reported in the translingual literature, none of the L2 studies cited above focused on authentic student texts in specific institutional contexts (Donahue, 2013).

Aiming to understand the relevance of translingual theory and practice in light of students' products and experiences, we opted for a mixed methods approach. Mixed methods research can provide opportunities for representation and legitimation (Onwuegbuzie & Teddlie, 2003). Through the process of triangulating student products, background information, and self-reports, we sought to represent the students' subjective as well as measurable (potentially more generalizable) aspects of our students' college writing experience.

The following questions guided our inquiry:

1. How does the writing of Chinese multilingual students develop in a mainstream English L2 context with respect to linguistic accuracy, syntactic complexity, and clarity?
2. Does pre-college achievement as measured by tests (SAT, TOEFL) predict any aspect of writing development in college for L2 students?
3. What factors mediate student writing development for English L2 students? Specifically, what strategies do L2 students rely on and how do these evolve over time?
4. What evidence of translanguaging do student writing products and self-reports provide for? What role does the L1 and/or its culturally-specific writing norms exert on students' development and confidence as writers in an L2?

Participants and their Educational Context

Our small liberal arts college is located in suburban countryside several miles north of a thriving financial hub in the Southeastern United States. Ranked tenth among liberal arts colleges and with an acceptance rate hovering around 20 percent, it was described as "most selective" by U.S. News and World Report. International students at the college, less than 9 percent of the student population, have all the same curricular options as the general student population. Chinese international students comprised 28 percent of the international student population and 6.8 percent of the total student body at the time of writing (2016–2017 school year).

In the past five academic years, we have invited all first-year Chinese international students to participate in our study. Each year, a majority (75 percent or more) have participated. This chapter focuses on the progress of our first research cohort, the graduating class of 2016, at the end of their junior year. These nine students represent 75 percent of the Chinese international students in the class of 2016 and the educational backgrounds and disciplinary interests typical of this population at our college, as shown in Table 2.1.

Table 2.1. Participant backgrounds and fields of study

Pseudonym	Major and minor (if any)	English exposure in high school
Karina	Political Science major	Chinese national high school plus one year in U.S. high school
Helen	Economics major	Chinese national high school plus one year in U.S. high school
Kyle	Mathematics and Chemistry major	Chinese national high school; one English as a Foreign Language class per year
Li	Math major Economics minor	Chinese national high school; one English as a Foreign Language class per year
Camile	Chemistry major	Chinese national high school; one English as a Foreign Language class per year
Tan	Philosophy major Communication Studies minor	Chinese high school plus one year in U.S. high school
Celia	Economics major Math minor	Chinese national high school; one English as a Foreign Language class per year
Victor	Math and Economics major	Chinese foreign language school, more than one English course per year
Hogan	History major	Chinese national high school; one English as a Foreign Language class per year

Although a few participants completed some high school as exchange students in the United States, all of them, ostensibly, are products of China's national education system and its English language curriculum. Most began studying English either in elementary or middle school and continued to do so in high school either as a subject or in a foreign language school, where they received additional coursework. We consider them advanced L2 writers because of their years of English language study, and TOEFL iBT scores, which range from 100 to 108 (average =105); similarly, their verbal SAT scores range from 530 to 730 (average = 630).

Data Collection Procedures

From their freshman through junior year, the cohort of international students submitted an untutored writing sample from courses they took each academic term. If students were not required to write papers in a given term, we accepted other extended writings such as special project proposals or internship applications. In collecting samples of student work from both classroom and non-classroom contexts, we aimed to capture both the varied topics, genres, and disciplines in which student wrote and the strategies whereby they negotiated their identities in the writing process.

For our qualitative data, we conducted and audio-recorded oral interviews with the students, some face-to-face and others via Skype, after the conclusion of their junior year. Our interview protocol consisted of 18 questions, shown in the appendix, derived from theoretical notions about translanguaging (Canagarajah, 2013) and previous scholarship on writing self-concept, development and strategies of English as a Second Language students (Ching, 2002; Martinez et al., 2011; Mastan & Maarof, 2014; Usher & Pajares, 2008; Zimmerman & Pons, 1986;).

Quantitative Analysis

In the section that follows, we define the performance descriptors of L2 writing proficiency studied and the specific tools we used to measure them.

Linguistic accuracy

We recognized that examining accuracy (i.e., grammatical errors) in student work reflects a conventional monolingual approach to L2 writing efficacy. In our study, we also wanted to build on, rather than cast aside, L2 research (Atkinson et al., 2015). In L2 research and practice, accuracy is a common, albeit controversial measure of L2 writing development. In this study, we measured linguistic accuracy by counting grammatical errors per clause (Bardovi-Harlig & Bofman, 1989; Fischer, 1984; Storch 2005, 2009). Concluding in an earlier research phase (Campbell et al., 2013) that the process of both counting and assigning grammatical categories to errors produced results too disparate (Polio, 1997) to be pedagogically useful, we focused solely on counting errors. We read the papers and identified errors independently, only re-examining results if they differed by more than 20% between readers, and recorded the final counts on ATLAS.Ti by entering them as a summary variable on a spreadsheet that would ultimately be imported to SPSS for statistical analysis.

Complexity

Another common performance descriptor, syntactic complexity, may be measured to evaluate L2 development (Ortega, 2003). Syntactic complexity can be measured by length of production unit, amount of coordination, and sentence complexity (Lu, 2011, 2015; Ortega, 2003; Wolfe-Quintero et al., 1998). We measured sentence complexity according to the number of clauses per sentence, as computed in Version 3.3.1 of L2 Syntactic Complexity Analyzer (2014) developed by Xiafei Lu at Penn State University. This computational system automatically analyzes syntactic complexity in written English (Lu, 2010). We hypothesized that, with greater exposure to English and more writing opportunities, both accuracy and complexity would increase between freshman and junior year.

Clarity

One atypical discourse-analytic marker included in our study is clarity. Because conversations with faculty, tutorials with students, and analysis of feedback on student writing revealed that a lack of comprehensibility—not grammatical error or even concerns about intercultural rhetoric (Kaplan, 1966)—most impeded perceptions of efficacy in student writing, we decided to evaluate this aspect of student prose. Our use of "clarity" and measurement therefore differs from both traditional and contemporary uses. Traditionally, writing handbooks and style guides cite awkward shifts in tense, voice, and sentence syntax as well as repetitive or inexact word choice (in other words, usage practices) as impediments to clarity. We reject this definition, as scholars in rhetoric and composition (Barnard, 2010; Crowley, 2006) have done, on account of its culturally-embedded prescriptions on academic style and register (Kreuter, 2013). In our research, we define clarity simply as a textual site of communication breakdown, a sentence in a paper that, without authorial input, we could not understand—even with speculation. Further, instead of designing our examination of clarity issues as studies have approached grammatical accuracy, assuming a uniform standard and expecting high interrater reliability, we expected that our subjective relationships to the text and the English language would impact our findings.

We read the 54 student papers for sentence-level problems with clarity independently first and, afterward, deliberated until we reached consensus. In sociolinguistic and translingual terms, these conversations involved negotiation for meaning between readers of different language and disciplinary backgrounds and the texts of our multilingual Chinese writers. Our final results were recorded in ATLAS.Ti software version 7.5.2 and subjected to quantitative analysis in SPSS version.

Quantitative Analysis

We evaluated whether the difference in mean accuracy, complexity, and clarity scores in the 54 papers collected over six semesters from our nine students were statistically significant by conducting a single group one-way repeated measures analysis of variance (ANOVA). In order to measure the strength and direction of the linear relationships between accuracy, complexity, and clarity, we calculated Pearson's Correlation coefficient.

All interviews were transcribed and subsequently analyzed through an iterative process of independent coding and group norming. We first read and assigned categories to random transcript samples independently and then submitted these preliminary categories to the group for further refinement. We met again to deliberate about categories before concluding our second round of individual transcript analyses (Hruschka et. al., 2004). For this chapter, we examined the relationship between our categories and translingual theory, as well as in view of our quantitative data.

Results

Development of Accuracy, Clarity, and Complexity

We compared the likelihood of grammatical error per clause (accuracy score) over six semesters. As shown in Table 2.2, the one-way ANOVA yielded a significance value of .032 ($p < .05$) with a sphericity level of .106 ($p = .106$).

Table 2.2. Descriptive statistics and ANOVA on mean accuracy scores

Semester	Mean	Standard Deviation	One-way Repeated ANOVA
1	76.59	32.29	$F(5,40) = 2.739, p = .032$
2	66.28	25.12	
3	54.19	20.71	Test of Sphericity $p = .106$
4	68.13	39.62	
5	47.37	23.60	
6	38.40	.56	

Overall, accuracy scores decreased significantly over six semesters. The mean difference also shows linear relationships, or a steady decrease in grammatical errors, from semester one through semester six, with the exception of an increase between semester three and semester four as shown in Figure 2.1. After pairwise comparison through a post-hoc test, no pairs of semesters emerged as significantly different.

For syntactic complexity, we compared the mean number of clauses per sentence over six semesters as shown in Table 2.3.

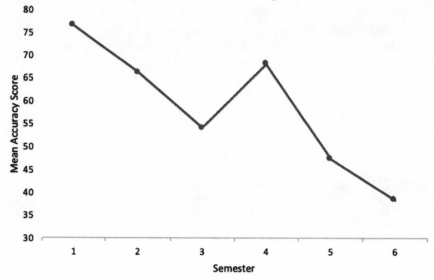

Figure 2.1. Chart for Mean Accuracy Scores over the Six Semesters.

Table 2.3. Descriptive statistics and ANOVA on syntactic complexity

Semester	Mean	Standard Deviation	One-way Repeated ANOVA
1	1.94	.266	F(5,40) = 1.645, p = .171
2	1.92	.16	
3	1.78	.18	Test of Sphericity p = .024
4	1.64	.26	
5	2.05	.38	Greenhouse-Geisser
6	2.01	.67	F(1.917, 15.338) = 1.645, p = .226

The one-way repeated ANOVA test reported in Table 2.3 produced a significance value (p) of .171 with a sphericity level of .024. However, there was no overall significance between means at different semesters (p = .226). We can, therefore, conclude that syntactic complexity did not increase significantly over six semesters. As Ferris (2003) and Ortega (2003) have noted, substantial changes in syntactic complexity for L2 writers require at least a year of post-secondary instruction. Even after three years, syntactic complexity might not increase significantly; however, these English L2 students succeed in a traditional monolingualist environment, suggesting, as others (Crossley & McNamara, 2014) have noted, that syntactic complexity is only one way of assessing sophistication in writing.

Finally, in comparing the likelihood for clarity issues per sentence (clarity score) over six semesters, the one-way repeated ANOVA and the tests of within-subject effects yielded a significance of .002 as shown in Table 2.4. After testing for sphericity (p = .011), we used a correcting factor, Greenhouse-Geisser, which was significant (p = .011). The means decreased from semester one through semester six with the exception of an increase between semester three and four (see Figure 2.2). In other words, as students wrote across time, problems that interfered with reader comprehension texts decreased. Noticeably, standard deviation scores decreased drastically in semesters five and six compared to previous semesters.

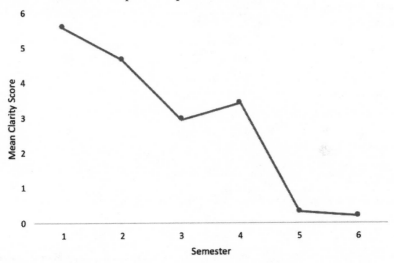

Figure 2.2. Chart for the mean clarity scores over the six semesters.

Table 2.4. Descriptive statistics and ANOVA on mean clarity scores

Semester	Mean	Standard Deviation	One-way Repeated ANOVA
1	5.57	4.33	$F_{(5,40)} = 4.787$, p = .002
2	4.65	4.39	
3	2.95	2.96	Test of Sphericity p = .003
4	3.41	4.24	
5	.31	.63	Greenhouse-Geisser
6	.19	.56	$F_{(2.859, 22.874)} = 4.787$, p = .011

Overall, results show that clarity problems decreased significantly, suggesting that communication breakdowns in student writing, as judged by readers from different language and disciplinary backgrounds, decreased over the six semesters. Specifically, problems with clarity decreased every semester with the exception of the fourth semester—typically, the spring of their sophomore year—when our students are pressed to declare their majors and commonly encounter both increasingly challenging disciplinary content and specific practices for communication. Their struggles in this semester may have manifested in decreased writing clarity, reflecting the predictably uneven development of "novice" writers (Sommers, 2008, p. 158) facing greater and shifting cognitive and rhetorical demands.

Although accuracy and clarity improved while syntactic complexity did not at the level of means across semesters, correlation analyses revealed relationships between the three sets of results: accuracy-clarity, syntactic complexity-clarity, and accuracy-syntactic complexity. Accuracy and clarity were strongly positively correlated (Pearson Correlation = .708), with significance at the .034 level. In other words, as errors in grammar diminish, so do problems with clarity.

In contrast, accuracy and complexity were negatively correlated (Pearson Correlation = -.956; p = .000), suggesting that students made fewer grammatical errors when they produced more syntactically complex sentences. Although research (Biber et al., 2011; Ortega, 2003; Wolfe-Quintero et al., 1998) challenges the assumption that L2 writers will produce more clauses at higher levels of language proficiency, our findings suggest that when advanced L2 writers in English *do* increase their number of clauses, a stronger command of SWE grammar may allow these to manage them successfully.

Influence of pre-existing factors (SAT and TOEFL Scores)

An analysis of students' SAT scores-accuracy, students' SAT scores-syntactic complexity, and students' SAT scores-clarity, revealed no correlation between pre-existing student performance on standardized tests and college writing performance. Expecting SAT scores to correspond to first-semester college performance (Mattern et al., 2012), we further explored whether there was a negative linear relationship between the two sets of scores of the first semester and SAT scores.

Table 2.5. Pearson Correlation for first semester's accuracy scores and SAT Scores

		SAT
First Semester Clarity	Pearson Correlation	-.686
	Significance	.0419
First Semester Accuracy	Pearson Correlation	-.696
	Significance	.0379

Table 2.5 shows that students with higher SAT scores produced texts with fewer clarity and grammar problems in the first semester. Beyond the first semester, however, there was no correlation.

Furthermore, we found no correlation between students' TOEFL scores-clarity, TOEFL scores-accuracy, and students' TOEFL scores-syntactic complexity. We did find a negative correlation between first semester accuracy scores and the TOEFL scores (Pearson Correlation = -.788) with a significance level of .012 (p = .012) as well as a negative correlation between second semester accuracy scores and TOEFL scores (Pearson Correlation = -.773) with a significance level of .015 (p = .015). That is, similar to the SAT, students with higher TOEFL scores produced fewer grammatical errors than their counterparts with lower TOEFL scores in the first two semesters only.

Qualitative Results

The interviews covered multiple topics, beginning with the amount and extent of writing produced through the junior year and including questions on the student's writing processes, changes to the process over six semesters, and types of support used, when and how, as well as questions about L1 and L2 confidence. Key results with an emphasis on second language and translingual concerns are reported in the section that follows.

Opportunities to Write

Knoch et al. (2015) found that their undergraduates did limited writing over three years of university: students studying in the institutional subdivisions of medicine, dentistry, health sciences, business, or economics were required to produce little to no writing. Such was not the case for our participants. Student majors and specific course choices over three years led to a wide variety of writing experiences and differing amounts of writing, but even as juniors in their majors, with the exception of Kyle (Math and Chemistry) and Camile (Chemistry), the students reported doing moderate to substantial amounts of writing for courses. Moreover, those not assigned writing for class continued to write for professional and personal purposes in both Chinese and English outside of class.

Changes in Writing Process

Echoing findings from fluency research (Chenoweth & Hayes, 2001), most participants reported that writing had become easier and less time consuming than it had been initially. Karina reported considerable confidence in L2 academic writing after three years of study:

> [W]hen I think back to my freshman year, I remember my first paper ever, I was so, like so nervous and so anxious. I [couldn't] express myself very well in English, so . . . I wrote a Chinese like outline and like translated it to English, which is, which . . . [didn't] help very much. I [didn't] really get really good grades, and it [took] a lot of time for me like to translate between languages and stuff. But now, I don't even write an English outline. I just do my research and record all the- the bibliography and all works cited and stuff and then just write it. And I don't even really check my grammar. It just flows out.

While not all nine students voiced Karina's confidence, eight commented that their English L2 speaking, reading and writing skills had all increased substantially while their reliance on L1 support had diminished. In contrast, Celia felt that her writing had remained "about the same" since she came to our institution—despite evidence to the contrary from her scores for clarity, accuracy, and complexity—because her written work continued to receive the same grades.

Resource Use

As Leonard (2014) notes, multilingual writers are not "fixed and stable" (p. 228) in the linguistic resources they bring to writing occasions, but flexible depending on rhetorical demands. Participant comments suggest that their need for writing support resources reflects a similar flexibility. Overall, participants reported that their need for and/or use of resources, whether technological or tutorial, had diminished over time. When asked if they used electronic resources, such as a thesaurus, concordancers, Word tools, or an electronic translator, when writing, Li, Camile, and Celia mentioned Word's autocorrect feature, while Karina, Camile, and Hogan turned to dictionaries on occasion. After the first year, students did not report using electronic translating programs. As Li explained,

> I used to use Google translator but after- for the first year maybe, but after I [found] out the translation is not as accurate or . . . it [didn't] make sense most of the time. So, also I [relied] a lot on that; I feel like . . . it kind of [blocked] my

> ideas because sometimes when it [gave] me translations and
> they [had] like different words and I [felt] like, I [felt] like I
> [became] more like focused on the wording and the gram-
> mar, the grammatical like, things, instead of like trying to get
> the flow of the idea which I really want to do.

In other words, Li felt that the translator impeded her ability to focus first on
conventional higher-order concerns (depth of ideas, development of ideas).

Helen echoed Li's concern about inaccuracy, commenting that translator
use in the first year had kept her from learning subtle distinctions between
words. Tan, who attended part of high school in the United States, went
beyond rejecting translation programs to stress the importance of not reading
any class materials in Chinese, a practice which she believed had impeded her
ability to succeed in the English L2 environment during her first year.

In terms of help-seeking behaviors, students described a range of strategic approaches contingent on need and time. Eight consulted professors to discuss class content and assignment parameters, seek advice about
sources or rhetorical models, or preview a working thesis. Victor singled
out these discussions as the most pleasurable part of the writing experience,
explaining,

> I mean, definitely it is not enjoyable because . . . when you
> are . . . dealing with a paper or assignment, you are trying to
> just get it done before the deadline or something. But, . . .
> when [what] you're trying to do [for] a paper is to figure
> out an idea, talk to the professors and well if you guys agree
> on something and you feel it's very exciting maybe do some
> research on it; that's definitely one enjoyable thing in the
> whole writing process.

In addition to discussing ideas and research with professors, Hogan, Karina and Li mentioned having had professors who willingly discussed style and
grammar as well, and Helen reported reviewing graded papers with faculty to
learn what had worked and what had not worked. Not all students mentioned
frequent or useful contact with their professors. For example, Celia sought
feedback from her professors at multiple stages in the writing process but felt
that they weren't sufficiently directive in comments and/or gave suggestions
too near deadlines to help her improve as a writer.

All participants reported that the second language specialist, with whom
they could make hour or longer appointments, provided a helpful mix of
open-ended and directive assistance. In Karina's estimation,

> . . . the most important thing she did was not like helping me to write anything that she thinks I'm trying to say, but asking me what I want to say, and like ask me to verbally say it. Because I feel like the way I say it and the way I write it are very different. And the way I write it, I always want to make things more complicated when I write it out. So if I say it clearly, and if I can express myself well to her, and then she just records whatever I said, it really looks much better than the original text I wrote myself.

Karina's comment emphasizes the difference between oral and written communication and also reveals the give-and-take characteristic of the specialist sessions. This process of collaborative meaning-making was often time-intensive, especially in the first year, when students spent a total of 95.75 hours (11 hours, average) working with the language specialist.

While the second language specialist's strategy of asking students questions to help them clarify wording and recording these responses was considered helpful, her attempts at reformulation, in which teacher rewrites student sentences in order to analyze them and develop greater accuracy, could be disconcerting at times. Kyle, in particular, mentioned anxiety during tutorials in his first year:

> [W]hen we were working together I was always bothered by the idea that [she] corrected my papers so much that it [didn't] show my work anymore . . . Like I was so afraid that I mean [the specialist tutor corrected] my work so much; I mean, I was afraid, oh my God this doesn't sound like what I wrote and I was so afraid at how, how my work actually turned into [hers] . . . that was like my biggest fear when I was writing my essay then coming to [her].

The fear and lack of confidence Kyle expressed was anticipated by Ferris (2010). In presenting studies on reformulation and its appeal to second language acquisition researchers, Ferris (2010) argued that, even if it were shown to be a more effective way of improving student accuracy than corrective feedback, "reformulation puts teachers' words into students' mouths (or pens or word processors) . . . [and] is thus antithetical to the larger goal of helping students explore their ideas and develop their own voices" (p. 190).

Another option for students seeking support comes through the writing center, which is staffed by peer tutors with majors in many disciplines and provides half-hour appointments. Victor explained that his interest in this tutoring depended on his confidence in a subject:

> Yea so I think the main reason we sought help [was] . . . the first maybe middle paper, and get a bad grade, and the professor's advice . . . is get some help. . . . But first year I definitely, you know, [sought] help a lot because I [was] a new, like, writer for whatever style I [was] trying to write and definitely [wanted] to learn more. But when you go into sophomore year and like so junior year especially when you go into a specific subject. I think firstly that the writing style, you know doesn't require a lot of . . . writing help anymore.

When students felt confident, they generally did not want tutoring. Students also reported working with center tutors mainly on grammar, style, and citation issues. However, even when they preferred to focus on style with peer tutors, students did not want someone to "fix" articles and tenses, as has been reported in writing center literature (Blau & Hall, 2002). Helen, who repeatedly stressed her desire to use not just accurate but aesthetically effective diction, explained that

> the writing center tutors . . . I would go to . . . are the ones who are very particular about word choices and very particular about structure, I mean in terms of sentence structure, not the whole structure of the essay. I found them to be really helpful, and they tend to be the philosophy or English majors. Um, but in terms of other tutors, . . . I think it's less helpful compared to professors . . . because they are used to helping students who just simply don't know how to write, who don't know how to form arguments or grammar mistakes, which, those things are not my primary concern.

Tutors who viewed Helen as a student writing in English as a second language who needed remediation did not meet her interests in stylistic revision, a situation she experienced even more strongly during her study abroad experience:

> this year I tried to talk to one of the writing tutors in the center . . . at [a college in London] but it was funny because she look at me and thinking, wow, she's from China, and doesn't really- she expects I don't know that much . . . because the level of English the Chinese students here speaks are a little

> bit—I would say it's a little bit lower than [at our college]. So she saw me and she kind of expects that I didn't really speak that much English and/or write that much English and she saw my paper and was like, wow this is really good, but to me that was a very rough draft, it was not good at all, there was too many mistakes with the way I wrote . . .

While noting that perhaps "priorities" (e.g., expectations) for student writers differed between our institution and her abroad institution, Helen experienced the tutor's assumptions as a kind of L2 profiling, a behavior that reduced tutor expectations and denied her useful conversation about aesthetic and rhetorical improvement. In contrast, she felt that sessions with the second language specialist at our institution built on the assumption that Helen wrote well in English and wanted to write with style and grace.

The Role of L1

Most students said that L1 had little to no overt role in their academic writing. "In my first year," according to Li,

> I didn't think in English, but in Chinese when I was doing the planning but . . . like now, I think in English too. I think that's better because it's quicker, also . . . in [the] first year, . . . one of the reasons that my wording [was] so awkward [was] I [thought] in Chinese then I [translated] . . . But so basically the Chinese grammar is different than the English.

Li cites both efficiency and clarity as reasons to use English for academic purposes. The language in which students learned material also impacted language use. Helen noted that her choice of conversational language depends on purpose and context. Others explained that they used English for academic work, while communicating with family and friends in Chinese. In his interview, Kyle explained that he wrote poetry in Chinese.

While English may be the lingua franca for academic discussions, rhetorical preferences within disciplines sometimes felt and continue to feel confining. In Karina's words, "in my freshman year, I was more creative, and I was more, I was braver in, I guess trying out new things, trying out new techniques, and in making sentences that are not [dry], but more in a creative way to express myself. But now, I'm more, I don't like to experiment. I just want to write my sentences clear." Karina indicates that in adopting a hegemonic monolingual value for the clear, concise, and "dry" argumentation favored in academic SWE, she experiences what she suggests is a loss of autonomy and linguistic agency.

Overall, participants reported feeling as if their L2 growth was accompanied by a comparable loss of academic competence in their L1. Hogan's extended answer to this question reveals a complex relationship between his L1 and L2 use and his chosen adjustments to the campus monolingual environment.

> When I first [came] to America . . . [and was] formulating my ideas in my mind, I always like [thought] in Chinese of what I should write and what kind of things I should look for and what kind of ideas I actually put down on my paper. I think there was a transitional period where I was forcing myself to think in English first, so for example like if like I pick up a book . . . I will think . . . first like the Chinese word for book first and then translate that to English . . . but then there was like a transitional time probably about half a year to a year [when] I was forcing myself that everything I see or that everything I read into my mind like I need to recognize the English first . . . And right now like [for the past] two years [everything] . . . like everything like I am thinking . . . or talking [about] . . . or writing. English always comes first in my mind.

Keenly aware of shifts between his linguistic abilities in L1 and L2, Hogan described responding with a deliberate attempt to maintain his L1 competence. Victor, in contrast, expressed language confidence related to exposure and function:

> Definitely [when] writing in Chinese [I am] more confident because [I wrote] it for like 80 years [sic] and yea, [I] know most of the characters that are used. . . . Because when [I'm] writing in English using single sentence[s], [I] can express [myself] clearly, but for some complicated situations or longer phrases, Chinese would be a better way to communicate it. English for me is more of a way to write academically, properly. . . . If you want me to write a poem or novel or whatever [in English] I have no confidence to do that. In Chinese maybe I am confident to write that. . . . *It would be a great novel.* (emphasis ours)

His characteristic humor aside, Victor clearly distinguishes between situations for L1 use and L2 use, with L2 use preferred for what he perceives as straightforward and necessary communication or for academic work.

Translanguaging

Examples of translanguaging commonly show speakers or writers switching between languages, integrating them in a communicative act that draws on two or more languages to create a hybrid (Ayahs, 2018; Lu & Horner, 2013). The students interviewed for this study provided examples of translanguaging in conversation with other Chinese speakers, as in Helen's comment about speaking with another woman in her economics course. In writing, student comments suggest that visible translanguaging happens less often, primarily when class content provided opportunities for use of cultural knowledge or specific Chinese language. Both Kyle and Camile reported drawing on their L1 for some assignments. Whereas Kyle reports translanguaging specifically when referring to Chinese historical figures or locations, Camile's description suggests a stage in her drafting process during which she fluidly draws on both languages:

> [I write] certain things in English and certain things in Chinese. Because it depends on the class. But like for Buddhism, a lot of things are related to Chinese ideas, so it is easier to write Chinese. Because Buddhism, especially classical Buddhism, it has many texts in like ancient Chinese, not ancient Chinese writing, but like, you know, like those poems or old stories, those kind of styles. It's very simplified, so you can just summarize a lot of things in one or two characters. Yeah, so that's how, that's when it's easier to write Chinese words.

Unclear from her response is how she goes from hybrid text to final form in submitted papers. Both Kyle and Camile discuss their translanguaging choices as easy or efficient strategies ("more quickly") as well as contingent upon class content. Their description of choices contrasts to comments offered by students included in the Ayash study included in this collection.

Even though students seldom deploy their L1 in final written products, course content that allows students to draw on their L1 culture clearly mattered to Celia, whose interview responses reflect challenging and difficult experiences in the English L2 setting. She found opportunities to draw on her cultural background a particular comfort, explaining: "I think my strength is knowing like the different culture. [Not] necessarily the language helps enrich the content of my writing [but] when I was taking the Chinese detective, fiction, and film course, I'm like *I can write about this.*"

Discussion

In our mixed methods, longitudinal study of a cohort of advanced Chinese L2 writers, we found that students' writing grew notably in terms of accuracy and clarity but not in syntactic complexity. For the most part, as the quality of student writing developed, so did their reported confidence and strategic competence in academic writing in a traditional monolingual environment.

The students' stories are complex. In comparison to an idealized multilingual writer who creates hybrid text from multiple linguistic traditions, such as the three writers profiled by Bou Ayash (2019), the English L2 writers we studied inevitably translanguage at the topic and conceptual levels, but rarely at the lexical and rhetorical level on the page, where cross-language transfer from Chinese to English, and vice-versa, is often perceived in traditional SWE environments as "interference." As some participants noted, they grew as L2 academic writers but felt a corresponding loss of L1 confidence. Yet in contrast to the multilingual students featured in Ayash's analysis (2019), our participants, did not voice desire to push back against Western academic writing conventions and instead spoke of wanting to write in a rhetorically appropriate and disciplinary way.

Overall the L1 loss should be understood as contingent on their situation as international students trying to succeed in an L2 context. Unlike domestic multilingual and immigrant students who are pressured to adhere to a monolingual norm, most of our participants expect to return to China after graduation, suggesting that their L1 loss may not be permanent. They've learned new academic concepts and information in English and may not know how to talk about these things in their L1, which would make them feel less confident when they return to China to work, as studies and anecdotal evidence suggest. With workplace experience, however, they will learn the appropriate technical vocabulary and ways of talking about the topic at hand.

Second language scholarship has moved beyond a simplistic view of "other" (e.g., non-American) academic writings, such as that presented in early studies of contrastive rhetoric (Kaplan, 1966). At the same time, research illustrates clear differences in expectation, genre, and rhetorical preferences between academic writing in American and China (Mina & Cimasko, this collection; Sullivan, 2012; Wu & Rubin, 2000). Our students remarked on these differences. In Camile's words,

> I was so surprised when I just got here and then I learned [from faculty] about how . . . English writers like to give out the ideas in the beginning . . . as a thesis sentence . . . [but]

sometimes in Chinese writing, you want to save more [of the argument to lay out] like as you read along.

Just as the five-paragraph form taught in secondary systems across the United States is not necessarily well-received in college, L2 writing strategies taught in an L1 environment may not work. Our students realized this early. Kyle spoke directly to these differences at one point.

> [i]n freshman year, I [would get assigned a paper] I [would] make sure that I [saw] the specialist tutor at least once for each paper before I hand it in, just because I was at a very like total [starting] point at writing an English essay and yea and for a lot of things that I feel good about- for example, grammar or sentence structure that I feel it is extremely reasonable and logical [to put it that way for the tutor] and other American people it's it may be bizarre and weird to actually read it. I think one of the most common mistakes I made was that I tend to write a sentence super long. About like extended to like three rows for a single sentence and I thought it was extremely fine and like logical, and actually, *that's actually something we were taught when we were English learners back in China,* that you should always use a lot of, you know, [substance] in your sentence to, you know, make it better, to make it more complicated so that you know it actually can kind of reflect that you are very good at manipulating sentences and [running them together]. . . .[Such sentences] could be very confusing for native [L2] speakers.

The insights that Kyle and his peers shared about their L2 writing development reflect increased strategic competence, a hallmark of translingual agency. Canagarajah (1999) describes the learning strategies that lead to successful language acquisition as a "curiosity toward the language, the ability to intuit linguistic rules from observation of actual usage, a metalinguistic awareness of the system behind languages, and the ability to creatively negotiate meaning with speakers and texts." (p. 91). In their submitted papers, our participants did not exhibit translingual strategies at the syntactic or grammatical level touted in many studies (Canagarajah, 2013), but we argue that, in this language context, they were by no means passive conduits or victims of English-only pedagogy. They learned to exploit resources (faculty, the campus writing center, the second language specialist) to their benefit, transforming the assumptions and pedagogies that they initially encountered. In response to these students' needs, the second language specialist has shifted to more negotiated pedagogies and a greater focus on clarity over correctness. At the same time, the writing center has adapted to meet students' requests for directive feedback that addresses the rhetorically appropriate and disciplinary ways of writing preferred in the SWE context.

In contrast, we must note that translingual agency manifests differently in foreign language settings. In one study of native English-speaking writing faculty at Chinese universities (Shi, 2009), professors reported resistance from students, whose concerns about national examinations and emphasis on form undermine Western EFL process-oriented and communicative-focused approaches. In such a context, the EFL teachers—not the students—must adapt their teaching methods to the local context.

Limitations

While faculty evaluations as manifested by grades suggest a high degree of achievement for our L2 writers, we did not analyze argument or content knowledge and do not offer evidence to link linguistic growth to L2 rhetorical efficacy because we were unqualified to evaluate content knowledge and ideas forwarded in the texts about which students were writing. In addition, our research did not address whether the extent of growth in clarity and accuracy in the students' writing would have been possible without student willingness to embrace the hegemonic expectations of a predominantly English speaking campus community. Yet even in such an English-dominant institutional context, students seized opportunities to exercise agency, seeking assistance when they wished it on their own terms. As confidence in English L2 academic writing increased, their sense that they needed support through the writing process (from invention through revision) decreased.

Moreover, we must concede that our study focuses on a highly privileged group of L2 writers, high-achieving at home, successful abroad, and with considerable control of their language choices. Consider, for example, a remark Helen made in response to her sense of L1 loss.

> And of course I still read, and still write, trying to write a bit,
> but it depends on where I am, in China I write in Chinese
> a lot more and in English-speaking countries I write a lot
> more in English, just because the environment, um . . . you
> can't have both, so I try to read as much Chinese, I write as
> much Chinese as I can when I'm in China, and I have this

> good friend who studied literature, she sends me things, and I try to catch up.

Though multilingual writers conforming to monolingual disciplinary expectations, these students are also mobile, moving between cultures on a frequent basis. Privilege enabled them to study at a highly selective liberal arts college that provides a writing and discussion intensive monolingual environment yet continue to choose to maintain L1 fluency.

Lessons Learned

Through this study, we better understand how our L2 writers from China learn to navigate the writing-intensive demands they face in a traditional SWE environment as well as how we can support them. Their growth as writers testifies to a resilient, persistent approach to L2 writing growth and strategic use of a variety of campus resources. We are better equipped to encourage faculty toward what Horner (this collection) terms a "post-monolingual state." Through the lens afforded by student interviews, we have also become more confident that faculty support their L2 student writers despite a lack of exposure to a translingual disposition. Finally, we better understand the limited reliability of standardized measures for admission, which predict first-year performance but not beyond.

The implications of this study are greatest for L2 specialists and writing center educators who support translingual approaches in theory, but struggle to balance its call for students to challenge dominant ideologies about correctness and standardized language rules (Horner et al., 2011) with institutional pressures such as those expressed by Bobbi Olson (2013) when asked to "clean up" a multilingual student's paper so that "no trace of her status as a non-native English speaker remained, which is exactly what her instructor wanted and expected." (p. 1). Our research has provided evidence of what composition and L2 researchers have argued for decades: that students will continue to progress as writers, even when we hold back from discussing every error; limiting error-correction to instances in which communication breakdowns (problems in clarity) occurred in student texts does not prevent students from developing grammatical accuracy. Such a finding should reassure well-intentioned, mainstream faculty who want to support multilingual students but worry that they cannot address every language issue they encounter in papers. Furthermore, we hope that findings showing multilingual students are able to progress with respect to grammatical accuracy over the course of three years prompts faculty to rethink notions of fairness in evaluation and grading.

Even in monolingual institutional settings such as ours, a translingual approach that "encourages reading with patience, respect for perceived differences within and across languages, and an attitude of deliberative inquiry" (Horner et al., 2011, p. 304) is not only desirable but possible. We can help multilingual students "translate" the ideas they want to express in English through open-ended questions about meaning and intent. A modified language experience approach in which the specialist or peer tutor records the student's oral clarification of specific passages and, with the writer, considers whether this version should replace the original, can balance the open-endedness of such sessions with the explicit, direct instruction that multilingual students often request (Williams & Smith, 1993). In other words, making room for student voices does not mean we should refrain from "translating" the dominant academic culture's assumptions about language and rhetoric for them. A truly empowering translingualism would help students decide when to push boundaries and when to remain within them.

Above all, we have learned not to engage in writer profiling by engaging in assumptions about student needs and desires. Our results also suggest caution before embracing translingual approaches that eschew *any* directive tutoring. Some students want to adapt their rhetoric and style to American contexts. Others, cognizant of the American preference for plain and concise prose, still prefer to focus on developing a sophisticated, syntactically complex SWE style. For example, consider Hogan's ambitions as a writer:

> . . . when I am thinking about writing or thinking of myself as a writer is when I find something in the historiography that is hotly debated, and I want to be part of that debate and that's when I conceptualize myself as a scholar, not as an undergrad who is learning from all the scholars. Like I am a peer of [my, my own peers]. That's when I pay attention more to my style, I want to develop that Ph.D., you know that Ph.D. style writing.

In our quest to apply translingual approaches, listening also means the willingness to honor student requests and desires, even if they run counter to our instincts or agendas.

References

Atkinson, D., Crusan, D., Matsuda, P. K., Ortmeier-Hooper, C., Ruecker, T., Simpson, S. & Tardy, C. (2015). Clarifying the relationship between L2 writing and translingual writing: An open letter to writing studies editors and organization leaders. *College English, 77*(4), 383–386.

Bailey, S. (2012). Tutor handbooks: Heuristic texts for negotiating difference in a globalized world. *Praxis: A Writing Center Journal, 9*(2), 1–8.

Banes, L. C., Martínez, D. C., Athanases, S. Z. & Wong, J. W. (2016). Self-reflective inquiry into language use and beliefs: Toward more expansive language ideologies. *International Multilingual Research Journal, 10*(3), 168–187.

Bardovi-Harlig, K. & Bofman, T. (1989). Attainment of syntactic and morphological accuracy by advanced language learners. *Studies in Second Language Acquisition, 11*(1), 17–34.

Barnard, I. (2010). The ruse of clarity. *College Composition & Communication, 61*(3), 434–51.

Blau, S. R. & Hall, J. (2002). Guilt free tutoring: Rethinking how we tutor non-native-English- speaking students. *The Writing Center Journal, 23*(1), 23–44.

Bruce, S. & Rafoth, B. (Eds). (2009). *ESL writers: A guide for writing center tutors* (2nd ed.). Heinemann.

Campbell, S., Fernandez, R. & Koo, K. (2013, October 17–21). Supportive mainstreaming of Chinese L2 writers at a small liberal arts college in the United States. In T. Silva & P. K. Matsuda (Chairs), *L2 Writing in the Global Context: Represented, Underrepresented, and Unrepresented Voices* (Symposium). 12th Symposium on Second Language Writing, Shandong University, Jinan, China.

Chenoweth, N. A. & Hayes, J. R. (2001). Fluency in writing. Generating text in L1 and L2. *Written Communication, 18*(1), 80–98.

Canagarajah, A. S. (1999). Interrogating the "native speaker fallacy": Non-linguistic roots, non-pedagogical results. In G. Braine (Ed.), *Non-Native Educators in English Language Teaching* (pp. 77–92). Lawrence Erlbaum Associates.

Canagarajah, A. S. (2006). The place of world Englishes in composition: Pluralization continued. *College Composition and Communication, 57*(4), 586–619.

Canagarajah, A. S. (2011). Translanguaging in the classroom: Emerging issues for research and pedagogy. *Applied Linguistics Review, 2*, 1–28.

Canagarajah, A. S. (2013) (Ed.). *Literacy as translingual practice: Between communities and classrooms.* Routledge.

Carroll, L. A. (2002). *Rehearsing New Roles: How College Students Develop as Writers.* Studies in Writing and Rhetoric. Southern Illinois University Press.

Ching, L. C. (2002). Strategy and self-regulation instruction as contributors to improving students' cognitive model in an ESL program. *English for Specific Purposes, 21*(3), 261–289.

Crossley, S. A. & McNamara, D. S. (2014). Does writing development equal writing quality? A computational investigation of syntactic complexity in L2 learners. *Journal of Second Language Writing, 26*, 66–79.

Crowley, S. (2006). *Toward a civil discourse: Rhetoric and fundamentalism.* University of Pittsburgh Press.

Donahue, C. (2013). Negotiation, translinguality, and cross-cultural writing research in a new composition era. In A. S. Canagarajah (Ed.), *Literacy as Translingual Practice* (pp. 150–161). Routledge.

Ferris, D. R. (2003). *Response to student writing: Implications for second language students*. Routledge.

Ferris, D. R. (2010). Second language writing research and written corrective feedback in SLA. *Studies in Second Language Acquisition 32*(2), 181–201.

Fischer, R. (1984). Testing written communicative competence in French. *Modern Language Journal, 68*(1), 13–20.

Fishman, J., Lunsford, A., McGregor, B. & Otuteye, M. (2005). Performing writing, performing literacy. *College Composition and Communication, 57*(2), 224–252.

Garcia, O. (2009). Education, multilingualism, and translanguaging in the 21st century. In T. Skutnabb-Kangas, R. Phillipson, A. K. Monhanty & M. Panda (Eds.), *Social justice through multilingual education* (pp. 125–139). Multilingual Matters.

Grimm, N. (1999). *Good intentions: Writing center work for postmodern times*. Heinemann/Boynton Cook.

Herrington, A. & Curtis, M. (2000). *Persons in process: Four stories of writing and personal development in college*. NCTE.

Horner, B., Lu, M., Royster, J. J. & Trimbur, J. (2011). Opinion: Language difference in writing: Toward a translingual approach. *College English, 73*(3), 303–320.

Hruschka, D. J., Schwartz, D., Cobb St. John, D., Picone-Decaro, E., Jenkins, R. A. & Carey, J. W. (2004). Reliability in coding open-ended data: Lessons learned from HIV behavioral research. *Field Methods, 16*(3), 307–331.

Kaplan, R. B. (1966). Cultural thought patterns in inter-cultural education. *Language Learning, 16*(1), 11–25.

Knoch, U., Rouhstad, A., Oon, S. P. & Storch, N. (2015). What happens to ESL students' writing after three years of study at an English medium university? *Journal of Second Language Writing, 28*, 40–52.

Lape, N. (2013). Going global, becoming translingual: The development of a multilingual writing center. *The Writing Lab Newsletter, 38*(3–4), 1–6.

Larsen-Freeman, D. (2006). The emergence of complexity, fluency, and accuracy in the oral and written production of five Chinese learners of English. *Applied Linguistics, 27*(4), 590–619.

Leki, I., Cumming, A. & Silva, T. (2008). *A Synthesis of Research on Second Language Writing in English*. Routledge.

Leonard, R. (2014). Multilingual writing as rhetorical attunement. *College English, 76*(3), 227–247.

Lu, M. & Horner, B. (2013). Translingual literacy, language difference, and matters of agency. *College English, 75*(6), 582–607.

Lu, X. (2010). Automatic analysis of syntactic complexity in second language writing. *International Journal of Corpus Linguistics, 15*(4), 474–496.

Lu. X. (2014). *L2 syntactic complexity analyzer (Version 3.3.1)* [Computer Software]. http://www.personal.psu.edu/xxl13/downloads/l2sca.html.

Lu, X. & Ai, H. (2015). Syntactic complexity in college-level English writing: Differences among writers with diverse L1 backgrounds. *Journal of Second Language Writing, 29*, 16–27.

Martinez, C. T., Kock, N. & Cass, J. (2011). Pain and pleasure in short essay writing: Factors predicting university students' writing anxiety and writing self-efficacy. *Journal of Adolescent & Adult Literacy, 54*(5), 351–360.

Mastan, M. E. & Maarof, N. (2014). ESL learners' self-efficacy beliefs and strategy use in expository writing. *Procedia-Social and Behavioral Sciences, 116,* 2360–2363.

Matsuda, P. K. (2006) The myth of linguistic homogeneity in U.S. college composition. *College English, 68*(6), 637–651.

Matsuda, P. K., Canagarajah, A. S., Harklau, L., Hyland, K. & Warschauer, M. (2003). Changing currents in second language writing research: A colloquium. *Journal of Second Language Writing, 12*(2), 151–179.

Matsuda, P. K., Saenkhum, T. & Accardi, S. (2013). Writing teachers' perceptions of the presence and needs of second language writers: An institutional case study. *Journal of Second Language Writing, 22*(1), 68–86.

Matsuda, P. K. & Silva, T. (1999). Cross-cultural composition: Mediated integration of US and international students. *Composition Studies, 27*(1), 15–30.

Mattern, K. D., Patterson, B. F. & Kobrin, J. L. (2012). The validity of SAT scores in predicting first-year mathematics and English grades (Research Report 2012–1). The College Board.

Olson, B. (2013). Rethinking our work with multilingual writers: The ethics and responsibility of language teaching in the writing center. *Praxis: A Writing Center Journal, 10*(2). http://www.praxisuwc.com/olson–102/.

Ortega, L. (2003). Syntactic complexity measures and their relationship to L2 proficiency: A research synthesis of college-level L2 writing. *Applied Linguistics, 24*(4), 492–518.

Ortmeier-Hooper, C. (2008). English may be my second language, but I'm not "ESL." *College Composition and Communication, 59*(3), 389–419.

Polio, C. (1997). Measures of linguistic accuracy in second language writing research. *Language Learning, 47*(1), 101–143.

Ray, B. (2015). "It's beautiful": Language difference as a new norm in college writing instruction. *College Composition and Communication, 67*(1), 87–103.

Shi, L. (2009). Chinese-Western "contact-zone": Students' resistance and teachers' adaptation to local needs. *TESL Canada Journal, 27*(1), 47–63.

Sommers, N. (2008). The call of research: A longitudinal view of writing development. *College Composition and Communication, 60*(1), 152–164.

Sommers, N. & Saltz, L. (2004). The novice as expert: Writing the freshman year. *College Composition and Communication, 56*(1), 124–149.

Sternglass, M. (1997). *Time to know them: A longitudinal study of writing and learning at the college level.* Routledge.

Storch, N. (2005). Collaborative writing: product, process, and students' reflections. *Journal of Second Language Writing, 14*(3), 153–173.

Storch, N. (2009). The impact of studying in a second language (L2) medium university on the development of L2 writing. *Journal of Second Language Writing, 18*(2), 103–118.

Sullivan, P., Zhang, Z. & Zheng, F. (2012). College writing in China and America: A modest and humble conversation, with writing samples. *Conference on College Composition and Communication 64*(2), 306–331.

Usher, E. L. & Pajares, F. (2008). Sources of self-efficacy in school: Critical review of the literature and future directions. *Review of Educational Research, 78*(4), 751–796.

Williams, J. M. & Smith, G. G. (1993). The case for explicit teaching: Why what you don't know won't help you. *Research in the Teaching of English, 27*(3), 252–264.

Wolfe-Quintero, K., Inagaki, S. & Kim, H. (1998). *Second language development in writing: Measures of fluency, accuracy and complexity.* University of Hawaii Press.

Wu, S. & Rubin, D. (2000). Evaluating the impact of collectivism and individualism on argumentative writing by Chinese and North American college students. *Research in the Teaching of English, 35*, 148–178.

Yang, W. & Sun, Y. (2015). Dynamic development of complexity, accuracy and fluency in multilingual learners' L1, L2 and L3 writing. *Theory and Practice in Language Studies, 5*(2), 298–308.

Zimmerman, B. J. & Pons, M. M. (1986). Development of a structured interview for assessing student use of self-regulated learning strategies. *American Educational Research Journal, 23*(4), 614–628.

Appendix

Structured Interview Questions (Adapted from Zimmerman & Pons, 1986)

General/Preview

1. What are your major, minor and concentration (if any)?
2. How has your year been? What sorts of courses have you taken? What writing assignments have you had, if any?
3. How has this year compared to freshman and sophomore years with respect to writing and your English language development as a whole?

Writing Strategies

4. Describe your writing process from the time you receive a writing assignment to the point of final submission.
5. Do you use any resources regularly when you write? For example, do you use material resources such as a thesaurus, concordancers (Corpus of Contemporary American English), Microsoft Word tools, Google, an electronic translator, etc.? What about people resources such as your professor or tutors?
6. How has your use of these different resources (material and people resources) changed over time? For instance, perhaps you went to a professor or a tutor each time you had a paper as a freshman but now only go for longer papers.

7. What do you consider to be the role of your native language in your writing process, if any? Do you, for example, jot down translations or ideas in Chinese on the margins of your books or in your notes or perhaps draft in Chinese before writing out your paper in English? When do you find your native language a resource? If it's ever a hindrance, explain why.
8. What kind of writing do you do outside of class? If you write outside of class, how often do you engage in the different kinds of writing you describe?
9. If you were to give an incoming Chinese international student tips for getting good grades on papers at Davidson, what would you say? What about advice for becoming a better writer?

Writing Self-Efficacy and Self-Concept

10. How much do you enjoy the writing process? Explain your answer.
11. How competent do you feel as a writer in English overall? And in Chinese? Explain why you feel this way?
12. What do you consider your strengths and challenges when writing in English? What about in Chinese? How have these strengths and challenges changed since freshman year?
13. How do you think you compare to other Chinese international students at Davidson? How about to American students?

Curricular and Instructional Issues

14. As you think back to your freshman year, how did your choice to take the WRI 101 in fall or spring impact your writing development, if at all?
15. At other institutions, international students must take special sections of first-year writing. How do you believe having to take mainstream writing courses alongside native English-speakers has influenced your development as a writer?
16. What impact do you believe your curricular choices (e.g., choice of major, courses, study abroad, etc.) have made on your writing development? Which courses helped you the most? Which helped you in other ways but did not contribute to your growth as a writer?
17. What impact do you believe certain ways of teaching or mentoring have had on your writing? Please explain.
18. What role, if any, have your peers (Davidson students or study abroad friends and classmates) had on your development as a writer? Please explain.

3

Expectations, Mismatches, and Translingual Dispositions in Teaching Multilingual Students

Lilian W. Mina
Auburn University at Montgomery

Tony Cimasko
Miami University

With the goal of expanding on translingual opportunities for student writers, this chapter discusses (mis)matches between the experiences and expectations of international multilingual students in a U.S.-based ESL composition program and the program's actual goals and pedagogies. The study found that students are generally receptive to the writing pedagogies within their classrooms, but there are important misconceptions about the role of composition courses, and frustrations in connecting with domestic L1 English users for academic and social purposes. We find that although instructors and students alike are already engaged in translanguaging work in many ways, they are missing opportunities for more. The chapter concludes with recommendations on how to encourage the opportunities that a translingual disposition towards pedagogy presents in a college writing program.

Keywords: ESL composition, student expectations, translanguaging

A translingual approach, or disposition, recognizes that language use is fluid; for instance, speakers and writers often move between languages, modes, and other affordances as they see fit for their own communicative and rhetorical success in a given context. In part, this fluidity reflects and facilitates a language user's movement between social and cultural contexts. A translingual disposition, then, calls for a shift in our conceptualization and worldview of language diversity, language, culture, and practices. In social contexts, language users make meaning by drawing from their rich

DOI: https://doi.org/10.37514/INT-B.2020.0438.2.03

repertoire of communicative resources, but the adoption of translingually oriented curricula in post-secondary writing programs is still relatively limited, especially in writing programs that have typically placed multilingual students in designated ESL classes. In this project, we offer the case of one institution and interrogate the degrees to which the program could shift its policies and pedagogies to a translingual approach. In scrutinizing the program, we aim to offer implications and recommendations for other writing programs that are open to the adoption of translingually oriented curricula and practices.

While an essential part of this project is seated in the desire to learn more about the international L2 students enrolled in Miami University's ESL Composition program, the primary purpose, in regard to student linguistic diversity, is to better understand how a translingual pedagogy can more completely prepare students for academic writing. Thus, interrogation of the benefits and drawbacks of drawing on translingually oriented curricula and practices in the program at Miami University shaped our approach to data collection. We began with an examination of the needs assessment data that were collected as part of the standardized curriculum of both the English Composition program and the ESL Composition program. Specifically, we were interested in Nation and Macalister's (2010) suggestions for examining necessities, shortcomings, and student wants as a means of understanding their needs. While student "shortcomings" are often identified through the placement process when they first enter the university, student "wants" remain unidentified in the program's current model of needs assessment. As such, we positioned our data collection to move beyond student "shortcomings," which are too often associated with deficit-model paradigms, to focus instead on student wants and expectations.

Aiming to identify international L2 student wants and expectations and potential (mis)matches between their wants and the program's existing goals and pedagogies, we conducted a program-wide mixed-method study. The findings of this study, though cited briefly in this chapter, worked as the springboard for our recommendations for pedagogical approaches that align with translingually oriented curricula and practices in the ESL Composition program. After reviewing the relevant literature and our research methodology, we present a synopsis of our thematic findings about student experiences, expectations, and responses to the program requirements. We end this chapter with a critical discussion of how to acknowledge the translingual disposition in framing and shaping the recommended curricular changes and teacher training inspired by our findings.

Review of Literature

Student Experiences

Scholars have emphasized the need to understand the prior educational experiences of multilingual students, and particularly their literacy practices, as a condition for selecting better pedagogical approaches to teach these students. Ferris and Hedgcock (2014) claim that many international students find undergraduate writing coursework daunting due to their previous experiences with reading and writing in English. They encourage teachers of writing courses to be aware of students' pedagogical histories in order to craft creative pedagogical approaches that address them. Similarly, Canagarajah (2011) asserts that pedagogies for multilingual students should be developed based on student practices, and Spack (2004) cautions against a pre-designed curriculum that makes assumptions about multilingual learners without any validation of these assumptions. Furthermore, Garcia and Wei (2014) theorize the positive validation of students' experiences, and explain that multilingual students can only establish new language and writing practices in "interrelationship with old ones" (p. 79). They believe that students use their learning and language histories and complex sets of needs and expectations to "invest," using Norton's (2000) term, in learning new practices to achieve these expectations. Transferring previous learning experiences requires integrating old and new language practices in order to create a repertoire of resources that the learner will use in the new learning context, in this case, ESL Composition classes. Therefore, in order to understand whether or not the ESL Composition classes are conducive to the transfer of learning experiences, it was necessary to assess students' expectations and experiences before making program-level changes in pedagogy.

Beyond making pedagogy meaningful for learners, transparently acknowledging past experiences adds a wealth of knowledge and skills to the writing classroom. Canagarajah (2013) urges teachers to build on the strategies that multilingual students have developed instead of "imposing their own understanding of literacy" (p. 9). He calls these strategies "resources" that both teachers and students can use in the classroom. Advocating for a translingual approach in writing, Shipka (2016) furthers this argument and considers difference as a resource. Within Shipka's view, the disparate educational, linguistic, and cultural experiences multilingual students possess can, and should, be utilized as resources that may potentially enrich the writing classroom. Collectively, Canagarajah's and Shipka's argument challenge writing teachers to change their approaches in order to acknowledge different cultural practices, languages, and modes of composing. Further, teachers should combine these resources of difference with more critical and reflective practices in order to help students "engage with the dominant norms" of the institution (Canagarajah, 2013, p. 9). Thus, it is imperative to unpack and understand the experiences that students bring into the ESL composition classroom before making any decisions regarding program mission, curriculum design, and/or pedagogical practices.

Student Expectations

In addition to students' educational experiences, their varied goals and expectations may inform their engagement and willingness to participate in many activities in a writing class (Ferris & Hedgcock, 2014). As such, both teachers and students need to work towards understanding and adjusting their writing class expectations (Ferris, 2009). The need for this understanding and adjustment drives this project, which empirically examined students' expectations to inform possible curricular and pedagogical changes. For example, students and instructors may have conflicting expectations of support for and feedback on writing class work. International multilingual students are concerned about their English language performance and expect extensive language instruction in their writing classes (Evans et al., 2009; Zamel, 2004). Many other aspects of the culture of U.S. writing classes may be problematic for international students. Continuing her discussion, Ferris (2009) alerts writing teachers that international students do not expect to "formulate opinions and arguments" (p. 13) for their writing assignments because this skill may not be a requirement of their previous language-oriented instruction.

Acknowledging this complex relation between students' previous educational experiences and current expectations challenges teachers to create more encompassing pedagogies that will engage students from diverse backgrounds and with a wide spectrum of experiences and expectations. For example, Gilyard (2016) suggests asking multilingual students to compose a translingual literacy narrative/history in which they document how they or someone they know has shuttled between the boundaries of language either locally or globally, academically or socially, in writing or in speaking. Such an assignment would invite students to reflect on their "trans"language and/or "trans"national experiences, forming their own unique opinions on those experiences.

This brief review of literature on international multilingual students' prior experiences and current expectations from the ESL Composition classroom illustrates that Canagarajah (2013), Shipka (2016), and Gilyard (2016) have pluralized student differences, thus advocating for a translingual approach. The question remains about how a translingual approach can transform ESL composition classrooms in a meaningful and productive way that improves their ability to address multilingual students' experiences, while building on their expectations from the writing class. The remainder of this chapter answers this question.

Context of the Study

The study was conducted in Miami University's ESL Composition program, part of the university's English department. The program's two first-year courses, ENG 108 and ENG 109, form a year-long writing sequence that most new international undergraduates follow. ENG 108 is a writing and U.S. cultures course, with much of the curriculum giving attention to individual rhetorical modes, such as summarizing, defining, describing, and arguing before moving into more complex texts such as a group multimedia project that combines multiple modes. ENG 109 emphasizes rhetoric by starting with personal rhetorical experience and examining the rhetoric of a text before attempting alphabetic and multimedia projects designed around the expectations of particular audiences. Placement in the two courses is based on a test designed and administered by program faculty.

The objectives of the ESL Composition program are divided into specific areas of academic writing including critical thinking, audience awareness, research and reading skills, and language conventions. Students in this program are encouraged to draw from a rich and extensive repertoire of linguistic, cultural, and technological practices as they maneuver their way through the new academic context of a U.S. university and complete the two courses. Program objectives and course descriptions emphasize the importance of students considering multiple cultural points of view, and to move beyond language accuracy to thinking about more complex aspects of writing (Jones & Landis, 2018). Theoretically, as Bou Ayash (this collection) also finds, this program is outwardly inclusive of the translingual practices students have developed before arriving to the program, such as their cultural and technological knowledge and practices. In reality, however, the emphasis is very much on English in American (or more broadly Western) contexts. This discrepancy between the program description and its enactment signals a more monolingual than a translingual approach.

Research Questions

This chapter draws on the results of our survey of the experiences and expectations of international undergraduates enrolled in an ESL composition program that was growing quickly at the time our study was conducted. Specifically, the study sought to answer the following questions:

1. How do previous English language learning experiences and early connections with classmates at the university contribute to creating expectations of first-year ESL composition classes among international students?
2. How do these students respond to the challenges of their ESL composition classes, both individually and through connections to peer communities?
3. What points of alignment and misalignment exist between these students' experiences and expectations, and the ESL Composition program's curriculum design and pedagogy?

Participants

Of the students participating in this study ($N = 279$), an overwhelming majority (96.4%) of them were from China, followed by three students from South Korea and one each from Japan, Pakistan, India, the United Arab Emirates, Russia, Sweden, and Germany. After obtaining IRB approval, students were recruited through their writing course instructors and consented their participation before completing the survey.

Data Collection

The four-page paper-based survey was composed of 22 multiple choice and short-answer questions organized into three sections. The questions addressed students' national and L1 backgrounds, time spent studying in the US and at the university, English language education in their home countries, perceptions of their own English language abilities, expectations of ENG 108 and 109, surprises that they had encountered, and their patterns of networking and studying with domestic and international students. Instructors in their respective ENG 108 and 109 sections distributed the survey. Students were given twenty minutes to complete the survey, after which instructors collected the anonymous surveys and immediately delivered them to the researchers.

Data Analysis

With the goal of meeting Canagarajah's (2011) and Spack's (2004) aim of making instruction more responsive to students' communicative realities a fundamental feature of a translingual approach to teaching writing, we examined the verbal data inductively, searching for patterns in the matches and mismatches between students and the program. In line with this approach, all data were transcribed verbatim without revisions to the language of any survey respondent's writing, unless a part of a response was illegible. Data from the survey were entered into a spreadsheet program, with codes assigned to each short answer multiple-choice questions. For example, the answer to our question about the number of years spent studying in the US was divided into four columns ("This is my first semester," "Less than one year," "One-two years," and "More than two years"), and for each survey respondent a score of 1 was entered in the corresponding column. This allowed us to make an initial identification of broader patterns in the response. Each of the researchers then read written responses to open-ended questions and compared them with the broader patterns emerging from the quantitative responses for triangulation of data and possible explanations of those responses. We paid particular attention to comparing present classes and past home country experiences (for example, amount of English language writing done prior to and in the U.S. writing classes) to find potential correlations or causational links.

Students' Experiences

The overwhelming majority of participants (83 percent) had had some prior experience with university-level academic work in the US, although most of that had come from Miami University, during the semester at the university preceding our research. Regardless of their U.S.-based experiences, all participants had received English language instruction in their home countries for an average of eight years, going back to elementary school. More than half characterized that instruction as mostly or entirely academic in nature, but a sizable minority saw their English instruction as being equally split between academic (texts written to fulfill course requirements, especially longer and more formal texts) and non-academic English.

Student responses indicate that the dominant academic genres they experienced prior to entering U.S. writing classrooms were highly structured and standardized forms of writing, particularly TOEFL and other standardized test essays and the five-paragraph essay form. In English as a *foreign* language (EFL) settings, where all participants received their prior English instruction, writing of this kind is frequently a prime determinant of academic and professional advancement, and the justification for making it the focus of curricular attention is clear (Reichelt, 2011). Upon entry to U.S. universities, which are English as a *second* language contexts, standardized tests of English proficiency are suddenly no longer relevant, and writing assignments are likely to be unfamiliar even when the language development level of the assignments is appropriate. Responses about the writing areas students needed help with, when in their home countries, also point to this potential mismatch, with 59 percent of students having been far more concerned about local-level, accuracy-oriented problems of vocabulary, grammar, and mechanics rather than global-level of generation and organization of content. When students encountered difficulties and sought out focused help for their writing in their home countries, they chose to primarily consult teachers, formal internet sources, and more fluent friends and seniors, rather than peers working at the same language level. Combined, these preferences may be interpreted as an orientation toward perceived English language authority.

Expectations of First-Year ESL Writing Classes

The second half of the survey included a direct question that asked, "When you came to ENG 108 or 109, what did you expect of the class?" About 90 percent of participants expressed their eagerness to improve their English skills broadly defined. Moreover, we noticed a clear orientation among students to "learn and think in American way," "write like a native English-speaking student and have American writing habits," and "accept American culture as soon as possible." These statements, on the one hand, display an interest in learning and improving language skills in order to function more effectively in a cross-cultural environment. Students appear to believe that their success is contingent upon and achieved by assimilating the linguistic practices of their American counterparts. On the other hand, these statements may reflect students' fear of failure due to their perceived lack of linguistic ability (Ferris, 2009), or even worse, lack of native-speaking competence. These interpretations were consolidated upon realizing the emphasis, reported by many students in their written comments, on improving grammar, vocabulary, and word choice, equating these with a totality of writing skills. These findings are consistent with those of the study by Evans et al. (2009), indicating that international students have concerns about their English language proficiency and integration into American culture.

Perceptions of Pedagogies in First-Year ESL Writing Classes

Students were also asked, "What have been the most surprising aspects of the class so far?" in the areas of teaching practices, class activities, and assignments. Upon analyzing students' responses to this question, a number of themes stood out: modalities of teaching and writing, assignment content, and interaction dynamics. Students manifested their surprise at the use of less traditional technologies and media, such as social media sites and games. Other students seemed fascinated by the multimodal teaching materials used in presenting class content, including movies, cartoons, and PowerPoint presentations.

Interaction patterns and dynamics in ENG 108 and 109 classes also surprised participants in our study. These patterns included engaging in interactive group work and discussions, a common practice in first-year writing classes. Interactive group work practices were perceived as novel because they gave students the freedom to express ideas and opinions about topics of discussion. As one student put it, "We can give our own opinion every time." Students expressed their fascination with such opportunities to share their thoughts either in whole-class discussions or in small-group activities. Students also seemed to agree that the level of engagement in class discussions and group work activities varied. While many praised their classmates on their active participation in discussion, others showed their frustration at some of their classmates' silence and resistance to talking, or how many students "never said a word." They described that silence as boring or undermining their learning experiences. This problem of silence or reluctance to participate in class discussions and activities may be interpreted in relation to the earlier finding that students seemed largely keen on improving their English language proficiency. The silence lamented by some students may be due to students' shaky confidence in their English language skills and their perception of their linguistic difference as a deficit rather than a resource (Canagarajah, 2013; Shipka, 2016).

Such students want to move closer to the standards by aspiring to "think and write as American," as one survey respondent worded it, thus signaling a potential dismissal of their translinguality for the sake of standards. Many other respondents shared this perspective on American and native-speaker standard use of English as part of their course expectations. "I expected to have more chances to improve . . . by communicating with my professor and classmate," one student noted, adding, "However, I ended up with a class full of Chinese students (sad smiley face)." "Small groups work with Americans in order to practice English" was a similar priority for another student. In another response, a desire to "help me to correct the habit which may be 'Chinglish' in writing" emerged, and another wrote, "I thought it would teach me to express ideas in a more native style" (underlined by participant). One student reported even deeper differences and a need for native-like writing: "Because Chinese and Americans have different thinking/logical when they write message. I hope to learn how to write message like Americans people."

Another point of agreement among most participants was on the value of peer review. Many students wrote that peer review was a whole new experience for them. Although not many students described the peer review process in their respective classes, they highlighted the benefits of peer review in improving their essays or their English in general. Some students found peer review to be helpful for identifying their writing mistakes, mostly sentence-level errors. Although not surprising, given students' obsession with grammar and vocabulary, it was interesting, as these same students reported relying heavily on the review of authority figures, prior to their U.S. educations.

Experiences Outside the Classroom

When our participants looked for academic support outside of the classroom, a majority of them routinely showed a preference (57 percent) for working with peers from their own country to address writing and other academic concerns, working with Americans far less frequently (28 percent), and working with internationals from other backgrounds (15 percent) only occasionally. These patterns are similar, but not identical, to their socializing patterns, in which students prefer to spend their spare time with fellow nationals. The academic support that the students find in these peer groups is very widely distributed across problem areas, from large-scale content and discourse issues to local grammar and conventions concerns, with no single problem being more frequent than others. In their responses to the question about the communities with which they interact, only a small portion of students stated that they actively sought the company of Americans for English language practice, expressing widely divergent experiences. A few found their interactions to be quite positive, calling their American contacts "friendly" or "pretty cool," and others seemed to have connected with American students of similar ethnic backgrounds. This finding is similar to Andrade (2006), who found that international students prefer social relationships with people from their home countries if available, and that they may have close friendships with domestic students in the case of absence of opportunities to socialize with students from their countries.

The Translanguaging Conversation

Numerous mismatches were identified between international students' earlier experiences and expectations and the goals and practices of the ESL Composition program in which they studied. The most important of these in the data was the nature of their pre-university EFL instruction, in China and elsewhere. The survey results point to a majority of learners having received limited writing instruction, and that writing instruction was considered as non-academic, mostly formulaic, and primarily concerned with grammatical and lexical accuracy, unlike the rhetorical orientation of their writing courses. Broadly, translingualism, in prioritizing the intersections of audiences and writers over formal accuracy and reproduction, is one of many pedagogical directions that would fit the philosophy of the ESL Composition program. Offering a translingual approach to writing for linguistically diverse students in the program, though, would initially present students with another element that does not match their prior experiences. Instructors would be obliged to address this mismatch by openly discussing the benefits of such an approach; with this kind of scaffolding, students can eventually shift their focus from mastering the "standard" English language and "thinking and writing like an American" to perceiving language as a diverse resource (Canagarajah, 2016) that can be used rhetorically to achieve various goals. Discussing the concept of correctness within the translingual disposition with students, or putting an emphasis on clarity rather than correctness as Campbell, Fernandez, and Koo recommend (this collection), can be a feasible and productive pedagogical intervention to solve these deep-rooted problems.

Peer support coming from non-native users of English, rather than native-speaking Americans, is a prime example of translanguaging that is already in practice in the program even though it was not initiated by program faculty. The linguistic, social, and experiential support offered by other language learners can frequently be as or more useful than what is offered by native speakers, and can provide advantages that are unavailable otherwise (Árva & Medgyes, 2000; Medgyes, 1994; Rogers et al., 2016). Gilyard (2016) strongly criticizes strict English-only language policies and curricula adopted in some institutions because they may be dismissive of the rich linguistic repertoire international multilingual students bring to the writing classroom. He describes multilingual students as constantly experimenting with multiple languages in the various contexts in which they find themselves. The Miami ESL Composition program could easily build on students' proclivity toward multilingual language use by explicitly approving and encouraging students to continue pursuing it.

The study findings identified a clear orientation toward TOEFL and TOEFL-like standardized test writing in English as a foreign language instruction. This may also be partially responsible for the "speak and write like an American" opinions that highlighted many of the student responses; only non-L1 English foreigners take the TOEFL test; therefore, students may reasonably conclude that "foreignness" in language performance will inevitably be perceived as a problem by native users of English. A sense of foreignness and of native-like performance as the only worthwhile goal of second language development may also explain why a significant number of students do not fully appreciate the emphasis on writing versus other skills, namely oral English and communication skills in ENG 108 and 109. A translingually oriented curriculum would not entirely ignore this background, but would acknowledge the advantages of language accuracy, but as one of a myriad of tools available for rhetorical success, contingent upon their particular audiences and purposes.

Among our results, we have found that students bring a wide continuum of prior English educational experiences to their U.S. studies, particularly in writing, some that create more present or future potential areas for translanguaging than others. While some students bring a substantial familiarity with academic writing activities, others have very limited exposure to such writing and may be comfortable only with informal and spoken forms of the language, opening up opportunities for multimodal composing. However, these incoming students are uniform in expecting improvements in their academic English skills in first-year writing courses; most of their concerns center on local-level issues of grammar and vocabulary, though, with less concern about more global aspects of academic discourse. Divergences between the program and students regarding their appreciation of and responsiveness to American teaching styles, class dynamics and assignments, and cultural differences suggest possible difficulties in introducing more translanguaging. Finally, whether students are generally successful in their writing courses or they have more difficulties, they find some support among peer communities. By and large, these contacts are students from their own countries or regions. Interactions with Americans and with international students from elsewhere are much more limited, and tend to be non-social in nature, due in part to perceived attitudes of disinterest or intolerance among the Americans they meet. Although our study did not go into detail about out-of-classroom practices, it is not difficult to speculate that students would be immersed in translingual work at these times, as they move between papers and textbooks in standard written English and verbal and electronic exchanges about those papers in their first languages.

At the same time, the translingual approach considers language as just one of the many semiotic resources to which students have access (Canagarajah, 2016). Building on students' interest in non-traditional technologies provides an obvious opening for a wider array of compositional tools. Shipka (2016) argues that incorporating a translingual pedagogy will shift the focus to composing practices that entail utilizing all these possible resources as students compose multimodal texts. Yet, Shipka warns against utilizing such tools only for their own sake, what she calls the "agency of things" (2016, p. 251). Using technologies must be connected to audiences and purposes; to make the shift away from simply being effective writers to being effective composers, instructors need to foster an approach from a position of communicational fluency. Starting with students' fascination with the technology, instructors can build activities and reflective exercises that allow students to hypothesize about audience needs and responses when different media are employed. Since the vast majority of students regularly engage in multimodal literacy practices outside their academic work through social media, electronic gaming, and other digital and non-digital activities, bringing the kinds of multimodality that they typically use and care about has the potential to encourage them to look beyond writing accuracy toward broader issues of messaging and audiences.

Implications of the Study

The first of two implications to emerge from the study is that courses and curriculum have room for modification. Curricular and course expectations, objectives, and outcomes can often be antithetical to a translingual approach. Changing composition courses and the curriculum as a whole in translingual ways would more clearly recognize and respect linguistic differences. One potentially useful avenue is a framework recently proposed by Shapiro et al. (2016). In their work, writer agency is the specific outcome; in other words, an effective curriculum creates the "optimal conditions" for students to build their awareness of available resources for composing, awareness of the need to take action in a set of rhetorical circumstances, and the authority to act (Shapiro et al., 2016, pp 32–33). "Noticing" (Shapiro et al., 2016, p. 33), or the ability to analyze and evaluate a set of circumstances and the options available for responding, is the first step in writers exercising agency.

Beyond agency, mismatches like those that emerged from our study between students' expectations and existing program objectives and pedagogies can be addressed by bringing other translingual approaches into writing curricula. Many students may enter first-year composition courses without explicitly understanding their nature, focus, and objectives. Devoting more time at the start of a course or even earlier to explicating these characteristics would contribute even more to creating dialogues with students, to explore and negotiate under what circumstances they should write and speak in English or rely on other languages, when they should pursue traditional writing or bring in other modes of composition, and when other tools could be appropriate and effective.

Mismatches between international students' expectations of integrating into American academic and social culture and a scarcity of opportunities for communication with American students suggests that other benefits of translingual pedagogy can be realized by bringing international and domestic students together in the same writing classrooms, rather than placing them on separate tracks. Acknowledging the importance of integrating international students into U.S. universities, Matsuda and Silva (2011) called for a "cross-cultural composition course" that would ideally be taught by an instructor who is trained to teach both populations of students (p. 253). More recently, Canagarajah (2016) recommended that writing teachers adopt a translingual approach in their writing classrooms. Such an approach entails capitalizing on students' resources, including multiple languages and language varieties. Also, enhancing the cross-cultural environment in which students study and live requires bringing students' languages, cultures, and technologies to the forefront of the writing classroom. Greater involvement with domestic students and members of the local community would be achieved in the classroom, contribute to international students' verbal and non-verbal social language growth, and expose domestic students to a more diverse group of students. Andrade (2006) suggested that there is a need for increased interaction between domestic and international students for more meaningful intercultural learning for both groups. She rightly argued that interaction in educational activities can contribute to improving cultural understanding.

The second major implication that we see in the study results is that proposed curricular changes call for substantial teacher preparation. Instructors are not always ready to teach courses incorporating translingual approaches even if they are committed to the outcomes that translingual approaches would offer. Canagarajah (2016) encouraged teachers to "negotiate translingual writing" within programs that may be adopting a stricter monolingual ideology and norms (p. 268). It is important for programs engaging in this type of training to not offer this as a one-time event, but as ongoing learning to train faculty and staff to respond to new and wider populations, reflecting the fluid and expanding nature of translingual communication.

Recommendations

The translingual approach to teaching writing respects students' languages and cultural backgrounds (Canagarajah, 2013; Horner et al., 2011). Focusing on pedagogy that positively presents translanguaging and gives students tools that they can use as needed in the future may be a more productive end. Students will become more appreciative of their ability to use more than one language to communicate efficiently across contexts. Allowing students to use their multiple languages seamlessly to construct texts would make for an invisible but fruitful way of shuttling between those languages (Canagarajah, 2013).

Agency is an important goal of a translingual writing curriculum. However, among students similar to those that participated in our study, this may be a greater challenge. Test preparation and memorization with limited critical analysis were common traits of their writing education experiences, and the limited amount of writing that they did in the past makes noticing in written texts more difficult. Frequent in-class activities that encourage more analysis of sample texts and rhetorical situations would be beneficial. Many of the students in our study cited their interest in the range of media—digital media in particular—that their instructors bring to the classrooms, so another important outlet for agency is to be found here. In situations where the broader requirements of a program or a department limit how often new media can be used in major projects, low-stakes writing done between projects as preparation or as reflection is far more open. Allowing students to go beyond the usual choices of email or forum posts for daily assignments or to comment on what they have learned could encourage more unexpected, creative, and insightful work (Shapiro et al., 2016). Ferris (2009) suggests that low-stakes writing tasks (such as, but certainly not limited to, blog posts, reading responses, note-taking activities, and posts to social media sites) motivate students to write fluently without being intimidated by risking their grades. Some of these assignments may focus on the culture of writing courses, and they may also invite students to use multiple languages.

Enhancing the cross-cultural environment in which students study and live requires bringing students' languages, cultures, and technologies to the forefront of the writing classroom in order for all students to value and appreciate diverse experiences and engage with translingual approach in writing. As students discuss and write on cross-cultural topics, asking students to utilize their language varieties as well as their cultural ones means students will have to make more rhetorically informed decisions and choices appropriate for the composing situation and the audience to which they are writing. Moreover, if and when multilingual students interact with mainstream students whom they perceive as "American" and "native speakers," they will realize that "standard" English is such a myth (Matsuda, 2006) and that "American" students' use of multiple language varieties can be almost identical to international students' use of multiple languages. Instructors may be in a position to work with international students on how to better connect with their domestic counterparts, and to reach out to the domestic population of their institution to encourage more cross-culture contact, and to advocate against intolerant attitudes like those that were encountered by some of our study's participants.

Many kinds of opportunities exist for instructors and program administrators to bring student and program expectations into greater alignment. Unlike junior students in Campbell, Fernandez, and Koo's study (this collection) who wanted "to write in a rhetorically appropriate and disciplinary way" (this collection), first-year students in our study had a narrower focus on sentence-level concerns. Incorporating lessons on rhetoric early in a course may contribute to shifting students' expectations and goals from the courses. Likewise, in the months between a student's acceptance to a U.S. university and their first day of class, writing instructors and administrators can collaborate on conveying more explicit information on the expectations of writing courses ahead of time. Sharing detailed course descriptions, using social media to network with incoming students, and encouraging students to engage in short and informal reading and writing activities just prior to the start of a semester are just a few possibilities. Early exposure will strengthen students' familiarity with the new standards and help them adjust their expectations of the program. All of these discussions of the expectations of a translingual course would also make explicit that student writers will have access to a range of linguistic and non-linguistic composing tools.

Preparing teachers for these proposed curricular changes and for translingual practices requires careful consideration. For example, training will enable instructors to understand the rationale and value of adding translingual components before they are asked to practice them in their own classrooms. Training should also give program administrators a chance to anticipate and respond to resistance from instructors to practices that may involve a greater time commitment to prepare, read, comment on, and grade. The number of high-stakes projects in a single course and the time allotted to them should be adjusted accordingly, in order to assure equity for instructor workloads. Furthermore, offering mixed sections of first-year composition classes requires substantial teacher training. The overwhelming majority of instructors at the site of our study have been trained to work almost exclusively with multilingual students, whereas instructors outside the program have very limited, if any, training or experience with multilingual students. This is not a unique situation to in first-year composition courses. Thus, it is essential to train both groups of instructors to teach composition to diverse student populations.

Arnold's (2016) experience at American University Beirut can be a good model to start a much-needed conversation on translingualism. She reported that the responses to the translingual approach were quite diverse, attributing these varied reactions to the fact that most of those writing instructors had been trained in ESL and EFL contexts and on SLW research that pays excessive attention to students' linguistic "problems" and how minimizing these problems is seen as a sign of success for both the student and teacher. Discussion of articles that form the foundation of the translingual approach should be incorporated into suggested teacher training as a response to the kinds of student concerns, expectations, and frustrations expressed in this study. The questions participants in Arnold's study raise are legitimate, coming from multilingual teachers teaching multilingual students whose language proficiency is questionable and who see "their future success depends on their mastery of standard English only" (2016, p. 80).

Finally, complementing the translingual pedagogy's development of student agency, instructors should learn more about the students with whom they work. Just as their ability to evaluate and choose alternatives for composing texts and for communicating about those texts is based on noticing, so too instructors would do well to notice more about their learners' individual, cultural, linguistic, academic, technological, and other backgrounds beyond simple measures of writing and reading ability. Knowing these details as well as students' academic goals enables the development of more useful and more powerful pedagogy.

References

Arnold, L. R. (2016). "This is a field that's open, not closed": Multilingual and international writing faculty respond to composition theory. *Composition Studies, 44*(1), 72–88.

Árva, V. & Medgyes, P. (2000). Native and non-native teachers in the classroom. *System, 28*(3), 355–372.

Canagarajah, S. (2011). Codemeshing in academic writing: Identifying teachable strategies of translanguaging. *The Modern Language Journal, 95*(3), 401–417.

Canagarajah, A. S. (2013). Introduction. In A. S. Canagarajah (Ed.), *Literacy as translingual practice: Between communities and classrooms* (pp. 1–10). Routledge.

Canagarajah, S. (2016). Translingual writing and teacher development in composition. *College English, 78*(3), 265–273.

Evans, N. W., Carlin, D. B. & Potts, J. D. (2009). Adjustment issues. In M. S. Andrade & N. W. Evans (Eds.), *International students: Strengthening a critical resource* (pp. 25–41). Rowman & Littlefield Education.

Ferris, D. R. (2009). *Teaching college writing to diverse student populations.* The University of Michigan Press.

Ferris, D. R. & Hedgcock, J. S. (2014). *Teaching L2 composition: Purpose, process, and practice.* Routledge.

Garcia, O. & Wei, L. (2014). *Translanguaging: Language, bilingualism and education.* Palgrave Macmillan.

Horner, B., Lu, M.-Z., Royster, J. J. & Trimbur, J. (2011). Language difference in writing: Toward a translingual approach. *College English, 73*(3), 303–321.

Jones, J. B. & Landis, W. (Eds.) (2019). *Miami Composition teacher's guide.* Hayden-McNeil Publishing.

Matsuda, P. K. (2006). The myth of linguistic homogeneity in U.S. College composition. *College English, 68*(6), 637–651.

Matsuda, P. K. & Silva, T. (2011). Cross-cultural composition: Mediated integration of U.S. and international students. In P. K. Matsuda, M. Cox, J. Jordan & C. Ortmeier-Hooper (Eds.), *Second-language writing in the composition classroom: A critical sourcebook* (pp. 252–265). Bedford/St. Martin's.

Medgyes, P. (1994). *The non-native teacher.* Macmillan Publishers.

Nation, I. S. P. & Macalister, J. (2010). *Language curriculum design.* Routledge.

Norton, B. (2000). *Identity and language learning: Gender, ethnicity, and educational change.* Pearson Education.

Office of the Registrar. (2015). *Course list.* http://www.admin.muohio.edu/cfapps /courselist/.

Reichelt, M. (2011). Foreign language writing: An overview. In T. Cimasko & M. Reichelt (Eds.), *Foreign language writing instruction: Principles and practices* (pp. 3–21). Parlor Press.

Rogers, P., Zawacki, T. & Baker, S. (2016). Uncovering challenges and pedagogical complications in dissertation writing and supervisory practices: A multi-method study of doctoral student advisors. In S. Simpson, N. Caplan, M. Cox & T. Phillips (Eds.), *Supporting graduate student writers: Research, curriculum, and program design* (pp. 52–77). University of Michigan Press.

Shapiro, S., Cox, M., Shuck, G. & Simnitt, E. (2016). Teaching for agency: From appreciating linguistic diversity to empowering student writers. *Composition Studies, 44*(1), 31–52.

Shipka, J. (2016). Transmodality in/and processes of making: Changing dispositions and practice. *College English, 78*(3), 250–257.

Spack, R. (2004). The acquisition of academic literacy in a second language: A longitudinal case study, updated. In V. Zamel & R. Spack (Eds.), *Crossing the curriculum: Multilingual learners in college classrooms* (pp. 19–45). Lawrence Erlbaum Associates.

Zamel, V. (2004). Strangers in academia: The experiences of faculty and ESOL students across the curriculum. In V. Zamel & R. Spack (Eds.), *Crossing the curriculum: Multilingual learners in college classrooms* (pp. 3–17). Lawrence Erlbaum Associates. 3–17.

4

Translingual Approaches as Institutional Intervention: Implementing the Single-Language Writing Group

Yu-Kyung Kang
Gonzaga University

This chapter describes the development of a single-language writing group in a U.S. university writing center where 80% of its clients are international students. A single language writing group challenges ubiquitous immersive language philosophies and offers a monolingual means of engaging students in translingual dispositions. Specifically, this chapter reviews the author's own ethnographic research on Korean students' English encounters and illustrates how a Korean single-language writing group helped students experience their first language as a resource rather than a barrier in developing academic writing. Notably, the group workshops fostered translingual dispositions as they allowed the students to situate their language ideologies and practices in their history as Korean transnationals. The author argues that non-conventional literacy support acts as an institutional intervention contributing to the literate ecology of students' transnational experiences.

Keywords: translingual disposition, language ideologies, U.S. higher education, writing center, international students

The number of undergraduate international students attending U.S. higher education institutions has risen sharply over the past decade. Reflecting this nationwide trend, the total number of foreign students at the University of Illinois Urbana-Champaign (UIUC) has doubled (from 4,964 in fall 2005 to 10,381 in fall 2015); these students make up 22.3 percent of student enrollment. With such growth, students, faculty, and staff have scrambled to adjust and attend to dramatic demographic changes in and outside of the classrooms. To compensate for such dramatic increases, units, departments, and programs that provide literacy services and support (e.g., the first-year writing program, the linguistics department) frantically and substantially increased the number

DOI: https://doi.org/10.37514/INT-B.2020.0438.2.04

of classes and instructor/graduate TA hires. But despite efforts of people on the frontlines, many multilingual international students are without sufficient language resources and literacy support to develop academic writing skills at the university. Consequently, in an institutional space that is both welcoming and exclusionary, international students become more socially, culturally, and academically segregated.[1]

The Writers Workshop (WW), the campus writing center at UIUC, is a primary source of campus-wide literacy support for all members of the university. Reflecting the very sharp increase in the number of international undergraduate students, between fall 2005 and spring 2014, the percentage of the undergraduate students with ESL/multilingual backgrounds coming to the WW increased from 54.7 percent to more than 80 percent. In response to this dramatic increase in demand for literacy support for our culturally, educationally, and linguistically diverse student body, WW put efforts into providing improved academic services for the growing population. For instance, the WW revamped regular in-house services, developed new services, and collaborated in new ways with units and programs across campus (Kang, 2018, p. 133). The ESL writing groups, a new service, were part of the WW's broader efforts to accommodate the increasing number of international students visiting the writing center. Specifically, the Korean *single-language writing groups*, which are the focus of this chapter, were first facilitated in spring 2012, and were a continuation of "ESL writing groups" that were offered in previous semesters at the WW.

In this chapter, I describe the Korean *single-language writing group* (SLWG) and argue that, in this writing group, Korean international undergraduate student writers were able to develop a translingual orientation to their English academic writing, even as they spoke predominantly in Korean. This translingual orientation countered the deficit ideologies that dominated their English writing experiences in their transnational journeys. The writing group, taking place as a series of workshop sessions, fostered translingual dispositions as they allowed the students to situate their current academic writing experiences within Korean language ideologies and their history as Korean transnationals. Although most second language research stresses

---

1   The time period focused on in this chapter coincides with my time at UIUC. As of fall 2017, according to the Office of International Student and Scholar Services at UIUC, the number of international students reached 10,834 with a slight decrease (by 7 percent) in the undergraduate enrollment from the previous academic year. This is the first sign of decrease in the enrollment of international undergraduate students in more than a decade.

the effectiveness of immersion learning (i.e., that the target language is best acquired through immersion in the target language), this chapter illustrates how the SLWG helped students experience their first language, Korean, as a resource rather than a barrier in honing English rhetorical flexibility. This chapter, thus, seeks to contribute to the current conversation on and development of translingual approaches and pedagogies by highlighting the importance of providing learning spaces (both physical and psychological) and by suggesting that a translingual approach to writing, can invite and empower multilingual students to negotiate and unsettle existing language ideologies through the mixing of languages and by using one's first language.

I elaborate on the Korean SLWG as an experimental undertaking that aimed to hone a translingual disposition among the students by helping them break away from the deeply rooted self-deprecating English ideologies acquired over the course of their national and transnational educational journeys. In the following sections, I describe the research that led to the idea for SLWG, including my research with jogi yuhak students at the university, which demonstrates that these students need a space where they can explore their past and present ideas and practices surrounding English and language in general. By understanding and respecting individual literacy experiences, I contend that the writing group helped students reflect on ideologies that debilitated their own English language learning, thus helping students take ownership of English and their English literacy practices. I suggest that such unconventional methods of literacy support, such as the Korean SLWG, act as institutional interventions, which contribute to the development of students' transnational experiences.

Evidence-Informed Theory

In the field of Writing and Composition Studies, the 1974 College Composition and Communication resolution "Student Rights to Their Own Language" was NCTE's first call to embrace language diversity. With this initiation, the exploration and pursuit of linguistic diversity has been active in Writing Studies and its adjacent fields. In January 2011, with the publication of "Language Difference in Writing" in *College English*, "translingual," a relatively new term to the field, took center stage. Horner et al. called for a paradigm that promoted linguistic diversity and opposed traditional *monolinguistic* approaches to writing (i.e., those approaches which fetishize Standard English or Edited American English) in our college writing classrooms. As translingual scholars acknowledge, the movement to promote, accept, and practice non-*monolinguistic* orientations to language has long been explored across various disciplines (e.g., bilingual studies, translation studies) under labels such as "bilingualism," "multilingualism," and "plurilingualism."

Although the big ideas behind the translingual approach have been gaining attention and momentum in the past few years, more recently, there have been tensions over what the outcomes of the approach might (or should) look like in our college classrooms, and in students' writing. For example, within composition classrooms, Matsuda (2014) criticized translingual scholars ("tour guides") for promoting translingual writing which he views as a "problematic trend . . . luring" scholars and teachers ("tourists") with alien writing . . . obscure[ing] more subtle manifestations of the negotiation as well as situations where writers make the rhetorical choice not to deviate from the dominant practice" (pp. 482–483). I see his concerns as understandable; many pedagogical strategies of the translingual approach have so far more or less focused on code-switching or code-meshing as their end product. And, although translingual scholars have presented *living* translingual literacy practices in various communities in the United States and around the world (e.g., Bou Ayash, 2013; Canagarajah, 2002; Young & Martinez, 2011) and introduced pedagogical applications providing tools, evidence, and guidelines for teachers, tutors, and learners (e.g., Hanson, 2013; Jerskey, 2013), much of this research has exemplified "putting together diverse semiotic resources for meaning" (Canagarajah, 2013a, p. 6). Through my experience as a teacher-scholar with training in both L2 and writing studies, I see the translingual approach as a productive tool in helping L2 student writers make conscientious rhetorical choices whether to deviate or confirm to the dominant practices (e.g., Standard English or Edited American English).

The motives and rationale behind the Korean SLWG emerged well before the current "turf battle" broke out between second language studies and translingual approaches (see Canagarajah, 2015; Matsuda, 2014). In fact, the writing group emerged initially less from a theoretical alignment with translingual theory than from a felt sense that Korean students needed a space where they could be mentored in fluent Korean about their linguistic, literate, and rhetorical practices and ideologies. In addition to the visible aspects of translingual literacy, such as the meshing of languages in writing, the translingual approach also points to the less-visible *dispositions* that "constitute assumptions of language, attitude toward social diversity, and tacit skills of communication and learning" (Canagarajah, 2013a, p. 5). This orientation, according to Canagarajah (2013a), "includes an awareness of language as constituting diverse norms, willingness to negotiate with diversity in social interactions, and attitudes such as openness to difference, patience to co-constructed meaning and acceptance of negotiated outcomes in interactions" (p. 5). Not only was this disposition scarce in the Korean undergraduate students, but, as my own research revealed, their narrow perceptions of the language was stunting their English literacy usage and development overall at the university. Thus, the SLWG was an experiment to address the students' specific ideologies. My exploration of the Korean SLWG dovetails with conversations that are surfacing in the growing body of translingual literature, not solely because the writing group used the Korean language, the students' first language, as the main medium to talk about language and writing, and not because the study presents how students used their more familiar semiotic resources to produce writing—in fact, they did not code-mesh in their academic writing. Instead, I argue that the writing group developed *translingual dispositions* by understanding and attending to their particular monolinguistic English language dispositions, which had been shaped by national and transnational experiences. I claim that the Korean SLWG was a translingual site for Korean undergraduate students with particular language ideologies and literacy practices.

Research Informing SLWG

The felt sense I note above prompted a path of inquiry for my research and pedagogy. I proposed, designed, implemented, and studied the Korean SLWG guided by preliminary findings from my larger longitudinal ethnographic and auto-ethnographic research on the literacy and rhetorical practices of South Korean (henceforth "Korean") undergraduate students with jogi yuhak experience prior to their matriculation at UIUC. Jogi yuhak, which literally means Early Study Abroad in Korean (traditionally, the phrase "study abroad student" referred to students studying abroad for undergrad or grad school), is a popular transnational educational migration trend that has been prevalent in Korea since the mid 1990s, and that has also been gaining popularity in other East Asian countries, such as China and Taiwan. This trend has sent thousands of pre-college students, even as young as elementary school, to English-speaking countries—including the US, Canada, New Zealand, Singapore, and Malaysia—for their schooling. The purpose of my research was to examine this Korean phenomenon at UIUC, where Korean students had become the second largest international student group (second to Chinese international students). More than 80 percent of approximately 700 Korean undergraduate students had gone through some part of their elementary and/ or secondary educational years studying abroad in a school where English is the official language before enrolling at the university (Kang, 2018).

My curiosity about the jogi yuhak and the literacy practices of Korean undergraduate students with pre-college study abroad experience also stemmed in part from my own personal and professional experiences. As a Korean with jogi yuhak experience in the 1980s and as a returning international student in the early 2000s, I was fascinated by the changing characteristics of the Korean student population during my graduate studies at UIUC. Through teaching and tutoring in ESL classrooms, first-year writing classrooms, and the WW, I was intrigued by the subtle and stark differences of their literacy and language practices and needs in comparison to traditional Korean undergraduate students without jogi yuhak experience. Thus, from fall 2011 to spring 2013, I looked into the ways these students' literacies and literate selves developed as they negotiated and navigated U.S. college life. In order to understand and provide an in-depth articulation of their literate lives, I collected and analyzed data from numerous informal and formal observations in learning and social settings, conducted individual and group interviews of students, faculty and administrators, and collected various personal and institutional artifacts.

During my research, as well as in my personal and professional encounters with many traditional and Korean international students with jogi yuhak experience, I discovered that it was rare to see these Korean students using English amongst their Korean peers. It was as if it was an unspoken rule. This insight is what led me to consider a university academic writing group facilitated not in English but in the students' first language (L1), Korean. To most second language (L2) scholars and teachers, the decision to use the students' L1 as the primary oral communication in an English-language learning context might seem counterintuitive; however, to others the use of one's L1 may seem obvious, considering its convenience to the speakers. My decision to use Korean in the writing group, was based on neither L2 literature nor convenience, but on the particular English ideologies these students carried with them. To understand the literacy and rhetorical practices of these students, it is important to understand how the language ideologies that shaped these practices were constructed in the history and context of the local and global.

First, one must consider a key characteristic of the Korean students with jogi yuhak experience (henceforth post-jogi yuhak students). Most of the students in the study felt that they lacked the English competency they thought they should have acquired during their many years studying abroad. Students did not feel that they had lived up to the promise of the jogi yuhak project—a nationally fetishized transnational education project premised by the belief that earlier is better (and immersion in the target language is best) for language acquisition. Because they believed they did not accomplish the goal of acquiring "perfect" English skills, they hid their English language (abilities) from others, other Koreans in particular, as much as they could (Kang, 2016).

So, in their everyday literacy practices among their Korean peers, English words and phrases may have come up sporadically in casual settings, but elsewhere, Korean was the language of choice.

Such literacy practices—the choice not to use the English language amongst Korean peers—of the post-jogi yuhak students should not only be understood within the U.S. university context alone, but also within the Korean national context—how English has been taken up, how it is used, and why people choose to use the language in Korea (Shim & Park, 2008). In other words, it is important to understand the language ideologies behind the practices constructed locally and globally. In Korea, English has come to be perceived to be one of the key "skills" to a successful life (on the personal level) and as part of the nation's survival strategy (on the global level). This strong belief has plagued the nation and its people with yeongeo yeolpung ("English Fever"), the relentless pursuit of English exemplified by the massive English education market, English villages, English-only kindergartens, split-tongue surgery,[2] and jogi yuhak—to name a few expressions of this "fever." It has become so extreme that the value of English exceeds its practical use, as English is more or less contained within specific linguistic domains such as popular culture but not used much in the everyday lives of the people (Park, 2009; Park & Abelmann, 2004). According to Park (2009), many Koreans have a "strong belief about English and Korean's relationship to the language [which has] led [to] a heavy pursuit of English at all levels of society, thus constructing English as a hegemonic language" (p. 4). Within this social construct, another important aspect is that English has been equivalent to the "white" west. In other words, many South Koreans consider white people in and from the western nations (specifically the US and UK) to be "native" speakers and the owners of the English language. This is exemplified in the common hiring practices of English private institutions in Korea: for marketability, "white" instructors/teachers are preferred regardless of their educational background and teaching qualifications.

Considering this dominant linguistic ideological construct, it is understandable that post-jogi yuhak students, despite the geographical, cultural, and educational heterogeneity of the students' pre-college experience, share

---

2   A oral surgical procedure known as frenectomy, eliminates the presence of the lingual fernum (muscular tissue that connects the bottom center of the tongue to the floor of the mouth). Mostly in the early 2000s, Korean and western media reported on the use of this procedure on children ages 0 to 9 to "enhance" their English pronunciation (the "R" sound, in particular) in the midst of joki yeongeo yeolpung ("Early English Education Craze") which persists today.

homogeneous notions of "good English" or rather "doing English well"—literally translated from Korean "영어를 잘하다." For most of the participants in the study, regardless of the foreign country in which they were educated in English, "doing English well" means doing English like an American, or to be more exact, doing English like a bek-in (a Korean word that literally means *white person*).

This is how Sun, one of the participants in my study, responded to my question about what it means to do English well.

> Sun: To me, doing English well is communicating, no, I mean no difficulties in communicating, exchanging intentions/meanings when talking with foreigners, and also, for me, when the pronunciation is good. I tend to think that [someone is] doing [English] well if the pronunciation is good when communicating.
>
> Me: *Do you mean when talking like American (mikook Saram)?*
>
> Sun: Yes, sounding like an American.
>
> Me: *Whom do you mean by Americans exactly?*
>
> Sun: American white person (bek-in) without question.

Sun spent most of his teenage life in Malaysia (with frequent visits to Korea during breaks like most transnational Korean students). Since the age of 11, until coming to college in the US about a month before, Sun attended international schools with classmates from countries such as China, India, Korea, Malaysia and the US. Although he lived in a demographically and linguistically diverse environment both in and out of school, he was very firm about what was acceptable and what was not in terms of "doing English well," particularly among white people and in official school settings.

> When I'm by myself, when I go to a restaurant or in my [first-year composition course] and there are more "bek-in," then I feel extremely "unsecure." I don't feel "secure." Although I know how to do the English, I get this feeling right smack at the beginning, "I am not good at English compared to them." And when I feel I'm lesser than them, it makes me freeze and I don't say anything. You know, I talk a lot, I'm a VERY talkative kid but when I'm with "bek-in," I don't talk.

Sun's insecurity with English language use can be explained by English language ideologies shared by Koreans—*self deprecation*. According to Park

(2009), *self deprecation* is an "ideology that views Koreans as lacking sufficient competence to pursue English meaningfully" and a term applied to "cultural and social constructions of linguistic competence in order to understand how a community may subordinate itself within a hierarchical relation of power through the mediation of such constructions" (p. 26). Interestingly, the students in the study demonstrated lack or avoidance of English language practices not only among white peers, but also more frequently among their Korean peers with whom they spend most of their time. Because they do not want to be judged or evaluated poorly for their English competency, they rarely speak English with one another (Kang, 2015). This "white gaze" that hinders the students from using English among Americans is also imagined among their Korean peers.

Most Korean undergraduate students in the study felt they lacked the English competency that they should have acquired during the many years studying abroad. The negative sense of their own English abilities and their representations of English as owned by white Americans led me to implement the SLWG with the Korean undergraduate students. I chose the Korean language as the main medium to accommodate the students' practical and psychological language preference because my research showed that, in terms of academic English support, these students did not have a space for fast, fluent, meta-talk about language, about literate practices, and about rhetorical issues (Kang, 2016). They needed the richness and comfort of their first language to negotiate the complexity of their academic immersion in English. As evidenced in my research of a Korean student organization's achievements, the students, who carried self-deprecating English language ideologies, needed Korean, the language that helps them feel confident and respected (Kang, 2015). With these preliminary findings from my research, I was motivated to explore, design, and facilitate a literacy learning experience that took into account this ambivalence towards English and explored the educational, cultural, and linguistic histories these students brought with them.

De-constructing Ideologies

With evidence and justification provided by my ethnographic study and from my administrative work at WW as the ESL Services Coordinator, in spring 2012, I organized and began a SLWG for Korean undergraduate students. The writing group was one of many services that the writing center provided to students, faculty, and staff on campus. Despite campus-wide general and target promotions, only eight students came to the information session; seven students participated until the end.

As stipulated in the announcement/flyer (see Appendix B), the overarching goal for the SLWG was to attend to students' own questions pertaining to U.S. academic writing. To participate in the writing groups, the students had to attend the information meeting before the first session and agree to attend all four sessions of the workshop. At the information meeting, I handed out a student information sheet (see Appendix C) to collect their personal information, including English literacy/education background and their personal goals for the workshop. At the hour-and-a-half workshop sessions, the first half was used to introduce and go over the topic of the day and do some controlled practice with resources found on writing websites (e.g., Purdue OWL). For example, in the first session, we reviewed elements of *rhetorical situations*. Students then analyzed the rhetorical situation of a sample paper individually and then as a group. In the second half of session, the students had to analyze the rhetorical situation of their own writing and discuss the resultant analysis as a group.

Although the structure of each one-and-a-half-hour session was relatively fixed, the development of topics for each session was a fairly organic process. The topic of the following session was decided through discussion during the previous session. If during a session, however, a topic other than the topic previously decided upon should come up, we would adjust our discussion and attend to student concerns by discussing and/or searching for resources online. The topics we considered included organizing ideas, understanding different kinds of writing tasks, understanding instructors' responses, and using sources. In this process, students were encouraged to explore and reflect on their English literacy experiences. In the sections that follow, I explore the how SLWG became a translingual site where students were able to identify and navigate the largely monolinguistic ideologies behind their language development.

Judgmental English

Although I had designed the workshop for the students to use Korean as their primary medium of communication, I did not announce this during the information session nor did I make it explicit in the workshop. As anticipated, the students' reluctance to communicate/speak in English was noticeable from the beginning. It was in a part of the workshop, which was devoted to peer review activities, when the students' avoidance of using English in their sharing (or not sharing) of English writing became clear. Despite several in-person and email reminders to bring their current in-progress writing to the second session, only one student arrived with his writing (and that writing example turned out to be a polished edited version already submitted for a course in the previous semester). My curiosity as to why the students did not bring their papers was partially answered during that same session. As I elaborated on the usefulness of peer reviews and asked what the students thought, there was silence. Then Min, who did his early study abroad in New Zealand, broke the silence in a quiet voice: "I don't show it to my Korean friends because I think they are just going to judge [my English]." All smiled and nodded at Min's response. Then Hyun jumped in right away and said, "It's not only that but I don't think the writing will get any better [with their feedback]." And all nodded again. In addition to the fear of being judged, the students refrained from seeking help from their Korean peers because they had doubts about not only their own English, but also about their peers' as well.

Getting to the Roots

As we were reviewing one student's draft on the fourth day of the workshop, Dahae, a senior in psychology, expressed frustrations with her repeated use of the word "because" and her inability to diversify sentence structure. As she began to talk about her frustrations, she partly blamed the "habit" of using "because" on her past "TOEFL Training." When I encouraged her to elaborate, she said:

> I think because I lack "expressive ability," when I want to add explanation I think I use "because" a lot. I used *because* a lot [in TOEFL writing]—to show the relationship [between sentences]. [We were taught in the TOEFL writing training that we] needed to use a lot of *reasoning* [in U.S. academic writing].

With Daehae's remark, something clicked and the group had a lively discussion about the influence of "TOEFL training." TOEFL (Test of English as a Foreign Language) is a standardized English proficiency test that, according to ETS (Educational Testing Service[3]), "measures your ability to use and understand English at the university level. And it evaluates how well you combine your listening, reading, speaking and writing skills to perform academic tasks" ("About the TOEFLiBT," n.d.). Although the cut off score

---

3   ETS is the world's largest private nonprofit educational testing and assessment organization that develops and administers various achievement and admissions tests, including TOEFL and GRE, in the United States and 180 countries (ETS, n.d.).

might vary, most higher education institutions require TOEFL scores. I use the phrase "TOEFL Training," commonly used by Koreans as TOEFL is not only required in applying to higher education institutions abroad, but it is pervasively used as a gatekeeper in the education and corporate world in Korea. Furthermore, most Koreans preparing for the TOEFL exam and all the students in the group had one experience or another with rote TOEFL training at a TOEFL hagwon—private English learning institutions ubiquitous in Korea and perceived as mandatory to receive high scores on the TOEFL exam. The students acknowledged that the TOEFL training gave them the impetus to start thinking about the American academic essay, but also how the past training had been a deterrent in writing in college. They resented how the training limited the ways they structured and organized essays and stymied their word and phrase choices.

The lively conversation naturally extended to other English learning experiences in Korea and their transnational educational journey. The TOEFL training was just one small window into the culture of English language in Korea—how English language is taught, how ideologies surrounding English are constructed, and how (narrow) conceptions of the language are reinforced in Korea by Koreans at home and abroad. As post-jogi yuhak students who were brought up and educated in the eye of the English fever/tornado, it was a chance for them to step back and view the metalinguistic landscape and factors that influenced their English language lives. As they were reviewing their own and peers' writing, they were also reflecting on their related past and current literacy educations. One student shuffled through vague memories about his first private tutoring experience before kindergarten, another frowned remembering his strict middle school English teacher posting test scores for all to see, and one even shed tears as she recalled her first week studying abroad in a foreign land. During this animated session, the students went through their papers eager to identify other remnants of the TOEFL training and their English "training" in Korea and abroad. With this motivation, the students were now eager to share their papers. It was an opportunity for the group to think about language and language use with their own past experiences and literacy histories; it was an opportunity for them to engage with their existing dispositions and to make room for translingual ones.

Rhetorical Flexibility through Translingual Dispositions

Many of the students wrote on their information sheets that they wanted to learn "writing skills," and improve their "expressions." Despite these students' secondary education in English speaking countries and first-year writing requirements at the university, it was disheartening (but not that surprising), to find students with confined definition of what good writing is—in their words, paragraphs of "native-like perfect English" with flawless "expressions," grammar, and mechanics. As they had longed to talk "accent-free" like a bek-in, their long-term goals was to write "accent-free" like an American. Because the students were overtly concerned about getting pronunciation and writing "right," they had been missing the opportunity to critically explore and experiment with the language in the meaning-making process.

With continuous encouragement and discussions about the benefits of peer-review and their own culturally-conditioned conceptions surrounding English, the group gradually became a space that was safe enough for most of the students to share their rougher drafts. Encouraging students to consciously and continuously put aside their concerns about being judged resulted in spending more of our time talking about the rhetorical use and impact of phrases and words at the sentence level. For example, we would stop at a seemingly simple word like "about" and use dictionaries and thesauri to explore the connotations involved in the use of other options such as "regarding," "concerning," or "with reference to" and the consequent impacts on sentence-level meaning. Or students would compare words like "next" and "following" and examine which word might best suit the writer's intentions. At this point, their concerns were not about sounding or writing like a bek-in but more about making rhetorical choices and thus developing a rhetorical identity for themselves in learning and using the English language in their writing. As the students were now open to translingual *guidance*—a pedagogy that encourages rhetorical identity above "perfect" English—it afforded them with the opportunity to find themselves not as incompetent language users through their white gaze, but as legitimate users of English making rhetorical choices.

In a follow-up individual interview, Won expressed how it was very refreshing to "spill her secrets to the world."

> Wow! I had so much to say. I really like the way we conversed. It was good just for the fact that I was able to share my concerns. I, first, felt that I gained something, gained confidence and will. [I thought to myself] so, it's not just me but others have these worries too. I realized by talking about such issues and I look back [on my past experiences]. I don't think I could this could have happened if it was done in English.

The writing group sessions, at one point or another, all seemed like therapy sessions. It was a space for students to share their concerns, reveal anxieties, and also devise strategies to cope with their literacy realities. Overall, the sessions provided a safe space to process their language and literacy practices. Won affirmed my initial hypothesis regarding the writing group with her last statement: use of L1 would facilitate the writing development process by lowering students' anxieties that were driven by self-deprecating English language ideologies. The use of L1 lowered language anxiety and promoted deep thought and honest expression between the members. But more importantly, the Korean language afforded them the opportunity to break out of their self-deprecating ideologies and deficit identities as English language learners because the use of L1 enabled them to develop rhetorical identities in the language learning process. Using English became just more than memorizing, regurgitating, and mimicking the language of the bek-in. The students' L1 provided them with the conceptual space to explore and use English on their own terms and with their own intentions.

I had a chance to meet up with Won roughly a month after the writing group ended. During our hour-long conversation, Won reflected on her English experience during her jogi yuhak days in Arkansas and her experience after SLWG at the university. She mentioned that, now, whenever she felt inferior among her white peers because of her English, she consciously and intentionally reminded herself, "It's okay. I don't have to 'do English' that way [like a bek-in]. It's my second language. They don't know how to speak Korean. So it's okay." She admitted it was not easy to go against her "natural instincts." She also mentioned how she had more freedom to use English without being too worried about "sounding foreign." Although she seemed ambivalent and less confident from time to time about her stance even during our meeting, it was certain that her translingual disposition was growing— not only affecting how she used English, but also various aspects of her life as a U.S. college student and as a global citizen.

Translanguaging as a Process

Despite concerns that the translingual movement might be a "fad" prompting "linguistic tourism" (Matsuda, 2014), a translingual disposition is being welcomed by many who have been longing for explanations and remedies for working with the language diversities in their composition classrooms. Some second language scholars have expressed concerns that translingual pedagogies do not consider the students' choices—for instance, the choice to learn "Standard" written/spoken English—and that they, instead, will enforce using students' other language or languages. It is important to note that in the Korean SLWG, I did not tell students what language or languages to use. I simply indicated they could use Korean and created a context where that choice would include all present. I also did not encourage them to use Korean in their academic writing. Students negotiated and chose the linguistic resources that aligned with their learning goals. Use of L1 allowed students to put anxieties aside and become more reflective about the process of writing in English. Ultimately, however, all academic writing produced and refined in this group was in English. As such, the Korean SLWG had no end-products/writing that had visible translingual semiotic elements.

I do not wish to argue here that the SLWG is a one-size-fits-all remedy for all international students or multilingual students. A series of Chinese SLWGs that the writing center ran after the success of the Korean SLWG offers a useful perspective here. The first of these groups had a Chinese facilitator, and the latter two groups each had a non-Chinese speaking facilitator (me and another WW tutor). Although the groups were successful in attending to student writing needs, the use of the Chinese language was not a key element in terms of tapping into their language ideologies and practices. Compared to the Korean students, Chinese undergraduates in the group were less concerned about not being able to produce "perfect" English. According to McNamara (2018), Chinese students at UIUC are more focused on asserting their power as consumers to "secure some yield on their educational investment" (p. 4). Thus, they inadvertently acknowledge their level of English competency (or lack there of) by proactively claiming literacy support to broaden their "linguistic and cultural horizon" (McNamara, 2018, p. 9). Therefore, the Korean SLWG, which catered to the specific language ideologies derived from a particular transnational educational experience (jogi yuhak), may not provide specific tools for teaching all multilingual students; rather it offers evidence for the importance for teachers to investigate, acknowledge, and utilize the language ideologies and practices of a particular group or groups of students by "[resisting] thinking of identifying students and our teaching in terms of fixed categories of language, language ability, and social identity" (Canagarajah, 2015, p. 622).

The writing group, during its development stage, was scheduled for one hour-and-a-half workshop per week for four weeks. Upon students' request, however, it was extended to two hours a session for six weeks in total. The six-week period was a valuable time for identifying students' past and present literacy contexts and the language ideologies that they had been exposed to or had conformed to. Rather than hiding behind their anxieties of incompetency, overwhelmed by the power of monolinguistic English ideologies, the students used the space to negotiate their Korean and English literate identities. The group offered an example of what Pratt (1991) calls *safe houses*, "social and intellectual spaces where groups can constitute themselves as horizontal, homogeneous, sovereign communities with high degrees of trust, shared understandings, temporary protection from legacies of oppression" (p. 40). For Korean undergraduate students, the SLWG was a *translingual safe house* "for hearing and mutual recognition . . . to construct shared understandings, knowledges, claims on the world that they can then bring into the contact zone" (Pratt, 1991, p. 40). Thus, helping them "move beyond a consideration of individual or monolithic languages to life between and across languages" and language ideologies (Canagarajah, 2013b, p. 1). SLWG functioned as a safe house where Korean students, as they proceeded on their transnational education journey, began to acknowledge and negotiate pre-conceived monolingual and translingual language orientations in their own past and present literacy and rhetorical practices.

Conclusion and Implications

The US has been one of the most resistant countries in the world to embracing multilingualism. The world has been accommodating the dominance of our monolingualism for decades now, but that era is ending and we need to forge a new translingual stance in the anglocentric world and in our language pedagogies. As language diversity is becoming a norm in higher education institutions across the US, scholar-teachers have the obligation to advocate for and cultivate linguistic diversity in our students' lives. Non-conventional literacy support, like the Korean SLWG, acts as an institutional intervention contributing to the literate ecology of students' transnational experience and these translingual approaches must take into account the dynamic global and institutional contexts in which they are applied.

U.S. higher education institutions are seeing an unprecedented number of students from abroad. These students from abroad are bringing not only languages but also ideologies surrounding the English language. This chapter has examined how a Korean *single-language* writing group, an experimental learning group at the campus-writing center, was translingual in nature on a few different levels: students' first language, Korean, was used voluntarily by the participants as the primary communication medium; their Korean and English language practices and ideologies were examined; and the participants were able to deal with monolingual ideologies that hindered their English language development. Talking about their literacy histories and the ways nationalism and global capitalism have influenced English language learning was productive in cultivating translingual dispositions in Korean undergraduate students, particularly with jogi yuhak experience. This group allowed these students to confront some of the self-deprecating English language ideologies they carried with them. The writing group provided a space for students to explore and negotiate their preconceived notions about English language and its use, and thus was a tool to help them forge more flexible rhetorical identities (rather than limiting linguistic identities).

Many pedagogical textbooks emphasize the importance of *knowing* the students we teach. My study echoes this notion and further details what this *knowing* might entail for different student groups and individuals. In the case of Korean undergraduate students at UIUC, it was pertinent to examine and recognize students' literacy and rhetorical practices in both learning and social settings at the university, in Korea, and at their respective early study abroad locations. It was with in-depth knowledge of the particular and peculiar literacy and rhetorical practices, and the language ideologies behind the practices that I was able to create the SLWG for the Korean undergraduate students. Therefore, the writing group is not a solution that will necessarily help meet the needs of all multilingual international students. The results of this experience, however, should serve as an impetus for scholar-teachers to seek to learn the needs of our multilingual/translingual students from abroad and to use this knowledge in effectively designing writing curriculum and instruction.

References

Bou Ayash, N. (2013). Hi-ein, Hi جو or جو Hi? Translingual practices from Lebanon and mainstream literacy education. In S. Canagarajah (Ed.), *Literacy as Translingual Practice: Between Communities and Classrooms* (pp. 96–103). Routledge.

Canagarajah, S. (2002). *A geopolitics of academic writing*, University of Pittsburgh Press.

Canagarajah, S. (2013a). Introduction. In S. Canagarajah (Ed.), *Literacy as transnational practice: Between communities and classrooms* (pp. 1–10). Routledge.

Canagarajah, S. (2013b). *Translingual practice: Global Englishes and composition relations*. Taylor & Francis.

Canagarajah, S. (2015). Clarifying the relationship between translingual practice and L2 writing: Addressing learner identities. *Applied Linguistics Review, 6*(4), 415–440.

ETS, (n.d.). About the TOEFL iBT® Test. https://www.ets.org/toefl/ibt/about?WT.ac=toeflhome_aboutibt_180910.

Hanson, J. (2013). Moving out of the monolingual comfort zone and into the multilingual world: An exercise for the multilingual classroom. In S. Canagarajah (Ed.), *Literacy as Translingual Practice: Between Communities and Classrooms* (pp. 278–286). Routledge.

Horner, B., Lu, M., Royster, J. J. & Trimbur, J. (2011). Language difference in writing: Towards a translingual approach. *College English, 73*(3), 303–321.

Jerskey, M. (2013). Literacy brokers in the contact zone, year 1: The crowded safe house. In S. Canagarajah (Ed.), *Literacy as translingual practice: Between communities and classrooms* (pp. 197–206). Routledge.

Kang, Y. (2015). Tensions of the local and global: South Korean students navigating and maximizing U.S. college life. *Literacy in Composition Studies, 3*(3), 86–109.

Kang, Y. (2016). English-Only when necessary: Literacy practices of Korean undergraduate students at a "global" university [Doctoral dissertation, University of Illinois at Urbana-Champaign]. IDEALS. Illinois Digital Environment for Access to Learning and Scholarship. http://hdl.handle.net/2142/90767.

Kang, Y. (2018). Expanding the role of the writing center at the global university. In S. K. Rose & I. Weiser (Eds.), *The Internationalization of US Writing Programs* (pp. 132–148). Utah State University Press.

Matsuda, P. K. (2014). The lure of translingual writing. *PMLA, 129*(3), 478–483.

McNamara, T. (2018). Diminishing returns at corporate u: Chinese undergraduates and composition's activist legacy. *Literacy in Composition Studies, 6*(1). http://dx.doi.org/10.21623%2F1.6.1.2.

Park, J. S. (2009). *The local construction of a global language: Ideologies of English in South Korea.* Mouton de Gruyter.

Park, S. & Abelmann, N. (2004). Class and cosmopolitan striving: Mother's management of English. Education in South Korea. *Anthropological Quarterly, 77*(4), 645–672.

Pratt, M. L. (1991). Arts of the contact zone. *Profession, 33*–40.

Shim, D. & Park, J. (2008). The language politics of "English fever" in South Korea. *Korea Journal, 48*(2), 136–159.

Young, V. A. & Martinez, A. Y. (2011). *Code-meshing as world English: Pedagogy, policy, performance.* NCTE.

Appendix A

Korean Single-Language Writing Group Announcement Flyer

Navigating Academic Writing:

Writing Groups for <u>KOREAN</u> Undergraduate Students

Would you like to talk about U.S. academic writing in your own language?

Do you sometimes wonder what your writing assignments mean?

Do you struggle to talk with your professors and classmates about writing?

Would you like to practice U.S. conventions of using sources?

Then you would want to join <u>Navigating Academic Writing</u>, FREE writing groups hosted by the Writers Workshop. These groups are specifically for writers whose first language is Korean and will meet in a 4-week session. Topics will be tailored to your needs but may include organizing ideas, understanding different kinds of writing tasks, understanding instructors' responses, and using sources. The sessions will be led by an experienced Writers Workshop consultant who understands struggles with writing in English. In order to participate, you **must** attend the informational meeting on **February 2** (Thursday) at **3:00 pm** to sign up and you **must** attend all four sessions. Students who have participated in <u>Navigating Academic Writing</u> in the past are not eligible.

Informational Meeting:
    Thursday, February 2, 2012

Writing group sessions:
    Thursday, Feb 9
    Thursday, Feb 16
    Thursday, Feb 23
    Thursday, March 1
    3:00 p.m. to 4:30 p.m.
    Room 251 Undergraduate Library

Email ykang5@illinois with the subject "Writing-Group-Korean" by **February 1** to attend the informational meeting.

Appendix B

Student Information Sheet

NAVIGATING ACADEMIC WRITING

KOREAN UNDERGRADUATE WRITING GROUP / Spring 2012

Name: _____

Email: _____

Phone:_____

Major: _____ Year in School: _____

Age:_____

Writer's Workshop ID Number (if you have one): _____

Our group will meet on Thursdays from 3:00–4:30 pm on February 9, 16, 23 and March 1. Attendance is required at all 4 sessions.

- What courses are you currently taking that require writing (please list)?

- How long have you been speaking English (When did you come to the States or another country where English is the first language to attend school)?
- How long have you been writing and/or reading in English?
- Have you received any specific writing instruction in English? What type (ESL classes, IEI, coursework elsewhere, etc.)?
- What kind of writing projects are you currently working on? Please describe in detail. (For example, course assignments.)
- What concerns do you have regarding writing in English and/or academic writing?
- What areas do you most want to improve in your writing?
- What writing subjects do you want our Undergraduate Writing Group to address? (For example: American academic writing conventions, citation and source use, paragraph organization, common English grammar areas that challenge Korean writers, etc.)

Part 2: Investigations of Deliberately Translingual Pedagogy

5 Translingual Pedagogy and Anglophone Writing Instruction in a Swedish Department of History

Thomas Lavelle
STOCKHOLM SCHOOL OF ECONOMICS

Maria Ågren
UPPSALA UNIVERSITY

This chapter describes a pedagogical approach to Anglophone writing instruction brought about by the growing use of English as an academic lingua franca. In order to meet the needs of relatively experienced academic writers located in Sweden but with diverse national and linguistic histories, that approach relies upon three central tenets: 1) learning-and-teaching is a process of *collaborative inquiry,* 2) participants' experience with *lingua-franca communication* and its associated dispositions constitutes a resource to be supported and leveraged, 3) the work of writing takes place in *conceptual spaces* where writers make textual decisions, spaces that can be enlarged and structured through strategies that help student writers activate the prior knowledge derived from their linguistic, rhetorical, and educational backgrounds. This chapter describes these three pedagogical tenets, illustrates them with classroom examples, and ultimately demonstrates that this approach aligns closely with translingual theory and so supports writers as they draw, in their Anglophone writing practice, upon the translingual strategies they regularly, but perhaps not always consciously, employ in their lingua-franca communication.

Keywords: English and academic lingua franca, collaborative inquiry, lingua-franca communication, conceptual spaces, graduate students

The pedagogy we describe in this chapter evolved to meet the needs and abilities of a specific community of academic writers. The members of this

DOI: https://doi.org/10.37514/INT-B.2020.0438.2.05

community, primarily graduate students in history programs, are academically accomplished, all having earned bachelor's degrees and some, advanced degrees. They all are multilinguals, including a few traditionally seen as native speakers of English. Alongside Swedes, the writers in our classes come from a long list of countries, so many come with experience of differences in educational cultures, academic conventions, and their rhetorics. Finally, and importantly, all use English as an academic lingua franca and use it with a disposition attuned to communication across traditional language boundaries. In other words, they all translanguage routinely and without the conflicts that often accompany this strategy in "monolingual" environments. Accordingly, we developed a pedagogy that does what any pedagogy sensitive to this group's needs must do: help these writers extend successful practices from spoken domains into Anglophone academic writing, where dominant conceptions of language (and academic success) represent English as a reified system that demands conformity.[1] Our particular pedagogical choices, therefore, represent a specific application for this community of a more general translingual strategy that acknowledges and harnesses student writers' prior knowledge, experience, and linguistic/rhetorical competence. It follows that these choices also evolved in dialogue with a growing body of research on language and writing generally known as translingual approaches (e.g., Cangarajah, 2013; Cooper, 2014; Creese & Blackledge, 2010; Garcia & Wei, 2013; Horner, 2011, 2016; Horner & Lu, 2012; Horner & Trimbur, 2002; Lu, 1994; Lu & Horner, 2013; Matsuda, 2013; Pennycook, 2008, 2010). Through that dialogue, we have identified a representation of English—including its uses and users, and the ideological networks they exist within—that is a valid and valuable basis for making and articulating specific pedagogical decisions.

In what follows, we first describe briefly the circumstances that created a strategic need for Anglophone writing instruction in the Department of History at Uppsala University. Next, we identify and briefly defend the three theoretical commitments, i.e., translingualism, that have informed—and continue to inform—our efforts to support Anglophone writing within our target

---

[1]   The use of *Anglophone* throughout this chapter simply reflects, at one level, a common international expression referring to the use of English and the people using it, particularly when the speakers/writers involve are multilinguals and English represents only one part of their linguistic repertoire; see for instance Flowerdew, 2007; Garcia Ramon, et al., 2006; Ho, 2010; and Lillis & Curry, 2010 for examples. At another level, the expression *English* and permutation of it, such as *English medium*, *EFL* and *ESL*, are entangled, as Horner points out, with default interpretations that suggest "a language fixed in form and meaning" (2011, p. 303); we are working here to complicate such default interpretations.

community. Briefly, these are commitments to a de-essentialized conception of language and languages (i.e., it foregrounds language as performance and backgrounds language as system), to a recognition that the performative representation inherent in this de-essentialized conception of language, like all other representations, operates ideologically, and to an acknowledgment of language users' strong individual agency in carrying out this performance. Finally, the core of our chapter then describes the three tenets of our pedagogy: instruction framed as collaborative inquiry, instruction aimed at maintaining and leveraging our students' lingua-franca dispositions, and instruction built around learning objects that focus our writers' prior knowledge and that help organize the conceptual space in which they exercise agency. Before concluding, we assess the transferability of our approach to other settings, with particular attention to the United States, where monolingual ideologies occlude the translingual realities.

Anglophone Writing in Uppsala's Department of History

The twenty-first century brought to Sweden, as to many other countries, pressures to internationalize institutions of higher education that had historically been largely national, local-language-speaking organizations. Those pressures accelerated organic processes already underway to increase student exchanges, graduate-student recruitment, cross-border research cooperation and the adoption of Anglophone course literature, particularly in some faculties (such as medicine, natural science, and business) and in larger universities.

Nationally, this pressure led to a revision of degree structures to follow those defined in the Bologna Accords, which aimed to facilitate student mobility across European universities (see Schriewer, 2009 for a description and critical appraisal). At Uppsala University, it also led to increases in the recruitment of international students to master-level programs and the hiring of international faculty, post-doctoral fellows and Ph.D. candidates, along with growing expectations that faculty publish their research internationally. In each of these cases, "international" connotes non-Swedish speaking and by implication, reliance on lingua franca uses of English for academic work (cf. Lillis & Curry, 2010, pp. 6–7).

Parallel to these university-wide responses to academic globalization, there were within the Department of History two rationales for creating a larger role for Anglophone writing instruction, one disciplinary and one ethical. The disciplinary rationale reflected the changing nature of historical research. The research community had moved away from conceptualizing academic history solely as a narrative about the past, particularly the past of a people or a nation, where a national language was self-evidently the suitable medium. Instead, they conceptualized academic history as framing and answering questions about *societies* in the past, which makes necessary comparisons to similar, but not identical, developments in other parts of the world and which in turn requires the use of an academic lingua franca for engagement with the international research literature (Lavelle & Ågren, 2010, p. 216). Informed by these disciplinary changes and by the growing numbers of history graduates in Sweden pursuing international careers (particularly those earning master's and doctoral degrees), the ethical rationale acknowledged the need for graduates to present their work in English and the department's "responsibility today to give students what they will require for success . . ." (Lavelle & Ågren, 2010, p. 203).

In this context, the authors met in 2003 when Ågren (a historian) arranged a half-day workshop for Ph.D. students on writing academic history in English. She invited Lavelle (an applied linguist) to address the linguistic dimensions of second-language writing alongside speakers on Anglo-American historiography and Anglophone rhetoric. This relatively holistic workshop for graduate writers proved successful, and in its wake the department, through the authors, has organized Anglophone writing instruction for various target groups in various formats.

These have included additional doctoral workshops and, from spring 2004 through spring 2007, regular half-day seminars for master's students. In fall 2007, those seminars gave way to a master's-level elective course, Academic Writing in English, which carries the standard 7.5 credits, one quarter of a semester's full-time workload. Since 2014 there has been a similar course for doctoral candidates offered collaboratively with other history departments in the Stockholm-Uppsala region. Alongside this instruction, writing-in-English workshops have also taken place in interdisciplinary research units hosted organizationally in the department, where formats varied and participation is open to senior and junior faculty, post-doctoral research fellows and Ph.D. candidates.

These target groups—graduate students for the most part with post-docs and faculty in much smaller numbers—we have come to believe, are best served with the evolving translingual pedagogy described below.

A Translingual Lens

The success of our pedagogy (i.e., our writers seeing themselves as textual decision makers and going on to make decisions that successfully support their aims as writers) depends in large measure on an accurate representation of what English is and is not. We draw for such a representation upon a body of translingual theorizing that takes a strong position on the nature of languages, most specifically a position on what they are not, not "single, stable, monolithic, internally uniform sets of forms" (Horner, 2014, p. 1). Instead "languages exist only in and through their speakers, and they are reinvented, renewed and transformed in every interaction, each time that we speak" (Calvert, 1999, 2006, quoted in Cooper, 2014, p. 15). English, from this de-essentialized perspective, is not a closed system to master (or be mastered by), but a network of social practices—many durable, some transient and all, like other social practices, deeply embedded in their performative contexts. This position highlights a gap between dominant, common-sensical representations of language and languages and the more accurate representations offered by linguists, educationalists, and composition researchers. Increasingly, that gap is seen as a question not of language theory, but language ideology, and writ large, inaccurate essentialist representations of language underwrite an equally misleading ideology of literacy (see Horner, 2016; Horner & Lu, 2014). Scholars working with translingual approaches, such as Horner and Lu (2013), Canagarajah, (2013b) and Garcia and Levia (2014), therefore explicitly frame translingualism as an ideology in contrast with and opposition to the rigid monolingualism mentioned above and discussed below. Finally, a performative conception of language also requires and posits agentive, decision-making speakers/writers/readers/listeners, language users, who, in other words, shape language and linguistic exchanges. A translingual lens, then, represents English (and other languages) as performative rather than essentialist, insists on the ideological relevance of representation, and affirms the agency of speakers and writers regardless of whether they choose to follow or flout conventions, norms and social expectation.

Cooper (2014) provides a succinct expression of a translingual representation of languages. She begins by denying reification: "Language does not exist as an entity. Language is not a code, not a means of expression, not a resource," and continues by affirming sociality: "[w]hat we call language consists of practices—patterns of behavior—that arise out of interactions" (p. 14), a position Cooper integrates into a larger framework for social analysis via Bourdieu's notion of durable dispositions. She emphasizes that this argument has been made elsewhere, by Wittgenstein, Heidegger, Bakhtin and Davidson among others. Beyond philosophy, it is also made in sociolinguistics, where Pennycook (2010) cites Canagarajah (2007) to define English not "as a system out there" but as "a social process constantly reconstructed" to account for environmental factors (p. 9). In educational research, Creese and Blackledge (2015) also marshal various sociolinguistic insights to rule out both homogeneity and stability (Bloomaert & Rampton, 2011) and the notion of separate bounded systems (Jørgensen et al., 2011) as viable starting points for the study of languages and their uses. On that basis, Creese and Black-ledge conclude instead that "[t]he idea of *a language* . . . may be important as a social construct, but it is not suited as an analytical lens through which to view language practices" (2015; p. 20, emphasis in original). We conclude, therefore, that another lens is also required to teach and to talk about the language practice that is academic writing.

Because essentialist conceptions of language have powerful ideological functions and deep ideological roots, a translingual lens also requires an ideo-logical dimension. While language ideologies are "neither simple nor mono-lithic" (Creese & Blackledge, 2015, p. 25), their consequences for multilingual writers are well documented. In composition studies, translingual theorists have consistently recognized and resisted those effects. Horner, et al., (2011) makes the case that the ideology of monolingualism (as the essentialist ide-ology underwriting English-only policies and attitudes is typically called in American composition research) treats languages as discrete and uses that separation as the basis for rankings and hierarchies among dialects and ver-naculars of English, with strongly negative consequences for speakers whose usage differs from so-called standard English. Lu and Horner (2013) are even more explicit about the "[t]he continuing denigration of subordinated groups through attacks on their language" (p. 583) and the role language ideology plays in this denigration. Beyond translingual work, research has documented these consequences along at least two parameters: external effects and internal effects. The former manifest, for example, as impacts on grading in university courses (Land & Whitley, 1989; Nielsen, 2014; Severino 1993), on placement and access to for-credit courses (Inoue, 2017; Matsuda & Silva, 1999), and on opportunities to publish (Flowerdew, 2007; Lillis & Curry, 2010). The lat-ter manifest as alienation and loss of confidence (Rubin & Williams-James, 1997), anxiety (Leki, 2007) and pressure to conform (Severino, 1993), the last of which speaks most directly to questions of writers' experience of agency.

In translingual literature, it is Lu and Horner (2013) who provide the fun-damental argument for strong writer agency. That argument adopts a tem-poral perspective on language users' relationship with language and begins by deploying Butler's (1997) position that in using language speakers/writers create it; each "site of articulation," in her terms, is where a language either continues to exist or not. Lu and Horner (2013) dovetail that performative understanding with Giddens' notion of structuration, where social structures and individual actors operating among those structures are mutually depen-dent and co-constitutive. In translingualism, the "structures" are languages, instantiated as durable dispositions, and the actors are speakers/writers and their interlocutors. Some acts of language creation, then, are transient and others remain as "seeming regularities of language . . . best . . . understood not as the preexisting rules determining language practices but, rather, as the products of those practices: an effect of the ongoing process of sedimentation" in which agentive speakers/writers participate (Lu and Horner, 2013, p. 588).

This de-essentialized, performative view of language drives the translingual commitment to strong writer agency, and as we shall see below in discussing our third pedagogical tenet, we aim for the experience of agency to percolate into most aspects of our writers' writing. The extent of linguistic agency is, however, subject to question even from scholars broadly sympathetic to a translingual agenda in research and teaching. On the basis of linguistic inequality (Blommaert, 2005) or vital materialism (Jordan, 2015; Guerra & Shivers-McNair, 2017), these scholars argue for constraining the role of human agency in analyses of writing practices. Ultimately, however, none of these challenges to writer agency deny it outright, but offer instead ways to modify and complicate that role analytically, and so a strong sense of writer agency remains—alongside a de-essentialized and ideological understanding of English—a centerpiece of the theory informing our pedagogy.

Translingualism in Practice

The preliminary point of this section is first, to clarify how the three tenets of our pedagogical practice (leading collaborative inquiry, foregrounding lingua-franca experience and dispositions, and structuring conceptual spaces for active writerly decision making) relate to the three theoretical commitments we have adopted from the translingual research discourse (that accurate representations of languages are de-essential and performative, that all representations of language are positioned ideologically, and that the exercise of linguistic agency is inevitable even if it is unconscious and inconspicuous). With those relationships in place, the section describes the stream of interventions characterized by each tenet and shows how those interventions follow from our theoretical commitments.

Collaborative inquiry exists as a general approach to organizing teaching and learning, and it is, therefore, potentially applicable to many kinds of content. In our courses and workshops, students' texts are the objects of inquiry, yet even so, the possibility remains that such an inquiry could seek and find in student writing linguistic forms, rhetorical moves, or genre features that either match or fail to match so-called standard English, academic conventions, or disciplinary norms. Of course, such an inquiry would conflict completely with our theoretical commitments, and so to align collaborative inquiry with a translingual take on language, we focus the inquiry on the relationship of linguistic forms to linguistic norms (accurate representation), the values informing those norms (ubiquitous linguistic ideology), and the outcomes of writerly decisions (inevitable agency).

A similar point applies to our second stream of intervention, the foregrounding of lingua-franca experience and dispositions. That foregrounding leverages the sociolinguistic fact that all our writers use English as a lingua franca, both in the academy and in other endeavors. Their experience guarantees a familiarity with multilingual interlocutors and with well-documented lingua-franca dispositions and communication strategies. That familiarity, whether tacit or explicit, obviates the need Horner identifies to "*develop* attitudes and strategies for reading and writing aligned with . . . successful use of ELF" (2011, p. 302, emphasis added). In a similar vein, our writers consciously see themselves as "contribut[ing] to the transnational flow of literate activity," an awareness that Roozen (this collection, Chapter 6) highlights for his students. In fact, improving the success and reducing the difficulty of those contributions is what typically brings students to our courses and workshops. However, as becomes clear below, favorable experience, dispositions, and self-awareness provide no guarantee of success.

Finally, our third stream of intervention deploys learning objects that expand and enrich the conceptual space where our writers make the decisions that constitute their writing. Again, that space is available for many kinds of thinking about writing; in fact, given their prevalence, "essentialist language ideologies seep into any conceptual or institutional space not actively occupied by an alternative representation, behavior, or practices" (Lavelle, 2017, p. 194). Therefore, our interventions saturate these conceptual spaces with open questions about the nature of language, about the operation of language ideology, and, especially, about authorial choices and their effects as experienced by immediate readers—peers and instructors—but also to more distant gatekeepers.

Instruction as Collaborative Inquiry

Biggs & Tang (2011) identify collaboration between and among teachers and students as one of four necessary conditions for conceptual change, which in turn is essentially synonymous with effective learning. This is because collaborative "dialogue elicits those activities that shape, elaborate and deepen understanding" (Biggs & Tang, 2011, p. 24). Elmgren and Henriksson endorse this characterization and emphasize the changing role of the teacher in collaborative inquiry (2014). This changing role, however, extends beyond a collaboration-transmission binary, as Horner (2011, 2016) seems to suggest, and its complexity can be captured in a number of ways. Ramsden (2003), for instance, frames transmission-based teaching as the base of a three-part hierarchy, where it is superseded and subsumed first by facilitative teaching, which primarily organizes students' learning activities, and then by collaborative approaches, where "[t]eaching is comprehended as a process of working cooperatively with learners to help them change their understanding" (p. 110). Lavelle (2008) locates "transmission" within a four-part taxonomy of teaching roles (transmitter, developer, facilitator, transformer), where collaboration follows most naturally from the facilitator role.

However one frames or labels the teaching role, the educational literature cited above makes clear that collaborative inquiry is a methodology, and as such, it is available for the learning and teaching of any subject. Therefore, our second and third tenets yoke this method to a specifically translingual writing pedagogy. Our syllabus relies rather little on delivering predetermined content, and even the assigned types of writing are, rather than ends in themselves, means for exploring textual decisions and the factors that influence them, including speculation about their putative reception. More specifically, our classroom practice consists largely of workshops and seminars where we negotiate various aspects of the texts students submit, for example, their meanings (both semantic and social), their intended audiences, their relationships to other texts operating in the same or similar contexts, and, significantly, the decisions that created them. As detailed below in our descriptions of lingua-franca dispositions in the classroom and of the learning objects used to explore conceptual space for conscious decision making, these negotiations are wide ranging and multi-faceted. Largely student driven, negotiations may address any formal choices from the lexical through the discursive or rhetorical, and be either wholly compliant with or resistant to institutional and disciplinary conventions.

Because our inquiry explores openly what constitutes successful Anglophone writing for a particular group in its own specific sets of circumstances, the pathway of any given exploration cannot be fully planned or predicted. Instead, our courses can and do take surprising, unsettling, yet nevertheless insightful turns. For example, in a course for doctoral candidates on writing academic history, we read a dissertation successfully submitted at another Swedish university and asked would this pass in Uppsala. While our answers remained necessarily speculative, our inquiry shed light on a range of topics relevant to dissertation writers, including reader dispositions, tolerance for innovation, explicit versus implicit assessment criteria, and the interplay between English lexis and syntax on one hand and Swedish expectations and rhetorical culture on the other.

Unsurprisingly, the effects of and conditions for collaborative pedagogy extend beyond the teacher's role and classroom management to include the institutional positioning of courses and the attitudes of everyone involved in a given workshop, seminar series, or course. Participation in all our activities is voluntary. M.A. and Ph.D. courses are pass-fail electives with no prerequisites, and our workshops and seminars for more senior scholars carry no costs for their departments or research projects and thus no obligation to document achievement or involvement. Tellingly, one graduate-student course evaluation claimed, "this is the only course I've ever taken where all I had to do was improve." Simply put, we face none of the institutional impediments reported for other translingual innovations, where to varying degrees institutional architecture of various kinds impedes pedagogical initiatives (see e.g., contributions by Malcolm et al., and Gallagher & Noonan in Horner & Tetrault, 2017).

Instead, we meet groups of writers with relatively high degrees of intrinsic motivation, which we find complements collaborative inquiry and, according to Biggs and Tang, "drives deep learning and the best academic work" (2011, p. 36). In addition, these well-motivated academics share other characteristics that make them willing and capable collaborators. They see themselves as (emerging) experts in their fields and to some extent accomplished writers, almost all having completed at least an undergraduate thesis or substantial term papers in some language and others with theses, dissertations, or articles behind them. Moreover, through the needs analyses incorporated into our teaching, we see that participants' concerns closely mirror our own: simply improved academic writing—where the terms of improvement are specific to each writer—on those occasions when writers choose to (or must) disseminate their research or submit coursework in English. However, as will become clear below, even in this highly favorable collaborative environment, essentialist linguistic ideology generates challenges for our translingual pedagogy and the writers it exists to support.

Lingua-franca Dispositions

Research literature characterizes rather well the dispositions associated with successful lingua-franca communication, both generally and in settings where English functions as the lingua franca. They are dispositions that have two sides: one primarily passive and associated with tolerance, acceptance and patience, the other associated with active meaning making. Canagarajah and

Wurr (2011) cite Khubchandani's characterization of lingua-franca commu-
nicators in South Asia as "accepting the other on his/her own terms" and
"develop[ing] positive attitudes to variations in speech" (p. 2). Similarly, in
their review of research on English as a lingua franca (ELF), Jenkins et al.
(2011) find a "strong orientation towards securing mutual understanding
regardless of 'correctness,' for instance by employing [Firth's (1996)] 'let it
pass' and 'making it normal' strategies" (p. 293). The active yang to this passive
yin is the "putting forth of one's own efforts" to "achieve [the interlocutors']
common interests" (Khubchandani, quoted in Canagarajah & Wurr, 2011,
p. 2). In ELF research, this is observed as "active monitoring" to preempt
misunderstanding, which interlocutors carry out because they do not take
mutual comprehension for granted, but rather acknowledge it as the worked-
for outcome of cooperative meaning making (Jenkins, et al., 2011).

As pointed out above, our students have experience with lingua-franca
communication and dispositions, but nevertheless, it remains a challenge
for them to maintain those dispositions throughout our instruction. In general terms, this is unsurprising since, as Horner points out, dispositions, too,
are performative and exhibit the fluidity of performance and positioning
rather than the stability of ingrained characteristics (this collection). More
locally, some of our writers' dispositional fluidity concerns the "common
interest" Khubchandani correctly identifies as central to many lingua-franca
exchanges. Specific interests naturally vary greatly, from general "communicative objectives (Canagarajah, 2007, p. 95) through the utilitarian "function of
transmitting information effectively and efficiently" (Ehrenreich, 2010, p. 418)
and the broader transactional and interpersonal work of "furthering corporate
activities and maintaining social relations" (Kankaanranta, 2006, p. 218) to
the "demanding communicative business" that speakers get done in academic
settings (Maruanen, 2006, p. 128). In each case or category, it is a common
interest or shared enterprise that provides a higher-order rationale to support
both tolerance and cooperation.

For reasons we only partially understand, however, the context of writing instruction adds to our students' difficulty in sustaining consistently
this higher-order common interest or shared enterprise. One simple reason is that most of our courses and workshops enroll, alongside historians
and history students, writers from related disciplines such as archeology,
ethnography, anthropology, art history, comparative literature, or media
studies. Thus, a student of early modern social history may struggle to com-
mit consistently to active meaning making when reading a paper on the
methods of ancient archeology. In other words, our observations suggest
that if and when engagement wanes for a disciplinary point being made,

it becomes more difficult for participants to identify and honor a shared communicative enterprise.

Beyond differences in disciplinary knowledge and engagement, attention to writing as artifact—to written products—contributes to the erosion of the common interests or goals essential to a lingua-franca disposition. As our classroom conversations turn inevitably to words, sentences, paragraphs, introductions, and genre, the risk grows that reified conceptions of language take hold and linguistic form becomes a discursive end in itself and thereby usurps the role of higher-order interest or enterprise. Such shifts in conversational priorities, however temporary, discourage the tolerance for wide-ranging language difference that typically characterizes our classroom interactions.

The mechanism is likely complex by which form and convention usurp the superordinate discursive position in what are typically and ideally tolerant, let-it-pass lingua-franca exchanges. Participants' habits probably play a role. Malcolm's analysis, for example, of her translingual pedagogy, identifies in her students' peer reviewing ingrained attention to formal conventions that she refers to as "concessions to monolingual reading and writing practices" (2018, p. 112). In Uppsala, our participants typically bring with them, in addition to their lingua-franca experiences, many years of classroom experiences of learning English and other languages, experiences that not only inculcate a certain focus on form, but for successful learners, as many academics are, also represent an investment in static, reified and numerable representations of language and languages. So, in addition to habits of various kinds, the social capital that these investments represent also conflict with a lingua franca disposition. Finally, even the institutional labeling of our instruction as *writing in English*—while sometimes necessary to describe what we do—suggests too, as Horner observes, expectation of "conformity to a language fixed in form and meaning" (2011, p. 303). The effects of habit, prestige, and institutional labeling are of course entangled in a network of linguistic ideology more complex than we can untangle here, but one lesson relevant to pedagogy is that because essentialist representations will fill any available space not actively occupied by an alternative conception of language, lingua-franca dispositions require support and encouragement.

Therefore, in order to support an alternative, i.e., translingual, conception of language in day-to-day pedagogy, and thus support our participants' tolerant and cooperative dispositions, we draw, in our collaborative inquiry into student texts, on Blommaert's notion of voice to help sustain a shared enterprise that remains explicitly superordinate to any exploration of forms and conventions. For Blommaert, "voice is an eminently social issue" (2005, p. 68), which differs markedly from conceptions of voice prominent in American composition studies; those conceptions foreground individual expression and individualism, as outlined and critiqued by Ramanathan and Atkinson (1999). As a social issue, Blommaertian voice foregrounds communicative success or failure and the social conditions, including power relations, that facilitate or hamper such success. More technically, voice is the successful "perform[ance of] certain discourse functions" (Blommaert, 2005, p. 71). Critically, that success depends at least as much upon readers' dispositions as it does on a writer's management of language forms. In Blommaert's case studies, texts that match readers' expectations—expectations for linguistic correctness or narrative ordering or simply appearance—achieve uptake and execute discourse functions; their writers are granted voice. Texts that do not meet such expectations are denied uptake and perform misaligned discourse functions or none; their writers are not granted voice. Within this power dynamic, writers work to "creat[e] favourable conditions for desired uptake" (Blommaert, 2005, p. 68), but voice, being heard and understood, remains a social question because ultimately it is readers who either grant voice to a writer or deny it.

In our instruction, Blommaert's theorizing supports the maintenance of lingua-franca dispositions and helps resist the seepage of essentialist conceptions of language into our classroom discussion of participants' texts. At one level, this social model of communication simply provides participants with a reminder of the sociality of academic communication. At another level, the social construal of voice provides an additional focal point for our collaborative inquiry and thus a new shared enterprise when (inter)disciplinary curiosity waivers. Collectively, we ask what creates favorable conditions for a writer's uptake. Efforts to answer that question require that we foreground the intellectual work done in a text. It also requires that we include in our inquiry consideration of other readers—gatekeepers such as thesis or dissertation supervisors, journal editors, grant-giving bodies—and their reading dispositions and expectations.

Lingua-franca dispositions, then, are neither stable nor unconstrained and uncontested; they are nonetheless an affordance that follows from the explicitly multilingual environment where we teach. The pedagogical interventions they require are protection and promotion. In and of themselves, however, these dispositions do too little pedagogical work. The kind of learning we aim for only occurs when lingua-franca dispositions are used to envoice the writers of specific texts.

Lingua-franca Dispositions in Our Classrooms

The following paragraph (sentence numbering added) is paragraph two in a 5,000-word conference paper written by a Ph.D. candidate in history who participated in one of our workshops. The paper is an engaging study of Swedish internment camps in operation during the 1940s. It is rich in empirical detail and theoretically grounded. The paper opens indirectly, with a paragraph on the rollback of "civic rights and liberties" in the US and other Western countries following the September 11 attacks in New York, a paragraph that closes by citing Swedish authorities' criticism of such measures, particularly the Guantanamo Bay prison camp, which is called a violation of international law. What, if anything might keep a reader from granting this writer voice?

(1) This official Swedish stand has recently been questioned after revelations of an illegal extradition of two Egyptian citizens to the CIA and Egypt in 2004. (2) The question has been raised what Sweden really keeps on its own back yard. (3) With what right do we criticise others and what does our own recent past look like? (4) Extremely few people know that the Swedish state during the Second World War and for some time thereafter set up and operated fourteen prison camps for civilian foreigners whose principal design was all but identical to that of Guantanamo Bay. (5) The first of these camps was set up by the Swedish government in March of 1940. (6) The motivation was the threatening international situation. (7) Upon decision by the Swedish national board of health and welfare, foreigners could thereafter be indefinitely imprisoned in camps without trial. (8) The imprisonment needed not be motivated and could not be appealed, and at most around 1,500 foreigners were imprisoned. (9) The system constituted a fundamental break with internationally accepted western legal principles.

In accounting for loss of voice, Blommaert emphasizes that semiotic resources do not always move successfully, i.e., the failure in place y of forms and strategies that were discursively effective in place x (2005, p. 157). Horner explains similar breakdowns in terms of readers underestimating the difficulty inherent in meaning production (2011, p. 302) and "powerful ideological views about what does and does not constitute 'correct' writing" generally and for a particular genre (p. 305). Lillis and Curry highlight the effects of "indexical clustering . . . where specific language and rhetorical features are refracted through ideologies of location," both geographic and linguistic, in disqualifying or dismissing certain texts and authors (2010, p. 153).

Acknowledging a degree of friction present in all communicative exchanges (Horner, 2016, pp. 107–108, p. 148), we envoiced this writer (let's call him Bengt) and co-create meaning rather comfortably. In the opening sentences (1–3), Bengt shares his indignation and levels indirect charges of hypocrisy at the Swedish state. By introducing hypocrisy over a "camp," he dramatically anticipates the pending revelation in sentence 4, and he extends the parallel between the 2000s and the 1940s with both the final reference to "accepted western legal principles" and the justification for the camps in the name of national security during a "threatening international situation." Finally, in the passage that elaborates on this revelation (sentences 4–9), Bengt outlines his empirical findings with little friction and no obvious cause for devoicing beyond perhaps the semantic shading of *motivation* and *motivated* toward *justification* and *justified*, which is how the Swedish cognates are used, and the relatively light use of sentence-to-sentence transition marking typical of Swedish academic writing, both of which may be "indexical" in the Lillis-and-Curry sense.

But our teaching-and-learning objectives turn less on *our* granting voice to our writers—a given—and more on the imagined reactions of the readers informing Blommaert's, Horner's, and Lillis and Curry's analyses. On that basis, our workshops and seminars collaboratively explore writers' choices and their putative relationship to voice without, we believe, slipping into an assimilationist posture. In the following treatment of this sample, we provide an idealized account of our workshop discussion of how Bengt might create favorable conditions for voice, i.e., for this text to carry out his intended discourse functions and intellectual work, including consideration of potential obstacles to this outcome. By an idealized account, we mean a selection of comments made and questions posed in class augmented by the inclusion of issues and reflections relevant here, but not raised by anyone in real time during the actual seminar. We idealize in this way in order to maximize the illustrative potential of this example in a short chapter.

One site in this excerpt for such exploration is Bengt's early show of indignation. Workshop participants struggled with this particular discourse function in this context; it could, they proposed, possibly jeopardize Bengt's voice with academic readers. More specifically, we asked whether and how the indignant tone of exposé and tabloid journalism best supports the other intellectual work his paper does.

Bengt, as it happened, was happy to revise the tone and content of his opening once they were discussed, but because writing instruction for us is largely a collaborative process of foregrounding and informing writers' choices, we consider here a scenario in which Bengt had chosen to prioritize his indignation and highlight governmental hypocrisy. On one hand, if the greatest risk to Bengt's voice follows from readers associating this tone and message with other genre, general strategies for revision could revolve around overcoming those associations or incorporating them into an academic analysis through more active hybridization. On another hand, it may be that for less cooperative readers this passage proves immobile, incorrect, or indexical of foreignness or rhetorical immaturity and thereby license a devoicing (in Blommaert's, Horner's, and Lillis and Curry's terms, respectively). If so, one possible trigger or excuse for this breakdown is the indignant rhetorical question in sentence 3. As a rhetorical question, it evokes certain expectations that are only partially met: the paper does describe what "our own recent past look[s] like," but it does not explore at all the philosophical issue being framed here, whether a social critic must always have an impeccable moral resume. Moreover, "our recent past" may mark the "locality" of the text (Lillis & Curry, 2010) and risk being dismissed as "parochial" (Flowerdew). Another challenge to voice here is the backyard metaphor, which we cooperatively see as occupying some of the same semantic terrain as the familiar glass-houses idiom and the mote-beam-eye injunction of Luke 6:42. Like the businessman Ehrenreich quotes regarding a lingua-franca exchange between colleagues, we "sort of understand" and are content with that understanding (2010), but we are obliged to acknowledge not all readers are cooperatively disposed or satisfied with this kind of understanding. With respect to voice and instruction, our challenge is to support an agentive writer deciding whether to retain an innovative passage, modify it, or remove it. The point of that instruction is not to advocate one path or another, but to create as rich an appreciation as possible for the roles forms can play in the work of meaning making at any given textual site.

In our classrooms, lingua-franca dispositions support collaborative inquiries into specific texts and the question of voice. Implicitly, those dispositions contribute to the process of inquiry as guarantors that in our workshops and seminars every writer is granted voice. While this support draws largely on the passive, tolerant side of a lingua-franca disposition, "active monitoring," also contributes to our collaborative inquiry, for instance when participants test interpretations, identify misunderstandings, pose questions, and propose alternatives. Typically done with reference to voice, this monitoring always defers to writer agency in weighing the tradeoffs involved in choosing, for instance, to express indignation or not, to harmonize dissonant connotations or not, to flout or follow convention in collocations like *civic rights*. Yet despite their contributions to students' understanding of writing decisions and their potential consequences, these explorations have limitations that require an additional, complementary stream of translingual writing pedagogy.

Conceptual Space for Writers' Agency

That complementary stream follows from our third tenet and thus provides a set of tools designed to expand the conceptual space where writers make decisions about their texts and their uptake, i.e., voice. We introduce these tools as learning objects to guide our student writers through a three-step process. First, they marshal the prior knowledge they have already acquired while writing in their range of other languages, rhetorical traditions, and educational cultures. Second, they organize the conceptual space constituted by that knowledge into a network of specific writerly options. Third, they make writing decisions by weighing the complex tradeoffs associated with each option. Our definition of learning objects is the simple one that Churchill (2007) ascribes to the term's earliest uses: "curriculum content . . . broken down into small, reusable instructional components that each address a specific learning objective" (p. 479). While the learning objects we deploy are relatively familiar and straightforward, the learning outcome they support—for writers to make active and informed decisions about how best to negotiate the uptake of their texts—is complex and elusive.

Some features of this complexity and elusiveness are well documented. One is that uptake and voice, as discussed above, are inherently social and shifting phenomena. Further, because complexity and diversity lie at the heart of lingua franca communication, criteria for success are "constructed in each specific context of interaction" (Canagaragah, 2007, p. 925). Moreover, although scholars from Firth (1996) to Canagaragah (2013) have identified the success of lingua-franca communication with strategies rather than forms, mastering a catalogue of strategies provides no guarantee of voice as the success of any strategies depends upon the specifics of shared enterprises, audience expectations, and a host of other factors. There is, in other words, no playbook to follow.

Without such a playbook, we work instead to support student-writers' context-specific decision making. Some of that work consists in helping our writers see themselves as decision makers, which does not always come naturally or easily to them. All have studied a range of languages and most have encountered some kind of prescriptive writing instruction; in those endeavors, the identities ascribed to and assumed by students are more likely to be rule-follower and pattern-matcher than decision maker. So as will become clear, we infuse our instruction with a vocabulary of agency, of choice, of volition, and decision making.

Typically, we address four domains for agency: genre, paragraphs, sentences, and vocabularies, each of which simply names heuristic contexts in which writers enact their writing, i.e., contexts for organizing, framing and executing different kinds of decisions. As a first illustration, we discuss how our instruction tries to create conceptual space for agentive decisions about genre, and in doing so we can address a potential objection to our learning objects.

To stimulate our writers' creation of conceptual space about genre, we employ as a learning object the prescriptive modeling of various genre and their components presented by Swales and Feak (2012). By way of background, we observe that with broad individual variation, our students do only a fair job of answering questions like: What do Dutch editors expect when they commission a book review? or What counts as an effective introduction in a Swedish or Polish research paper? Obviously, we pose such questions to activate and then document the genre knowledge our writers already have, so they can bring it to bear on their performance of genre in Anglophone texts. These same student writers are much more expansive, however, in responding to the prescriptions Swales and Feak offer, for example, on book reviewing: introduce the book, outline the book, highlight parts, provide commentary, prescriptions complete with two or three recipes for executing each of these general aims (2012). Based on their experience with reviews and reviewing in other languages and setting, some students concur, others prefer summative rhetoric throughout, still others want to begin with strong evaluative statements, and so on. Responding to a prescriptive prompt reactivates and focuses their genre knowledge, the first of our three phases. Reactivated, their thinking about book-review content and its possible arrangement moves on to concrete options, for instance, what *other* moves are possible and how might they be instantiated and arranged. Finally, they consider for each option potential effects, including effects on the granting of voice, and how, informed by those considerations, they can execute specific decisions about the performance of the book-review genre in their own texts, i.e., how they exercise active and conscious writerly agency.

Despite our efforts to see our writers always as decision makers, it is possible, even reasonable, to criticize the use of learning objects derived from prescriptive materials as inevitably prescriptive and thus incompatible with translingual pedagogy and active decision making. The prescriptive guidelines of Swales and Feak (2012) draw heavily on Swales' own analysis of genre, and Horner's (2016) discussion of that analysis provides a way both to understand and deflect such criticism. Briefly, Horner uses Swales' analyses of various genre to show how descriptions of textual practices reify language use as stable (and thus misleading) representations. Swales' models are "transformed from terms of analysis to terms of practical prescription" (2016, p. 83); whatever their original function, "the representation then comes to serve not as a heuristic but as an empirical observation against which . . . practice is judged" (2016, p. 83). Horner's translingual reading reiterates our point made above, that essentialist representations of language seep into any uncontested arena. In resisting this reification of practices into so-called larger "units of discourse," he foregrounds the emergent character of any constituents these analyses produce and thus their limitation. Foregrounding of this kind encourages practitioners, like our student writers, to act "not simply within but with and on the [patterns of constituents] identified" (Swales, 2016, pp. 85–86).

This working with and on the provisional constituents of, say, a book review is precisely what happens through the three phases of students' work with conceptual space for conscious agency. The marshalling of prior knowledge contextualizes Swales' genre models, and any model, as simply one normative take on Anglophone writing. The identification and organization of options underscores their emergent character and the inherent limitations of each, those derived from models and those derived from experience. Finally, in weighing the effects of following or flouting normative takes and then making their textual decisions, our student writers do what Horner ultimately calls for: they recognize their agency and the mutually constitutive relation between themselves and the partial, provisional models they are continuously revising (Horner, 2016). This reading of Horner's interrogation of reified genre shows that in the context of a translingual pedagogy—one that promotes writers' roles as decision makers and supports their lingua franca dispositions through collaborative inquiry into questions of voice and uptake—any learning objects properly used can help to shape space for conscious and active agency.

The learning object we deploy to create similar space around the composition of sentences is a simple grammar for writers that foregrounds the role clauses play in meaning making yet resists essentialist associations of sentence-level language description with correctness and error. In other words, we talk about clauses as sites of performance where writers do intellectual work by profiling certain things, concepts or people as participants in various kinds of actions and relationships. While our own grammar for writers is an original composite of functional, cognitive, and traditional approaches, there are prescriptive takes on clauses in books such as Fish (2011), Lanham (2006), or Williams (1995), and it is possible to treat those models as we treat Swales and Feak (2012) on genre. Whatever model serves as a starting point, our learning objective remains conscious and active decision making as an outcome of a three-phase process of conceptual change.

To illustrate this process in a setting where clauses and sentences provide the heuristic context, consider [1] below, excerpted from a master's students' paper for an exercise on framing, executing and evaluating sentence-level decisions.

[1] In his book *Vichy Syndrome*, Henry Rousso, who is a French historian specialising in the events of the Second World War, analyses the evolution of French memory about Vichy France, commonly seen by historians as exceptional studies into French history.

Our grammar for writers identifies Anglophone norms that privilege, for instance, formal features such as relative proximity among obligatory element (e.g., subjects, predicating verbs, and direct objects) uninterrupted by optional elements like adverbials and non-restrictive modifiers and right-branching clauses, i.e., clauses that begin with relatively brief, relatively simple, and relatively familiar constituents and add constituents with more length, complexity, and novelty as a clause unfolds across a page. Obviously, these norms are not universal, and our writers generate any number of alternatives. In that light, we explore collaboratively the placement in [1] of the information given as the non-restrictive relative clause, "who is . . . Second World War." The students in question were uniformly happy with the writer's decision: although the author-profile clause does postpone the central predication of this sentence and separate it from the subject, our writers felt that this information was necessary, that no other position was more attractive, and that postponement does not add difficulty to the meaning-making process. A second decision we discussed concerned "commonly seen by historians as exceptional studies into French history," where many student readers found it difficult to identify exactly what concept or element was in fact "seen . . . as exceptional." Most alternatives offered disambiguated the reference by creating some kind of apposition linking, say, "a topic commonly seen" or "a period commonly seen" with either "the evolution of French memory" or "Vichy France." In each case, we collaboratively weighed communicative pros and cons for the specific options generated.

Interventions and learning objects of this kind provide a description of clausal constituents that stimulates students to activate and focus what they know about these constituents and their relationships in their languages other than English. They initiate discussions that draw upon that collective knowledge to frame networks of possible options for drafting or revising specific English sentences in specific Anglophone situations. Finally, they make conscious choice, however provisional, by weighing the perceived advantages and disadvantages for voice and uptake of competing syntactic alternatives.

A similar process unfolds around the creation of conceptual agency space for decisions about composing paragraphs. Our learning object simply models possible relationships among sets of sentences formatted as a visual paragraph. Introducing this object, again, catalyzes three stages of conceptual change. In our classes, the prior knowledge students marshal coalesces around notions of unity, singularity, or consistency, which seem therefore to be central to the semantics of the paragraph. For our writers, that abstract unity, like the abstract constituents of book reviews, can manifest in many different ways: a central issue given early and elaborated later, a summative wrap pulling together an inductive discussion, a step-wise linear progression proceeding logically or chronologically, and so on. Once generated, this collective understanding of how paragraphs *might* be composed helps to organize the conceptual agency space where writers make decisions about specific paragraphs in specific texts.

The following paragraph on the history of copyright embodies any number of decisions, including those shaping perception of harmony or dissonance between visual marking and propositional content.

(1) The common law "copyright tradition" focuses on the encouragement of productivity in return for economic remuneration. (2) This school of thought concentrates on the labour and skill invested into the creation to produce the copyrighted work. (3) Commentator Lauraine Nocella noted that the common law tradition, which subsists in the United Kingdom, "considers the interests of the public who pay the royalties and aims to protect the work and balances the interests as economic nature." (4) The first statute within the UK to recognise copyright can be traced back as far as the Statute of Anne of 1710. (5) This early legislation enabled the copyright holder to prevent "others from dealing with his work to the public without his consent." (6) Scholar William Cornish noted that the Statute of Anne was to promote the interests of London's publishers from fierce competition, and this could further support those who argue that the common law fails to offer the author protection of his work, by failing to protect the moral rights of the author, which is at the core of the continental view. (7) The continental view, apparent within French law, considers the rights of the authors as the fundamental issue

that requires protection. ⑧ The moral rights of the author are of great importance as the "artist is personally involved in his work, with consequences for him, and the art-enjoying public, that transcends the realm of purely commercial concerns" which transpires within the common law copyright tradition. ⑨ The moral rights from continental Europe concentrate on the relationship between the author and his work, and the creation will reflect the author's personality. ⑩ The birth of moral rights came from the 1789 Revolution in France where prior to the Revolution rights of printing were granted by the King through the notion of censorship. ⑪ The Revolution brought about the abolition of the monopoly relating to privileges and moral rights were founded. ⑫ These moral rights are distinct from economic rights in the sense that moral rights cannot be assigned; this has proved to be a major difference between the continental and common law traditions.

Two general responses to this paragraph emerged in classroom discussion. Some commentators were comfortable with the degree of harmony manifest here and pointed to the apparent symmetry in contrasting the common and civil-law traditions and in the strength of sentence 12 in forging a unified understanding of the two. Others read the paragraph as more binary than unitary, thus with a dissonant relationship between format and content. In doing so, they pointed to the richer level of detail in sentences 3 through 6, underscored the scholarly treatment of common law contra a more impressionistic treatment of civil law, and questioned the efficacy of sentence 12 in unifying the two elaborations because of its paragraph-final position and its mix of familiar, backward-looking information and new concepts, specifically the *assignment* of rights. These contrasting readings transcend rather quickly the relatively pedestrian question of paragraph unity—when the writer sees that if she wants to harmonize content and layout, she can add a comparative opening sentence something like or instead of 12—and go on, first, to identify options for the overall composition of this passage and, then, provide guidance for weighing those options.

Moreover, this collaborative classroom inquiry provides a reminder about the questions, comments, summaries, re-framings, and interpretations lingua-franca interlocutors would employ in a *conversation* about copyright law. However, because writing is not literally a conversation, writers like ours gradually learn to anticipate or even postulate putative feedback of this kind and incorporate it into their writerly decision-making processes. Given the well-documented context dependency of lingua-franca communication, such anticipation is necessarily approximate, even speculative, work, but paragraph-level decisions constitute an arena where our student writers combine the exercise of their writerly agency and an awareness of the sociality of voice and uptake.

Given the prominent role translation plays in thinking about translingual writing pedagogy (in this collection and elsewhere), it is fitting to close this section with an illustration of how our third tenet expands and enriches conceptual space for writerly decisions about lexical translation. As historians, our student writers must make decisions about translation across languages, across time, and across cultures. They do the first when, for example, German source material uses Erbe to cover the entire semantic field shared for English by bequest, inheritance, and heritage. They do the second when, for instance, translating the Swedish term stånd, which referred from the middle ages to the 1860s both to social groupings of people broadly like classes or castes and to the parliamentary representatives drawn from each group. It is, in other words, a term whose referents no longer exist and whose meaning-making relies upon ideologies and social relationships that belong to another era. They do the third as words cross cultural boundaries and their resonances change, for instance with the Russian олигарх, which translates literally as oligarch. However, in Russia it can connote everything from the despotic, corrupt associations Anglophones bring to the word to more neutral or even positive inflections more typical of, say, magnate, representative of big business, or even economic and political elite.

Our instruction supports these decisions with a learning object that initiates the three-stages of conceptual change for student writers. In this case, the object is the lists each student produces of difficult translation decisions that she or he wants to explore collaboratively. That exploration begins with collective reaction to the lists and the problems they pose. Typically, the reaction resembles a word dump, which draws on all the linguistic resources present in a group, lists of words from Swedish, Finnish, Turkish, or French that cover, say, an example mentioned above, Erbe, and the semantics of probate. After having expanded the conceptual space available by marshaling a body of prior lexical knowledge, students translate the new candidates into English and in doing so structure the conceptual space with options beyond those mentioned above, for instance, legacy, birthright, or endowment. With concrete options in place, the student writer who nominated Erbe for collaborative inquiry can weigh tradeoffs framed by criteria suitable for translation, for example, denotational and connotational range, relative brevity or relative comprehensiveness.

The Mobility of a Translingual Pedagogy

The translingual pedagogy for Anglophone writing described above rests on our three tenets: that learning and teaching proceed optimally through a process of collaborative inquiry; that our student writers arrive with lingua-franca dispositions, which are valuable for their writing but which also require support because like all dispositions they are performative and thus fluid; and that rather traditional learning objects can help students develop conceptual spaces for the active and conscious exercise of writerly agency. Indirectly, but no less importantly, those tenets rest in turn on three theoretical commitments regarding the nature of languages. They are 1) that languages are performed and thus best represented as networks of social practices and misrepresented as stable, finite, essentialist systems; 2) that the choice among competing representations is always and inevitably ideological; and 3) that because language is performance, speaker agency is ubiquitous in this performance even when linguistic ideologies work to occlude it. It is, as we demonstrated above, a felicity to these theoretical commitments in our implementation of the three pedagogical tenets that makes ours a translingual approach to writing instruction.

Such a pedagogy has the potential to move widely and successfully primarily because the conception of language from which it proceeds applies universally. The applicability and desirability of our specific implementation in workshop formats and discussion-based seminars depend, of course, upon local conditions, for instance the particular capabilities of faculty, the willingness of students to participate in open inquiry, and not least the institutional architecture, which will inevitably reflect linguistic and educational ideology. Nevertheless, the pedagogy we perform at Uppsala University *should* travel because its intellectual premises are accurate and fair and *could* travel because its specifics—collaboration, disposition, and conceptual support for self-conscious agency—appear to suit prevailing needs and conditions in a range of local settings.

As outlined above, the validity of our premises receives increasing support in applied linguistic and educational research alongside similar work in composition studies. Exigencies of fairness are also well documented. In the US, nothing shows that more clearly than the reception of Horner, et al. (2011), where the authors make a case for fairer treatment of language difference via translingualism as a disposition and an ideology. In Asian-Pacific contexts, Pennycook's ongoing critique of standard English ideologies (2007, 2010) make a comparable case. In Europe, fairness meets de-essentialized understandings of language at the intersection of research on lingua-franca uses of English and analyses of globalization's negative impact on an already unfair distribution of linguistic resources.

One could argue that our implementation of translingual pedagogy certainly benefits from or even relies on local conditions. Our students come from or come to Sweden, where English is widely used yet not dominant, and so they arrive for instruction already equipped with self-conscious lingua-franca dispositions. We would reply that such dispositions are widely available, perhaps universal, but they are unacknowledged or even hidden. On Pennycook's reading (2008), all uses of English are lingua-franca uses because the so-called varieties native speakers share, standard or otherwise, are post-hoc constructions that deny the variation of English, variation that suggests instead an open set of local practices. Pennycook rests his claim, first, on the failure of both monolithic versions of English and pluri-centric versions (i.e., World Englishes) to account for the profound diversity of English actually in use. Moreover, this expanded understanding of lingua-franca uses captures performative similarities shared by English users all over the world (Pennycook, 2008). Even students in "monolingual" America have both dispositions for and experiential knowledge of uncodified language practices, although that experience is not always positive (Matsuda, 2006; Smitherman & Villanueva, 2003). In a word, the dispositions that we support in our students and pedagogically direct toward self-conscious agency are resources available for a translingual Anglophone writing pedagogy *anywhere*.

Given then that lingua-franca or translingual dispositions are essentially universal, what are the impediments to more wide-ranging implementation of a pedagogy like ours (or any that follows from a translingual representation of languages)? In his afterword to this collection, Horner points to the pervasive power of monolingualist language ideology; it is dominant, and it has cemented its dominant position despite millennia of lingua-franca communication and its attendant dispositions. More optimistically, he identifies translinguality as also pervasive, the condition of all speakers, just as Pennycook identifies all Anglophones as lingua-franca speakers.

We take Horner's latter point on ubiquity as an argument that a pedagogy like ours is in fact available to anyone; the specific linguistic histories students possess neither qualify them for nor disqualify them from this kind of learning and teaching. Their ideological stances, whether actively or passively adopted, may create challenges, but not prohibitions. Therefore, we speculate that a major impediment to the spread of translingual writing pedagogy, particularly in the United States, is the reluctance of writing teachers to give up the static, reified—and of course privilege-granting—representations of English that essentializing ideologies offer. Some of these reluctant teachers may actively and openly embrace something they call standard English. Others, as Kopelson (2014) explains, support the dominant essentialist take on language through indifference. Most others though are quiet, but active, essentialist, denying for example that speakers/writers/readers co-create meaning, ostensibly on the basis of their "field's history and its enduring legacy practices" (Jordan, 2015, p. 366). This group is large enough and influential enough for Jordan to conclude that a translingual stance on language "can remain a tough sell in rhetoric and composition" (2015, p. 366). However, his explanation in terms of "history" and "legacy practices" denies the agency of these quiet essentialists and minimizes the consequences of their ideological work. In contrast, Lavelle (2017), forwards Miller's (1991) indictment of composition programs and practitioners as complicit in sustaining and reproducing the dominant language ideology; he refocuses that indictment specifically on resistance to translingual pedagogy and explains the extensive complicity as the work of both programs and practitioners to defend actively their investments—symbolic as well as economic—in the ideology of standard English. In brief, there are obstacles to the diffusion of a pedagogy like the one described above, and those obstacles lie neither with student populations nor with pedagogical practices themselves but rather with the conflicting investments of reluctant teachers.

Conclusion

As we said in opening this chapter, the pedagogy discussed above evolved to meet the needs of a specific community of academic writers and in dialogue with a growing body of translingual research on language and writing. Because our community of writers consists primarily of graduate students and because graduate education generally calls for a large measure of conformity—to professional expectations, to disciplinary norms, and especially to established discursive practices—our highest priority among learning outcomes is that students can and do execute informed decisions about their Anglophone writing, an experience of agency to temper their experience of conformity. These decisions are variously course-grained or fine-grained, addressing the rhetorical aims of papers, theses, and dissertations, the whole-part relationships within those texts, the clustering of points and propositions into paragraphs, the arrangement of clausal constituents, and, not least, the selection of lexical items—words and phrases whose referents call for translation across languages, across time, and across cultures.

Our tripartite pedagogy reflects this priority. Our most concrete and specific curricular interventions revolve around the learning objects we employ to enrich our writers' conceptual space for conscious decision making. Those interventions take place in a context theoretically and ideologically informed so as to foreground and sustain explicit lingua franca dispositions. Both that contextualization and the interventions are themselves instantiated methodologically through workshop and seminar formats and through an overarching spirit of collaborative inquiry. Students and instructors alike genuinely want to learn about the communicative dynamics of the students' texts we discuss, for example their potential interpretations, their uptake, and their challenges. All three elements of our pedagogy can continue to evolve, particularly the central work with learning objects, which is potentially open ended.

Likewise, research on translingualism continues to evolve within various disciplinary research programs in linguistics, education, and composition, to name three. We have already identified our expansive view of human agency as one area for continued theorizing. Another is the status of dispositions, a concept that here straddles its everyday usage and its history in Bourdieu's social theorizing. The notion clearly does substantial work in our pedagogy and research, and more thorough examination, empirical as well as theoretical, will help it to do that work better. For instance, a richer understanding of dispositions and their relationships to specific institutional habitas may contribute to a fuller understanding of Blommaert's envoicing and devoicing (2005), especially as they are enacted in higher-educational settings.

References

Archibald, A., Cogo, A. & Jenkins, J. (Eds.). (2011). *Latest trends in ELF research*. Cambridge Scholars Publishing.

Biggs, J. & Tang, C. (2011). *Teaching for quality learning: What the student does*. The Society for Research into Higher Education.

Blommaert, J. (2005). *Discourse: A critical introduction*. Cambridge University Press.

Blommaert J. & Rampton B. (2011). Language and superdiversity. *Diversities, 13*(2), 1–22.

Butler, J. (1997). *Excitable speech: A politics of the performative*. Routledge.

Calvert, J. (1999). *Pour une écologie des langues du mond*. Plon. (A. Brown, Trans.). *Towards an ecology of world languages*. Polity.

Canagarajah, A. S. (2007). The ecology of global English. *International Multilingual research Journal, 1*(2), 89–100.

Canagarajah, A. S. (Ed.). (2013a). *Literacy as translingual practice: Between communities and classrooms*. Routledge.

Canagarajah, S. (2013b). *Translingual practice: Global Englishes and cosmopolitan relations*. Routledge.

Canagarajah, A. S. & Wurr, A. J. (2011). Multilingual communication and language acquisition: New research directions. *The Reading Matrix, 11*(1), 1–15.

Churchill, D. (2007). Towards a useful classification of learning objects. *Educational Technology Research and Development, 55*(5), 479–497.

Cooper, M. M. (2014). The being of language. In B. Horner & K. Kopelson (Eds.), *Reworking English in rhetoric and composition: Global interrogations, local interventions* (pp. 13–30). SIU Press.

Creese, A. & Blackledge, A. (2010). Translanguaging in the bilingual classroom: A pedagogy for learning and teaching? *The Modern Language Journal, 94*(1), 103–115.

Creese, A. & Blackledge, A. (2015). Translanguaging and identity in educational settings. *Annual Review of Applied Linguistics, 35,* 20–35.

Dryer, D. & Mitchell, P. (2017) Seizing an opportunity for translingual FYC at the University of Maine: Provocative complexities, unexpected consequences. In B. Horner & L. Tetreault (Eds.), *Crossing divides: Exploring translingual writing pedagogies and programs* (pp. 135–160). University Press of Colorado.

Ehrenreich, S. (2010). English as a business lingua franca in a German multinational corporation: Meeting the challenge. *The Journal of Business Communication, 47*(4), 408–431.

Firth, A. (1996). The discursive accomplishment of normality: On "lingua franca" English and conversation analysis. *Journal of Pragmatics, 26*(2), 237–259.

Fish, S. (2011). *How to write a sentence.* HarperCollins.

Flowerdew, J. (2001). Attitudes of journal editors to nonnative speaker contributions. *TESOL Quarterly, 35*(1), 121–150.

Flowerdew, J. (2007). The non-Anglophone scholar on the periphery of scholarly publication. *AILA Review, 20*(1), 14–27.

Gallagher, G. & Noonan, M. (2017). Becoming global: Learning to "do" translingualism. In B. Horner & L. Tetreault (Eds.), *Crossing divides: Exploring translingual writing pedagogies and programs* (161–177). University Press of Colorado.

García, O. & Wei, L. (2013). *Translanguaging: Language, bilingualism and education.* Palgrave Macmillan.

Garcia Ramon, M. D., Simonsen, K. & Vaiou, D. (2006). Guest editorial: Does Anglophone hegemony permeate gender, place and culture. *Gender, Place & Culture, 13*(1), 1–5.

Guerra, J. C. & Shivers-McNair, A. (2017). Toward a new vocabulary of motive. In B. Horner & L. Tetreault (Eds.), *Crossing divides: Exploring translingual writing pedagogies and programs,* (19–31). University Press of Colorado.

Ho, E. Y. L. (2010). Language policy,"Asia's world city"and anglophone Hong Kong writing. *Interventions, 12*(3), 428–441.

Horner, B. (2011). Writing English as a lingua franca. In A. Archibald, A. Cogo & J. Jenkins (Eds.), *Latest trends in ELF research* (pp. 299–311). Cambridge Scholars.

Horner, B. (2014). Introduction: Reworking English in rhetoric and composition— global interrogations, local interventions. In. B. Horner & K. Kopelson (Eds.), *Reworking English in rhetoric and composition—Global interrogations, local interventions* (pp. 1–10). SIU Press.

Horner, B. (2016). *Rewriting composition: Terms of exchange.* SIU Press.

Horner, B. & Kopelson, K. (Eds.). (2014). *Reworking English in rhetoric and composition: Global interrogations, local interventions.* SIU Press.

Horner, B. & Lu, M. Z. (2012). Toward a labor economy of writing: Academic frictions. In. J. N. Christoph et al. (Eds.), *Literacy, economy, and power: New directions in literacy research* (pp. 111–126). SIU Press.

Horner, B., Lu, M. Z., Royster, J. J. & Trimbur, J. (2011). Language difference in writing: Toward a translingual approach. *College English, 73*(3), 303–321.

Horner, B. & Tetreault, L. (Eds.). (2017). *Crossing divides: Exploring translingual writing pedagogies and programs.* University Press of Colorado.

Horner, B. & Trimbur, J. (2002). English only and U.S. college composition. *College Composition and Communication, 53*(4) 594–630.

Inoue, A. B. (2017). Using writing assessment to create the conditions for translingual pedagogies. In B. Horner & L. Tetreault (Eds.), *Crossing divides: Exploring translingual writing pedagogies and programs* (pp. 119–134). University Press of Colorado.

Jenkins, J., Cogo, A. & Dewey, M. (2011). Review of developments in research into English as a lingua franca. *Language Teaching, 44*(3), 281–315.

Johnasson, B. (Ed.), *Att undervisa med vetenskaplig föränkring—i praktiken!* [Teaching with a research foundation—in practice]. Uppsala University.

Jordan, J. (2015). Material translingual ecologies. *College English, 77*(4), 364.

Jørgensen, J. N., Karrebæk, M. S., Madsen, L. M. & Møller, J. S. (2011). Polylanguaging in Superdiversity. *Diversities, 13*(2).

Kankaanranta, A. (2006). "Hej Seppo, could you pls comment on this!" —Internal email communication in lingua franca English in a multinational company. *Business Communication Quarterly, 69*(2), 216–225.

Kopelson, K. (2014). On the politics of not paying attention and the resistance of resistance. In B. Horner & K. Kopelson (Eds.), *Reworking English in rhetoric and composition: Global interrogations, local interventions* (pp. 207–220). SIU Press.

Land, R. E., Jr. & Whitley, C. (1989). Evaluating second language essays in regular composition classes: Toward a pluralistic U.S. rhetoric. In D. M. Johnson & D. H. Roen (Eds.), *Richness in writing: Empowering ESL students* (pp. 284–293). Longman.

Lanham, R. A. (2006). *Revising prose.* Longman.

Lavelle, T. (2008). English in the classroom: Meeting the challenge of English-medium instruction in international business schools. In P. Mårtensson, M. Bild & K. Nilsson (Eds.), *Teaching and learning at business schools: transforming business education* (pp. 137–153). Gower.

Lavelle, T. (2017). The ins and outs of translingual work. In B. Horner & L. Tetreault (Eds.), *Crossing divides: Exploring translingual writing pedagogies and programs,* (pp. 190–198). SIU Press.

Lavelle, T. & Ågren, M. (2010). Academic writing in English—pedagogical answers to strategic challenges. In B. Johnasson (Ed.), *Att undervisa med vetenskaplig föränkring—i praktiken!* [Teaching with a research foundation—in practice] (pp. 202–218). Uppsala University.

Leki, I. (2007). *Understanding ESL students' academic literacy.* Lawrence.

Leung, C. & Street, B. V. (Eds.). (2012). *English: A changing medium for education.* Multilingual Matters.

Lillis, T. M. & Curry, M. J. (2010). *Academic writing in global context.* Routledge.

Lu, M. Z. (1994). Professing multiculturalism: The politics of style in the contact zone. *College Composition and Communication, 45*(4), 442–458.

Lu, M. Z. & Horner, B. (2013). Translingual literacy, language difference, and matters of agency. *College English*, 75(6), 582–607.

Makoni, S. & Pennycook, A. (Eds.) (2007). *Disinventing and reconstitution languages.* Multilingual Matters.

Malcolm, K. (2017). Disrupting monolingual ideologies in a community college: A translingual studio approach. In B. Horner & L. Tetreault, (Eds.), *Crossing divides: Exploring translingual writing pedagogies and programs* (pp. 101–118). University Press of Colorado.

Mårtensson, P., Bild, M. & Nilsson, K. (Eds.) (2008). *Teaching and learning at business schools: Transforming business education.* Gower Publishing.

Matsuda, P. K. (2006). The myth of linguistic homogeneity in U.S. college composition. *College English*, 68(6), 637–651.

Matsuda, P. K. (2013). It's the wild west out there: A new linguistic frontier in U.S. college composition. In A. S. Canagarajah (Ed.), *Literacy as translingual practice: Between communities and classrooms* (pp. 128–138). Routledge.

Matsuda, P. K. & Silva, T. (1999). Cross-cultural composition: Mediated integration of U.S. and international students. *Composition Studies*, 27(1), 15–30.

Mauranen, A. (2006). Signaling and preventing misunderstanding in English as lingua franca communication. *International Journal of the Sociology of Language, 2006*(177), 123–150.

Miller, S. (1991). *Textual carnivals: The politics of composition.* SIU Press.

Nielsen, K. (2014). Self-assessment methods in writing instruction: A conceptual framework, successful practices and essential strategies. *Journal of Research in Reading, 37*(1), 1–16.

Pennycook, A. (2007). The myth of English as an international language. In S. Makoni & A. Pennycook, (Eds.), *Disinventing and reconstituting languages* (pp. 90–115). Multilingual Matters.

Pennycook, A. (2008). Translingual English. *Australian Review of Applied Linguistics, 31*(3), 301–309.

Pennycook, A. (2010). *Language as a local practice.* Routledge.

Ramsden, P. (2003). *Learning to teach in higher education.* Routledge.

Rubin, D. L. & Williams-James, M. (1997). The impact of writer nationality on mainstream teachers' judgments of composition quality. *Journal of Second Language Writing, 6*(2), 139–154.

Schriewer, J. (2009). "Rationalized myths" in European higher education: The construction and diffusion of the Bologna model. *European Education, 41*(2), 31–51.

Severino, C. (1993). The sociopolitical implications of response to second language and second dialect writing. *Journal of Second Language Writing, 2*(3), 181–201.

Smitherman, G. & Villanueva, V. (Eds.). (2003). *Language diversity in the classroom: From intention to practice.* SIU Press.

Swales, J. M. & Feak, C. B. (2012). *Academic writing for graduate students: Essential tasks and skills* (3rd ed.). University of Michigan Press.

Williams, J. M. & Columb, G. (1995). *Style: Towards clarity and grace.* University of Chicago.

6 Mapping Translingual Literacies: Encouraging and Enacting Translingual Perspectives of Literate Life

Kevin Roozen
UNIVERSITY OF CENTRAL FLORIDA

Understanding translingual practice is not just relevant for those who physically immigrate across national borders and fluently speak multiple languages, but for everyone whose literate life is shaped by and contributes to the translingual flow of literate activity. This chapter traces one writer's continual re-use of languages, images, texts, and textual practices across multiple textual engagements including playing a Japanese video game, creating and maintaining a wiki site, teaching herself Japanese, crafting fan-fiction and fan-art, and illustrating a biology lab manual. Ultimately, the chapter argues that the writer's case illustrates the wisdom of Bruce Horner's call for attention to the translingual dispositions of so-called monolinguals. Further, for students, engaging such mappings makes visible the concrete ways their literate lives are informed by and contribute to the translingual flow of literacy, a crucial step toward understanding translinguality as the norm rather than the rare exception.

Keywords: translingualism, monolinguals, transnationalism, literate activity, literacy.

What has come to be recognized as the "translingual approach" to language use has been deeply invested in making more readily visible the ways that all people's communicative acts are implicated in the flow of language and literacy across the presumed borders of languages, cultures, and nations (Canagarajah, 2013; Horner et al., 2011; Jordan, 2012; Lee & Jenks, 2016). The abiding attention to the translingual character of all language practice, along with the fact that the communicative action we all participate in is shaped by and contributes to translingual and transnational networks, has been present since the earliest scholarship on translingualism. In outlining the central tenets of translingual-

DOI: https://doi.org/10.37514/INT-B.2020.0438.2.06

ism, for example, Horner et al. (2011) assert that, at its very heart, "a translingual approach argues for (1) honoring the power of all language users to shape language to specific ends; (2) recognizing the linguistic heterogeneity of all users of language both within the United States and globally" (p. 305).

The emphasis on the translingual nature of all language practice is echoed by Jordan (2012), who reminds us that "multilingualism is a daily reality for *all* students—all language users—whether they themselves use more than one language or whether they interact with others in settings of multiple language contact" (p. 1, italics in original). Jordan (2015) reiterates this point in a later publication when he defines a translingual approach as "an orientation to the ways in which all language users are capable of purposeful deliberation across codes, regardless of traditional attributions of nativity or competence" (p. 369). More recently, Lee and Jenks (2016) have argued that what they term "translingual dispositions," "are essential for all users of English in a globalized society, regardless of whether they are 'native' or 'nonnative' speakers of English" (p. 319).

But while the translinguality of all language users is routinely asserted in the scholarship, it does not tend to be reflected in Writing Studies' dominant accounts of translingual language practice. As Bruce Horner points out in his afterword to this collection, research focused on translingual practice has demonstrated a "persistent association, if not conflation, of translinguality with transnationality and translanguaging," leading to what he describes as a "seeming neglect, if not exclusion, of translinguality among ostensible U.S. English monolinguals [and] their linguistic or civic counterparts elsewhere" (p. 297, this collection). As a result, the accounts of translingualism and translingual writing that dominate our scholarship tend to depict people moving across linguistic, cultural, and national borders (Lorimer Leonard, 2013, 2014, 2015; Vieria, 2011). Despite a wealth of scholarship illuminating the ways that Web 2.0 technologies make it possible for people to participate in the global flow of language and literacy without leaving their own homes (Daniel-Wariya, 2016; Fraiberg, 2017, 2010; Monty, 2015), our common notions of translingual languaging and literacy remain grounded in accounts of people moving physically across the globe.

However fine-grained such accounts may be, coupling translinguality tightly to transnationalism creates potential problems. As Horner asserts, focusing our analytic attention solely on non-English speaking multilinguals serves only to reinforce "monolingualism's definition of language difference as deviation from a norm of sameness in linguistic form" (p. 298, this collection). The consequence, Horner asserts, is that translinguality

> risks being understood merely as a distinctive and distinguish-
> ing feature of the language practices of "multilinguals," and

hence something that "mainstream" (a.k.a English monolingual) teachers, students, and, well, people can dismiss as
irrelevant to normal life—at best a curious, exotic feature of
"others": transnationals, non-native English speakers. In short,
it can contribute to monolingualism's domestication of translinguality through its exoticization. (p. 298, this collection)

Ultimately, Horner argues, the exoticization of translinguality only reinforces
an "ideology of monolingualism" (this collection), the notion that monolingualism is the clear norm and that translingual practice remains a rare and
limited exception. To address this gap, Horner calls for increased attention to
the translinguality that textures the language and literacy of people who are
presumed to be monolingual (this collection).

As one response to Horner's call, in this chapter I examine the textual activities of one writer whose language and literacies do not immediately signal
the transnationalism that has characterized our dominant accounts of translingual writing, but that are indeed densely entangled in the translingual flow of
meaning-making. Using sample texts and excerpts from text-based interviews
collected during an extended case study of a young woman named Susanna and
her literate activities, in this chapter I trace her translingual textualities of over a
span of ten years, focusing especially on her weaving of Japanese language into
a variety of literate activities including playing a Japanese video game, creating and maintaining a wiki site, teaching herself Japanese, crafting fan-art and
fan-fiction, and, oddly enough, illustrating a biology lab manual.

According to Horner, one challenge of adequately rendering more readily
visible the heterogeneity of all language use is the tendency to examine language as existing "outside material social practices" (pp. 295–296, this collection), as occurring on some abstracted terrain rather than as people's actual,
concrete actings in the world. Elaborating, Horner states,

> For the removal of language from practice renders language
> a matter of timeless, immaterial forms (abstracted from the
> full ecology of communicative practice). It is the treatment
> of languages as immaterial forms that renders sameness in
> language the norm, since that sameness depends on the
> evacuation of the crucial elements of time and space from
> communicative practice—all that inheres in the notion of
> "utterance.". . . It is at the point of utterance that translin-
> guality enters as an insurgent view of language positing dif-
> ference in language as itself the norm rather than a deviation
> from the norm. (p. 296)

For Horner, studying language as abstracted from the messiness and complexity of people's concrete uses in the world tends to foreground homogeneity and sameness, and thus tends to obscure the array of heterogeneous elements that texture actual language use. Horner's insistence on examining people's concrete, material practices echoes Blommaert's (2010) claim that the proper focus of language use "should be the actual linguistic, communicative, semiotic resources that people have, not abstracted and idealized (or ideologized) representations of such resources. Our focus should, therefore, be on repertoires, on the complexes of resources people actually possess and deploy" (p. 102). Without close, careful attention to people's concrete, material practices in the world, it can be easy to overlook the heterogeneity that textures their language and literacy, particularly when those elements might be relatively unmarked.

In order to ground the inquiry into Susanna's languaging and literacy in her material social practices and in the full ecology of communicative practice, data collection for this case study involved developing a detailed sense of Susanna's richly literate lifeworld and the concrete texts and textual practices that mediate her engagements. The initial data collection (e.g., interviews, collection of sample texts, and observations) focused on the reading, writing, and other textual activities she was involved in for her fan activities. Our early interviews discussed her fan activities in broad, general terms, including her history of engagement with those activities. Initial data collection also included a literacy history interview intended to illuminate Susanna's various other literate activities.

Subsequent interviews addressing Susanna's fan activities and any other literate activities she mentioned during the literacy history interview led to more focused interviews about those textual engagements, and included collection of sample texts in whatever representational media were appropriate (e.g., hard copy and digital inscriptions, drawings, illustrations). Sample texts were crucial for text-based interviews that focused on Susanna acting with specific texts and textual activities rather than on her involvement with literate activities more generally. Our text-based interviews were often process- and practice-based in order to make visible the processes and practices Susanna employed in creating and acting with various texts. This ongoing series of interviews provided opportunities for the kinds of "longer conversations" and "cyclical dialogue around texts over a period of time" that Lillis (2008, p. 362) identifies as crucial for understanding practice within the context of a participant's history. They also allowed for what Stornaiuolo et al. (2017) describe as "the unprecedented, surprising, and meaningful to emerge in observations of human activity without predetermined and text-centric endpoints of explanations" (p. 78).

To map Susanna's translingual practice across time, space, and multiple representational media, these data were analyzed interpretively and holistically (Miller et al., 2003). I first arranged data inscriptions (i.e., sample texts, sections of interview transcripts, interpretive notes, copies of texts and images, etc.) chronologically in the order in which Susanna engaged with them. This analysis of the data generated a large number of histories reaching across seemingly different literate activities. Based on those analyses, I constructed brief initial narratives of Susanna's histories with practice across multiple engagements. Those initial narratives were reviewed and modified by checking and re-checking those constructions against the data inscriptions (to ensure accuracy and seek counter instances) and by submitting them to Susanna for her examination. At these times I often requested additional texts from Susanna, and frequently she volunteered to provide additional materials and insights that she thought might be useful in further detailing the re-use and resemiotization of discursive practices across different sites of engagement.

To represent Susanna's translingual practice, and also to make my own analytic practices more visible, I present the results of the analysis as a documented narrative (Prior, 1998) rather than as a structuralist analysis. Doing so allows me to present the history of Susanna's translingual practice in a coherent fashion without flattening out the richness, complexity, and dynamics of how this practice is semiotically remediated and continually reassembled across engagements. If attention to concrete, material practice stands to unpack the dense heterogeneities of languages and literacies tangled, untangled, and re-tangled together into what can seem like stable, autonomous homogeneities, the documented narrative functions as a way of following particular heterogeneous elements while also gathering them up into a somewhat coherent account of communicative practice. It is a way of discursively re-assembling heterogeneous elements in a way that identifies particularly salient ones and makes visible how and why they have become tangled together and to what effect. The documented narrative, in other words, offers a discursive way of fashioning accounts that make visible what Lee and Jenks (2016) refer to as "the multilayered and unpredictable ways in which translingual dispositions can manifest themselves" in people's literate activities (p. 318).

In the following pages, I first introduce Susanna and elaborate the mapping of her translingual practice. In the latter portion of the chapter, I briefly outline my efforts to invite learners to use the account of Susanna's experiences to examine their own translingual engagements, and then discuss the benefits that engaging with these types of mappings hold for learners and teachers.

Examining a Richly Translingual Life

At first impression, there is nothing about Susanna that immediately suggests what Lee and Jenks (2016) characterize as "an inherent plurality of language resources" (p. 318). A white female now in her mid-thirties, Susanna speaks with a soft, gentle drawl associated with the part of the southeastern United States where she was born and raised and where three generations of her family have lived, a region many refer to as "the deep south." While she did travel away from her hometown to pursue an undergraduate degree in English and then a master's degree in Rhetoric and Composition, both of those institutions were only a few miles away, and still located in very rural areas of the state. The same is true of the institutions where she taught college classes after completing her master's degree and then where she enrolled to pursue her doctoral work.

According to Susanna, she had only rarely traveled beyond the south-eastern US, and even then not for extended visits. Talking about her travels outside of the region, Susanna stated that "[o]ther than going somewhere to conferences, the only trips I've taken to other parts of the country were to Tucson and Mt. Rushmore." Despite her deep and extensive engagement with Japanese, Susanna had never traveled to Japan. Her only travels outside of the United States consisted of three trips to Europe: twice to travel to England and France for undergraduate study-abroad programs and once to Italy to visit a friend.

Susanna's initial engagements with Japanese language and culture centered around a series of video games called Aero Fighters, an English version of the Sonic Wings series of games originally released in Japan, that she played during her adolescent and early teenage years. The various versions of the game involve a series of heroes piloting different types of aircraft as they battle villains who are attacking sites around the globe, including major cities such as London and Tokyo and prominent locales including the Panama Canal, the North African desert, and the Grand Canyon. From the first time she played the game, Susanna was immediately taken by the action, the characters, and even the soundtrack.

As her interest and engagement with Sonic Wings grew, Susanna started collecting and playing the original Japanese versions of the games, and also started collecting advertisements and player manuals associated with the games. The games, and the materials she collected, quickly became more than a source of entertainment. They also served as a focal engagement for Susanna's interest in Japanese culture and language. In the sections that follow, I elaborate a number of instances in which Susanna's involvement with Japanese via Sonic Wings is woven into her literate engagements.

Assembling a Wiki: "I decided to base my practice wiki on Sonic Wings"

Ten years after her initial encounters with the game, Sonic Wings became the focus of a wiki Susanna created. At the time, Susanna was a graduate student teaching first-year composition, and she and some of the graduate students in her program had started toying with the possibility of having students create their own wikis as a writing assignment for the class. As Susanna explained, she and some of her fellow graduate students,

> had been talking about the possibility of using wikis in a comp[osition] class as a way of having an online portfolio where students could post and edit their own work. I didn't know wiki code very well, so I decided to try making a wiki as a way of learning it and of figuring out if it would actually work for a portfolio.

Susanna decided to use Sonic Wings as a focus for her wiki because, as she stated,

> Around the same time, I was listening to the Sonic Wings 2 soundtrack even though I hadn't been really interested in Sonic Wings in a few years, and it got me excited about the series again. I used to have a Sonic Wings web site years ago that attempted to do some of what the wiki does, like catalog the characters, mostly, so I decided to base my practice wiki on Sonic Wings and post the information I had from my old website.

Once Susanna's application to Wikia received approval, she immediately started mining her old Sonic Wings website for useful materials. According to Susanna,

> I started by adding the information from my old site, but a lot of it was incomplete or inaccurate, so I ended up playing through each game and recording all the characters, enemies, and aircraft as I went.

As she re-played the games, she also researched Sonic Wings online as a way of gathering as much information as she could about the game and other games related to the series. Since initially creating it in 2008, Susanna has worked steadily worked on the wiki over the past nine years. To date, her wiki consists of 255 pages offering information about the five different versions of the game, the game's main characters, soundtracks, codes and strategies for gameplay, and external links to publications about the games and other relevant information.

The wiki, available at http://sonicwings.wikia.com/wiki/Sonic_Wings_ Wiki, is a rich mix of prose and images, in both English and Japanese, from a wide variety of genres. Although much of the wiki is in English, Japanese is featured prominently in ways small and large. Throughout the wiki, for example, Susanna has included both the Japanese and English names for the game's major heroes and villains.

Japanese is featured much more prominently on the wiki in the many game-related materials Susanna collected and decided to include for her viewers. According to Susanna,

> Most of the materials I've collected are in Japanese, and there's a lot of them that were never officially put into English, like book-length strategy guides, soundtrack booklets, and screen-shots from games that were either not released in English at all, or where the text was either left out or changed for the English version.

Susanna is particularly proud of the Japanese versions of the many player manuals she has incorporated in the wiki. Elaborating on her decision to include the Japanese versions of the player manuals, even though the wiki was in English, Susanna stated,

> I wanted to include them because some of them are hard to find, so it's a good resource for the wiki to have; it gives people a reason to keep coming back to the site. Also, I like showing off my collection.

The page on the wiki devoted to Blaster Keaton, Susanna's favorite hero character in the Sonic Wings series, offers an example of the ways Japanese is woven throughout the site. Explaining her affinity for Keaton, Susanna stated,

> He was one of my first favorite Sonic Wings characters. I guess part of it is that he's better developed than many of the other characters. . . . So basically, I guess just because he's a funny, nice guy with a well-developed history. Plus, he's cute, and I've always liked robots anyway.

Viewers of Keaton's page on the wiki are greeted with an image and some basic information about his character set in a call-out box with a blue back-ground (see Figure 6.1). Beneath an image she grabbed from a version of the game, Susanna provides readers with the names Keaton goes by in both the human and robotic forms of his character (Blaster Keaton when he appears in his human body, and Robo-Keaton or Mecha-Keaton when he occupies his robot body) using both English and Japanese katagana. In another portion of Keaton's page, Susanna includes a series of additional screen grabs featuring Keaton, some which include brief phrases in English language, and some which include brief phrases in Japanese language.

Keaton, Blaster	
Japanese Name	ブラスター　キートン (Blaster Keaton - human), メカキートン (Mecha-Keaton - robot)
English Name	Blaster Keaton (human), Robo-Keaton (robot)

Figure 6.1. Image and basic information about Keaton's character from the Sonic Wings wiki.

Japanese appears much more substantially in the many game-related documents Susanna includes on Keaton's wiki page. The page from the player manual for Sonic Wings 3 (see Figure 6.2), for example, provides Keaton's name (which on this page is indicated as "Bluster Keaton," a play on "Blaster Keaton") in large katagana script vertically down the left-hand side of the page. The smaller script along the top lists one of the lines Keaton's character utters throughout the game. The smaller script, which consists of katagana, hiragana, and kanji, offers players information about Keaton's character's airplane. The three neat rows of script on the right side of the page offer specifications of some of the weapons at Keaton's disposal.

Figure 6.2. Page from the player manual for Sonic Wings 3 showing an image of Keaton's character and Japanese script.

In assembling her wiki, Susanna wove together text from multiple languages—including English and the three Japanese alphabets—multiple genres, and multiple representational media—including images, sounds, and her embodied experience of playing the video game.

The Sonic Wings wiki Susanna created, and her engagement with the video game upon which the wiki is based, are certainly intersections of language contact. Susanna's efforts at assembling the wiki are a fitting example of what Horner et al. (2011) describe as "shap[ing] language to specific ends" (p. 305). The images are also translinguistic and transnational in the sense that they too have been drawn from a Japanese video game and incorporated in Susanna's Sonic Wings wiki.

Translating Texts: "I've just about learned two of the Japanese alphabets"

Through her initial encounters with Japanese when she was young, including playing and learning about the Sonic Wings video games and watching a great deal of anime during her high school years, Susanna developed an interest in learning to read and write in Japanese. As a way of pursuing that interest during her undergraduate years, Susanna enrolled in an entry-level course at college, but she wound up dropping it early in the semester. As she stated,

I started taking Japanese as an undergrad but the beginning-level class was too advanced for me. Most of the other students had had Japanese in high school. So, I dropped it after a couple of weeks.

Susanna's work on the wiki renewed her interest in learning Japanese, and she decided to teach herself Japanese by translating chunks of Japanese language. Initially, Susanna indicated that "I don't know Japanese beyond . . . a few words I've picked up from Sonic Wings." She quickly discovered that translating Japanese demanded a great deal of time, so to make it more manageable she focused on very short passages of Japanese prose. She started with translating panels of Japanese manga she had been reading, and found that the overall story and the visual images offered in each panel helped her to better understand the language. When she felt like she was ready for slightly longer, more complex passages, she gravitated toward the materials related to Sonic Wings she had collected and included on her wiki. The relatively brief sections of text accompanied by images were well suited for translating as a way of learning the language.

Figure 6.3. Page from the player manual for Sonic Wings Special offering, an image of Keaton's character and brief descriptions of his key features in Japanese script.

One of the documents Susanna translated was a page from the player manual for the Sonic Wings Special version of the game (see Figure 6.3).

The page features a colorful, detailed image of Keaton's character from the game. Brief passages of katakana, hiragana, and kanji offer descriptions of his production specifications, weapons, technologies, means of locomotion, and other special features.

To translate the prose descriptions from Japanese to English, Susanna would type a phrase from the manual into an online translation service called Babelfish using Microsoft Japanese IME software which allowed her to type in the three Japanese alphabets. She had begun to memorize some hiragana and katakana, and relied on a print Japanese-English dictionary when needed. For the kanji, Susanna use jisho.org, an online Japanese dictionary. Once Babelfish offered the translated version, which was typically somewhat "garbled," Susanna would return to Babelfish and Jisho to clarify the meaning. Then she rewrote the phrase in "fairly standard English."

The translated version Susanna generated appears as Figure 6.4. Susanna translated all of the Japanese script in the original. She translated the large script at the top and the right-hand side of the page. She also translated the small script at the very bottom of the page. After inserting the descriptions she translated into the original document, Susanna also indicated that she Photoshopped the image so that the background portions of the translated portions blended into the original image.

6.4. The translated version of the page from the player manual Kate created.

Susanna indicated that even though the translations took an enormous amount of time and attention, she found doing these kinds of translations very helpful. Prior to her engagement with translation, Susanna indicated that she only knew the few words of Japanese she had picked up from playing the video games and putting together the wiki. After doing several of these translations, Susanna indicated the she felt like she knew a great deal more:

> I've just about learned two of the Japanese alphabets, hiriga-na and katakana, from having to look up so many characters, which makes typing them in to translate a lot quicker. . . . I've also learned a bit about airplanes and Japanese culture.

Susanna's translating work immerses her in the interplay of multiple languages, including the three Japanese alphabets and multiple versions of English, as well as images and multiple texts, both print and digital. With her translating, Susanna is also working at the intersection of multiple languages with a variety of technologies (print and digital). As they did in her wiki, (transnational) images play a key role in her translating work.

When she completed the work of translating the prose and Photoshopping the translations back in the original image, Susanna posted the finished version on the Keaton page (in the "artwork" section) of the Sonic Wings wiki. According to Susanna, she wanted to make it available to other Sonic Wings fans, who, like herself, are "obsessive enough to want to know the *real* story behind the plot and characters" but who could not read the Japanese versions of the documents or did not know anyone who could translate them into English.

Drawing and Writing Fan-fiction: "I liked the idea of using all of my favorite hero characters"

While working on the wiki and immersing herself in her translations as a means of learning Japanese, Susanna decided that she would write a fan-fiction novel sequel to the Sonic Wings series for National Novel Writing Month (NaNoWriMo). As it did with her wiki and her translating, her work on her novel included blending Japanese and English in a variety of ways. Susanna had written a few brief fan-fiction stories based on Sonic Wings, and she felt that writing a novel would provide her with the opportunity to explore her favorite characters from the game in more detail and extend the plot in some interesting directions. As she stated "I also liked the idea of using all of my favorite hero characters, rather than just a couple at a time like I had to do in stories."

Susanna's first step toward writing the novel involved creating profiles for the main characters she planned to include. These "character profiles," as Susanna referred to them, offered an image of each character, some basic information about them, and a brief version of their backstory that Susanna created from information available from the game and information that she made up.

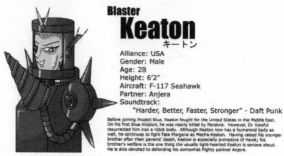

Blaster
Keaton
キートン

Alliance: USA
Gender: Male
Age: 28
Height: 6'2"
Aircraft: F-117 Seahawk
Partner: Anjera
Soundtrack:
 "Harder, Better, Faster, Stronger" - Daft Punk

Before joining Project Blue, Keaton fought for the United States in the Middle East. On his first Blue mission, he was nearly killed by Pandora. However, Dr. Kowful resurrected him into a robot body. Although Keaton now has a humanoid body as well, he continues to fight Fata Morgana as Mecha-Keaton. Having raised his younger brother after their parents' death, Keaton is especially protective of Hawk; his brother's welfare is the one thing the usually light-hearted Keaton is serious about. He is also devoted to defending his somewhat flighty partner Anjera.

Figure 6.5. The character profile Susanna created for Keaton's character in her fan fiction novel.

Intent on including Keaton's character in her novel, Susanna assembled a profile sheet (see Figure 6.5) using a wide array of the resources she had at her disposal from her extensive translingual history of engagement with Sonic Wings and with Keaton's character in particular. At the top of the sheet, Susanna included Keaton's name in both English and Japanese katagana. Commenting on her decision to list the Japanese version, Susanna stated that,

> For Keaton's [name] it's all katakana, and it just says "Keaton," not "Blaster Keaton." I can't remember why I didn't put his whole name. I put the Japanese on there to make it more official-like and tie it back into the Japanese original.

On the left-hand side of the sheet, Susanna included a digital image she had created of Keaton in his robotic body. Her drawing prominently foregrounds features she had encountered in the images she had seen and the descriptions she had read (and sometimes navigated simultaneously) while playing the game, creating and maintaining the wiki, and doing her translations, including his bright red, box-shaped robotic body, his detailed helmet, his drill arm and the spikes on his shoulder, and his electronic right eye. At the bottom of the sheet, Susanna included a brief paragraph that outlines Keaton's backstory. Like the digital image she drew, the information in Keaton's backstory material is laminated with Susanna's history of engagement with the character while playing and re-playing the game, working on the wiki, and teaching herself Japanese. As she stated while talking about developing the backstories for her hero characters, "Backstories and subplots for the good guys have come to me, too, the more I plan, play the games, translate, and so on." Susanna incorporated other representational media into Keaton's profile as well. The last item in the list of information beneath Keaton's names, for example, is a song by Daft Punk titled "Harder, Better, Faster, Stronger" that Susanna associated with his character in the novel because the title and lyrics indexed the robotic body his fellow heroes built for him.

Susanna also planned to include one of her favorite villains from the Sonic Wings series in her novel. According to her, Daio Ika, "is one of my favorite villains. It has an interesting backstory about being part fallen angel in humanoid form and part giant squid. And, it appears in a couple of different forms in the game."

Figure 6.6. The character profile Susanna created for Daio Ika's character in her fan fiction novel.

As she did with her profile for Keaton's character, Susanna assembled a sheet for Daio Ika (see Figure 6.6) by weaving together a wealth of resources from her richly translingual history with Sonic Wings and Daio Ika's character in particular. At the top of the sheet, Susanna listed the character's names in both English and Japanese. In Daio Ika's name in Japanese, the first two characters are kanji and the second two are katakana. The sheet features two different images of Daio Ika that Susanna created using her digital drawing tablet. The image on the left-hand side of the sheet is a representation of Daio Ika's weaker form, which consists of a teal-colored giant squid and a humanoid figure with six arms reminiscent of a Hindu deity. The image on the right-hand side of the sheet features Susanna's drawing of Daio Ika in its stronger form, which consists of a pink-colored squid accompanied by a humanoid figure of an angel with large feathered wings and two pairs of arms, one thin and one more prominently muscled. Like the

digital images she drew for the character, the descriptive backstory information Susanna included at the bottom of the sheet is textured by Susanna's
history of engagement with the character while playing and re-playing the
game and working on the wiki. According to Susanna, coming up with the
backstory information about the game's villain characters was much more
challenging than for the heroes, largely because the villains "have no backstory in the canon games." To generate the backstory information for Daio
Ika's character in her novel, Susanna indicated that she viewed and read as
much information about the character as she could, and then made sure
that she was "careful not to contradict anything that is said in the games"
or in any of the materials she had collected. As she had with Keaton's sheet,
Susanna also incorporated music into Daio Ika's profile. The last item in the
list of information beneath Daio Ika's names indicated a song by Voltaire
titled "Feathery Wings" that Susanna associated with the angelic humanoid
that was part of the character's stronger form.

Although not as readily visible as her translations, the translingual nature
of the profile sheets Susanna created while planning her fan-fiction novel is
apparent in the way she provided the characters' names in both English and
Japanese. The images Susanna created are also translingual in the sense that
they are based on representations of Keaton and Daio Ika she had seen while
playing the video game, while working on the wiki, and, again in the case
of the image of Keaton, while doing her translating. Perhaps not as readily
evident, the character profiles are also translingual in the sense that the information that Susanna offers in the "backstory" information on the character
sheet, even though it is written in English, is deeply informed by what she
had read and seen while assembling the wiki and, especially in the case of
Keaton's backstory information, while doing her translating.

By the end of NaNoWriMo, Susanna had finished 13 chapters of the novel,
which she titled *Sonic Wings Crusade*. The novel would eventually stretch to
18 chapters by the time she stopped working on it and posted it to an online
fanfiction site. But where Japanese and English had been blended together in
her wiki, in her translating activities, and in the character profiles she created,
Japanese is entirely absent from the prose of her novel, even passages that
specifically feature Keaton and Daio Ika. And where Susanna had deployed
images associated with the video game in her wiki, her translations, and in the
character profiles, those were entirely absent from the novel as well.

The novel's ninth chapter, for example, features a fierce battle between
Keaton and his partner, Anjera, and Daio Ika at Stonehenge. The extended
passages below, excerpted from that chapter, describe the moments when the
heroes identify the villain:

By the time the first visitors were beginning to file up through the underpass leading from Stonehenge's parking lot to the monument, Blaster and Anjera were already making fly-bys in their planes. Blaster was now wearing his fully robotic body as opposed to his humanoid one, just in case a battle did ensue. Keaton was quite proud of the shiny red body with its boxy chassis, powerful weapons, and titanium-enforced helmet to protect his human head.

"There is the angel image!" Anjera called now over the radio. Blaster looked down from his F-117 Seahawk, zooming in with his mechanical right eye to examine the image as he wheeled past it. There was no doubt now that it was the same angel as the one which appeared on Daio Ika: a short-haired, humanoid figure with large feathery wings, breasts, and four arms. One pair of arms, the set positioned slightly lower and to the front, was delicate, but the other pair was oddly muscular. All this was imprinted in the grass with painstaking detail.

From reading these passages, it is tempting to think that Susanna's translingual blending of Japanese and English does not extend into the prose of her novel. But even in the absence of visible traces of Japanese script and images associated with the Japanese version of the video game, I would argue that Susanna's novel is still richly translingual. In one sense, the translingual character of the novel is signaled by the theme and content of the novel, which, after all, is based on the video game. But it goes deeper than that. The translingual nature of the novel is also apparent in the way that the specific details Susanna employs in describing Keaton and Daio Ika are the very ones featured in, and that she herself has featured, in the images she created and in prose descriptions she crafted of these two characters.

Susanna's mention of the "boxy chasis" of Keaton's "shiny red" and "fully robotic body" in the first paragraph of the excerpt, for example, has been prominently featured in the Japanese game, in the many descriptions and images she assembled into the wiki, in the page from the player manual she translated, and in her character profile. The same is true of Susanna's later references to Keaton's "mechanical right eye" and his "large, sphere shaped hammer weapon," which have also been featured in those earlier engagements.

The same can be said of Susanna's detailed description of Daio Ika's character that appears in the third paragraph of the excerpt, in which the angel is characterized as a "short-haired, humanoid figure with large feathery wings, breasts, and four arms," with "[o]ne pair of arms, the set positioned slightly lower and to the front, was delicate, but the other pair was oddly muscular." These descriptive details have been prominently featured in images of the character in the video game, in the materials that Susanna assembled into the wiki, and that she represented in her drawing and in the prose of Daio Ika's character profile sheet. In short, even though Japanese script is absent, the prose of Susanna's novel is profoundly informed by Susanna's translingual encounters with documents and images from the original Japanese versions of the game.

Doing Scientific Illustration: "there were only two animal drawings I had available"

Susanna's engagement with the Japanese video game did not just texture her fan activities (the wiki, her translating, and her fan-fiction novel and fan-art), it also extended into her work illustrating organisms for the university's biology lab program. Susanna was one of four respondents to a flyer posted on a campus bulletin board seeking people to do scientific illustrations for the university's biology lab manual. Posted by the Lab Coordinator of the Principles of Biology Lab I, the laboratory component to the first in a sequence of two required introductory Biology courses offered at the university, the flyer sought people interested in doing some illustrations for the manual students used to accomplish the activities.

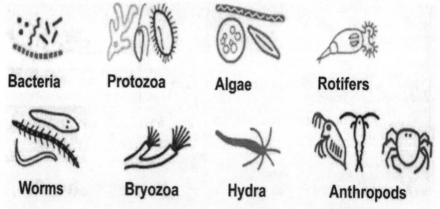

Figure 6.7. Selected illustrations from the previous edition of the lab manual.

According to the Lab Coordinator, the illustrations in the existing edition of the manual (see Figure 6.7) were not helpful in terms of allowing students to accurately identify the organisms they encountered in a particular lab activity that asked students to identify and draw organisms found in a drop of pond water. Commenting on the existing illustrations, The Lab Coordinator stated,

> You can see that they are really crude and they're very simple and they don't give you specifically what much of anything is. They're just not real helpful if the student wants to know what they are looking at.

Susanna had never done professional scientific illustrations, but she felt as if she had a good deal of experience illustrating characters or scenes from the fanfiction stories and novels that she had been writing regularly since her early childhood. Responding to the phone message she left, the Lab Coordinator contacted her and asked her if she had any samples of her drawing she could send him.

Figure 6.8. Susanna's pegasus frog image.

According to Susanna "There were only two animal drawings I had available to send for samples." One of the drawings (see Figure 6.8) Susanna selected was a winged frog she referred to as a "pegasus frog." As she explained,

> The pegasus frog is from an old educational DOS game named *Challenge of the Ancient Empires*. I adored it to the point of making a book of fan art from it and writing a really stupid fan-fiction. The pegasus frogs were my favorite monsters, so when I replayed the game some months ago, I wanted to draw one.

*Figure 6.9. Susanna's image of Daio Ika from the character
profile sheet she created for her fan fiction novel.*

The second picture Susanna chose (see Figure 6.9) was one of the images
of Daio Ika from the character profile sheet she created while planning her
fan fiction novel. Elaborating, Susanna stated, "The squid and deity picture is
from my . . . fan art; it's one form of an enemy named Daio Ika, the Japanese
name for Giant Squid. This particular picture was drawn to go on a Daio Ika's
profile picture for my fan novel."

Susanna's drawing depicts a large teal-colored squid with six flowing arms
and two longer tentacles. It also provides detailed rendering of the eye and
the funnel, or siphon.

To the Lab Coordinator, the drawings Susanna submitted, which he said reminded him of "cartoon animals, like a cartoon squid and a cartoon frog," suggested that she possessed the abilities to illustrate the organisms for the pond water activity: "I just wanted some samples to see how well she could draw, and I liked them, so I thought she could do a good job with the pond animals." Based on those drawings, the Lab Coordinator selected Susanna from among the four other applicants to create some new illustrations for the lab manual.

When he was satisfied with Susanna's illustrations, the Lab Coordinator pasted them, along with their Latin names for genus and phylum, into a document that would eventually be published in the revised edition of the lab manual (see Figure 6.10).

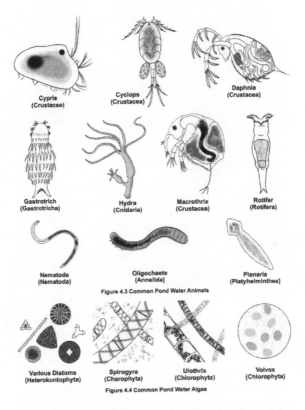

Figure 6.10. Page from the updated biology lab manual with Susanna's illustrations.

From the Lab Coordinator's perspective, Susanna's illustrations worked much more effectively in helping students to identify the organisms they encountered in the pond water. Reflecting on how the students in recent lab sessions performed on the pond water activity, he recalled that,

> [s]tudents were able to find and identify examples of cyclops,
> hydra, rotifers, nematodes, and we found some diatoms. So
> we were able to find about a third of them. The students had
> a really good time.

The Coordinator's comments suggest that Susanna's illustrations allowed lab students to more readily identify organisms that students using the representations in the lab manual had struggled to name. His comments also suggest that using Susanna's illustrations made the pond water activity much more engaging and enjoyable.

The page of illustrations bears no overt traces of Susanna's translingual work. And yet, her engagement with illustrations for the lab manual is translingual in a number of ways. First, it is Susanna's drawing from the character profile she created for Daio Ika that convinced the Lab Coordinator of her ability to draw the pond water organisms for the lab manual. In this sense, the drawing of Daio Ika, which is heavily informed by her encounters with images of Diao Ika in the video game and her own drawings of Diao Ika for the fan-fiction novel, paved the way for her work in scientific illustration. In other words, an image that had mediated Susanna's engagement with the Sonic Wings video game, her creation of the Sonic Wings wiki, and writing her fan-fiction novel came to pave the way for her engagement with scientific illustration.

Second, I would argue that Susanna's style for drawing the pond water animals—the conventions she uses—are also translingual in the sense that they are also heavily informed by her encounters with images of Diao Ika in the video game and her own drawings of Diao Ika for the fan-fiction novel. Consider, for example, the close similarity between how Susanna drew the flowing arms and tentacles of the squid in the Daio Ika image and the waving arms of the hydra she drew for the lab manual. Consider as well the similarity between Susanna's rendering of the squid's arms and tentacles and the body of the nematode and oligochaete as well as some of the interior features of the daphnia and macrothrix she drew for the lab manual. In other words, Susanna's representational practices themselves are translingual, and point to what Lee and Jenks refer to as "the multilayered and unpredictable ways on which translingual dispositions can manifest themselves" in people's literate activities (2016, p. 318).

Susanna has not traveled across the geographic borders of the United States and Japan, and thus her life's traversals do not follow the transnational migrations that dominate Writing Studies' accounts of translingualism and translingual writing. And yet, as this detailed mapping of Susanna's material texts and textual practices has illuminated, her literate activities are deeply and densely textured with translinguality. In assembling the wiki, doing her translations, creating fan art and fan fiction, and even illustrating organisms for the lab manual, Susanna displays the kinds of abilities that scholars have come to identify with a translingual disposition. For Horner et al. (2011), such a disposition demonstrates an "openness to linguistic differences and the ability to construct useful meanings from perspectives of them" (p. 308) and a "deftness in deploying a broad and diverse repertoire of language resources, and responsiveness to the diverse range of readers' social positions and ideological perspectives" (p. 308). For Canagarajah (2013), a translingual sensibility is evidenced by "an understanding of the production, circulation, and reception of texts that are always mobile" and that reach across languages, cultures, ethnicities, and nations (p. 41). Susanna's wiki, her translations, her fan art and fan fiction, and her work on the lab manual signal her openness to and facility with deploying a wide array of linguistic and semiotic resources and her responsiveness to a diversity of readers/viewers. Those texts, and the textual activities from which they emerge, likewise index Susanna's attunement to the far-flung networks across which they circulate.

Pedagogical Implications

For students in the classes I teach, this detailed tracing of Susanna's texts and practices functions as a kind of model for us to closely examine the various texts that we create and act with across our academic, professional, and everyday lives. After walking students through Susanna's multiple encounters with translingual practice from playing Sonic Wings, to creating and maintaining a wiki site, teaching herself Japanese, crafting fan-fiction and fan-art, and illustrating a biology lab manual, I invite students to use this mapping of Susanna's translinguality to look carefully at our own concrete, material engagements with language and literacy in "the messy, complex, and rather unpredictable . . . sociolinguistic world in which we live" (Blommaert, 2010, p. 27). As a way to keep our examinations grounded in the material conditions of our linguistic practice, we collect specific texts that animate our textual lives and consider the specific processes and practices from which those texts emerge, always with an eye toward identifying instances of language difference, however small or fleeting they might seem. In keeping with this mapping of Susanna's literacies, we trace our uses of particular heterogeneous elements across the full ecologies of our communicative practices, always with an eye toward following those elements as fully as we can across time, space, and representational media.

The mappings we generate, which tend to identify and trace our own rich histories with a wide variety of engagements with translingualism, continually remind me of all that can be obscured or rendered completely invisible, subordinated, or entirely ignored, when we do not pay close attention to people's concrete, everyday encounters with language difference. They also continually serve as a reminder that we need to continually interrogate what Vershawn Young (2004) describes as the faulty assumption that some languages "are so radically different" as to be "incompatible and unmixable" (p. 706), which he argues is a crucial step toward democratizing attitudes regarding people and the linguistic resources they employ.

Based on their own mappings and those of their classmates, students are frequently surprised at the dense translinguality they can see in their own lives. One of the things students are surprised to find is the variety of different languages they routinely act with, even though they do not consider themselves to be fluent in those languages. Like Susanna's initial encounters with Japanese in playing Sonic Wings and creating the wiki, students' mappings make visible the wide array of languages that animate their textual lives. One student, for example, while closely examining the sheet music she used to practice the flute, was surprised to find multiple Italian terms on every page, and even more surprised that she had a fairly confident sense of what those terms indicated, even though she would not claim to "know" Italian. Another student, while studying images of the various tattoos adorning his and has classmates' bodies, was surprised to find characters from a wide array of languages.

While these kinds of findings initially prompt some insightful discussions about what it means to truly "know" and "be able to use" a language, those conversations tend to quickly give way to insights about the very concrete ways we are all actively and agentively shaping language to our own ends rather than just using the language already presented to us, that in our actual blendings and mixings and transformations of language, we are not just acting with language as we encounter it, but rather acting upon it by refashioning it for our own purposes, investing it with our own intentions, reusing it for our own needs.

In addition to making visible the multiple ways that language contact comes to be woven into our lives, or to quote Bakhtin (1986), the multiple avenues through which "language enters life through concrete utterances . . . and life enters language through concrete utterances as well" (p. 63), engaging with these kinds of mappings helps reinforce and enhance our understanding that "translingualism" is, at its heart, "not about the number of languages, or language varieties, one can claim to know. Rather, it is about the disposition of openness and inquiry that people take toward language and language difference" (Horner et al., 2011, p. 311).

Another thing that students find somewhat surprised to see in their mappings is the wealth and variety of translingual semiotic resources they act with in addition to spoken or written language. In talking through why they find this somewhat surprising, students commonly mention that the term "translingual" tends to orients them toward attending to spoken or written language so much so that they tend to overlook the various other modes they use in their meaning making. Like Susanna's use of the images and music that originated in the Japanese versions of the game, students' mappings make visible a host of semiotic resources from across the globe that animate their everyday meaning making. One student, while examining some of the images of her own favorite video game characters, was surprised that she could discern subtle details in the images that signaled intertextual connections not only to previous versions of the game, but also to manga and anime publications. Another student, while listening closely to the music on her playlist, was surprised to encounter not only lyrics from other languages that she had not previously noticed but also various musical stylings, tempos, and rhythms associated with cultures and ethnicities from across the globe. In this sense, engaging with detailed mappings of our actual communicative practices can provide us with more realistic, and more accurate, conceptions of how people actually language, which is crucial for recognizing that issues of translingualism are relevant to each of us.

In his afterword, Horner notes that "propulsion toward translingual orientations requires pushing against monolinguist tenets: friction is both necessary to and an inevitable product of movement" (this collection). The discussions that emerge as students and I talk about Susanna's translingual practices and our own mappings of our translinguality are not infrequently textured by such frictions. Like all classrooms, mine are populated by students who readily value their exposure and engagement with language contact and those who, as Lee and Jenks (2016) describe, are more "guided by ideological assumptions that privilege ethnocentric or monolingual standards of English" (p. 328). And, just because people recognize the translinguality that textures their lives does not mean that they immediately regard it as a valuable resource for making meaning in the world. Ultimately, though, my sense is that careful attention to people's material engagements with translingual writing, making, and doing—their being and becoming across embodied languages and literacies in the world—can help us challenge representations of language grounded in the ideology of monolingualism, a key first step toward fashioning language and literacy instruction increasingly relevant to the production of people and practices in and for the twenty-first century.

References

Bakhtin, M. (1986). The problem of speech genres (V. W. McGee, Trans.). In C. Emerson & M. Holquist (Eds.), *Speech genres and other late essays* (pp. 60–102). University of Texas Press.

Blommaert, J. (2010). *The socioloinguistics of globalization.* Cambridge University Press.

Canagarajah, S. (2013). Negotiating translingual literacy: An enactment. *Research in the Teaching of English, 48*(1), 40–64.

Canagarajah, S. (2016). Translingual writing and teacher development in composition. *College English, 78*(3), 265–273.

Daniel-Wariya, J. (2016). A language of play: New media's possibility spaces. *Computers and Composition, 40,* 32–47.

Fraiberg, S. (2010). Composition 2.0: Toward a multilingual and multimodal framework. *College Composition and Communication, 62*(1), 100–126.

Fraiberg, S. (2013). Reassembling technical communication: A framework for studying multilingual and multimodal practices in global contexts. *Technical Communication Quarterly, 22*(1), 10–27.

Fraiberg, S. (2017). Pretty bullets: Tracing transmedia/translingual literacies of an Israeli soldier across regimes of practice. *College Composition and Communication, 69*(1), 87–117.

Fraiberg, S. & Cui, X. (2016). Weaving relationship webs: Tracing how IMing practices mediate the trajectories of Chinese international students. *Computers and Composition, 39,* 83–103.

Guerra, J. (2016). Cultivating a rhetorical sensibility in the translingual writing classroom. *College English, 78*(3), 228–233.

Horner, B. (This collection). Afterword. In A. Frost, J. Kiernan & S. B. Malley (Eds.), *Translingual affordances: Globalized approaches to the teaching of writing* (this collection). The WAC Clearinghouse and University Press of Colorado.

Horner, B., Lu, M., Royster, J. & Trimbur, J. (2011). Language difference in writing: Toward a translingual approach. *College English, 73*(3), 302–321.

Jordan, J. (2015). Material translingual ecologies. *College English, 77*(4), 364–382.

Kelley, B. (2016). Chocolate frogs for my betas!: Practicing literacy at one online fanfiction website. *Computers and Composition, 40,* 48–59.

Lee, J. W. & Jenks, C. (2016). Doing translingual dispositions. *College Composition and Communication, 68*(2) 317–344.

Lillis, Theresa. (2008). Ethnography as method, methodology, and "deep-theorizing": Closing the gap between text and context in academic writing research. *Written Communication, 25*(3), 353–388.

Lorimer Leonard, R. (2013). Traveling literacies: Multilingual writing on the move. *Research in the Teaching of English, 48,* 13–39.

Lorimer Leonard, R. (2014). Multilingual writing as rhetorical attunement. *College English, 76*(3), 227–247.

Lorimer Leonard, R. (2015). Writing through bureaucracy: Migrant correspondence and managed mobility. *Written Communication, 32*(1), 87–113.

Miller, P., Hengst, J. & Wang, S. (2003). Ethnographic methods: Applications from developmental cultural psychology. In P. M. Camic, J. E. Rhodes & L. Yardley (Eds.), *Qualitative research in psychology: Expanding perspectives in methodology and design* (pp. 219–242). American Psychological Association.

Monty, R. (2015). Everyday borders of transnational students: Composing place and space with mobile technology, social media, and multimodality. *Computers and Composition, 38,* 126–139.

Prior, P. (1998). *Writing/disciplinarity: A sociohistoric account of literate activity in the academy.* Erlbaum.

Roozen, K. (2009). From journals to journalism: Tracing trajectories of literate development. *College Composition and Communication, 60(3),* 541–572.

Scollon, R. & Scollon, S. (2003). *Discourses in place: Language in the material world.* Routledge.

Shipka, J. (2016). Transmodality in/and processes of making: Changing dispositions and practice. *College English, 78*(3), 250–257.

Vieria, K. (2011). Undocumented in a documentary society: Textual borders and transnational religious literacies. *Written Communication, 28*(4), 436–61.

Young, V. A. (2004). Your average nigga. *College Composition and Communication, 55*(4), 693–715.

7 Dialogic Openings for Recreating English

Marylou Gramm
UNIVERSITY OF PITTSBURGH

In this chapter, the author argues that the student-teacher conference is crucial for fostering international undergraduates' translingual writing as it facilitates collaborative, inquisitive close readings of drafts, enabling students to exploit fertile grammatical deviations to engender analysis. The author describes two instances of students' specific translingual constructions, (1) "fancy people dignity" and (2) "appreciate" used simultaneously as verb and adjective, and shows that by negotiating language, form and meaning in the conference, students develop the cognitive and creative potential of their linguistic innovations.

Keywords: translingual, linguistic innovation, dialogic, student-teacher conference, composition pedagogy

Translingual and Dialogic Approaches

Contrary to monolingual strategies and assumptions, as this collection theorizes and as established in the work of Bruce Horner, Min-Zhan Lu, Jacqueline Jones Royster, and John Trimbur (2011), the translingual disposition in composition "takes the variety, fluidity, intermingling and changeability of languages" to be the norm and the notion of a universal standard English to be a political myth: "A translingual approach sees difference in language not as a barrier to overcome or as a problem to manage, but as a resource for producing meaning . . . expressively, rhetorically, communicatively" (pp. 305, 303). While "the aim of traditional writing instruction has been to reduce 'interference,'" translingual pedagogues understand that "deviations from dominant expectations need not be errors; that conformity need not be automatically advisable" (Horner et al., 2011, pp. 302, 304). This approach calls for instructors' close readings of students' texts (Trimbur, 2016) to explore deviations as pedagogical opportunities and to support students in meaningfully manipulating and transforming conventions rather than simply pursuing so-called linguistic standardization.

DOI: https://doi.org/10.37514/INT-B.2020.0438.2.07

In this chapter, I describe my translingual dispositions, specifically employed during student-teacher conferences, which encourage the translingual composing of two international writing students from Mainland China, one in an ESL composition class that employed a translingual course design and the other in a writing intensive, upper-level, literature course for all undergraduates. The narratives of these conferences are from my field notes, written during and immediately following each conference. Like other teacher-scholars in this collection, I consider forms that translanguaging can take in undergraduate writing and the impacts that it can make on undergraduates' critical thinking about their texts, building on such earlier analyses as Lu's "Professing Multiculturalism: The Politics of Style in the Contact Zone" (1999) and Suresh Canagarajah's "Negotiating Translingual Literacy" (2013). Canagarajah (2013) has noted the need for more of this work, reflecting that "some scholars have started complaining that advances in theorization of translingual practices have far outstripped pedagogical implementation" and that such pedagogies would, in turn, generate "useful insights into communicative practices" (p. 12). Answering Canagarajah's call, I explain (1) how translingual dispositions in my student-teacher conferences promote the development of my students' linguistic innovations; (2) how translanguaging can signify the mark of a writer's cognitive work and, therefore, is a particularly fertile place for investigating a writer's unelaborated ideation; and (3) how students can use these innovations to articulate and advance thinking in their essays while their diverse English grammar remakes English. When students are guided and encouraged to develop the rich potential of their translingual writing by a facilitator, translanguaging works as a catalyst for their critical thinking in writing about the literature they read, their lived experience, and their linguistic innovation. In contrast, when we dwell primarily on errors as deficits, particularly with students who hail from what Goffman (2005) has termed "face-work" cultures, we risk eroding their sense of dignity as writers and amplifying their feelings of anxiety about composition (Shaughnessy, 1977 as cited in Lu, 1994, p. 448). By encouraging students to explore the creative potential of their fertile deviations during our face-to-face conversations, we give student writers the vital opportunity to develop knowledge of diverse conventions and help them to build a sense of literary dignity, to acquire a text-based-face born of the social interaction between readers and writers as those writers contribute to the evolution of the language that they use.

The impact of my conferences with students on the development of their translingual innovations correlates with scholarship documenting the power of teacher-student face-to-face dialogue (compared to written comments) in catalyzing multilingual students' revision processes (Gitzen, 2002; Goldstein

& Conrad, 1990; Liu, 2009; Young & Miller, 2004). I believe further that direct conversation with students in conferences in which we closely examine their inventive rhetorical, syntactic, and semantic choices in their essays effectively supports their translingual experiments. Through our conference exchanges—my questions and their reflections about their unconventional and intriguing language choices—students endow their translingual forms with efficacy and meaning. Pivotal moments of dialogic exchange during our one-on-one discussions of their drafts launch students' revision processes as they develop a heightened consciousness of their translingual forms as discursive resources for expanding meaning in their essays.

In further support of my student-teacher conferencing choices, I offer here the specifics of Horner, Lu, and Canagarajah's work that speak directly to this dialogic pedagogy. In arguing that all writers, including international students, are refashioning language as they use it, Horner and Lu (2013), raised a profound, inclusive, and germane question: Why is it that deviations in writing by so-called "mainstream" writers "are perceived as creative" innovations, "while deviations in writing by those identified as belonging to subordinate social groups are taken as manifestations of the writers' lack of knowledge or fluency with 'the standard'" (p. 583)? A common (monolingual) response is that the poetics practiced by native users of English deviate meaningfully and intentionally, while the nonnative apprentices who have not mastered the tools of the trade deviate without consciousness. But both of these assumptions are quite often untrue. The poet's creative unconscious is frequently at work, and the apprentice—if one takes the time to ask her—has often applied her tools quite meaningfully even if that meaning is not immediately recognizable or fully articulated in its initial incarnation. Lu's essay, "Professing Multiculturalism: The Politics of Style in the Contact Zone," (1994) maps one of the earliest translingual pedagogical applications treating grammatical and rhetorical deviations from the perceived standard as stylistic innovation. In an approach to revision that has students explore the various meanings inherent in their grammatical idiosyncrasies, Lu leads class discussions that prompt students' thoughtful negotiation of stylistic choices. The revision of Lu's student's ostensibly erroneous phrase, "can able to," is not corrected according to "one's knowledge of or respect for the authorities of a dictionary English versus colloquial English" (1994, p. 453). Though revisions conforming to currently accepted forms (e.g., "is able to") are discussed, students spend equal time exploring the various meanings of the inventive phrase, "can able to," which is uniquely designed to communicate "conflicting attitudes toward a belief in the transcendental power of the individual" whose agency is potentially curtailed as it depends upon an authority's permission ("can") and not just upon intrinsic ability ("able to") (Lu, 1994, p. 453). Lu's pedagogies offer support for my decision to treat student writers, as we converse about their drafts, with the same authority and creativity as published authors who do not "passively absorb and automatically reproduce a predetermined form" or deserve to have their idiosyncratic writing regarded as the result of "the not-yet 'perfectly educated' [and] solely in terms of 'error'" (Lu, 1994, pp. 455, 447).

While Lu (1999) describes negotiated literacy occurring among students in classroom discussions of a translingual text, and Canagarajah (2013) empha-sizes negotiations among students via their written responses to peers' trans-lingual experiments, I focus on my negotiations in conferences with students that were crucial to their translingual revisions. In dialogic conferences, I pro-mote the creative possibilities inherent in students' unusual syntax, semantics, and rhetorical moves. As my descriptions of our conferences show, from the questions I ask them, students discover the signifying power of their linguis-tic deviations and become the ultimate decision-makers about strategies for revision. In my experience, focusing our dialogue on the creative potential rather than on the dissonance of students' apparent deviations not only fos-ters students' engagement and confidence in writing but also promotes their creativity and critical thinking—central to my writing program's goals.

A Translingual Curricular Design

At my home institution, the University of Pittsburgh, the stated goals of our English Department's first-year composition courses—creative, critical inquiry about language, form, and meaning—are inherent to translingual writing. These goals shape our required first-year seminar in composition as well as the precursor composition workshops for native English speakers multilingual English speakers who place into them based upon SAT scores and an on-campus language proficiency test respectively. Articulated more specifically in our statement of "Goals for First-Year Composition" (2016) on the English Department's website, our curriculum engages students in writing as a creative form of critical inquiry; in considering (in writing) problems that emerge from a thoughtful examination of their lived expe-rience, their observations, and their reading of diverse texts; in developing ideas and analysis that reflect close attention to their own and others' specific language choices; and in revising by using strategies that productively chal-lenge conventions and reflect an awareness of the relationship between style and meaning. I carry these goals into the curricular design of my current ESL Workshop in Composition, the course for international first-year and transfer undergraduates, as well as into my responses to student compositions in the writing-intensive literature courses that I teach in our English department. In both types of courses, I ask students to use their languages innovatively in order to critically inquire into the conflicts and complexities within their own experiential narratives and those of published authors.

In what follows, I will discuss two case studies of Chinese students translanguaging—the first, Xiao Ming, in my ESL composition workshop and then Shiwei Li, in my upper-level, writing intensive literature class.[1] Both Xiao and Shiwei hail from mainland China—the predominant international population at the University of Pittsburgh, comprising nearly five percent of our students (University of Pittsburgh, 2018). I describe how Xiao and Shiwei translanguage by transferring into their Englishes Mandarin topic-comment structures and indeterminate parts of speech respectively. Starting with my conference with Xiao and from his revisions, I show how he uses an innovative translingual phrase to develop critical thinking about his narratives. First, however, I briefly outline the curricular design that generated Xiao's work.

My ESL Workshop in Composition takes translanguaging, translation, and transculturation as the central focus of inquiry for the course and the theme of our reading and writing. The class is subtitled "Transporting Home," a metaphor for students' and published authors' experiences of linguistic mobility. While Horner and Lu (2013) caution against assigning discrete languages to geographic spaces such as "nation," "school," or "home," I ask students to consider their first language or languages as *mobile* homes (along the lines of what Blommaert (2010) has called "mobile resources"), which they transport and mesh interactively with other languages in new contexts, thus renovating each time they compose. This theme of mobility presupposes a translingual disposition, for it highlights students' linguistic fluidity, imagining that they and their non-discrete languages are unendingly "en route." The course description of my syllabus suggests that each student embodies and carries within multilingual resources (rather than a fixed code) including language(s) learned from childhood onward and knowledge of a local English. These languages "are now," as Canagarajah (2006) put it, "traveling" and creatively combining with English words, syntax, and rhetorical structures commonly used in our southwestern Pennsylvanian academic locality, and thereby enriching and animating the student's compositions and languages (p. 590).

Students in this ESL Workshop in Composition course analyze the evolving roles of their languages in their lives in their first essay, a language autobi-

---

1   Both Xiao Ming and Shiwei Li gave written permission for their writing and conversations to be reproduced in this article, which IRB found sufficient given the limited nature of this qualitative study.

ography, and then explore the un/translatability of a metaphorical expression from their native tongue into English in the second essay. Finally, the third essay assignment—the one that lead to Xiao Ming's fruitful translanguaging which I discuss in the following section—asks students how interpreting a (self-selected) English language text can lead them to alter their perspective on a difficult experience of leaving home—however they currently define home in their lives. As I will show, probing unconventional passages in Xiao's writing during our conferences made me realize the potential for face-enhancing dialogues for students. My interactions with Xiao illustrate how teachers and students can work together to explore translingual innovations in their drafts.

Text-Based Face in ESL Workshop in Composition

A freshman in my ESL Workshop in Composition class in fall 2014, Xiao Ming struggled to analyze the meanings of his well-crafted narratives and conferenced with me more than once to try to understand what it would entail, as he put it (in his final portfolio reflection on his struggles in the course), "to search and dig out your idea and have more critical thinking." However, embracing Xiao's translingual neologism, "fancy people dignity," which appeared in his very first draft of the essay about a difficult experience of leaving home, ultimately helped him to practice critical thinking in this essay.

When I queried his phrase in our conference, Xiao explained that he had transferred Chinese grammar into the English, "fancy people dignity," because he had conceptualized it in his first language and then translated. Several studies, as noted by Leki (1992) and Whalen and Menard (1995), have documented the constraining effects of linguistic processing on the conceptual production of L2 writers, suggesting their need to revert to L1 or the commingling of L1 and L2 in order to generate concepts. In Yingliang Liu's (2009) interviews of Chinese undergraduate writers studying at a southwestern U.S. university, she found even her most successful student "thinking all in Chinese when she drafted the thesis," another "drafting an outline in Chinese in her mind," and her most challenged student drafting the entire composition in Chinese, which resulted in many Chinglish sentences (pp. 143, 148, 150). As a trace of Xiao's cognitive processing in Chinese emerged in his translingual innovation, "fancy people dignity," this phrase became fertile ground for investigating Xiao's unelaborated ideation; as I show in the following narrative of our conference, this translingual conceptual marker, when probed, enabled Xiao to analyze his narrative.

When we first met in conference to discuss Xiao's first draft, as we took turns rereading it aloud, I asked him how he responded as a reader of his own work, and he said he was unsure how to develop the critical thinking missing in it. (As noted, this had been his struggle throughout the semester.) To that end, I had in mind three critical inquiries for him to consider: (1) What is the significance of the isolation you suffered in your new middle school in Hangzhou (the capital of Zhejiang province, much larger and wealthier than his former hometown of Xiaoshan, where Xiao—as conveyed in his essay—had grown up and enjoyed prestige and popularity)? (2) What does your unconventional phrase, "fancy people dignity," mean? (3) How does O. Henry's story, "The Last Leaf," which you reference, change your perspective on your experience of exclusion in Hangzhou? Because I sensed that the first and third questions were most abstract and difficult, and more importantly because I wanted to ground our conversation in what Xiao *had* accomplished rather than focusing on lacunae, I began with Xiao's own language, his fertile unconventional phrase, "fancy people dignity." Among the other minor deviations, its meaning seemed most provocative to me because the notion of Xiao's dignity, amid what he otherwise lamented in this essay as experiences of humiliation and grief in his new exclusive school, struck me as contradictory and therefore intriguing. As I show in what follows, exploring his invented term led Xiao to compose sentences in his essay that addressed my other two inquiries (about the significance of his isolation in his new school, and the meaning of the O. Henry story he had incorporated in his essay). In our conversation, through unpacking his phrase, he was able to discover how his translingual neologism contained in a compressed and poetic form much of his unstated analysis.

In order to prompt a student to explore the richness of their linguistic deviations, I often have to identify the deviation which they have not noticed or identified as unconventional. Thus, before Xiao unpacked the meaning and significance of "fancy people dignity," I had to draw his attention to the term's unusual formulation. This moment in our conference enabled me to instruct Xiao in conventional English usage, and it enabled Xiao to instruct me in his ways of transporting Chinese grammar into his English. I noted that except in compound nouns (such as homework) and collocations (such as mother tongue), current academic English users more frequently modify nouns with adjectives rather than with other nouns, which are often coordinated with prepositions (Biber et al., 2002). I learned from Xiao that grammatically, "people dignity" transfers into English one type of Mandarin topic-comment (noun-noun) structure (Chen, 2009). Moreover, possessive nouns, Xiao told me, are not always marked grammatically in Mandarin, just as he omitted the possessive and did not mark the subject distinct from the possessive in fancy people dignity; both parts of speech can be understood implicitly through context cues in Chinese (Ross & Ma, 2006). I believe that Xiao gained authority as he instructed me about Chinese, and I experienced what Lee and Jenks (2016) have referred to as "learning opportunities" for instructors "doing" translingual dispositions (p. 338).

During the course of our conference about his first draft, Xiao created aloud a new meaning for "fancy people dignity" after he learned from me that this phrase, minus the apostrophe, eschews the possessive (people's): he suggested to me that he would like to use that missing apostrophe (missing possessive) "to convey that fancy people don't possess such dignity even though they may hope they do." Xiao said that he "liked hinting through the missing apostrophe [and s] what fancy people were missing since it would allow the reader to discover my meaning." Thinking out loud further, he mused that via this inventive phrase, he would like to imply that "one's so-called dignity exists only in the eyes of others who put that dignity onto you." In turn, others can take it away, as Xiao expressed in his essay when he recounted how his new Hangzhou classmates stripped his dignity: "their arrogant look in the eyes haunted in mind all of the time." During our conversation, when I questioned the unconventional "haunted *in* mind" (rather than haunted my mind), Xiao explained that he meant to insinuate that he had internalized or "took inside their arrogant look;" their judgment had lodged *in*side him; it was a sense of self projected into him by others, yet a judgment owned by them, by "*their* arrogant look." I understood from these explanations that his translingual invention, "fancy people dignity," minus the possessive, implicitly emphasizes that lack of self-possession because the fancy person does not possess and cannot conjure the dignity ascribed or denied by others.

Practicing close reading of students' drafts alongside them is a crucial part of the process of developing their translingual writing. Therefore, regarding Xiao's loss of dignity, at this point in Xiao's conference-revelations, I drew attention to his repeated use of the term "face" in his essay and asked why he had not used the more commonly translated Chinese term "to lose face;" the word "face" appears repeatedly in his first draft, though not explicitly as a psycho-social term, at his moment of greatest humiliation when none of his Hangzhou classmates included him in the working groups they were obliged to form in order to collaborate on the teacher's "social lesson." Remembering his predicament, Xiao had recalled in his essay:

> Sitting there alone, the teacher asked the class: "Is there any-
> one who's willing to chose Xiao as their desk mate?" Repeat-

ed loudly, no one answered. I lowered my head, covering my *face* with my bare hands. My *face* blushed. I even felt that there was real fire burning on my *face* . . . I felt like tens of thousands of unwilling and mocking eye sights were coming from all these students, taking me as a pathetic loner. (Emphasis added.)

Considering the importance of student autonomy during the conference and in post-conference composing, I want to highlight that in his revised essay, Xiao decided not to refer explicitly to the social implications of the recurrent word "face" in his essay, that is to say, he did not refer to loss of face, which continues to be a commonplace mode of expressing attainment or loss of repute even in twenty-first century post-economic-reform-era China (He, 2012; Mao, 1994; Pan & Kadar, 2011). Instead, Xiao opted to express his loss of social status and humiliation through the unconventional term he had composed before we met, "fancy people dignity," because during our conference, I maintained a translingual disposition, continually encouraging Xiao's innovation and independent choice as a writer. I was not commenting in the margins of his essay draft as an implicit evaluator: "What does fancy dignity mean? It's unclear." Or "why not use the term loss of face since you repeat 'face?'" And he was not a student confronting and considering such comments in solitude, uncertain of what his teacher might value or not value. As he had planned aloud in our conference, Xiao later went on to revise his draft and opt for the phrase "fancy people dignity" rather than the term face precisely because, as he declared to me, "I want to stress that the lost dignity was never my own in the first place;" in other words, by excluding the possessive mark he wanted to stress that fancy people dignity was neither possessed nor earned.

Yet as a reader of Xiao's final draft—revised after the conference yet evidently very much informed by our conversation—it seems to me that Xiao, through his "fancy people dignity" innovation, nonetheless conveys the concept of "face" implicitly. From my reading of Xiao's revision and Chinese notions of face, I would argue that there are two general sources of face indirectly implied, and they are worth defining so as to value Xiao's possible implications. According to the definition by Hsien Chin Hu (1944) reiterated by David Yau-fai Ho (1978) and Jun Liu (2001), face—in Chinese, mìanzi 面子—is social prestige acquired through an authoritative title, a high examination score, or other material public attainment, and face—in Chinese, liǎn 脸—is respect due to reputation for moral deeds (Hu, 1944; Ho, 1976). In both cases—material or moral—face is (like Xiao's definition of "fancy people dignity") granted by others on the basis of one's admirable action; "a sound míng-yù [reputation] must be *earned*" (Ho, 1976, p. 875, emphasis added). And even if earned, "Chinese face . . . is 'on loan. . . from society' not permanently owned by its bearer" (Goffman, 1967, p. 20 as cited by LuMing Mao, 1994, p. 460).

After the conference, Xiao developed in his revision (quoted below) a definition and narrative elaboration of "fancy people dignity" that places an emphasis on "fancy," that is, on the purely material basis of Xiao's status (or face) in his previous school in Xiaoshan and, moreover, on the fact that the wealth that he displayed he had not "earned." Stressing the importance of his material display (mìanzi) in establishing "fancy people dignity" in the eyes of his Xiaoshan classmates, Xiao recounted in his revision how he had used his family's wealth to acquire friendship and social respect rather than attaining them by means of his own moral agency (liǎn). In the following revised passage, Xiao recalled the outlay of toys that had garnered him approval among his young friends in Xiaoshan, a strategy that failed in his new school in Hangzhou because he could not achieve "fancy people dignity" where more affluent students possessed a larger collection of fancy things. I highlight especially the definition in that passage, which begins to transform his story into critical thinking, an achievement for Xiao in the course enabled by our dwelling in our conference and his dwelling in his essay on his translingual invention:

> In Xiaoshan, they worshipped or adored me for what I had owned. And my mother spoil me a lot: giving me money to buy some toys. Sharing these toys with my friends in town because not everyone has toys as much as I have, I was adored from them. The feeling of being the upper class had already cultivated my vanity and my so-called "fancy people dignity," *a dignity and popularity that resulted from my superior social status.* However, in the new environment (Hangzhou), when I first came to class, they didn't come to say hi to me and ask me to share toys with them. Some of they even have more toys than me. Without confidence, I lost the way to make friends. The feeling that I was isolated and despised by my new classmates depressed me so much that I didn't even do well in my subjects. (Emphasis added.)

Embracing the translingual view that English does not have to have its apostrophe or coordinated nouns in his revision, Xiao defined his neologism, using, in his revision (above) the convention of the appositive clause that I had recently offered to students during a class discussion of various sentence structures—"a dignity and popularity that resulted from my superior social status." He extended the narrative about the toys that had enabled him to "cultivate" his vanity and seem to possess dignity, showing how socially situated and contingent on others his dignity was, such that later in Hangzhou, the decline in relative value of his toys deprived him of dignity. From Xiao's translingual term, "fancy people dignity," minus that expected possessive, he hoped that a close reader might infer that he *never* possessed such ephemeral and socially contingent dignity and that dignity is not one's own when it is owned only by means of conspicuous consumption. In Xiao's oral elaboration during our conference (prior to revising his essay) he explained "dignity is not earned or possessed by the fancy people; it is given by others who adore you simply because of your display of wealth." Xiao's translingual phrase, identified by me but then endowed with meaning by Xiao, first orally during our conference and then in his revisions, allowed him to intimate his discovery of the hollowness of this way of acquiring admirers.

In order to complete this essay assignment, which (as noted previously) asked students to explain how reading an English-language source altered their perspective on a dislocating experience, Xiao turned at the end of this same essay to O. Henry's story "The Last Leaf." Having heard in our conference Xiao orally develop analytical meanings of his translingual phrase (while he took notes on his draft in English and Chinese on what he said), I finally voiced my third question: How does O. Henry's story, "The Last Leaf," which you reference, change your perspective on your experience of exclusion in Hangzhou? In response, Xiao said he was "proud of his translingual invention, fancy people dignity," and—embracing a translingual disposition—he decided to exploit it further as a resource. Xiao decided in the conference that he could use "fancy people dignity," as he put it, "in contrast to O. Henry's story." In other words, he could use it to introduce O. Henry as a counter-narrative to his own. As revealed in Xiao's revised passage, written after the conference and quoted below, O. Henry had led Xiao to realize that he believes friendship must be built among strangers through one's moral and nonmonetary actions. What follows is a brief synopsis of O. Henry's story and an explanation of how Xiao used it to extend his critical thinking about alternatives to "fancy people dignity."

In O. Henry's "The Last Leaf," prestige is acquired posthumously by a moral and unsolicited act of generosity by the elderly, unsuccessful, painter, Behrman, who dies after suffering a freezing storm throughout the night in order to paint the image of a leaf outside the window of his neighbor Johnsy, an image that keeps the dying Johnsy alive after she has vowed to succumb to pneumonia when the tree in her window loses its final autumn leaf. Through his sacrifice in creating this "masterpiece," Behrman achieves a dignity through moral rather than monetary or professional accomplishment. In the revision that follows, Xiao imagined O. Henry had helped Xiao to overcome the miserable memory of his social dislocation in middle school by realizing that "fancy people dignity" fails to cultivate genuine human connections, and that we must strive to create interpersonal bonds (*liăn*) not material display:

> Mr. Behrman could sacrifice his own life only to bring some more hope to help the girl to survive, so *why can't we* do more for our families or friends? When we are complaining about the estrangement between people, *why we couldn't* be the first to break the ice and show our welcome and kindness to them? . . . My embarrassment, estrangement, loneliness, the sense of being isolated and the emptiness was caressed by a warm stream of Mr. Behrman's gift to Johnsy: Love, sacrifice, and strong faith to strive for living on. These complex and mixed elements in the story became an invisible but somehow truly existed man, patting my head, scolding me in a soft yet strict voice . . . Instead of asking for something empty like fancy people dignity from some people, *shouldn't I first* learn how to give? *The reason why* I didn't make new friends was because I didn't show my welcome or friendliness to them. *I was like the dying woman* who gave up hope and stopped trying to find another way to connect. And this story, however, worked for me as the last leaf that the old painter had painted for her. It filled my heart with hope, confidence to make new friends. It was like a shelter and my final peaceful place, revealing the true, the good and beautiful to me. Wealth is an empty test, not everyone judges by it. (Emphasis added.)

In this revised passage, I want to note how Xiao used his revelation about the emptiness of "fancy people dignity" to ponder O. Henry's story and introduce important expository elements: rhetorical questions ("Why can't we . . . ? Why we couldn't . . . ? Shouldn't I first . . . ?"), analogies ("I was like the dying woman"), and explanations ("The reason why . . . "). However, weeks later, in our end-of-semester conference, I questioned Xiao about his uplifting, inspirational concluding sentences: "this story . . . filled my heart with hope, confidence to make new friends . . . revealing the true, the good and beautiful to me. I noted their "positive moral message" about "soundness of character," which I later learned, according to Sullivan et al. (2012), in their multi-voiced article about college writing in China and America, is a common rhetorical feature and overall aim in much Chinese undergraduate writing. Contributor Fenglan Zheng acknowledges that in China, "it is a writing teacher's responsibility to help cultivate positive . . . emotions among students" (Sullivan et al, 2012, p. 325), emotions such as Xiao's "hope," "friendliness," and "the true, the good, and beautiful" way of "do[ing] more for our . . . friends." Though I suggested that Xiao deepen his analysis of the problem of seeking "fancy people dignity" rather than concluding with an inspirational solution, I ultimately respected Xiao's expressed wish not to change this contrastive rhetoric in his conclusion. For in dialogic negotiations with students, rather than striving for conformity to American academic conventions of critical inquiry, I want to help them recognize options and develop a meta-cognitive awareness of the linguistic and cultural rationales for those that they choose.

Appreciating English in a Writing Intensive Literature Course

What happens to students' translingual approaches after they leave our composition classrooms? What is the potential for translingual learning transfer in other courses that prioritize writing among their requirements? My answer to those as yet unplumbed questions in transfer studies (Leonard & Nowacek, 2016) is provisional since they require data about a range of course settings, and my discovery here pertains to one, my writing intensive, upper-level, "Women and Literature" course, and the writing in that class in spring 2014 composed by Shiwei Li, a senior from mainland China, majoring in Math and Economics, who had taken my ESL Workshop in Composition class in 2011 and was able to continue her linguistic creativity within the "safe house" of my class, where she knew the instructor would welcome translingual experimentation (Canagarajah, 1997; Pratt, 1991). I want to explore Shiwei's writing and the role of our conferences in her revision as an illustration of what the translingual composing process and outcome can look like in a literature class situated outside of the disciplinary boundaries of composition.

In the essay assignment that Shiwei undertook in "Women and Literature," I asked students to compose an argument about their close reading of a metaphor concerning gender in any of the literary texts that we had read, and to imagine the author's purpose in using the metaphor. That Shiwei chose to engage with Virginia Woolf's "A Room of One's Own" is not irrelevant, and I stress her choice of text thanks to Jay Jordan's (2015) argument that we must pay attention to "Material Translingual Ecologies," to the material context that enables translingual writing. Though Jordan's ecologies emphasize bodies, sensation, and other ambient factors, I want to highlight the textual ecology of Woolf's "Room" as an agent in Shiwei's translingual endeavor. For Woolf's is an essay that famously defies conventions in order to open the literary landscape to women just as Shiwei's text admits a trans-rhetorical and translingual disposition of her own once she gains guidance about translanguaging in our conference dialogue.

The first paragraph of Shiwei's essay, "Selfless Angel or Angry Devil?" immediately departs from conventions of Anglo-American literary criticism. Instead of highlighting her thesis, Shiwei has placed us in a scene with Woolf, much as Woolf begins "A Room of One's Own" placing us "by the banks of a river:"

> Walking along the beautiful campus of Oxbridge on a Saturday afternoon, a female student thought about the masters of literature. The birds were singing and the sun was shining. She decided to go to the campus library to follow the footsteps of Lamb, who also studied in this college a hundred years ago. She imagined she could take a look at Thackeray's manuscript and a lot of other masters' works in the library. However, the guard refused her entry into the library, like she had a contagious disease. This unbelievable scene actually happened during the time period Virginia Woolf lived in, as she recorded in her famous book, *A Room of One's Own*.

When I paused in rereading Shiwei's essay aloud with her, at the outset of our conference, to query this unconventional opening, I learned from her and (later from scholars of contrastive rhetoric noted by Sullivan et al., 2012), that what Shiwei did here evokes one traditional form of a Chinese rhetorical opening, in which the writer links emotions and natural scenery. Sullivan et al. (2012) draw on the work of contrastive rhetorician, Xiaoming Li (1996), to explain that in Chinese compositions, human emotion (qing) is traditionally couched in nature (jing): "All descriptions of natural objects or scenery are for the sake of expressing emotions" (Li, 1996, p. 87 as cited in Sullivan et al, 2012, pp. 324–325). Shiwei linked qing and jing through juxtaposition, contrasting the indignant *"unbelievable* scene" where Woolf is refused entry and the cheerful singing birds and shining sun. At the same time, in this intro, Shiwei narrated rather than argued what becomes a key point in her essay—that Woolf tried stylistically and literally to follow in the footsteps of male writers like Lamb and Thackeray. I learned all of this—the student's manipulation of a traditional Chinese introduction and her implied thesis—by asking Shiwei, in person, why she wrote this introduction, why she began by describing Woolf's walk.

What if I had not asked Shiwei about these unconventional rhetorical choices and, instead, had simply required their revision? (What if I hadn't asked Xiao about the meaning of "fancy people dignity," but had simply placed an apostrophe s after people?) Conferencing with our students allows for a genuine dialogue in which we can ask them about the roots and the reasons for their deviations from conventions rather than (via commenting on the paper) editing or simply flagging them, and, in turn, students can teach us about their translingual, trans-rhetorical innovations. Through such dialogue, instructors can discover value in an opening paragraph that invites us into a mood and a scene rather than an explicit argument.

Shiwei's plan in the essay—as she explained it to me further in conference—was to continue to escort her reader on a walk alongside Woolf on her campus tour. Along the way, Shiwei analyzed the gendered metaphors that arise when misogyny obstructs Woolf's steps. The following passage, which contains a fertile translingual deviation, comes from a section of Shiwei's essay about the guardian angel who denies Woolf entry into the Oxbridge library without a patriarchal pass; it marks the place in Shiwei's first draft where I made my main inquiry about Shiwei's translanguaging during our conference, and it led Shiwei to expand her ideas about Woolf's manipulation of language:

> The guardian man were protecting the treasure only belongs to men. All those book, all the fancy foods, all the **appreci-ate** words were only for men. Woolf used word "kindly" and "regretted" when she talks about the guardian's attitude, but I also noticed the word "deprecating." Is this weird that she used two opposite adjective to describe the guard man? As I think, the kindly and regretted emotion was just the surface of the guardian. The man pretended to be polite, but inside his heart, his attitude was deprecating. He looked down upon Woolf, and as sensitive of Woolf, she could see through this hypocritical immediately. (Emphasis added.)

Though there are several somewhat distracting grammatical deviations in the final lines of this passage, I decided to query just one: Shiwei's intended meaning of "the appreciate words" in "All those book, all the fancy foods, all the appreciate words were only for men." I focused on "the appreciate words" because the phrase seems to have the most elusive and richest potential meaning about language, and language is Shiwei's continual concern in her essay. One could read Shiwei's misplaced verb, "appreciate," monolingually, as an error to be changed to the adjective "appreciative," a deviation arising from Chinese according to Shiwei. Chinese verbs, themselves, do not change to indicate their adjectival form but are generally accompanied by the generic character—的 de; sometimes the generic de is omitted, and the intended part of speech is simply understood from the context (Ross & Ma, 2006).

But instead of seeking to correct her phrase, "the appreciate words," working translingually in our conference, I asked Shiwei: what do you mean here by "appreciate?" It was a descriptive rather than a corrective question. In response, Shiwei asked me what appreciate could mean. We investigated the meanings and usages of appreciate in the dictionary, and I asked Shiwei which she intended. "I want them all!" was her ambitious response. Shiwei decided to continue her unconventional usage of this word—"appreciate"—and to exploit its dual meanings in order to deepen her ideas about Woolf's figurative language. In her revision, begun orally in conference and completed in writing later on her own, some of the other deviations in Shiwei's passage disappeared as she dwelled on and developed this section of her essay. Shiwei composed these revisions to her second paragraph after we had met and investigated the meanings of "appreciate" and how she could use them to justify her translingual innovation. Shiwei's (italicized) revisions show that encouraging translingual approaches catalyzes language acquisition, analysis and revision.

> The guardian man w*as* protecting the treasure *that* only belonged to men. All those book*s*, all the fancy foods, all the "appreciate" words were only for men. *I mean "appreciate" here as both a verb (appreciating) and an adjective (appreciative). Apparently, only the men are permitted to make their words grow in value so words are appreciating in men's writing. But Woolf is appreciative of words too as she works with them creatively.* She used the words *"kindly"* and *"deprecating"* to show the man pretended to be polite, but inside his heart, his attitude was deprecating. He looked down upon Woolf, and she could see through this *hypocrisy and reveal it to us.* (emphasis added)

What I might have read monolingually only as a mistaken usage of "appreciate" became for Shiwei in this translingual approach an opportunity to make meaningful her view of Woolf's appreciation of the creative possibilities for manipulating language. Building upon her translingual innovation, Shiwei went on to argue about Woolf's ability to manipulate language, an appreciation of language that Shiwei contended in her essay Woolf had learned by following in the footsteps of literary men.

By selecting Shiwei's intriguing, unconventional, opaque word as the focus of inquiry for our conference and pursuing a collaborative, close reading and inquiry of it in her first draft, I encouraged her to exploit a fertile grammatical deviation by thinking critically and creatively about its possible meanings. Such a translingual pedagogy gives writers like Shiwei and Xiao opportunities not only to learn or review conventions but, moreover, to challenge conventions in order to enhance their linguistic creativity and develop their thinking. Students dwell on their sentences and make close reading of their own prose a habit of mind, discovering that as language learners, they have the same ability to revise language (as well as their text) that all language users do (Horner et al., 2011). They exploit their fertile textual deviations, engendering ideas and contributing to the now worldwide enterprise of reinventing English. These translingual processes and innovations confirm Lu's contention that "efforts to acquire—learn and use—standardized U.S. English can be . . . enhanced by critical engagement with it" (Lu, 2004, p. 25).

Conclusion: Dialogic Openings to Translingual Dispositions

Xiao's and Shiwei's revisions illustrate the translingual innovations students perform as a result of dialogue about language and rhetorical meaning in a student-teacher conference. Instructors with translingual dispositions help students to develop analytic purposes for their linguistic innovations. But these achievements require student-teacher face-to-face dialogues, in which instructors ask students their intentions, demonstrate our openness to rhetorical and linguistic fluidity, and then encourage students to make the most meaningful and informed choices.

However, translanguaging raises pressing concerns about reception among readers in composition and the academy. With those concerns in mind, I want to consider, in closing, the implications when writers choose or refuse to include textual cues to make their linguistic innovations readily intelligible by foregrounding their alternative meanings. After I encouraged Shiwei in our conference to make her translingual phrase in this literary analysis as reader-friendly as possible, she chose to signal to her readers by placing scare quotes around her unconjugated form of appreciate and subsequently explaining her dual usages of the verbal and adjectival forms of appreciate. Canagarajah (2006) has spoken of such translations for readers as "a form of compromise" that acknowledges the writer's awareness of "using the structure in a peculiar way for a unique rhetorical purpose" (p. 610). Might creative writers, however, sometimes leave their meaning implicit for the close reader of their essay to infer as Xiao has expected readers to infer, from his eschewal of the possessive punctuation in "fancy people dignity," fancy people's lack of self-possessed dignity? Would another reader have understood Xiao's intention without access to his oral elaborations in our conference? And, if not, if translingual writers choose not to qualify their meaningful deviations, then what are the institutional risks for teachers who support them and do not edit or downgrade such experimental rhetoric, diction, grammar, and syntax? To what extent should writers "compromise" to accommodate "autonomous literacy ideologies" (Canagarajah, 2013, p. 135) by adding explanatory footnotes or incorporating parenthetical cues about their unconventional language and grammar in order to increase the likelihood that their translingual practices are immediately intelligible to wider audiences, qualified in terms of assessment, and acceptable as writing for the university?

But what should writing be for in the university? Should it protect the ephemeral rule(s) of a mythical monolingual version of English, mythical because we know in the past it was created by the tongues of Germanic and Norman French invaders? And mythical today because we know that the evolution of Englishes continues rapidly as the real and virtual worlds flatten. As Englishes proliferate and attain official status and become commonly used across the globe (Crystal, 2003; Galloway & Rose, 2015), our graduates will increasingly need to be practiced at engaging with emergent linguistic forms, and translanguaging enables both our international and domestic students to develop their competencies in "negotiated literacy," preparing them as writers, readers and speakers for the growing hybrid forms—of Chinglish, Spanglish, Arablish, and others—among billions of people who use indigenous Englishes everyday as linguistic currencies. Might composition's disciplinary parameters be elastic enough to encompass translanguaging that blurs the generic boundaries between essay and poetic prose? Might composition be the "undisciplined" field (Banks, 2015; Horner, 2016) that leads the academy to recognize and engage the realities of global communication flourishing outside its ivory doors? If the university is willing to open itself to translingual dispositions, then face-to-face conferences will be crucial, for extended conversations in conference enable our students to translanguage meaningfully and with confidence, unlike limited margin and end-comments on an essay draft. Face-to-face dialogues allow instructors the chance to question our students' deviations, to learn from our students about the linguistic and cultural roots of these linguistic and rhetorical idiosyncrasies, and to encourage our students to see them as potential innovations, imagining together the meaningful implications of the compressed concepts that translanguaging can convey.

References

Banks, A. (2015, March 19) *Funk, flight and freedom. Conference on College Composition Communication Chair's Address. National Council of Teachers of English* [Video]. YouTube. https://www.youtube.com/watch?v=EYt3swrnvwU.

Biber, D., Conrad S. & Leech, G. (2002). *Longman student grammar of spoken and written English*. Pearson Longman.

Blommaert, J. (2010). *The sociolinguistics of globalization*. Cambridge University Press.

Canagarajah, A. S. (1997). Safe houses in the contact zone: Coping strategies of African-American students in the academy. *College Composition and Communication, 48*(2), 173–196.

Canagarajah, A. S. (2006). The place of world Englishes in composition: Pluralization continued. *College Composition and Communication, 57*(4), 586–619.

Canagarajah, A. S. (2013). *Translingual practice: Global Englishes and cosmopolitan relations*. Routledge.

Chen, P. T. (2009, June 6–8). *Topic and topic-comment structures in first language acquisition of Mandarin Chinese* [Conference session]. In Yun Xiao (Ed.), *Proceedings of the 21st North American conference on Chinese linguistics* (Vol. 1, pp. 165–177). Smithfield, RI: Bryant University. https://naccl.osu.edu/sites/naccl.osu. edu/files/NACCL–21_Vol._1—Po-ting%20Chen—pp._165–177.pdf.

Crystal, D. (2003). *English as a global language*. Cambridge University Press.

Galloway, N. & Rose, H. (2015). *Introducing global Englishes.* Routledge.

Gitzen, M. (2002). *Face to face: Conferencing as ESL writing instruction*. (Doctoral dissertation, Purdue University). Purdue University e-Pubs. https://docs.lib .purdue.edu/dissertations/AAI3114042/.

Goffman, E. (2005). *Interaction ritual: Essays in face to face behavior*. Transaction Publishers. (Original work published in 1967)

Goldstein, L. M. & Conrad, S. M. (1990). Student input and negotiation of meaning in ESL writing conferences. *TESOL Quarterly, 24*(3), 443–460.

He, Y. (2012). Different generations, different face? A discursive approach to naturally occurring compliment responses in Chinese. *Journal of Politeness Research, 8,* 29–51.

Henry, O. (1919). *The trimmed lamp: And other stories of the four million*. Doubleday, Page & Company.

Ho, D. Y-f. (1976) On the concept of face. *American Journal of Sociology, 81*(4), 867–884.

Horner, B. (2016). *Rewriting composition: Terms of exchange*. Southern Illinois University Press.

Horner, B., Lu, M-Z., Royster, J. J. & Trimbur, J. (2011). Opinion: Language difference in writing: Toward a translingual approach. *College English, 73*(3), 303–321.

Hu, H. C. (1944) The Chinese concept of "face." *American Anthropological Association, 46*(1), 45–64.

Jordan, J. (2015). Material translingual ecologies. *College English, 77*(4), 364–382.

Lee, J. W., Jenks, C. (2016). Doing translingual dispositions. *College Composition and Communication. 68*(2), 317–344.

Leki, I. (1992). *Understanding ESL writers: A guide for teachers*. Boynton/Cook Heinemann.

Leonard, R. L. & Nowacek, R. (2016). Transfer and translingualism. *College English Special Issue: Translingual Work in Composition. 78*(3), 219–227.

Liu, J. (2001). Constructing Chinese faces in American classrooms. *Asian Journal of English Language Teaching, 11*, 1–18.

Liu, Y. (2009). *ESL students in the college writing conference: Perceptions and participation.* (Unpublished doctoral dissertation). The University of Arizona, Tucson, AZ.

Lu, M-Z. (1994). Professing multiculturalism: The politics of style in the contact zone. *College Composition and Communication, 45*(4), 442–458.

Lu, M-Z. (2004). An essay on the work of composition: Composing English against the order of fast capitalism. *College Composition and Communication, 56*(1), 16–50.

Lu, M-Z. & Horner, B. (2013a) Translingual literacy and matters of agency. In A. S. Canagarajah (Ed.), *Literacy as translingual practice: Between communities and classrooms* (pp. 26–38). Routledge.

Lu, M-Z. & Horner, B. (2013b). Translingual literacy, language difference, and matters of agency. *College English, 75*(6), 582–607.

Mao, L. M. (1994). Beyond politeness theory: "Face" revisited and renewed. *Journal of Pragmatics, 21*, 451–486.

Ming, X. (2014). *The last leaf of endless hope* [Unpublished manuscript]. University of Pittsburgh.

Pan, Y. & Kadar, D. Z. (2011) Historical vs. contemporary Chinese linguistic politeness. *Journal of Pragmatics. Journal of Pragmatics, 43*, 1525–1539.

Pratt, M. L. (1991). Arts of the contact zone. *Profession, 91*, 33–40.

Ross, C. & Ma, J-h. S. (2006). *Modern Mandarin Chinese grammar: A practical guide.* Routledge.

Sullivan, P., Zheng, F. & Zhang, Y. (2012). College writing in China and America: A modest and humble conversation, with writing samples. *College Composition and Communication, 64*(2), 306–331.

Trimbur, J. (2016). Translingualism and close reading. *College English Special Issue: Translingual Work in Composition. 78*(3), 219–227.

University of Pittsburgh Department of English. (2016). *Goals for first year composition courses.* http://www.composition.pitt.edu/undergraduate/first-year -composition#.

University of Pittsburgh (2018). Fact Book. https://pre.ir.pitt.edu/wp-content /uploads/2018/12/FactBook2018.pdf.

Whalen, K. & Ménard, N. (1995). L1 and L2 writers' strategic linguistic knowledge: A model of multiple-level discourse processing. *Language Learning, 45*(3), 381–418.

Woolf, V. (1981). *A room of one's own.* Harcourt Inc. (Original work published in 1929)

Young, R. E. & Miller, E. R. (2004). Learning as changing participation: Discourse roles in ESL writing conferences. *The Modern Language Journal, 88*(4), 519–535.

8

When Multimodal Meets the Translingual: Case Studies from an Experiment with a Multiliterate Composition Pedagogy in a Globalized Writing Classroom

Santosh Khadka
CALIFORNIA STATE UNIVERSITY, NORTHRIDGE

This qualitative study presents two cases from an investigation into how diverse students in a sophomore level writing class in a large research university responded to a pedagogical approach framed around the idea of multiple literacies. The findings indicate that a multiliterate composition pedagogy can productively invite students to embrace a translingual disposition through multimodal and intercultural practices. More importantly, this pedagogical approach provides instructors with ideas and strategies to respond to their students' diverse linguistic, cultural, and rhetorical traditions while cultivating in them multiple literacy skills that they need to navigate the complex composition and communication challenges of the twenty-first century globalized world.

Keywords: Translingual, Multimodal, Multiliteracies, Intercultural Competence, Remediation, Media Convergence, Web Design

Demographic shift defines American higher education now. Changing student demographics nationwide speak to the fact that U.S. college classrooms are becoming increasingly diverse and globalized. The increasing presence of international students combined with growing domestic diversity in the academy has transformed American college classrooms into true "contact zones" (Pratt, 1991). This chapter argues that the demographic shift in higher education and increasing global interdependence call for invention and adoption of writing pedagogies and curricula that engage diverse students

DOI: https://doi.org/10.37514/INT-B.2020.0438.2.08

in intercultural, translingual, and multimodal literacy practices. It proposes a multiliterate composition pedagogy, informed by recent developments in media and new media studies, literacy studies, World Englishes, globalization studies, and intercultural communication, among others, as a approach for writing instructors to respond to students' diverse linguistic, cultural, and rhetorical traditions while cultivating in them multiple literacy skills that they need to navigate the complex composition and communication challenges of the twenty-first century globalized world. Through extensive discussion of two case studies, this chapter demonstrates that translingual, multimodal, and intercultural literacy skills can be cultivated in students through implementation of what I call a multiliterate composition curriculum and pedagogy. It also calls for writing programs to employ multiliterate strategies to help prepare students to take up the composing and communication challenges of the globalized world.

Multiliteracies Framework of Diverse Writing Classrooms

Reflecting on what diverse students need to navigate the complex twenty-first century world, many literacy scholars maintain that changed working conditions demand flexible and multiple skills and literacies—both old and new—in students when they join the workforce. Irrespective of who students are demographically, they require multiple literacies to succeed in highly globalized and mediated workplaces. James Paul Gee (2001), for example, highlights that students need to learn multiple literacies to meet the changing demands and dynamics of the workplace: Jobs "fit" for industrial capitalism, which required "relatively low-level skills and the ability to follow instructions" are "fast disappearing" and becoming "rare today—and will be rarer yet tomorrow" (p. 81–82). Stable management or professional jobs where "'one rose through the ranks' towards the top of the hierarchy . . . are scarce in the new capitalism, where hierarchies are flatter, people are as liable to go up as down, and people are expected to change jobs and fields several times in a lifetime" (Gee, 2001, p. 82). Such work environments demand multiple literacies, Swenson et al. (2006) concur, but, more specifically, they call for both older print and critical literacies, and new digital and multimodal literacies—not one or the other—in potential employees.

In the United States, specifically, there is increasing agreement among educators that we should attempt to cultivate multiple old and new literacies in students through our pedagogy and curricular design. It has been my experience that Jay Bolter and Richard Grusin's (1999) notion of remediation, and Henry Jenkins' (2006) theory of media convergence, in particular, are promising concepts; these pedagogical implementations are likely to sponsor all three forms of literacy—media literacy, computer literacy, and multimedia literacies—that Douglas Kellner (2004) foregrounds. Student engagement with those media theories can illuminate the relationship between old and new media technologies, and, at the same time, speak to the contemporary genres and forms of composition. For instance, Jay Bolter and Richard Grusin (1999) define remediation as the incorporation or representation of one medium into another, and claim that digital or new media are characterized by remediation because they constantly present the contents from old media like television, radio, and print journalism, in different forms and styles. A fascinating thing about remediation is that it does not just work in one direction, i.e., it is not always the case that only new media remediate the old, but, interesting enough, old mediums such as TV and films also appropriate digital graphics and other features of new media. Therefore, it can be said that new and old media constantly interact with one another in a number of ways. Correspondingly, remediation and media convergence as means and products of media evolution can be instrumental in scaffolding the difference and diversity our students bring with them to our classrooms and can provide our students with complex processes and modes of communication and composition.

To extend the idea further, a multiliteracies framework (New London Group, 1996), informed by recent developments in diverse interconnected fields, such as media and new media studies, World Englishes, intercultural communication, globalization, literacy studies, and rhetoric and composition, can provide us with valuable resources and insights for designing vibrant curriculum for diverse writing classrooms. A course or a course sequence organized around an array of literacies—essayist, visual, digital, multimodal, translingual, and intercultural—can encourage students to use their native cultural, linguistic, and media resources in the class while also preparing them for the many complex composition and communication challenges of the globalized world. Of particular value for curricular design could be insights pertaining to diverse writing conventions and styles around the world (World Englishes or translingual scholarship in rhetoric and composition); the notion of intercultural communicative competence, and two-way or multi-way adaptation of communication behaviors (intercultural communication); the four dimensions of new media—agency, divergence, multimodality, and conceptualization (new media studies), which, together, can empower students to become active producers of different media content for others, a shift from their position primarily as the passive consumers of media content created and disseminated by others.

Such an innovative and broad-based curriculum can effectively respond to the call of scholars such as Geoff Bull and Michele Anstey (2010), who maintain that today's students need to be multiliterate in order to survive and flourish in a globalized world. As Bull and Anstey (2010) argue, "[g]lobalization provides a contextual necessity for us to become multiliterate" (p. 175). Becoming multiliterate includes having the ability to bring forth and use plural literacies, such as visual, multimodal, academic, critical, and intercultural, among others, as and when needed (Bull & Anstey, 2010; Cope & Kalantzis, 2000; Hawisher & Selfe, 2006; New London Group, 1996; Selber, 2004). For writing students, being multiliterate also includes the ability to interact using multiple Englishes in English-speaking contexts and employ multiple writing and communication styles across cultures and disciplines. Moreover, for these students, being multiliterate also includes the ability to critically evaluate information and resources and use them ethically across contexts. So, overall, becoming multiliterate involves a rich repertoire of creative, critical, reflective, and rhetorical skills needed to successfully navigate the complexities of the globalized world.

Researching Multiliteracies in a Diverse Writing Classroom

In an attempt to experiment with the possibilities and limits of a multiliterate composition pedagogy, I drew insights and resources from multiple aligned fields, as stated above, and framed a course for my sophomore-level students with four units focused on different sets of literacies:

- critical, visual, and rhetorical (unit 1);
- essayist and information (unit 2);
- multimedia and intercultural (unit 3);
- multimodal and global (unit 4).

I also created my unit assignments—literacy narratives, and rhetorical analysis of a media artifact (unit 1), argument essay (unit 2), remediation of argument essay into web form for local and global audiences (unit 3), and documentary film-making (unit 4)— and class heuristics with twin purposes in mind: providing space for students' native cultural, linguistic, and media resources, and cultivating multiple literacies in them along the way. The student population of the class included thirteen domestic American students (mostly monolingual) while seven other students hailed from different parts of the world—two from Puerto Rico, one from South Korea, two from Mexico, one from Haiti, and one from India. There was diversity even among domestic American students in terms of race, class, and literacy traditions let alone among international students who were brought up in completely different cultural, linguistic, and academic traditions.

Research Methods

The site for this research was a sophomore-level writing class offered in the spring of 2012 at a research university in the northeast US, and as a teacher-researcher, I solicited volunteer student participation for an IRB-approved research study. Fourteen of twenty diverse students representing six nationalities and multiple linguistic and cultural backgrounds participated in the research. My report here is based on a larger study for which I gathered multiple layers of data through interviewing, observation, and artifact analysis to better understand the complexity of the participants' multiliteracy practices.

I conducted semi-structured, video-recorded interviews with all the research participants four times, the number of interviews corresponding with the number of course units. My choice of the interview was to afford an in-depth exploration of student participants and their literacy practices. In order to maintain consistency across interviews, I used the same set of questions (see Appendix) for each of the interviewees, and asked follow-up questions, as needed, about her or his literacy, cultural, and linguistic traditions and strategies or processes used to complete the particular project at hand. I had the interviews transcribed later by a trained transcriptionist in order to use them as a data source in the analysis process.

I also maintained a reflective research journal throughout the semester, recording my thoughts and perspectives on the course and educational praxis in the class: What worked and what did not work in the class? Why did (or did not) the activities, assignments or teaching approaches work as well as they might have? What changes should be made to the course artifacts, assignments, or pedagogical approaches for future classes? Maintaining the research journal afforded me the opportunity to keep track of emerging meanings, perspectives, and interpretations; to reflect on the connections across sources; and to "uncover the patterns and explanations needed to answer your research question[s]" (Blakeslee & Fleischer, 2007, p. 184). This method also allowed me to record students' informal or oral feedback on course components and delivery styles.

In addition, rhetorical artifact analysis constituted another important part of my research method. For analysis, I collected multiple sources of data—student papers and portfolios, reflections, in-class writings, formal/informal notes, blogs or other online postings, and websites and multimedia compositions. I then triangulated those data with data from other sources, such as participant interview transcripts; course and unit goals; course materials including syllabi, assignment descriptions, assessment criteria, and writing prompts or heuristics; and my personal reflections and observations. I made triangulation a central part of my analysis because it is highly valued in qualitative research for its function of cross-verifying interpretations and research findings with additional testimonials.

Other factors that played into artifact analysis are my personal and theoretical lenses. My personal lens was one of a transnational researcher in the US. As a transnational educator in a U.S. research university, my positionality is implicated in this research. I also bring particular theoretical lens to this research—multiliteracies and its associated fields of study, such as globalization, intercultural communication, new media, media studies, and World Englishes. I use them as theoretical grounds while analyzing my research artifacts. When appropriate, I draw on pertinent ideas from the published literatures and accounts from these allied fields to seamlessly interweave the theory and praxis in my report.

Curriculum Design

My curriculum design followed a multiliterate approach to teaching composition. Each one of my four units took up a different set of literacies. The first unit, for example, was dedicated to learning from students about their literacy traditions, and cultivating critical and visual literacies (literacy narratives and rhetorical analysis of a media artifact were the major assignments). The second unit of my course asked students to explore the diverse facets of multiliteracies and its associated fields, such as globalization, intercultural communication, new media, and World Englishes for five weeks with an extended argument essay as the major assignment. The third unit, which I use as the main source of data for this chapter, was meant to introduce students to the notion of remediation (Bolter & Grusin, 1999) with some hands-on training with "repurposing" media (remediation was the major assignment). Students were asked to remediate their second unit argument essays into web forms in this unit. They produced two versions of the website in response to the assignment, which asked them to gear one version towards the general American public, while the other version was geared towards the specific communities of the students' peers. Students were asked to design the general websites first, share those with their peers, and only then redesign the website based on their peers' feedback. For the second version of the website, in particular, students worked for three weeks closely in groups of two; I tried to pair students from somewhat different backgrounds so that they could interact with one another and tailor their remediated websites to the expectations and the values of her or his peer. This particular project was intended to put students to work with multiple media or modalities, introduce them to convergence culture (Jenkins, 2006) and make them cognizant of the rhetoricity of different media (e.g., website vs. print), and the dynamics of intercultural and interracial communication. Unit four was dedicated to documentary production (collaborative documentary film-making project), where students in groups of three collaborated to produce a movie on controversial contemporary topics like Occupy Wall Street or the Trayvon Martin (shooting) case or the democratic movement in the Middle East. This unit encouraged students to work in collaboration with each other, work with multiple media, and learn multiple digital skills (camera work, editing, script writing), and presentation skills (they presented the projects to the class).

Data Analysis and Findings

I will report here on a sample of findings from the analysis of data collected, due to space constraint. Some select findings from the larger study have been discussed elsewhere (see Khadka, 2015, 2018). Here, I will specifically elaborate on the translingual, multimodal, and intercultural aspects of the remediation projects done by two particular students—Andre and Camila (fictitious names)—in the third unit of the course titled, "Remediation and Intercultural Literacy." Andre and Camila worked as peers for each other for the second version of the remediation project.

As briefly stated above, for the third unit of the course, I had remediation as the major assignment for which students had to repurpose their second unit argument essays into multimodal forms for two different audiences—the general American public ("general audience"), and the community of the peer ("specific audience") with whom she or he closely worked throughout the unit. My decision to have students design two versions of remediated text for two different sets of audiences, and to have self-identified monolingual students collaborate with self-identified multilingual students was inspired by Steven Fraiberg's (2001) idea of remixing texts for "local" and "global" audiences, and Ringo Ma's (2005) conception of two-way adaptation of communication behaviors. Even though Fraiberg and Ma come from different disciplinary backgrounds (Fraiberg works in rhetoric and composition, and Ma in intercultural communication), their frameworks or theories are highly productive for a globalized classroom. Fraiberg proposes a multilingual-multimodal framework of writing whereas Ma advocates for two-way or multi-way adaptations of communication behaviors by interactants in cross-cultural communication situations. For this assignment, I did not embrace these theories in their entirety, appropriating only Fraiberg's idea of multiple audience and Ma's idea of the reciprocal adaptation of communication behaviors. I foregrounded this adaptability of communicative strategies or behaviors to different communication situations in the assignment particularly because this ability is very crucial for successfully navigating the complex composition and communication challenges of the twenty-first century workplaces and the world, which are both highly mediated and constantly shifting.

The project culminated with a classroom presentation of both versions of remediation. Each student also composed a three-page-long reflection on various dimensions of the remediation process from audience to semiotic modes, diction, and style to selections of various design elements for different versions of the remediated text. I specifically asked them to consider how the media they chose for remediation shaped the message and content or, more explicitly, what changed or did not change during their remediation process, and, if anything did change, why. I wanted them to engage the dynamics of media and message, content and forms, audience and rhetorical choices, and the relationship between old and new media. Since students were producing two versions of the web text, I also asked them to explain their two target audiences, contexts and purposes for the two different designs, and the resources and languages (or language variety) that they chose for each of the two different web texts.

For scaffolding their remediation process, I provided relevant activities and resources meant to engage students with theoretical insights and hands-on experiences of remediation in different stages and forms. We watched a few videos on immediacy, hypermediacy, and remediation in the class; I asked students to read chapter selections from Bolter and Grusin's (1999) book, *Remediation: Understanding New Media,* and Jenkins' (2006) book, *Convergence Culture,* and a few chapters on website and document design from Anderson's (2011) *Technical Communication.* I also had them read some articles on intercultural communication styles and differences, and World Englishes. In addition, I had time allocated, for exploration and play, with some web design sites: WordPress, Wikispaces, Wix, and Google Sites. I divided the whole class into small groups of two, each group consisting of students from different cultural, linguistic, or literacy backgrounds in order to encourage "two-way adaptation" of stylistic and design preferences.

Students were required to design two versions of their website—the first for a general American audience and the second for their partner's community. This assignment engaged students in digital and intercultural and translingual literacy practices and sensitized them to a number of vital aspects of media and composition, such as the affordances and expectations of different media; the relationship between media and audiences, old media and new media, and media and semiotic modes; rhetorical choice of design elements in light of audiences and purpose; and cross-cultural difference in design conventions. Interestingly, this was the first multimodal writing assignment of the course that asked students to draw on their native linguistic, cultural, and media resources; students stated that they learned useful digital and multimedia skills in addition to rhetorical and stylistic dimensions of remediating an academic essay into a multimodal website. The multimodal met multilingual, or to use Horner et al.'s (2015) terms: transmodal converged with translingual in this particular unit and assignment. Almost all of the students stated in their reflections, and interviews with me, that they enjoyed working digitally on a website; for most of them website design proved to be a valuable experience. Many expressed their excitement that they learned something useful for their lives, and for many this was their first encounter with web design applications like WordPress and Google Sites. Many were even not aware that those applications existed, and that they could design their own personal websites.

Case Studies: Andre and Camilla

Andre and Camila were two students in my class who came from different literacy, linguistic, and cultural backgrounds. Andre is an African American male student. A self-identified monolingual English speaker, his entire education was completed in the US. Camila is a Puerto Rican female student; her first language is Spanish. She is bilingual, and completed high school at a Spanish-medium school in Puerto Rico, with English as a subject in the curriculum.

As required, Andre designed two versions of websites remediating his argument essay about the impacts of digital technologies on critical thinking abilities—the first was directed towards a general American public audience and the second targeted to his peer, Camila. While remediating his argument essay into a web form for a general American public audience, Andre considered a number of things: "viewers look briefly at a website and try to look for something that catches their eye without having to read a lot of content. Once that attention is caught, then the reader will actually dive into that portion of the website and it's [sic] content" (from his reflection blog post). Considering the general audience for the website as opposed to the scholarly audience for the earlier argument paper, he reports that he "changed the wording from academic to the average dialect" (blog post) for the website. He says that he also "placed pictures and videos into my site to capture the attention of the "browsing" viewer" (blog post). About other design choices, he says he chose a blue background for the site because that particular color "brought a calm and inviting vibe to my website" (blog post).

For the second version of website, however, his peer, Camila informed him that Puerto Rican people are mostly bilingual and speak both Spanish and English. Andre states that knowing the fact that Puerto Rican people also speak English was "a sign of relief" for him because he then found that he didn't have to "translate my website in Spanish" (reflection). He did not want to translate the entire website because doing that would have "changed the meaning of my website because certain idioms in English can't be translated over and I'm poor in Spanish" (blog reflection). Camila in her reflection blog writes that based on her learning in her high school, she suggested that Andre make some particular changes on his first version of the website in order to make it look more appealing to her home community in Puerto Rico. She wanted the font color to be made black from blue for the sake of contrast. She also wanted him to move link and menus in the page from right to left because titles in left is considered "formal" design in her community. Another change she requested was replacing comic pictures in Andre's first website with real pictures of real people. In asking for this change, Camila had this rationale: "even though comics convey messages in a fun way, pictures actually shows [sic] the persons, like the readers, and the readers can relate to those people in the actual pictures" (Camila's reflection blog). While her revision suggestions to Andre are focused more on interface design and color scheme, she, however, does not link them explicitly to any aspects of Puerto Rican culture. Even my attempt at cross-verification did not go anywhere. My effort to locate sources—scholarly and popular—that could fill the gap she left yielded virtually nothing, leaving me wondering whether her suggestions had any cultural grounding. In this sense, it can be the argued that these two students' conjecture about Puerto Rican culture is less officially informed than Andre's understanding of design preferences of the African American community, as discussed below.

In an interview with me, Andre says that he had some rudimentary experiences working with websites and could make some basic websites with templates available online, but he had never worked with WordPress or Google Sites to design websites. So, designing a full-fledged website was a completely different experience for him. He, however, knew that consideration of audience was the "biggest factor when it comes to media" (interview), therefore, he "added on to the visuals because it's a website and everyone wants to look around for the things that pop up and catch their attention. I tried to add a few images on each page that really catches the person's attention and also bring my humor into it" (interview). Moreover, Andre and Camila had some interesting moments working in collaboration, as Andre recounts:

> I put my title to the right, I had a blue background, which is not common, as it's a bit hard to see. I could see it, but she changed it. She put it to her culture, put everything in the left hand margin, which is ironic. When I went to her website I changed it to how my website kind of looked and she changed mine to how hers looked so when we looked at them together it was like every title I had in the middle and I took hers from the left and put it in the middle. We changed each other's and how our cultures affected our choices.

This exchange between Andre and Camila is salient from multiple points of view. First of all, this interaction shows that the participants are in the process of learning cross-cultural values and communication styles. They are seen negotiating cultural codes and design preferences for different audience expectations. Both Andre and Camila work to articulate the semiotic and stylistic preferences in terms of each other's community. These students are taking a translingual approach to the project. For instance, Andre is clearly trying to understand and adapt the outlook of his second web project to the design needs and preferences of Camila's Puerto Rican community. Camila's translingual disposition is even more explicit in that she is a multilingual student herself, and, as we will see, she went extra miles in attempting to understand Andre's not-so-common design choices.

Andre himself found the remediation assignment to be eye-opening, as he says: "often times, you do not think about how different people communicate with each other; you are always in your own niche or society so you are used to how people talk, but to think about how other people talk to each other is eye opening so it makes you think of the website, how they want it to look" (interview). This realization of variation in cross-cultural communicative and design conventions is at least the beginning of a deeper understanding of how complex and challenging the task of communicating across diverse audiences and contexts is in this globalized world. All of our students would benefit immensely if they could understand what it takes to effectively communicate across contexts, and also translate that understanding into actual communication practices as and when situations ask for such practices. This combination of multiple literacies would enable them to become productive members of dynamic workplaces and communities around the world.

Like Andre, his peer, Camila, also produced both versions of the remediated website centered around her argument essay topic: how innovations in media and technologies have transformed the ways we conduct businesses and services in the contemporary world (examples given include movie industry and humanitarian relief works). As assigned, her essay was targeted to the American general public, while the remediated version was tailored to the design preferences of her peer's community. In the remediation process, she says that she left the introduction from her argument essay as it was on the website because she "wanted people to know that the claims and proofs given were real" (reflection blog). For the general American public, she chose a "neutral color" and font. In terms of design, Camila says, she used a formal pattern:

> The basic stuff as in the header goes in the top left corner; indent when starting a new paragraph, and consistency in the font color, size, and style. A pattern I followed was making an index on the left side bar with the topics touched throughout my essay where one could click and the website would direct you specifically to that topic (like the Wikipedia style).

Camila also reflected on the impacts of medium on the content and presentation style, and made necessary adjustments for the medium of the web, as she says:

> When one writes a research paper in a blank word document one has to be formal because it is normally going to be handed in as a professional work, and also because the reader (teacher) is expecting formality . . . But when one is transmitting the information through a website one has to remember all the distractions that exists [sic]. . . This is why the colors, images, videos, and links play such an important role, because in the websites there are no expected readers other than the ones who are interested . . . when you create a website you have to retrieve your readers by making your website intriguing and interesting.

Camila's reflection speaks to her sensitivity towards transmodal and transcultural communicative differences. Her understanding of different communicative contexts and conventions for an argument essay as opposed to a remediated website targeted to a particular community is testimony to the fact that she is increasingly attentive to the factors that make a genre or form of communication different from others, and how each form or medium of communication is situated within a host of contextual factors which need to be addressed in order to make a particular act of communication effective and meaningful.

The second version of her remediation was targeted to Andre's community. Andre, an African American male student, comes from New York State, and he suggested that she add a video in the introduction. The video was Apple's first commercial, and that was added there, as Andre says, to "spice up the intro a little bit" (Andre's blog reflection). In Andre's view, that addition "makes sense because the whole context is how the media has changed our lives and certain aspects . . . but it is interesting to see how we started, with this adding humor to the website" (Andre reflection blog). Andre suggested another change on the "Kony page" in her website—adding a picture of Africa with the colors and a fist in the middle. The "Kony Page" in Camila's website explains how the Kony 2012 documentary produced by Invisible Children, Inc., became viral in social media and how that led to intervention by United States and African Union to end the forced recruitment of child soldiers by Joseph Kony, the notorious Ugandan militia leader. Camila readily accepts his suggestion because she understands the rationale behind his suggestion as:

> The reason of this specific picture is because Andre comes from an African American background and the colors represent his past and heritage, while the fists represent the unity and how Andre is unified with his past, or how African nationalism works as a symbol system for African Americans. This fits right in because the Kony movement is about Africa and Unity of all the nations through the social media.

Another change suggested was the font color. The original font color in her website was white as contrast to a black background, but Andre asked her to change it to blue "because they stand out and seem more inviting to the reader" (Andre cited in Camila's blog reflection). "The last change made was the addition of the picture in the conclusion . . . that says "the end" concluding with all the information provided" (Camila blog reflection). Camila's concluding page on her site was the last tab from left to right ordering of her web pages. It could be hard to imagine a concluding page in a website because a website generally follows matrixed organizing patterns where content is linked in numerous ways, but Camila followed a sequential structuring of content, which reflected the organization of her argument essay completed as the first installment of the remediation project.

According to Andre, while providing feedback to Camila's website, he was confused because he "thought it was great the way it was and also I really didn't know what audience I come from" (Andre's reflection blog post). So, he says, he had to turn the mirror onto himself in order to reflect where he comes from and how he perceives media. He further adds:

> But I actually saw in this project how different certain audiences are. My audience or at least I've grown up doing is putting the title of a section in the middle of a page, whether it is a website, or just classroom notes. But my partner, she was taught to always place her titles on the left hand margin. So when we traded websites I found myself taking all of her left handed titles and placing them in the middle and she took my centered titles and pushed them to the left. I found that a little humorous and interesting how the audiences we belong to really control what we think is aesthetically pleasing. In the end, the audience has the power over remediation and how media is displayed to them.

Looking at Andre's comment here, it becomes evident that the remediation assignment leveraged Andre's self-actualization as well as his intercultural competence (Chen & Starosta, 2008). He had to self-introspect and study his own community to see what specific language or cultural characteristics define him and his community.

His peer, Camila, gained similar insights about media, audience, and cross-cultural design conventions working on this assignment, as she writes in her reflection blog post:

> [t]his unit made me realize the importance of the channels where we portray our context and the difference in each different media. Even though it was the same context everything else changed, from the font color and size, to the pictures, and even the way it is read. I enjoyed this project because I did not only learned [sic] about creating a website or how the information should be portrayed differently but I also learned about Andre's background and how to adapt a certain website to a certain cultural background. In addition I learned about my culture because while I was trying to figure out how to explain it or how to portray it I actually learned more about my culture and the standards back home.

As these students reported, this assignment encouraged self-reflexivity and introspection. While explaining their culture, language, or community's design preferences, they looked inward to see what cultures, languages, and traditions they come from and what different values they hold in coming from those cultural, linguistic, and ethnic backgrounds.

As becomes clear from the general examination of the remediation projects, as well as a closer look at some specific student projects, students practiced multimodal, visual, translingual, and intercultural literacies when working on these projects. This assignment also initiated the process of two-way adaptation—learning from both self-identified monolingual and self-identified multilingual students—of design conventions of some other cultures and communities, and the ways of tailoring web designs to these conventions. The adaptation process was supported by resources drawn from multiple fields, such as intercultural communication, new media, World Englishes, and technical communication, and assigned to the class as unit and course materials. The videos on mediation and remediation, book chapters on remediation (Bolter & Grusin, 1999), media convergence (Jenkins, 2006) and website design (Anderson, 2011), articles on intercultural communication style (Ramsey, 1998) and World Englishes (Bhatt, 2001), together with student research and collaboration provided useful frameworks for students to understand the process of adapting communicative styles to different rhetorical and/or cultural context(s).

Conclusion

Through extensive discussion of two case studies, this chapter demonstrates that a multiliterate approach to teaching writing can cultivate multiple literacy skills, including translingual, intercultural, multimodal, and digital skills, among others—qualities highly desired in individuals looking to join a work force shaped by globalization. The instructional work and investigations I have done specifically show that a multiliterate composition pedagogy, informed by recent developments in media and new media studies, literacy studies, World Englishes, information technologies, and intercultural communication, among other strains of thought, can help teachers better respond to the diverse linguistic, cultural, and literacy traditions students bring with them to the classrooms. This pedagogical approach also equips instructors with resources and strategies to make their curricula and pedagogical tools and techniques very engaging and productive for diverse students. As a result, students learn multiple literacies—from critical, analytical, and information to multimodal and intercultural, which are needed to successfully navigate the communicative and composing challenges of the highly mediated and globalized world.

References

Anderson, P. V. (2011). *Technical communication: A reader-centered approach.* (7th ed.). Wadsworth Cengage Learning.

Anstey, M. & Bull, G. (2006). *Teaching and learning multiliteracies: Changing times, changing literacies*. International Reading Association.

Bhatt, R. M. (2001). World Englishes. *Annual Review of Anthropology, 30*, 527–550.

Blakeslee, A. & Fleischer, K.. (2007). *Becoming a writing researcher*. Lawrence Erlbaum Associates.

Bolter, J. D. & Grusin, R. (1999). Remediation: Understanding new media. The MIT Press.

Bull, G. & Anstey, M. (2010). Using the principle of multiliteracies to inform pedagogical change. In D. R. Cole & D. L. Pullen (Eds.), *Multiliteracies in motion: Current theory and practice* (pp. 141–159). Routledge Taylor and Francis Group.

Chen, G & Starosta, W. J. (2008). Intercultural communication competence: A synthesis. In M. K. Asante, Y. Miike & J. Yin (Eds.), (pp. 215–238). Routledge.

Cope, B. & Kalantzis, M. (Eds.). (2000). *Multiliteracies: Literacy learning and the design of social futures*. Routledge.

Cope, B. & Kalantzis, M. (2009). New media, new learning. In D. R. Cole & D. L. Pullen (Eds.), *Multiliteracies in motion: Current theory and practice* (pp. 87–104). Routledge Taylor and Francis Group.

Fraiberg, S. (2010). Composition 2.0: Toward a multilingual and multimodal framework. *College Composition and Communication, 62*(1), 100–126.

Gee, J. P. (2001). Literacies, schools, and kinds of people educating people in the new capitalism. In M. Kalantzis & B. Cope (Eds.), *Transformations in language and learning: Perspectives on multiliteracies* (pp. 81–98). Common Ground Publishing.

Hawisher, G. E. & Selfe, C. L. (2006). Globalization and agency: Designing and redesigning the literacies of cyberspace. *College English, 68*(6), 619–636.

Hawisher, G. E., Selfe, C. L., Moraski, B. & Pearson, M. (2004). Becoming literate in the information age: Cultural ecologies and the literacies of technology. *College Composition and Communication, 55*(4), 642–692.

Horner, B., Selfe, C. & Lockridge, T. (2015). Translinguality, transmodality, and difference: exploring dispositions and change in language and learning. http://intermezzo.enculturation.net/01/ttd-horner-selfe-lockridge/index.htm.

Jenkins, H. (2006). *Convergence culture: Where old and new media collide*. New York University Press.

Kellner, D. (2004). Technological transformation, multiple literacies, and the revisioning of education. *E-Learning, 1*(1), 9–37.

Khadka, S. (2015). (Teaching) essayist literacy in the multimedia world. *Composition Forum 32*. https://compositionforum.com/issue/32/essayist-literacy.php.

Khadka, S. (2018). A broad-based multiliteracies theory and praxis for a diverse writing classroom. *Computers and Composition: An International Journal 47*, 93–110.

Ma, R. (2005) Communication between Hong Kong and mainland Chinese: Rethinking cross-cultural adaptation. *International and Intercultural Communication Annual 28*, 197–213.

New London Group, The. (1996). A pedagogy of multiliteracies: Designing social futures. *Harvard Educational Review, 66*(1), 60–93.

Pratt, M. L. (1991). Arts of the contact zone. *Profession*, 33–40.

Ramsey, S. J. (1998). Interactions between North Americans and Japanese: Considerations of communication style. In M. J. Bennett (Ed.), *Basic Concepts of Intercultural Communication: Selected Readings* (pp. 111–130). Intercultural Press.

Selber, S. A. (2004). *Multiliteracies for a digital age*. Southern Illinois University Press.

Swenson, J., Young, C., McGrail, E., Rozema, R. & Whitin, P. (2006). Extending the conversation: New technologies, new literacies, and English education." *English Education, 38*(4), 351–369.

Appendix: Unit-Wise Interview Questions

Unit 1: Literacy Narrative and Rhetorical Analysis Interview Questions

Alphabetic and Digital Literacy Narrative Assignment

1. What were your goals for the literacy narrative? Were your goals different for the alphabetic narrative from the digital one? If yes, how or why?
2. Can you explain the process in which you started each of the narratives? What kinds of revisions did you undertake, if any? Why?
3. Did you encounter any challenges while composing them? How would you describe them? How did you resolve them?
4. How was assignment one different from or similar to the ones you were used to doing? How would you describe this assignment in relation to other writing assignments you have done so far?
5. How many languages do you speak? Is English your mother tongue/first language? Did your exposure to other languages and cultures in any way affect the way you composed your narratives? How?
6. Where and when did you learn to work in or with computer? When and how did you encounter Internet?
7. Anything else you want to share about your literacy narrative?

Rhetorical Analysis of a Media Artifact Assignment

8. What digital artifact did you choose for rhetorical analysis? Why?
9. What critical and rhetorical concepts, terms and tools did you find helpful in your analysis of the digital artifact? What concepts and terms from the assigned texts were useful?
10. While composing rhetorical analysis of your digital artifact, did you do anything new or different than what you would do in similar assignments in the past?

11. How do you view or approach that or similar artifact now? Did you always think that way?

12. What readings or texts did you find particularly productive or revealing in this unit? Why?

13. How do you evaluate rhetorical analysis assignment or the unit as a whole?

Unit 2: Argument Essay Interview Questions

14. What topic did you choose for the argument essay and why?

15. How did you narrow down the topic or research question/s?

16. How did you decide on your scholarly and popular sources? How did you decide what images to use in your essay?

17. Can you tell your experience of primary data collection? Who did you interview or what site did you visit for data collection?

18. Did the direction or focus of your essay change after you wrote the proposal? When, how and why?

19. How is this assignment similar to or different from unit one assignments (rhetorical analysis and literacy narratives)?

20. In responding to this assignment, did you draw on your language/variety, culture, and/or writing style? In what ways?

21. Did this assignment teach you any skill that you think will be useful—for life, for your career?

22. What did you like or did not about this assignment?

23. Do you have any other comments on this assignment?

Unit 3: Remediation Projects Interview Questions

24. What writing and digital composition (blogging, Wiki and website design, etc.) experiences did you have before joining this class? Did those practices and skills help you anyway to complete unit 2-argument essay and unit 3-remediation projects? How?

25. While remediating unit 2 argument essay into a digital form, what kinds of changes did you make? Why? Did ideas about audience and media lead to those changes? Anything else? (diction and other resources, e.g., textual, audio and visual)

26. Tell me the composition and revision process of your unit 3 projects?

27. What kinds of cultural and linguistic resources (first language, English variety, images, audios, videos, etc.) did you use in your unit 3 project? How?

28. What opportunity did this assignment (remediation projects) provide you in terms of learning new skills or practicing your existing skills?
29. What factors guided/shaped your first and second version of your website?
30. How do you explain the differences between the argument essay and the remediated website? And how do you explain the differences between the first version (for the general American public) and the second version (your partner's community) of your website?
31. What assigned texts from this unit did you find significant and why?
32. Do you have any other comments on this assignment?

Unit 4: Documentary Film Making Group Project Interview Questions

33. How do you compare the processes of making a documentary film, composing a web-based text, and writing an academic paper?
34. How do you describe the experience of working in a group? Did you encounter any challenges while working with your collaborators?
35. How did documentary filmmaking compare to other kinds of composition?
36. How did you collect and decide on the resources to be used on the documentary film?
37. What kinds of cultural, linguistic, and other resources did you use in your project? How?
38. While composing the documentary film, did you encounter any challenges? How did you resolve them? What literacy or composition practices from the past helped you with this assignment?
39. Did you do anything new or different in the assignment than what you would do in similar assignment in the past?
40. How do you evaluate this assignment? Could it have been replaced by other assignment/s? If yes, what kinds of assignment/s?
41. Any other comments on this assignment?

Overall

42. What expectations did you have for this writing course when you first joined it? How did you form those expectations? Were your expectations met by the course content and its delivery?
43. What do your friends in other classes say about their writing classes or composition in general? How do you compare your composition experience with theirs?

44. What do you think should a writing class focus on? Why?
45. Do you have any other thoughts on this course? Any suggestions or critique?

Part 3: Translanguaging Practices

9 Expressions of Monolingual Ideology and Translingual Practice in an Online International Collaboration Project

Zsuzsanna Bacsa Palmer
GRAND VALLEY STATE UNIVERSITY

Translingual pedagogies exist based on the premise that effective communication involves engagement with all available linguistic and semiotic resources. However, many students have been socialized to subscribe to a monolingual ideology that asserts a clear separation between languages. I present an analysis of the different textual and multimodal expressions of both monolingual ideology and translingual practice observed in an online blog writing project between Hungarian and U.S. students. The chapter argues that a cosmopolitan theory-based project design and online discussions between students of varying national and linguistic backgrounds can effectively challenge monolingual language ideology and presents strategies for using such methods to promote a translingual disposition.

Keywords: monolingual ideology, translingual practice, cosmopolitanism, multimodal, online collaboration

If we accept Garcia and Levi's (2013) definition of translanguaging as the "new *languaging reality*" which is *"original and independent from any of the 'parents' or codes"* (p. 204) we must take into account the pedagogical implications of this language ideology. Acknowledging that translingual approaches can only be successful outside of the long reigning influence of the monolingual ideology that posits a stark separation between languages is the first step towards effectively working with translingual practices in the classroom. For this reason, and as Mina and Cimasko assert (this collection), it is essential to understand the language ideology (the "parents" and "codes") that students bring into our classrooms and monitor how this ideology gets challenged

DOI: https://doi.org/10.37514/INT-B.2020.0438.2.09

when exposed to the translingual construct. This is especially important in collaborative projects across borders where monolingual and multilingual students from different cultural and linguistic backgrounds communicate with each other. The aim of this chapter is to describe the language ideologies students expressed through blog sites during such an online collaborative project and to describe whether and how these ideologies were challenged in students' online discussions

In order to teach students effective approaches for communication across cultures and languages, it is important to create environments where students can experience the challenges and rewards of transcultural communication in educational settings. Many initiatives, from study-abroad programs to collaboration across diverse campuses, have been successful in exposing students to linguistic and cultural diversity, but providing students with opportunities for contact with students from other countries can be difficult to set up in a face-to-face environment. However, Globally Networked Learning Environments (GNLEs)—a term coined by Doreen Starke-Meyerring and Wilson to refer to online spaces of collaboration (Starke-Meyerring & Wilson, 2008)—make connecting students in different countries easy and accessible, and allows for communicative engagement across cultures without changing physical location. GNLEs, according to Starke-Meyerring and Wilson (2008), provide a new, innovative vision for teaching transcultural communication skills, while at the same time preparing students for becoming global citizens through direct encounters with diverse student populations. Enhanced by the multifaceted communication tools in the Web 2.0 environment, students collaborate globally in classroom projects; thus, there has been an increase in facilitating such projects in the field of professional and technical writing (Anderson et al., 2010; Herrington, 2010; Herrington & Tretyakov, 2005; Maylath et al., 2008; Starke-Meyerring & Andrews, 2006; St. Amant, 2002). The studies cited here attest to the fact that these projects are an effective way to teach students practical approaches when communicating across cultures, as students personally encounter the challenges and rewards of working with peers from many different backgrounds. Through online contact with students from other countries, participants in such projects directly experience the need for creative communication strategies as they strive to arrive at shared meanings.

Research Design: A Cosmopolitan and Translingual Framework

This collaborative project between U.S. and Hungarian students was designed in the theoretical framework of cosmopolitanism (Appiah, 2006; Beck, 2006:

Canagarajah, 2013). Cosmopolitan principles dictate that one's prioritizing of an allegiance to humanity over local (i.e., national) allegiances results in greater respect for diversity based on a sense of global belonging. Thus, cosmopolitan theory provides an overarching theoretical framework that promotes an open attitude towards hybridity and diversity. For this reason, it can also serve as a basis for developing pedagogical projects aimed at teaching students successful communication practices in actual cross-border encounters. Elsewhere (Palmer, 2013), I explain that when the teaching of transcultural communication is situated in the cosmopolitan framework, it necessitates a pedagogy that goes beyond the traditional teaching approach to intercultural communication, an approach that is strictly focused on the cultural differences of those involved in transcultural encounters. Since a cosmopolitan outlook of dealing with diversity directly influences a person's communicative practices in a positive way, participants understand cross-border encounters as processes through which similarities and differences in cultures and language use are not viewed by an ethnocentric measure of appropriateness or correctness, but as different resources that each participant can draw on when collaborating. For example, two multilingual communication partners with a cosmopolitan outlook will take into account that, though both participants may speak English, extra efforts such as clarification, repetition, meaning checking, and meaning negotiation will be necessary to arrive at a shared understanding. This type of language use, where speakers and writers utilize their knowledge of different languages within the same communication encounter and reach shared meanings through linguistic negotiation, is already happening in many realms of our global world (see for example, Blommaert, 2010; Canagarajah, 2013; Pandey, 2013; Pennycook, 2010).

The principles of such negotiations are described in detail in Suresh Canagarajah's *Translingual Practice* (2013) where he also discusses the pedagogical implications of focusing students' attention on shared meaning and negotiation instead of cultural difference. Employing negotiations necessitates a teaching space where students are invited and encouraged to use their wide-ranging cultural, linguistic, and multimodal resources; such a space for employing negotiation fosters an environment where teachers and students alike let go of monolingual language ideology and its strict separation between languages. In this learning environment, the teaching of communication across borders is based on recognizing hybrid cultural identities involved in the transcultural communication process; it emphasizes cooperative action over coherence, and highlights a practice-based approach over a norm-, fact-, and proposition-based model. Thus, the teaching of transcultural communication includes the important process of overcoming the restrictions of monolingual ideology and the fostering of a translingual disposition. Whereas the term *intercultural communication* emphasizes total separation across cultures that can only be bridged by learning a new, totally separate language, the term *transcultural communication* highlights shared features of cultures and promotes the use of all available linguistic resources as exemplified by speakers who employ a translingual disposition While translingual dispositions have become a focus of research in recent years, what has not been as closely studied are the language ideologies that students bring to the classroom. This chapter works to fill this gap by describing the monolingual language ideologies many students expressed using different modalities in their blog posts, particularly as they described their identities during the initial phase of the blog exchange project between U.S. and Hungarian classrooms. Furthermore, the chapter demonstrates how some students moved beyond the limits of monolingual ideology during the subsequent commenting phase of this project, and represented translingual practice in their comments to their peers abroad. In this second phase of the project students were asked to comment on two of their overseas peers' blogs while making connection around shared identities and interests. Making these direct connections, in turn, opened the door towards creating higher levels of self- and other-awareness, which I suggest leads to a translingual disposition.

The Collaborative Project as a Research Framework

In this chapter, I explore student expressions of their translingual dispositions developed in an online collaborative project between U.S. and Hungarian students. I established the project together with Rita Kóris, a Hungarian professor of Business English, in order for our students to take advantage of the benefits of GNLEs to foster the development of transcultural and translingual communication skills. During the project, students in a Professional Writing class in the US at Davenport University, where I was the instructor, were connected through blog sites to students in Rita Kóris' advanced Business English class in Hungary at Pazmany University. Altogether, 52 students were involved in this collaboration project. Most students at Davenport University, 18 out of 22, were English monolinguals, while the remaining four students were immigrants or international multilingual students. All 30 students at Pazmany University were multilingual—as their International Relations major required them to pass advanced proficiency foreign language exams in two languages before graduation. All but one Pazmany student spoke Hungarian as their native language; however, their English proficiency varied based on years studied and time spent abroad.

In the first three weeks of the blog exchange project, all U.S. and Hungarian students were asked to explore their varied identities and language varieties in their "Identities and Languages" blogs. This assignment was crafted to encourage an appreciation of the ways in which students' many identities influence their transcultural communication processes. This aspect of the project invited students to consider the many identities people have outside of national origin and focus on similarities they have in other areas. The student blogs were all connected to the main project website, where students were able to view my "Identities and Languages" blog. At the beginning of the project, I modeled the structure and length of the blog post. After participants created their blog pages, links to each of these pages were listed on the main project website. Important to this assignment was the requirement that students also describe the specific language and word usage that they connected with each identity. This requirement was included so we could analyze how students connect different languages/language varieties to specific identities and determine whether monolingual ideology was evidenced in these descriptions.

In the subsequent three weeks, students were encouraged to explore all blog sites posted by their counterparts and were asked to post comments on two sites every week. Participants were also required to reply to comments that were placed on their own sites. The topic of the comments was not assigned; students were free to address any aspect of a partner student's blog page. Assigning a "response" post allowed for the examination of linguistic strategies students used as they created connections through commenting across borders. The hope was that this environment would foster translingual practice in the case of multilingual students and expose functionally monolingual students to this practice so that they could let go of prioritizing correctness and move away from monolingual language ideology.

Monolingual Language Ideology and Translingual Practice in Action

In psychology, an attitude is defined as a "disposition to react favorably or unfavorably to a class of objects" (Sarnoff, 1970, p. 279). In the case of language, Garrett (2010) states that we call these dispositions language attitudes, and that they can be directed towards certain languages, language varieties, and linguistic forms. Further, when these language attitudes are combined in a set of principles that explain values and assumptions about language in social reality, they become intrinsic and develop into what we call language ideologies. Monolingual language ideology, as emphasized by Horner in the *Afterword* of this collection, structures our thinking about languages and how they are separate entities based on an arbitrary look at linguistic elements (mostly words) that are separated from the context of their use. Horner asserts that the monolingual language ideology we are socialized into can be challenged by re-representing language through translingual practice. The focus of this chapter is to describe the ways in which participants, in their blog posts and blog responses, adhered to monolingual ideologies while they, increasingly, moved toward translingual practice.

In the first phase of the project, students created their blogs and described their identities on these initial blog posts. In this second phase, students were asked to place comments on a set number of blogs from the other country, but it was up to the students which blogs they chose to comment on. In these comments it became evident, that students not only made connections with others who had listed similar identities (for example, liked sports or nature), but that they also began to comment on language use and displayed language attitudes that showed a movement towards translingual disposition as described in the following sections.

Blog Posts: Monolingual Language Ideology and Translingual Practices

The blog assignment between American and Hungarian students asked them to first create a blog post to represent their different identities and second, in subsections, to describe the languages or language varieties that they associate with each identity. Once students understood that their different identities can overlap in cosmopolitan spaces with the identities of people from other cultures, they began to reveal their identities freely and described the characteristics and languages associated with these identities in great detail. It was here, on these initial blog posts, that monolingual language ideology was heavily represented, as students relied on the monolingual framework they had been socialized into to describe their languages. These initial blog posts were created as a response to the following assignment description in the course syllabus for both classes:

> To develop intercultural communicative competence, you will start out by understanding and mapping out your own cultural resources. For this reason, you will create a blog post that will describe your identities and languages. These you will tie to your cultural and ethnic heritage, your previous experiences, your involvement with professional and personal interest groups, etc. You will observe how each of these

aspects of you, or "identities" also connect with rich linguistic resources. For this reason, describe the languages/linguistic resources you use as you enact each identity.

For the research presented in this chapter, I analyzed 52 blog posts created as part of the project and analyzed the specific subsections each student included to describe the kinds of language they use when enacting that certain identity. An analysis of these subsections, along with follow-up interviews with several Pazmany students, provides insight into the language attitudes student held at the time of creating their blogs. For students who were functional monolinguals, this resulted in the description of different registers and the vocabulary associated with each certain identity. For students who were multilingual, the descriptions focused on the contexts in which they use the different languages they have acquired. Many students, especially at Pazmany University, connected their different languages to their school-identity. In fact, 20 out of the 37 students who chose to represent their student identity had descriptions about foreign language requirements in their major and the different languages they use as students. Connecting language skills with institutional identities indicates that foreign languages serve utilitarian purposes for these students.

The strong presence of monolingual ideology became even more obvious when Pazmany students discussed their identities as family members or their national identities, and connected their Hungarian language to these domains as shown in the following examples:

- "Of course we speak hungarian at home." (Blog #6)
- "I am proud of being a Hungarian girl. I speak Hungarian which is one of the most complicated languages all over the world." (Blog #18)
- "I'm 100% Hungarian, and we use hungarian language within the family." (Blog #14)
- "All of my family is hungarian so we speak hungarian with each other and I use hungarian when I speak with my friends." (Blog # 26)

In these statements the wording "of course we speak hungarian" and "I am 100% Hungarian" implies a strong underlying connection between nationality and monolingual ideology as speaking the language is a requirement for belonging to a nation. The writer of Blog #18 while showing her pride in the Hungarian language even lists some Hungarian words that she thinks "sound very special." One of these words is "randevú" a word originating in French. A strong positive attitude towards a class of objects as suggested by Sarnoff (1970) is clearly demonstrated in this example towards words that are perceived to be special and "100%" Hungarian. This highly exposed positive attitude towards a language (Garrett, 2010) results in a positive disposition towards Hungarian which makes the presence of monolingual language ideology very transparent in the words of this writer. As she designates her language as "special," an isolated system not influenced by other languages, she clearly subscribes to monolingual ideology and thus denies the interconnectedness of languages while, ironically, using a word as her example that her native language has borrowed from another language. This writer accepts the tenets of monolingual ideology without closer scrutiny, which supports the argument that language ideology, similar to all other ideologies, relies more on collective beliefs than on linguistic reality.

We can also see how one language connects to a specific national identity in the following example that comes from a Davenport university student who described a Bosnian-Serb identity:

> I use the Serbian language only around my immediate family here in the United States which consists of: my brother, mom, uncle, aunt and cousin. There are not too many people here that I know of that speak my language. I do speak in Serbian through social sites like Facebook or even applications like Skype. I would not say that im completely fluent, but I am able to hold a conversation. I have come a long way from when I didn't even speak English in first grade to now being able to communicate in two languages. (Blog #48)

The writer of Blog #48 connects his different languages to different contexts (Serbian language: only with family in US and relatives in Serbia; English language: outside of family in US and in school) which indicates a complete separation of languages that is in line with monolingual ideology. While this writer does not seem to associate a specific attitude with a language, his compartmentalization of languages and his pride of being able to learn English can be indicators that this writer does not perceive the interaction between his languages as beneficial.

There is also a multimodal example in the dataset of blogs that uses different languages, but still reinforces monolingual ideology. In this case, the student employs a pop music video which contains lyrics that challenge the idea of blending languages. On Blog #18, in the language subsection of the blog paragraph that describes the writer's Hungarian identity, the student posted a YouTube video by Emil RuleZ!, an alternative jazz performer in Hungary (Nyelvguru, 2014). Additionally, this blog post also features the word "randevú" as a Hungarian word referenced above. The video contains the music and text of the song *Hello Tourist* written and performed by Emil RuleZ!, and displays the picture of Chain Bridge in the background with the text of the song moving along with the melody line-by-line. The text of the song is mostly in English but it also contains Hungarian, German, French, and Italian words. Here is a short excerpt from the beginning of the song:

> Hello Tourist, du bist in Budapest, capitol of Hungary. For a little money I will show you this beautiful city. I am a Student, I am twenty-three, I study sociology, on the very famous Eotvos Lorand Science University. (Nyelvguru, 2014)

The inclusion of this video reinforces typical assumptions about language use, especially in pronunciation. Although the song is in English, it is sung with a very strong and overemphasized Hungarian accent (i.e., the presence of the Hungarian rolled "r" in English words, pronouncing a vowel where there is a silent "e" in English). This strong Hungarian accent is also recognizable in the words of the song that come from other languages. While words from different languages are mixed in this song, overemphasizing the accent highlights that there are impenetrable boundaries between languages. Thus the writer of Blog #18 by incorporating this video into her blog accentuates the importance of a divide between languages and through this reveals the influence of monolingual ideology. Making the choice of including this video, this student displays her positive attitudes towards her native language and her negative attitudes about the Hungarian language's connections to other languages. Because she has selected a video that emphasizes the "negative" or "laughable" aspects of what happens when languages get into contact with each other, she illustrates her negative disposition towards interactions between languages and emphasizes the linguistic "purity" that can be gained from monolingual ideology and from keeping languages separate.

Students' posts, in addition to associating language with nationalities, demonstrated awareness of language politics within a monolingual framework. One student emphasizes her political-language awareness when writing about her minority Hungarian identity:

> My motherlanguage is hungarian! In Transilvania approximatly 2 million people speak hungarian. At home with my parent's, freinds and seklers, we are talking in hungarian, but when we have to go in official places we have to speak romanian, or find somebody who can speak hungarian. (Blog #20)

For this student the stark separation of her two languages cannot only be explained by the prevalence of monolingual ideology, but is also supported by the political context that she lives in as a minority. Since Hungarian minority rights are not well supported by the Romanian government, this student's attitudes towards her Romanian language are negative. While in her everyday language use she very likely mixes both of these linguistic resources even within the same utterance, as a member of the Hungarian minority in Romania her national identity is closely connected to insisting on a complete separation of these two languages. Her attitudes towards these two languages are clearly expressed in her word choice and use of punctuation. Adding an exclamation mark after stating her native language was a way for her to emphasize that while she is from Romania, her language identity is closely connected with her "motherlanguage." In addition, incorporating the word choice "have to," with the meaning of the modal auxiliary "must," she highlights outside influences on her language choice and shows how language ideology goes beyond personal choice and plays a major role in state-sanctioned control of minority populations. Because she must speak Romanian in official places, it is not her choice, and, as is often the case with compulsory language use, negative attitudes are, inevitably, generated. These negative attitudes, then, stand in stark opposition with the positive disposition towards one's native language, further reinforcing the separation between languages and thus supporting monolingual ideology.

Granted not all writers conformed strictly to a monolingual ideology in their initial blog posts. A strong counter-example here is the multilingual writer of Blog #3 who is the child of Iraqi parents, but has grown up in Hungary. When she writes about her identity as a family member, she describes a situation where languages are constantly mixed:

> As I mentioned earlier we have our own multiple language. My parent prefer Arabic, we use more Hungarian, but you can find everything we ever learnt in it (French, German, Spanish and even Japanese). The most useful part of having two nationalities is that I know Hungarian just as goon (= *good*) as Arabic. I only use Arabic with my family. My dad sometimes pretends that he doesn't understand us until we do so, but because I use Hungarian more often those words pop in my head more quickly which leads to a mixed language. (Blog #3)

The orientation of this student to her different languages does the opposite of emphasizing the boundaries between them. As someone who experiences transcultural communication in cosmopolitan spaces on a daily basis, she acknowledges that she relies upon different linguistic resources in certain situations, especially with her family members to express herself. These different resources transgress several languages, and the writer of this blog approaches these resources with a utilitarian stance; she uses the word that comes to her mind first, whatever language it may belong to. This practical attitude towards different languages shows that this writer privileges communication and collaboration over reinforcing sharing values embedded into languages. Thus, she displays a translingual disposition that is essential for cosmopolitan practice. In her description, we cannot find any kind of value assignment to any of her linguistic resources; she understands that they are just resources at her disposal and thus she refrains from elevating any of her languages over the others or making a strong separation between them.

Such an orientation indicates a less significant influence of monolingual ideology on this writer's language use and implies an openness to the mixing of different languages. Such openness towards translingual practice is evident in the following description of a Davenport University student who was born in the Netherlands: "The language I use as a mediator is mostly English. I also throw in a little Dutch/English combo here and there when I speak with family" (Blog #46). Again, we can see here that the writer of Blog #46 uses different languages as resources in her identity as a family member.

Furthermore, some of the initial blog posts also include examples of a playful translingual disposition in the form of code meshing where participants incorporate words from languages or language varieties other than Standard English to represent their identities. This is often done by strategically placing non-English words into the Standard English text to better portray identities; such examples illustrate Canagarajah's (2013) stance that languages "provide creative resources to construct new and revised identities through reconstructed forms and meaning of new indexicalities" (Canagarajah, 2013, p. 199). Best exemplifying the code meshed connections between translingual practice and identity were particular word choices from two different site titles from the blog database. One of the Davenport University students, an international student from Iceland, used the title "svartahvitu" for her blog site (Blog # 49). "Svartahvitu" means black and white in Icelandic and is most likely used here to reference some element of the writer's Icelandic identity. The other site title example, "chupa la verga" (Blog #8), comes from a Pazmany University student. Although this is an obscene expression in Spanish, it is also used according to the Urban Dictionary website (Urban Dictionary, 2014) as a slang expression by certain groups in the US with the meaning of a greeting. While we cannot determine what exactly the blog writer meant when using this term, it is certainly the case that he brought new connotations to the description of his identity by using such a site title.

Additionally, several participants viewed the blog title or section titles as a useful place for incorporating different languages or language varieties. A Pazmany University student, for example, titles her whole blog" "My identities/identitásaim" (Blog #30), adding the Hungarian translation of the English word to her title. She then begins to introduce her Hungarian identity in the first section of her blog with the following statements: "My hungarian identity determine my life principally. It determines the way i think about the world, my preferences, and because of the language- how i can describe the things around me" (Blog #30). Based on this description it is understandable that for the writer of Blog #30 incorporating the Hungarian word that means "my identities" further accentuates her primary identity as Hungarian. A Davenport University student in Blog #50 uses the word "Yooper" (as someone from Michigan's Upper Peninsula, UP for short, who is called a Yooper), which only exists in a regional variety of English. Again, her usage of this word allows her to better describe the identity she introduces, rather than just introducing it with Standard English words.

Another example of a student who subscribes to a monolingual ideology on the surface, but in practice engages in translanguaging on his blog comes from Blog #8. Here, a Pazmany University student uses a nonstandard word: "\m/" in the title of the blog section where he describes his identity as a heavy metal music fan. According to the Urban Dictionary (Urban Dictionary, 2014) this is a "representation of the horns, a metal salute" that is used by heavy metal fans for affirmation. Using this non-standard word as the title of his blog section, the writer of Blog #8 is able to signal his insider status in this community and can incorporate connotations that would otherwise be left out of his description of this specific identity had he only used Standard English.

Another interesting case of incorporating different languages into the English blog text comes from Blog #47 where a Davenport University student who is a functional English monolingual ends his blog page with the following Hungarian sentence: "Szeretem a halat, így érdemes!" The title of the student's blog is "weeatfish" and the approximate translation of this Hungarian sentence is: *I like fish, so it is worth it!* The writer of Blog #47 was one of the students later interviewed, and when asked about why and how he incorporated this Hungarian sentence, he explained that he wanted to show that computers are able to make language barriers less of a problem, so he took a phrase that would go well with the "fish" theme on his blog and entered it into Google Translate. Although the Hungarian sentence is grammatically correct, it would require a very specific textual context for it to be actually meaningful; thus the writer of the blog not only displays the possibilities computer translations can offer, but he also demonstrates the limitations such programs have. Still, by reaching out to his audience of Hungarian students through incorporating their language into his blog, the writer of blog #47 works towards weakening language barriers that are supported by monolingual ideology.

The writer of Blog #9, a Pazmany University student, in an explanation of how he uses language(s) when playing the video game World of Warcraft, also describes and displays language practices that weaken monolingual ideologies:

> *Language:* Thats very intresting, because the game is an english language game, so we have many worlds what we dont translate. For example (Pull, heal, damage, tactic, talent, spell, the name of the spells), because its very funni if you try to translate to hungary. When we play together we use Team Speak 3 client, thats one program, like skype, we able to speak with each other during the game. When we doing "Raids" (we are playing in groups) we use very short phrases (DPS—damage per second,) because we have to react very fast to a different situations during the game. If u never heard about W.O.W. i show you one video how does it look like when we playing together. (Blog #9)

Following this description, the writer inserts a gameplay video that is posted on YouTube (Orseh, 2011). In the video a small text box in the bottom left corner of the frame appears that shows players' chats during the game. The following chat text from one of the video frames exemplifies how English and Hungarian mix during game playing activities and provides yet another example of the type of translingual practice that students involved in the blog project already apply in connection with their different identities:

> [Garlogg] whispers: ja és + ba még lány vagy . . . az mindig + pont
>
> To [Garlogg]: jaj ezt hagyjuk mert hidegrázást kapok tőle
>
> To [Garlogg]: de komolyan
>
> Ezetrol has initiated a ready check
>
> [Raid] [Zapphire]: RSC > Everyone has flask and food buff
>
> [Garlogg] whispers: :D
>
> [Garlogg] whispers: ez igy van és kész (Orseh, 2011)

As we can see in the above example, language choice is applied freely in this informal online environment. Languages mix without any type of attitudes attached to any of the languages involved or to the mixing of these languages. As players engage in the gameplay in this digital space, the language of the game is constantly intertwined with the language of the conversation between players, with and no trace of either positive or negative disposition. Due to the utilitarian purpose of language in action here, linguistic elements are purely viewed as resources players can rely on to achieve the same goal.

The representation of translingual practice described here and in the other examples from the blog texts above shows that while some students clearly display an overwhelming influence of monolingual ideology on their language attitudes, other students move away from it especially when establishing identities outside of the academic context. In the next section, we will first see examples of how participants in the commenting phase of the cosmopolitan pedagogical project first reaffirm the influence of monolingual ideology in their interactions. These examples, however, will be followed by descriptions of instances where students engage in negotiating practices that are the basic elements of a cosmopolitan outlook coupled with translingual approach to language use.

Expressions of Language Ideology and Translingual Practice

The 243 total comments created in the second phase of the blog project were analyzed to determine whether, and in what form, the language ideology that was represented on the student blog pages had been addressed in students' online discussions with their international partners. The comments were coded based on comment topic using Deborah Tannen's (1993) discourse analysis method. Tannen's approach to discourse analysis makes the connection between linguistic choices and culture very explicit. She describes the connection between mental structures and verbalization the following way: "on the basis of one's experience of the world in a given culture (or combination of cultures) one organizes knowledge about the world and uses this knowledge to predict interpretations and relationships regarding new information, events and experiences" (1993, p. 16). This organized knowledge, or structures of expectations, affects the linguistic choices one makes when speaking or writing, and can be reconstructed based on the linguistic elements of texts. Students' blog comments were analyzed by first identifying the comment topic and connecting this comment topic either to a single culture or to a combination of cultures. For example, comments that referred to the international sports scene reflected structures of expectations based on a combination of cultures. In this sports example case, these expectations were often supported by the writers' application of translingual practice in their comments.

As this chapter not only seeks to discuss how students used language during this project but also how they conceptualized language within their interactions, it is important to focus in on the comments first that referred to language. Through the analysis of all comments, most of which focused on the content of the blogs (e.g., sports, music), 25 comments were classified as "completely focused" on the topic of language, since these had at least two of the sentences referring to this topic. In terms of reinforcing monolingual ideology, in the 25 language comments, students often discussed foreign language learning in these comments, for example, how many years it took to learn a new language, and what languages the commenting partners speak and at what level. The following excerpt is representative of this type of comment:

> I am so intrigued that your english is so good! I know Spanish, but not enough to write a whole blog about! For that, I congratulate you! . . . Your blog is really good along with your english! (Comment on Blog #12)

While these comments approach language proficiency from a functional viewpoint, they are based on a strict separation of languages and prioritize mastery and control over a language as a system, thus reinforcing monolingual ideologies. When the student in the above example offers that "your english is so good," positive attitudes towards learning a language are displayed. However, these attitudes evolve into a disposition in which proficiency in languages other than one's own is valued. If that other language is English, the competency in that language is highly valued. These value systems, of course, do not arise in and of themselves; they are created by local and global power dynamics. Language attitudes are often invisible for that reason, as they are embedded in larger value systems. Nonetheless, language attitudes, as they are expressed not only in comments about language but also in actual language use, are the most easily detectable symptoms of hidden social values and attitudes. As monolingual ideologies represent a large investment of countries around the world into national identities, its prevalence and success is closely connected to a lens that sees the world through the eyes of separate and different nations and not as a whole

The tenets of monolingual ideologies also appear in the remaining six comments that were about languages and language varieties, in general, or related to certain characteristics of specific languages and language varieties. A comment exchange on Blog #49 illustrates how commenting partners discuss languages and reveal assumptions about them.

etelaky16 December 6, 2011 at 6:26 pm

Could you plese give me the answere if there are any resemblances between English and Icelandic language? I assume that in Iceland it is compulsory to learn English if I am not mistaken.

svartahvitu December 12, 2011 at 9:27 pm

There is no similarities between Icelandic and English. The only words that are the same are the new words that younger generations have brought into Icelandic, mostly swear words lol. Kids in Iceland start to learn English in School at the age of 9 or 10 I think, and people are learning English form the Tv-shows, the movies, and the Internet. Most Icelandic people speak English and we learn Danish as well in school.

The answer to the first commenter's question postulates languages as separate entities by relying on the borrowing model, where words from one language are borrowed to be used in another language. Here again, monolingual ideology is behind imagining languages as isolated systems that sometimes are enhanced by borrowing elements from other systems. In addition, the notion of compulsory language learning connects languages with power. Who can make learning a language mandatory? National education authorities that perpetuate the distribution of power through law that mandates that citizens "react favorably to a class of objects" (Sarnoff, 1970, p. 279), in this case a group of words and grammatical rules called the English language. Assumptions that languages can be made compulsory show a deeply internalized connection between language and power that is best represented by monolingual ideology through the collection of attitudes towards what has been codified as an isolated entity. Upholding monolingual ideology, however, demands mastery of code that is devoid of the speaker's context and limits the power of speakers to achieve effective communication through the linguistic resources they already have.

Despite the adherence to monolingual understanding of language on the surface of many of the comments, we found, in terms of the cosmopolitan attitudes the assignment was meant to engender, that students displayed an openness to languages and language acquisition, which is the first step towards understanding of translingual dispositions. The following comment exchange exemplifies the type of "open" language attitudes and assumptions that were expressed in students' comments:

> *adaydreaminggirl* November 28, 2011 at 7:29 AM
>
> Hi! Your blog is very interesting! :) I'm jealous because you can speak Spanish :D After graduating I plan to take language lessons in Spanish. It is so beautiful :) I heard that Portuguese can understand Spanish, but Spanish can't understand Portuguese. Is it true? Or it is just a legend? :) Erika

> *Juan the Interpreter* November 28, 2011 at 3:23 PM
>
> The Truth is that it depends on what type of spanish you speak, i can understand the Portuguese that the brazilians speak, but the actual Portuguese from Europe. Im glad you want to learn Spanish its a beautiful language that has such an amazing flow to it while you speak (Comments on Blog #36)

This exchange shows that students, while articulating some of their language attitudes ("It is so beautiful" and "it's a beautiful language that has such an amazing flow to it"), also question some of the beliefs they hold about languages through assigning expert status to the other commenter. This move points to the openness promoted by cosmopolitan values that encourages curiosity, and pursues knowledge not based on canonized standards, but on the personal experience of communication partners. It appears that within this commenting environment students are also willing to negotiate assumptions and meanings they previously associated with a language-related concept, thus they are willing to question linguistic standards. As mentioned earlier in the discussion about translingual practice (Canagarajah, 2013), the willingness to question assumptions, negotiate language codes, and use a practice-based approach which draws on all available semantic resources in cross-cultural communication encounters in search of a shared meaning is one of the important characteristics of a translingual disposition.

In addition to the 25 comments that were classified as having language as their main topic, 31 shorter comments displayed an open attitude towards language interrogation, as they concentrate on the meaning and usage of specific words. A Davenport University student comments: "I had to look up what a 'hostel' was. Is that a requirement for school?" (Comment on Blog #21) and from a Pazmany University student: "At the beggining of your blog you mentioned 'hobbyfarm'. Could you tell me what do you meant by it?" (Comment on Blog #33). In these two examples the comment writers rely on the blog writer to offer meaning. As students who are starting to develop translingual disposition, they assign expertise to their interaction partners and work with them to unpack the meaning in the context of the speaker. While the first commenter moves from the tools of standardized language (a dictionary) to finding out more about the context from their interaction partner, the second commenter assigns expertise to their partner early on while forgoing the standardizing power of a dictionary and appealing straight to the source of meaning. In another case, a Pazmany student in a comment on Blog #20 anticipates that her word choice might lead to questions, and she provides commentary on her word choice: "My two dogs are mongrels/mix dogs . . . I don't really know how do you call it, but I have found only these expressions on it." This comment was answered the following way by a Davenport University student: "Here mixed dogs are usually called mutts. They are often the best kind to have." This exchange shows that the commenting phase of the project where students interacted with each other also served as an arena where students displayed audience awareness and negotiated language use illustrating their growing reliance on translingual disposition in cosmopolitan interactions.

The meaning of the words "soccer" and "football" was also discussed several times in the blog comments. The following excerpt exemplifies how in a comment exchange initiated by a Davenport University student, participants go through elaborate questions and detailed explanations to arrive at a shared meaning.

> 1. juliehuser
>
> I found your blog very interesting. I do have a question however? You state that your brothers play football and that your boyfriend is a soccer coach, are you referring to the same sport? In the U. S. we call it soccer but I know other countries call it football, could you please let me know? My son plays soccer and my husband is a coach. Share a link with some information on soccer (football) if you could, as they are always interested in other countries and how they play soccer. Also at our university soccer is a big sport with a lot of international players on the teams—both boys and girls.

2. kitty0617

Yes, my brothers play soccer. In Hungary we call it football. Football or soccer may refer to one of a number of team sports, which all involve, kicking a ball with the foot to score a goal. Football play between 2 teams of eleven players with a ball. The game is played on a rectangular field of grass or green artificial turf, with a goal in the middle of each of the short ends. The goalkeepers are the only players allowed to touch the ball with their hands or arms.

The Pazmany student's answer clarifies that she uses both words, soccer and football, to refer to the same sport. This detailed explanation eliminates the possibility of the word "football" in this conversation referring to American football. Through this exchange the students involved in the interaction negotiate word meanings to ensure mutual understanding and thus exemplify how the negotiation of meanings is an essential prerequisite for the emergence of translingual practice in Canagarajah's (2013) terms. Coherence is not assumed, rather a meaning is agreed upon through negotiation. One of the students also pointed out in the post-project interviews that she discussed the meaning of soccer vs. football in her blog comments, saying that "we went back and forth a little bit on that one." Another Pazmany student is also very conscientious about soccer vs football in regards to using the right word when writing to a Davenport student. In his comment on Blog #49, he not only shows audience awareness, but assumes agency in language choice the following way: "I'm also a soccer (I still call it football) fanatic, on and off the pitch."

Participants in the blog project not only used verbal explanations to clarify word meanings but also utilized the affordances of the blog commenting interface and attached links to websites. A Pazmany student articulates appreciation for a link that was used to explain a word on Blog #50 by a Davenport University student: "The phrase "Yooper" was unknown for me, thanks for the link, it helped me to understand the meaning of it." Blog #50 also contains a picture of a wooden board in a forest that has the *Prayer of the Woods* carved on it in English. In reply to this picture, the same Pazmany student also posts the entire text of the *Prayer of the Woods* in Hungarian in her comment. The Davenport student then replies as follows: "Thank you for including the prayer of the woods in Hungarian, I really appreciate it. I am thinking about printing it out on a picture of woods and hanging it on my wall."

As the above examples show, many students found the commenting phase the most enriching part of the assignment. One of the Pazmany University students, later interviewed, explained: "So I thought that I write everything incorrect, and they will laugh and all, because we can't write correctly in English. So I thought this at the first moment. But after we started to comment on each other's blog I didn't find big mistakes in our comments. . . . First I thought that they will not understand but I realized that then they will ask what is it" (Interview #7). We can see that this student, once in contact with the other students through the comment feature of the blog, realized the possibility and importance of negotiations in communication encounters across cultures. This realization then freed her from concentrating rigidly on correctness and enabled her to focus on coordination and mutual understanding rather than concentrating on correctness for its own sake. The same interviewee then expresses this realization with the following words where she refers to Davenport students in the US as "they" and to Pazmany students in Hungary as "we"; for instance, "Because I realized that they are not interested in whether we write correctly or not. It was more important to relay information not whether it is done correctly. Because no one corrected us, so really they just wrote about the topic. I thought they would say, this is not correct, or something" (Interview 7). This statement illustrates that the commenting space served as an actual contact zone (Pratt, 1991) where some students were able to overcome restrictive monolingual ideology and use different languages, language varieties, and even multimodal means as communication resources in order to achieve mutual understanding.

Conclusion

The blog exchange project described in this chapter shows not only how entrenched the stark separation between nations and languages remains around the world, but also the way these ideologies get challenged in transcultural spaces. The understanding of varied identities through the cosmopolitan lens led to a pedagogical practice that enabled students in this GNLE to find many similarities between themselves and their counterparts—despite differences in national origin. This, in turn, allowed participants to challenge their assumptions about languages and meanings through conversations with other students across borders. Discovering what communication partners share often led to a more productive exploration of their differences, or what they do not yet share (Appiah, 2006). The layout of the blogs, which was based on describing different identity categories in separate sections, was conducive to helping students realize just how much they have in common with peers in another country. This provided students with a personal experience that supported their understanding of cosmopolitan principles and led to successful transcultural communication encounters.

The cosmopolitan outlook and translingual dispositions gained from this experience can be an asset when encountering cultural difference that often manifests itself as linguistic difference. For example, accepting multiplicity in language use, in the form of not adhering to standards, arose in the blog project when assumptions about language use and language ideologies were challenged in comment conversations between students. Accepting multiplicity in language use was also supported by the multimodal communication options of the blog interface. In fact, we can argue that the wide variety of linguistic and multimodal resources the project participants used in this transcultural context enabled the hybridity of these resources for communication to become more perceptible (see also Horner, Selfe & Lockridge, 2015). When students experience the practical value of cosmopolitan outlook and a translingual disposition, as they participate in communication encounters where collaboration is privileged over dominance and synthesis is achieved together, they are more likely to internalize these dispositions.

This more open, cosmopolitan attitude towards language appeared in the negotiations participants engaged in. The creativity participants displayed in using language(s) during the blog project could only emerge in a pedagogical space that de-emphasized a norm-based, Standard English approach. Creating classroom spaces based on cosmopolitan values in transcultural online environments thus can foster student's translingual disposition and can create the most optimal conditions in which they can learn successful communication practices across borders. Indeed, this is where translingual disposition and cosmopolitan outlook overlap. The goal of communication in cosmopolitan spaces is to overcome differences and enable collaboration based on what is shared between communication partners. Emphasizing differences, whether between people, cultures, or languages, cannot lead to collaboration. A cosmopolitan outlook coupled with translingual disposition is the best way to ensure collaboration, the completion of shared actions across languages and cultures.

References

Anderson, P., Bergman, B., Bradley, L., Gustafsson, M. & Matzke, A. (2010). Peer reviewing across the Atlantic: Patterns and trends in L1 and L2 comments made in an asynchronous online collaborative learning exchange between technical communications in Sweden and in the United States. *Journal of Business and Technical Communication, 24*(3), 296–322.

Appiah, K. A. (2006). *Cosmopolitanism: Ethics in a world of strangers.* W. W. Norton & Co.

Beck, U. (2006). *Cosmopolitan vision.* Polity Press.

Blommaert, J. (2010). *The sociolinguistics of globalization*. Cambridge University Press.

Canagarajah, S. A. (2013). *Translingual practices: Lingua Franca English and global citizenship*. Routledge.

García, O. & Leiva, C. (2013). Theorizing and enacting translanguaging for social justice. In A. Blackledge & A. Creese (Eds.), *Heteroglossia as Practice and Pedagogy* (pp. 199–216). Springer.

Garrett, P. (2010). *Attitudes to language*. Cambridge University Press.

Herrington, T. K. (2010) Crossing global boundaries: Beyond intercultural communication. *Journal of Business and Technical Communication, 24*(4), 516–539.

Herrington, T. & Tretyakov, Y. (2005). The global classroom project: Troublemaking and troubleshooting. In K. C. Cook & K. Grant-Davie (Eds.), *Online education: Global questions, local answers* (pp. 267–283). Baywood.

Horner, B., Selfe, C. & Lockridge, T. (2015). *Translinguality, transmodality, and difference: exploring dispositions and change in language and learning.* The University of Louisville Institutional Repository. https://ir.library.louisville.edu/cgi/view content.cgi?article=1083&context=faculty.

Maylath, B., Vandepitte, S. & Mousten, B. (2008). Growing grassroots partnerships: Trans-Atlantic collaboration between American instructors and students of technical writing and European instructors and students of translation. In D. Starke-Meyerring & M. Wilson (Eds.), *Designing Globally Networked Learning Environments: Visionary Partnerships, Policies, and Pedagogies* (pp. 52–66). Sense.

Nyelvguru. (2011, February 7). *Emil Rulez Hello Tourist* [Video]. Youtube. http://www.youtube.com/watch?v=6g26StE8N60#t=229

Orseh. (2011, September 10). Tenebrae—HC Shannox 10 [Video]. Youtube. http://www.youtube.com/watch?v=v4gUV1ecS9M.

Palmer, Z. B. (2013). Cosmopolitanism: Extending our theoretical framework for transcultural technical communication research and teaching. *Journal of Technical Writing and Communication 43*(4), 381–401.

Pandey, A. (2013). When "second" comes first—to the eye? Sociolinguistic hybridity in professional writing. In S. Canagarajah (Ed.), *Literacy as translingual practice: Between communities and classrooms* (pp. 215–227). Routledge.

Pennycook, A. (2010). *Language as a local practice*. Routledge.

Pratt, M. L. (1991). Arts of the contact zone. *Profession, 91*, 33–40.

Sarnoff, I. (1970). *Social attitudes and the resolution of motivational conflict*. Penguin.

St. Amant, K. (2002). Integrating intercultural online learning experiences into the computer classroom. *Technical Communication Quarterly, 11*(3), 289–315.

Starke-Meyerring, D. & Andrews, D. (2006) Building a shared learning culture: An international classroom partnership. *Business Communication Quarterly, 69*(1), 25–49.

Starke-Meyerring, D. & Wilson, M. (Eds.). (2008). *Designing Globally Networked Learning Environments*. Sense Publishers.

Tannen, D. (1993). What's in a frame? Surface evidence for underlying expectations. In D. Tannen (Ed.), *Framing in Discourse* (pp. 14–56). Oxford University Press.

Urban Dictionary (2014). Word definitions. http://www.urbandictionary.com.

10 Arabic, as a Home Language, Acts as a Resource in an English Writing Class: Borrowing Translation Strategies in a First Year Writing Course

Rula Baalbaki, Juheina Fakhreddine,[1] Malaki Khoury, and Souha Riman
AMERICAN UNIVERSITY OF BEIRUT, LEBANON

This chapter describes how home languages work as a resource for students in an English foundation writing course at the American University of Beirut, Lebanon. We describe writing tasks that require analysis of syntax, register, idiomatic, and cultural expressions as they are manifested in the specificities of usage in both Arabic and English texts. Our analysis of students' writing indicates that these writers became more consciously aware of using strategies; were better able to negotiate meanings; gained understanding of knowledge construction; and were more capable of producing meaning across language and cultural differences in their writing.

Keywords: translingual pedagogy, Arabic as a home language, writing practices

Our observation of an introductory translation course that primarily dealt with the rendering of Arabic literary texts into English initiated the idea of using home language texts, in lieu of English language readers, as the starting place for first-year writing (FYW). The translation activities we observed showed that students gained an ability to select, comprehend, and hone the syntactical and lexical elements of their translations. Inspired by the ground rules of this translation course, and supported by the literature on translingual

---

1   This chapter is dedicated to the memory of co-author Juheina Fakhreddine, who passed away in October 2018.

DOI: https://doi.org/10.37514/INT-B.2020.0438.2.10

and translocal theories and applications (Canagarajah, 2002, 2011, 2013; Creese & Blackledge, 2013; Grossman, 2010; Horner & Lu, 2007; Leonard, 2014; Ray, 2013), we repeatedly asked students to engage in translingual writing tasks where Arabic was L1 and English L2 (or even L3). Specific assignments called for analysis of syntax, register, idiomatic, and cultural expressions, as well as the specificities of usage in each language. The students worked on assignments involving close reading of texts in both L1 and L2/3, after which they produced thoughtful writing analyses, reflections, and responses in English.

By having students read texts in Arabic and employ them in developing their writing in English, we aimed to explore the benefits of using a translingual approach in our own context at AUB. Working with students who have complex language backgrounds, we implemented a pedagogical approach connected to translanguaging theories other scholars have developed but adapted for our own teaching and learning context. Examples from the students' writing demonstrate a translation-based translingual process and show that students were able to: analyze, negotiate meaning, and value their bilingual competency (Ferris, 2014); develop their language repertoires; reflect on their process while consciously using creative writing strategies to achieve their communicative objective across cultural differences (Canagarajah, 2006; Horner et al., 2011); discover the sensitivity to and awareness of sentence-level issues they possess (Ray, 2013); and appreciate the linguistic and cultural specificities that differentiate Arabic (L1) from English (L2) (Said, 2002).

This chapter includes a discussion of the pedagogical context and theoretical frame of the assignments, a discussion of pedagogy linking the current studies on translingualism to analysis of the students' writing, and a discussion of the place of the translation assignment in the current approaches to translingual studies and the suitability of its results for more thoughtful and engaged college writing practices.

Background

English is the language of instruction and the medium for communication across the context within which we work at AUB, "which bases its educational philosophy, standards, and practices on the American liberal arts model of higher education . . . and where [t]he language of instruction is English (except for courses in the Arabic Department and other language courses)."[2] Students take FYW courses (a sequence of English writing courses known as

2   See https://www.aub.edu.lb/Registrar/Documents/catalogue/under graduate09–10/university.pdf.

the Communication Skills Program) including English 102. In these classes, students are asked to meet the expectations of the course instructors in writing texts that adhere to grammatical accuracy, striving to "think in" English and use it exclusively. In other words, English is the only resource. Yet, most students and instructors may be using other languages such as Arabic, their home language, or French, which they have learnt at school, outside the writing class. In our case "translanguaging [becomes] a naturally occurring phenomenon" (Canagarajah, 2011, p. 402). Though our students are mostly Lebanese, there is a good number who come from other Arab countries and whose home languages are varieties of vernacular Arabic, which are different than the Modern Standard Arabic learned at schools in the Middle East and North African (MENA) region. Our students are mostly speakers and writers of English and Arabic, with some Armenian students, whose home language is Armenian, comprising a small percentage in our classes.

The Communication Skills Program at AUB is a service program through which all students have to pass in order "to satisfy university requirements and to meet the diverse literacy needs of AUB students. The program aims to educate students to use writing and reading for learning, critical thinking, and communication in academic and other social contexts."[3] Based on a certain scale and using the score a student obtains in a required English proficiency test, any student admitted to AUB is placed in one of the four courses that constitute the core of this program, one of which is English 102. English 102 "is designed to upgrade students' overall proficiency level in English and enrich their exposure to a range of discourse that develops fluency and accuracy in communication through reading and writing for critical thinking" (see Appendix A English 102 syllabus). It is the base course that caters to students with the lowest proficiency in English found acceptable for a student to function at AUB.

Given the university requirements and culture as well as instructors' expectations mentioned above, courses in the Communication Skills Program, including English 102, have always used monolingual English texts. The use of an Arabic text in English 102 and other courses in the program has historically been unthinkable, which renders the utilization of Arabic texts in an English course, the technique employed in our study, a major break away from conventions.

Theoretical Framework for Translation Assignments

Applied linguists and rhetoric and composition scholars value more than the product of students' writing believing that practitioners need to investigate

---

3   See https://www.aub.edu.lb/FAS/ENGLISH/COMMSKILLS.

what resources students bring to the writing classroom, including their experiences with and knowledge of languages. Canagarajah, among others, finds that these language resources interact dynamically with a new context they are brought into, changing it and undergoing change themselves (Canagarajah, 2013; Guerra, 2008).

Considering language difference as a resource, a translingual pedagogy attempts to train students to tune in to this difference and learn to navigate across language borders. Leonard (2014) advises writing and rhetoric teachers to remember that mono- and multilinguals actually differ "on amount and diversity of experience and use . . . [because] all language knowledge is socially contingent and dynamic no matter how many language codes one has access to" (Hall et al., 2006, p. 229). We suggest that a translingual approach, a communicative strategy which allows for broad "linguistic diversity" in different social practices, operates within this framework. Even when dealing with one language, students need, what Leonard (2014) calls, rhetorical attunement, "an ear for, or a tuning towards, difference or multiplicity" (p. 228).

FYW students often produce errors in written discourse, especially when they, understandably, think in Arabic and translate their ideas into English. In our study, the process of analyzing, responding, and reflecting in both languages was meant to have student writers examine their own writing rather than imitate model texts to discover how and why they could be reworking with a text "in response to specific contingencies" or "social circumstances" (Horner & Lu, 2007, pp. 154–155). By asking students to engage with their own texts at the sentence level, we hoped to raise their awareness of the "codes [the students] use" (Ray, 2013, p. 192) in a number of ways. First, we wanted them to "develop critical awareness of the choices that were more rhetorically effective" (Canagarajah, 2011, p. 402). Second, we encouraged students to treat their work "more consciously as active participants in the creation and re-creation of language" (Horner & Lu, 2007, p. 157) that was meaningful to them. Finally, we hoped that sensitivity to sentence-level language issues would become clearer to them, and they would be aware of how to better employ language and rhetoric to express their ideas effectively.

In addition, in our translation assignment we adopted one specific suggestion by Horner et al. (2011) by encouraging "renewed focus by students of writing on the problematics of translation to better understand and participate in negotiations of difference in and through language" (p. 308). Grossman (2010) believes that translation intensifies and expands a writer's discernment of style, technique, and structure by giving translators access to more than one national or linguistic tradition. The activities we worked on in our FYW classes were an attempt to deal with language difference in writing, to build on language variation and student resources (knowledge of Arabic in this case); to focus on the problematics of translation in teaching writing rather than eradicating those realities of difference as is the tendency in a monolingual approach.

The description of translation assignments and our initial analysis of students work follows. We present this analysis as case studies drawn from a larger study of 300 students' texts. We began with two research questions:

1. To what extent does a translation-related translingual activity develop students' critical awareness of rhetorically effective writing in English as they translate from Arabic?
2. To what extent does a translation-related translingual activity add to students' awareness of sentence-level choices?

For this chapter, we are most interested in a focus on the problematics of translation.

Translation Assignments

We first introduced translation assignments in the fall 2012 semester. This was the very first time Arabic texts had ever been assigned in a FYW classroom. Our purpose was to test whether integrating a translation component proves applicable in a FYW class. The excerpts assigned were from an Arabic detective story for young adults. Students read these excerpts and analyzed the diction, sentence structure, and idiomatic expressions used by the author, after which they translated words, expressions, and sentences into L2, reflecting on their choices to achieve a meaningful and faithful translation.

Following the 2012 pilot project, four instructors assigned translation projects in their English 102 classes, with a total student population of around four hundred, over two fall semesters, 2013 and 2014. Similar to the pilot, students were engaged in close reading of texts. They discussed and analyzed the cultural, lexical, and syntactic implications of these texts, before they set about translating selected short excerpts of these texts into English. In each of the semesters, a different text was selected. Fall 2013 semester students were first asked to analyze an Arabic selection from Wadad Cortas' memoir *Dunia Ahbabtoha* (*A World I Loved*) written in the early 1960s. Cortas rewrote her text in English before her death in 1979. The book was completely revised and edited for a western audience in 2009. The 2009 English version of *A World I Loved* was introduced and students analyzed the thematic and rhetorical choices made by the editors. The writing assignment for this activity was a compare-and-contrast essay that showed the similarities and differences between the writer's and editors' choices as well as a reflection that would reveal whether or not the Arabic reading helped students in comprehending the English text (see Appendix B for detailed instructions). In fall 2014, after analyzing an Arabic excerpt from Jabra Ibrahim Jabra's autobiography *Albi'r Al'ula* (*The First Well*), students worked on translating a short selection from the text and then compared their work to a published English translation. They wrote an essay to discuss whether this activity was helpful for them and reflected on their rhetorical choices during translation (see Appendix C for detailed instructions).

During the process of completing the translation assignment, the students worked collaboratively to construct meaning. In class, they worked in small groups to discuss the texts, translate excerpts, validate their choices, and revise their translations. The essays and reflections were written individually. Samples of their writings from the second and third phases were collected for data analysis since the assigned tasks were similar.

It is important to note that the cultural and emotional themes of Cortas' and Jabra's texts helped in introducing these translingual activities and invited students to connect to the authors' experiences as the excerpts would show later in the chapter. In *A World I Loved*, Wadad Cortas, the principal of an all-girls school, Ahliyya National School in Beirut, discussed her struggle to protect the Arab cultural and national identity through preserving students' use of Arabic. Cortas (2009) who fought against "French [language] gaining ground and putting Arabic in eclipse" (p. 80) believes that the use of Arabic is a sign of patriotism and a means of liberation from western colonialism. Jabra Ibrahim Jabra, a Palestinian writer, evokes in his autobiography, *The First Well*, nostalgia for the Arabic language and culture as the author vividly recalls his childhood and school memories during the 1920s in Bethlehem and Jerusalem. He expresses his fascination with Arabic language and its literature when he wrote "words glowed in my mind; they glittered like gold and sparkled like jewels. I imagined myself walking on colored silk carpets spread over the waves of a wondrous sea of dreams" (Jabra, 2012).

Analysis of Student Translation Work

Our discussion covers two fall semesters, 2013 and 2014, worth of students' written responses to the activities. Here we offer the examples of students' translation work that we feel best illustrates a translingual pedagogical potential. We have divided these student-examples into four main categories supported by rhetoric-composition theories related to translingual writing classes. The first category is writers' conscious use of strategies (Canagarajah, 2006), in which student writers bring the strategies that all writers use into the conscious, as opposed to the mechanical or unconscious, level. The second category is negotiation of meaning (Horner et al., 2011) and rhetorical attunement (Leonard, 2014), which student writers negotiate the differences between the linguistic specificities of their native Arabic, and those of English, thereby tuning in to these differences and coming to a decision about what to use and/or how to evaluate syntactical and lexical choices. The third category is construction of knowledge (Guerra, 2008; Horner et al., 2011) in which student writers make use of going through the stages of the activities to understand what they know and construct new ideas about what they write. The fourth category, making connections/improvising ways and producing meaning across language (and cultural) differences (Horner et al., 2011), takes the student writers to broader levels of attunement with the cultural, temporal, spatial, and linguistic aspects that two texts written in L1 and L2 may offer, thus bringing into their writing course a more well-rounded comprehension of academic and non-academic experiences. In short, the resistance and trepidation that might characterize any individual's first encounter with the very idea of using two languages in a writing classroom vanished as has been revealed in the student writers' responses.

Conscious Use of Strategies

The process of this translingual classroom activity started with introducing Arabic texts into English 102 classes. Students developed the ability and advantage of working together collaboratively on their "possible different textual realizations" (Canagarajah, 2006, p. 601) of the same Arabic text into English. Groups of students negotiated, contested, and (eventually) decided upon their texts together, selecting what they found most suited for the audience and rhetorical context. This exercise, in addition to the analysis of the original and translated texts, invites students to explore how their translation decisions are driven by a rhetorical context, enabling them to bring the strategies writers use, not excluding themselves as student writers, to the level of consciousness.

For example, after students translated an excerpt of the text into English, one of them wrote:

> As I translated the Arabic text into English, I discovered that my translation is different than the original. For example: في عصر احد الايام could be translated in many ways.

I translated it to "Once upon a time" while in the original version it is translated as "One afternoon". These simple dissimilarities have the ability to affect the whole meaning of the text. Additionally, the Arabic word ساحة could be translated into "square," "field" or "yard". Furthermore, مالس اي is an informal tactic that is used in Arabic [and] does not exist in English. So how would we translate it? What is the closest word we can write? These are the few questions we could ask ourselves while translating.

When student writers use one language to express their ideas, they might not be as readily aware of the strategies and processes that they are actually using to create the exact meaning. However, this student showcases that she is consciously aware of the strategies she employs to select her intended meaning.

When students in class had the chance to discuss and compare the different possibilities of translating a text and discussing how each textual representation is more suited for a certain audience and context, they were able to experience how "[t]he same language may be used to construct different texts if the language is used for different contexts and communities" (Canagarajah, 2006, p. 601), and they came to realize that "[e]quating one language with one discourse is terribly limited" (Canagarajah, 2006, p. 601).

Another student explained the choice of the text which he found most appropriate out of a number of possible other texts in the same language. He justified appropriateness by what the reader needs, or the context calls for:

First, the names were kept in their original pronunciation: "Yusuf," "Abdu," "Antar and Abla, etc." were not translated, as it sometimes happen[s] with some names. This gives the reader of the English translation a sense of what the people were called in their language. Also, some other names such as "the Box of the World" or "the Square of the Church of Nativity" were literally translated to keep an original touch to it. Adding to this, more technical words such as "magnifying lens," "spindle" or "paper tape" were also translated effectively in order to explain the box's mechanism as it was intended to be in the original text.

However, other words like "Yalla" and "Kaake"... were translated to "Ok" and "Cake" ... Sentence structures were not always respected. They were sometimes slightly modified to be understood by someone who reads English and does not know Arabic. For example, the listing of adjectives "large, blue, wooden box" was in the original Arabic "a box in wood large painted-blue". The order was changed in the English text to suit the linguistic needs of English speakers.

The examples above shows how student agency can consciously and knowingly departing from conventions. Here is another example that shows how students were able to question, and maybe demystify, certain conventions through a comparative analysis of an Arabic text and its translation.

In the Arabic version, it is understandable that the writer mentioned names of certain important characters in the Arab world. But including these names in the translation is of no use to the audience reading the translation as this audience is unlikely to be aware of the significance of these characters or even who they are. Thus, the English text translated from Arabic should not blindly copy everything the Arabic text has. It should omit what is confusing to its English audience.

The linguistic decisions students made and the decisions of other writers they reflected on (and sometimes challenged), as demonstrated in the excerpts, show the agency of the students, who were working with more than one language. The task gave them the opportunity to learn how to make decisions and to be "rhetorically creative"; for example, they strategically chose what needed to be transliterated from the original Arabic text and what needed to be idiomatic English. They considered, reflected, and defended their choices, which they based on what is needed for a certain audience, community, or context. As a result, they made choices consciously "from a range of different options to achieve their communicative purposes" (Canagarajah, 2006, p. 602). Thus, our study demonstrates how students' learning and language acquisition is achieved through a process of working with the language rather than simply applying strategies or techniques that are imposed on them. They experienced and consequently learned how "rules and conventions can be negotiated for one's purposes with suitable strategies" (Canagarajah, 2006, p. 602).

Finally, by digging for words and expressions, thinking of their different meanings and cultural implications, and consciously making linguistic choices driven by communities and contexts, students were able to "demystify certain conventions" and to "relate their writing to the social context," thus taking steps towards becoming "critical writers," who, we hope, with such praxis, would be well on their way "to shap[ing] their writing to achieve a favorable voice and representation for themselves" (Canagarajah, 2006, p. 603).

Negotiation of Meaning

One main feature common to writers (and translators) is that they both nego-tiate meaning in L1 and/or L2 (Horner et al., 2011) which we suggest pro-vides them with the ability to attune their rhetorical choices (Leonard, 2014) according to the meaning of the idea at hand. Given the linguistic specifici-ties of Arabic, a Semitic language that differs from English, not just in syntax and lexical origins, but also in the focus it places on syntax, lexis, eloquence, figurative language, and creativity, reading and translating, or analyzing the translation of Arabic/English texts necessitates that student writers engage in extensive negotiation and rhetorical attunement. The student writers in our project dealt with some of these specificities without necessarily referring to the finer lexical and syntactical terms or explanations. Most of the students in question had to deal with this kind of literacy in their Arabic classes, and it became a "latent" or "indirect" factor in their linguistic repertoire. For exam-ple, one student referred to "ya salam," an expression related to wonderment and enticement as ". . . an informal tactic that is used in Arabic that does not exist in English. So how should we translate it? What is the closest word we could write?" This question stems from the linguistic and folkloric existence of "al-Munada" rule in Arabic (similar to "Oh + proper noun" in English, a style that is no longer in up-to-date use). Awareness of the nonexistence of this form in English is the first step towards negotiating the equivalence, and tuning in to the linguistic differences.

Another student criticized the English translation of Jabra's text because it "lacks figurative expression compared to the Arabic text. The alliteration in Arabic gives the text special effects but the alliteration is absent in the English version." Awareness of this figurative feature and expecting to "enjoy" it in the English translation is an example of how the student writers, while criticizing the lack of the abundance in eloquent and figurative usage in L2, attune themselves to this rhetorical feature of English writing, at least as it occurs in the selected texts. One student went so far as to wonder whether the translation has "destroyed the magic of an original text."

Another student commented that this task provided them a chance to discover that "the English language is rich of words that are synonyms but can have different meanings . . . which helped me think more and search for the right and accurate words that could satisfy the meaning of the sentence." This element of "register," common to both Arabic and English writing, is a writing teacher's nightmare. In this exercise, many register-related negotia-tions were taken care of, since the tackling and juxtaposing of two languages elucidated the shades and levels of meaning in question. As a student wrote:

It was helpful to read a text and its translation because the original text will make us understand the real aim that the writer wanted to reach; it comes as a support for the English text. And the English text helped to enlighten the abstract and conceptual ideas present in the Arabic text.

Many student writers commented on the Arabic original of Cortas containing "sophisticated words [which] helped in strengthening her main topic which is patriotism and staying attached to our Arabic culture." A student wrote:

[T]he Arabic and English texts were similar and different at the same time. They were similar somehow in content and message . . . while they were different in word choices and audience . . . The message was clarified in the English text whereas in the Arabic text it was more detailed and complicated."

Another student wrote that in Cortas' text, "the choice of words was of a low level," and "the translator used diluted vocabulary." This is a clear reference to the lexical and syntactical differences between Arabic and English. The student writers embraced those differences at different levels of knowledge or awareness, yet their criticism or approval of one or the other worked towards their negotiating meaning and getting attuned to rhetorical modes.

Construction of Knowledge

When it comes to "constructing knowledge" (Guerra, 2008; Horner et al., 2011) of the specificities of usage in each language, students considered working with a text written in two languages as a source of enrichment. They viewed their L1 and L2/3 language(s) as valuable resources, as one of the students stated, "When we are working with several languages we are capable of saying and expressing ourselves in a more enriched and elegant way because each language can have characteristics that another one doesn't have." Another student wrote, "Both versions of the text present the reader with the same theme and ideas but each had different techniques in sending the message." A third student mentioned in the reflective essay, "using Arabic text in English course is helpful, students will understand the meaning of the text and the message that the writer wants to send. Then when they read the translation, they will have the opportunity to learn ways of writing in English." A fourth student wrote:

The aim of this course is to enrich students with English, set them on the correct path towards academic English courses, and enhance their writing for their future benefit. For me the activity which was most successful in achieving that was the translation activity. It helped clarify how to write what we thought in our mind, which is mostly in Arabic, in English. It clarified the vast differences in sentence structure; word choices; style; theme; idiomatic expressions and many more.

Students were negotiating meanings to translate effectively some Arabic excerpts into English, which expanded their communicative competence and created a space for them to express themselves more eloquently in English. They were reworking a text "in response to specific contingencies" or "social circumstances" (Horner & Lu, 2007, pp. 154–155), and were learning "language conventions with full awareness of how they are created and legitimated by use and cultural practices" (Hesford et al., 2009, p. 117). As students were comparing and contrasting L1 and L2 texts, they were constructing knowledge of how writers/translators modify their strategies to achieve rhetorical effectiveness and meet the needs of an audience from a different culture. One student pointed out in her reflection that Cortas' Arabic text uses charged and emotional words to empower her Arab audience. Another student observed that these charged expressions were lost in translation, and "made the Arabic text more like political oration, while the English text is more narrative and subjective."

Meaning Making across Language and Cultural Differences

From the examples that have been analyzed, we noticed that as our students were working in groups to decide on the best translation they could figure out for the excerpts they selected from the Arabic version of the texts. Throughout their discussions, they negotiated lexis and syntax and the cultural context within and across the different texts and audiences. We sought to adopt a pedagogical strategy that would enable them to adjust to the culture of the texts they dealt with while also considering the emotional factors that reflect the specificities of syntactical and lexical factors of L1 and L2. In this way, the classroom would be a space "to expand [students'] cultural views" (Hesford et al., 2009, p. 121) as they developed their language competence in English.

In the case of Cortas' *A World I Loved*, for example, students saw that the Arabic version contained more charged words and idiomatic expressions, which they could not easily find equivalents for to convey exactly the same emotional impact in English. One student wrote in her reflection: "Those feelings were totally shown and best described in the Arabic text '(دنيا أحببتها, مقدسي قراطس, 1960)' where the sentences were richer and more emotional. The use of charged words in [the] Arabic version clearly shows the emphasis of Cortas' purpose." This reflection shows the student's awareness of the purpose and audience in writing. It is clear that working on the Arabic text demonstrated to the student the bombastic use of Arabic diction and special expressions, as opposed to the simpler and more direct English counterparts.

In Jabra's *The First Well*, students also thought the word الكبار, which literally means "adults" in English, had more cultural connotations in Arabic. They were negotiating possible meanings like "wise," "people who were older," "those who had more wisdom," or "those who were more rational and they could learn or benefit from." They thought "adults" does not carry the cultural register as one student wrote: "the way the word [was used] in the Arabic version has its own style that was ruined in the English version." Similarly, a student wrote "I kept the word 'ya salam' an expression that means [in Arabic] that something is fascinating and amusing" since he could not find its equivalent in English. Another student wrote,

> This process was not easy; we found difficulty in translating some local linguistics . . . since the translation of such words will not reflect the exact meaning. [For example] التعريفة that is similar to pennies . . . does not reflect the true culture reflected by the original word.

Students were concerned with maintaining the cultural implications of the words and expressions, so they were consciously using strategies (Canagarajah, 2006; Grossman, 2010) while translating the Arabic text into English.

The above examples seem to resonate with the multilingual approach and are applicable in what students worked on to deal with differences among languages as "strategic and creative choices" that authors make in order to achieve "rhetorical objectives" (, 2006, as quoted in Horner & Lu, 2007, p. 149). We could see students constructing knowledge (Guerra, 2008; Horner et al., 2011) as they were responding to texts in a translingual context.

Students were also making connections and improvising ways to produce meaning across language and cultural differences (Horner et al., 2011). One Algerian student wrote in response to Cortas' text, "I recognized in those excerpts the atrocities from which, Algeria, my country suffered for more than a century under the destructive power of the same French colonizer."

Similarly, other students felt the nostalgia to the Arab culture and feared that they might be losing their cultural identity as they embrace the English Only approach. One student wrote:

We are gradually disconnecting from our Arab roots and this does not forebode a prosperous future for our Arab identities. We should be proud of our nation and embrace our cultures by using our language as a tool to prove to other countries that their languages are not more valuable than ours.

An Armenian student wrote:

Language was a mean[s] of protection for many nations in history [;] some nations are still in existence because of their commitment to their language[.] [A] very famous example [is] the Armenians that are a minority in this world but have used their language as a weapon.

These excerpts from students' writings reflect their emotional attachment to their identities and cultures, an aspect that we normally do not recognize when working with pure English texts. They reinforce the idea that as students "shuttle" between languages (Canagarajah, 2006) they notice the power of language and recognize that meaning is not fixed, making room for alternate translations.

Application, Implications, Limitations

This assignment responds to researchers' invitation to "take up language differences in composition" (Bawarshi, 2006; Horner et al., 2011). We suggest it is one example of how translingual praxis can attempt to address language difference in writing based on students' thoughtful appreciation of these variances. It provides a "favorable ecology" for students to develop their translanguaging skills (Canagarajah, 2011; Creese & Blackledge, 2010), and a safe space cultivated through the use of students' home language, to which they are often emotionally and culturally attached. Students, as such, could feel comfortable with their knowledge of their home language and could focus on constructing meaning, rather than feel anxious about producing "correct" and "standard" linguistic forms.

Such activities help students value what they already know and perceive this knowledge as an asset. It is based on the assumption that diverse linguistic backgrounds are a plus, departing from the previous view that speakers of English gain legitimacy only if they are monolingual "native" (or "native-like") speakers. Hence, learners of English who are speakers of other languages have to try, from their "inferior" and disadvantaged position, to approximate the status of a native speaker, as a result, stifling their true identity. The translingual activity, however, values the resources students have, primary among which is their multilingualism and the socio-cultural knowledge that comes with it, and allows students to embrace their identity and take pride in what they already know: their home language. It gives students a voice to share something considered valuable.

Moreover, this translingual activity helps students overcome their apprehension of writing in a second language, whose rules they have difficulty mastering, not only because it is foreign to them, but also because these rules keep shifting and oftentimes they are in the making as they are put into use. Students engage more in analyzing the lexis, the structures, and the cultural values in each idea they produce without focusing on the language errors as is often done in second language classes (Horner & Lu, 2007). They acquire the knowledge of "multiple conventions" rather than the "standard conventions" of the language. It is about acquiring the knowledge of how these conventions gain legitimacy in different historical periods, geographic locations and socio-cultural communities. It is discovering first hand that learning the conventions of one language is in many ways similar to learning the conventions of two or more different languages. More importantly, it is learning how to shift capably between different codes (be they varieties of the same or two different languages) as required by the rhetorical situation. This ability is invaluable in an increasingly globalized world, characterized by a perpetual pull between the local and global, where code-shifting, code-switching, and code-meshing have become survival skills.

This engagement of multiple languages ultimately responds to the call to pay greater attention to the problematics of translation in teaching writing (Horner et al., 2011). Thus, this assignment serves as a model of how translators, who are multilingual writers, can critically and creatively negotiate their rhetorical choices for effectiveness and communicative proficiency (Grossman, 2010). The processes that translators adopt and the strategies they employ work very well for student writers, who could borrow such processes and strategies to become more sensitive to context (cultural, academic, geographical, or historical), audience, and purpose requirements.

According to Edward Said (2002), "rhetoric and eloquence in the Arab literary tradition" (p. 222) are revered. He argues that this attitude of favoring eloquence in writing by the Arab-speaking population is, however, not favored in English speaking contexts. Whether this opinion is true or not, the practice our students received helped them deal successfully with this differ-ence and they were able to navigate between the language varieties.

Knowing that a wealth of knowledge is filtered when languages interact, it is significant to "envision and incorporate" non-native students' "multilingual and literacy repertoires as resources for learning" (Hornberger & Link, 2012, p. 274), and give them an opportunity to work with languages through a vari-ety of means before they can acquire the proficiency in English which enables them to adapt to university courses and later on to the global workplace (Sho-hamy, 2007). All excerpts from students' writing show the students' ability to express themselves using the appropriate lexis and syntax. The ability to compare and analyze texts and value the cultures they live or get exposed to is also revealed. In addition, the implications of the study on practitioners, cur-riculum designers, and the field of teaching writing and composition studies are worth mentioning.

At the macro-level, our analysis of student response to this assignment highlights the need to train students to work on more thorough and pro-found analysis of texts (be they monolingual or otherwise) to enable them to develop a more critical and conscious writing process, a subtler rhetori-cal sensitivity and a more astute ability to deal with different code shifts. It also helps students in maintaining a richer and more meaningfully learned and developed language repertoire. At the micro-level, most students showed enthusiasm and motivation to read and write about the texts they worked with. Students became aware that using the conventions of a certain language helps them reach new audiences of a different culture. As such, the activity helps in building cultural bridges. Besides, most students felt at ease in the class, reading or writing about issues and themes that matter to them (prob-lems encountered in their everyday life or nostalgic feelings); they seemed to develop a more positive self-perception, which could translate into a positive attitude towards language learning and writing.

Implications for Practitioners

It is necessary that teachers accommodate their teaching to meet students' diverse needs. Using the basic strategies of translation in a writing program would shift the focus from the "emphasis on the power of standardized lan-guages to an emphasis on the agency of language users" (Horner & Lu, 2007, p. 149) who would be able to make meaning of the language they employ. The outcomes promise benefits for writing teachers who choose to incorporate such translingual activities in their syllabi. Therefore, we encourage teachers who see the benefits of this approach to pay greater attention to the problematics of translation in teaching writing and figure out how to effectively approach language teaching in light of local conditions (Ferris, 2014). Creating the suitable environment that offers students multiple opportunities to help them "develop new habits of the mind" (Guerra, 2008, p. 301) throughout the writing process is thus recommended.

Implications for Writing Programs

The results we obtained, though in need of further verification, seem to indicate that collaboration with language departments would benefit a college writing program, thus calling for more inter- and cross-disciplinary writing programs, which incorporate more multi- and cross-language work. The aspect of writing where students draw on one another's resources and exercise positive interdependence is worth looking into. Thus, researching whether this kind of translingual activity facilitates collaborative writing processes and whether it enriches a written product is useful.

Implications for Researchers

The promising findings we obtained from our study open the door for more experimentation and research. Classroom studies need to be done that focus on the impact of using a home language and translation in a composition class, specifically in relation to meaning making, complexity of ideas, critical thinking, and linguistic forms in terms of competence and production. Though the reflections of most students in our study perceive such translingual activities positively, more focused and detailed studies are needed to find how such activities affect the actual quality of student writing.

Limitations

Yet this type of engagement presupposes a few limits to translation pedagogies. Minimally, the instructor needs to possess a knowledge of and appreciation for a plethora of suitable L1 texts that bolster the students' intellectual and emotive faculties in indulging in this kind of translingual writing, be that at the sentence-level or longer writings. Most importantly, at the programmatic level, and as many instructors prescribe to time-honored "English-only" class activities, skeptical teachers, who might view this added dimension as a "heretical" practice, would require specific encouragement and support to introduce non-English reading materials.

In programs where classes comprise very few speakers of Arabic (or other home languages), using this type of assignment might culminate in understandable resistance. True, the translingual activity employed here gave students the chance to learn the tools and strategies of translators in one small unit of the course; however, in order to check the impact, more than one activity should be experimented with over a given semester. Finally, due to our focus on merely exploring the effects translingual activities might have on students writing skills in an enrichment course, we have not carried out a systematic assessment. It might be helpful in future studies to measure, for example, via control versus experimental research methods, more accurately how this activity would impact the students' writing. The success or lack thereof of the experiment would be informed by repeating the experiment and tracing the students' performance in subsequent writing courses.

References

Bawarshi, A. (2006). Taking up language differences in composition. *College English, 68*(6), 652–656.

Canagarajah, S. A. (2002). Multilingual writers and the academic community: Towards a critical relationship. *Journal of English for Academic Purposes, 1*(1), 29–44.

Canagarajah, S. A. (2006). Toward a writing pedagogy of shuttling between languages: Learning from multilingual writers. *College English, 68*(6), 589–604. http://www.jstor.org/stable/25472177.

Canagarajah, S. A. (2011). Codemeshing in academic writing: Identifying teachable strategies of translanguaging. *The Modern Language Journal, 95*(3), 401–417. http://onlinelibrary.wiley.com.ezproxy.aub.edu.lb/doi/10.1111/j.1540–4781.2011.01207.x/abstract.

Canagarajah, S. A. (2013). Negotiating translingual literacy: An enactment. *Research in the Teaching of English, 48*(1), 40–67.

Cortas, W. (1965). اهتببحا ايند [A world I loved]. The Ahlia Publishing Company.

Cortas, W. (2009). *A world I loved*. (N. Gordimer & N. Cortas Said, Trans. & Eds.). Nation Books. (Original work published 1965)

Creese, A. & Blackledge, A. (2010). Translanguaging in the bilingual classroom: A pedagogy for learning and teaching. *The Modern Language Journal, 94*(1), 103–115.

Ferris, D. (2014). Review: "English only" and multilingualism in composition studies: Policy, philosophy, and practice. *College English, 77* (1), 73–83.

Grossman, E. (2010). *Why translation matters*. Yale University Press.

Guerra, J. C. (2008). Cultivating transcultural citizenship: A writing across communities model. *Language Arts, 85* (4), 269–304.

Hall, J. K., Cheng, A. & Carlson, M. (2006). Reconceptualizing multicompetence as a theory of language knowledge. *Applied Linguistics, 27*, 220–240.

Hesford, W., Singleton, E. & García, I. M. (2009). Laboring to globalize a first-year writing program. In D. Strickland & J. Gunner (Eds.), *The writing program interrupted: Making space for critical discourse* (pp. 113–125). Boynton/Cook Heinemann.

Hornberger, N. H. & Link, H. (2012). Translanguaging and transnational literacies in multilingual classrooms: A biliteracy lens. *International Journal of Bilingual Education and Bilingualism, 15*(3), 261–278. https://doi.org/10.1080/13670050.2012.658016.

Horner, B. & Lu, M. (2007). Resisting monolingualism in "English": Reading and writing the politics of language. In V. Ellis, C. Fox & B. Street (Eds.), *Rethinking English in schools: Towards a new and constructive stage* (pp. 141–157). Continuum.

Horner, B., Lu, M., Royster, J. J. & Trimbur, J. (2011). Language difference in writing: Toward a translingual approach. *College English, 73*(3), 303–321.

Jabra, I. J. (1987). البئر الاولى رئبئا *The first well: A beit lehem boyhood,* Jordan National Press.

Jabra, I. J. (2012). رئبئـلا ىلاولا ى *The first well: A beit lehem boyhood,* (I. J. Ballouta, Trans.) Jordan National Press. (Original work published 1987)

Leonard, R. L. (2014). Multilingual writing as rhetorical attunement. *College English, 76,* 227–247.

Ray, B. (2013). A progymnasmata for our time: Adapting classical exercises to teach translingual style. *Rhetoric Review, 32*(2), 191–209. https://www.tandfonline.com/doi/full/10.1080/07350198.2013.766853.

Said, E. W. (2002). Living in Arabic. *Raritan, 21*(4), 220.

Shohamy, E. (2007). Reinterpreting globalization in multilingual contexts. *International Multilingual Research Journal, 1*(2), 127–133.

Appendix A: English 102 Course Syllabus

American University of Beirut
Faculty of Arts and Sciences
Department of English

English 102: Enrichment Course in English
3 credit hours
Pre-requisite: English 100 or exemption

Course Description

English 102 is designed to upgrade students' overall proficiency level in English and enrich their exposure to a range of discourse. It develops fluency and accuracy of communication through reading and writing for critical thinking. Freshmen students should expect their final grade in the course to count toward their GPA. Sophomore students' final grade will only be counted toward their GPA in the semester they take the course and will later be dropped from their record.

Course Instructional Objectives and their respective Student Learning Outcomes

By the end of the semester, English 102 students will be able to:
- Communicate in a variety of settings and situations.
- Participate in group discussions and debates.

- Respond formally and informally to specific prompts on texts.
- Deliver presentations based on research and collaborative work.
- Read different genres critically.
- Identify writers' rhetorical techniques.
- Annotate, outline, summarize and paraphrase a variety of texts.
- Research self-selected and assigned topics using library and other resources.
- Compose unified, coherent and well-developed texts.
- Apply appropriate conventions of grammar and usage to develop accuracy and fluency.
- Incorporate learned information into the composition of texts.
- Draft, revise, edit and proofread written assignments.
- Reflect on own and others' writing, both for structure and content.

Appendix B: English 102 Activity, Fall 2013

Purpose:

- Compose unified, coherent and well-developed texts.
- Summarize and paraphrase a variety of texts.
- Respond formally and informally to specific prompts on texts.
- Apply appropriate conventions of grammar and usage to develop accuracy and fluency.

Task:

Read the Arabic version (pages 28–29) of "A World I Loved" by Wadad Makdisi Kortas, then work on the activities that follow: (1–1½ class sessions)

- Discuss the theme(s) raised in the text.
- Work in pairs or groups of three to discuss the following:
- Content and context
- Audience
- Sentence structure
- Word choice
- Idiomatic expressions
- Share your answers with the whole class.

Prepare an informal response to tell how the sentence structure, idiomatic expressions, and/or word choice help you come to terms with the text. Refer to evidence in the text to support your answers.

Read the English version of the same text by Wadad Makdisi Kortas, (pages 78–80), then work on the activities that follow: (1- ½ class sessions)

- Work in pairs or groups of three to discuss the following in comparison/contrast with the Arabic version: (make sure you paraphrase the ideas as you discuss them)
- Content and context
- Audience
- Sentence structure
- Word choice
- Idiomatic expressions
- Share your answers with the whole class and provide evidence from the two versions to support your answers.

From pages 79 OR 80 in the English version, choose one **paragraph** you think that it develops an important idea that appeals to you. (**Homework Assignment**)

- Circle the key words in that paragraph that enable you to form a comprehensive summary.
- Write the summary of that paragraph. (Attribute the ideas to the author)
- Revise the summary to make sure it:
- Presents a clear idea of the paragraph you have selected to summarize;
- Key words are used appropriately;
- Sentences are connected so as to create a flow between the ideas;
- Errors in grammar, spelling, and punctuation are minimal.

Develop a 250-**word response** to the idea presented in the paragraph you have summarized. Choose **ONE** of the following to include in your response:

- State why you think the idea is important/significant in our days; or why you think it is irrelevant now. Support your point of view by giving real life example(s) and by referring to the text itself for evidence.
- State how the comparison/contrast between the two versions of the text helped you (OR NOT) in understanding the text better. Justify your ideas by referring to specific evidence in the two versions.

Revise your response based on **the following checklist** to make sure you have minimal problems in content, organization and grammar.

Checklist to revise your response:

- My response relates directly to the paragraph I have summarized.
- I have stated a clear thesis statement to guide me as I develop my response.

- I have presented more than one piece of evidence to justify my ideas.
- Each sentence clearly states one idea/example.
- The sentences are logically linked to each other.
- The idea is clearly developed.
- A concluding sentence brings the response to a meaningful ending.
- Each sentence is capitalized and punctuated correctly.
- There are no run-on sentences, non-parallel structures, or fragments in the response.
- There is a correct sequence of tenses among the verbs in the response.
- There is no problem in subject-verb agreement.
- There is no problem with spelling

Note: Make sure you upload the summary and the response to Moodle by December . . . , 2013, and save a copy of your work on your USB for future use.

Write a reflective journal where you describe the process you worked on throughout the activity, analyze whether the activity has helped you achieve the learning outcomes and how, and whether you can make use of the skills and strategies you have practiced in other activities/courses.

Appendix C: English 102 Translingual Activity, Fall 2014

Purpose:

- Compose unified, coherent and well-developed texts.
- Summarize and paraphrase a variety of texts.
- Respond formally and informally to specific prompts on texts.
- Apply appropriate conventions of grammar and usage to develop accuracy and fluency.

Tasks:

- Read the Arabic version (pages 38–39) of *THE FIRST WELL by Jabra IbrahimJabra.*
- Discuss the theme(s) in the text (such as background, traditions, lifestyle, characters, etc.)
- Work in teams to discuss: sentence structures, word choices, idiomatic expressions, figurative expressions, etc., used in the text
- Share your answers with the class, providing specific examples from the text to support your answers.

Translate into English the second paragraph of p. 39 from the Arabic text. In teams, discuss individual translations, focusing on how you negotiated your sentence structures, word-choices, idiomatic, figurative and cultural choices, and any other feature the team deems interesting. Be sure to discuss challenges and benefits that you may have experienced.

(Individual translations prepared prior to team discussions).

Continued Activity (on translated text into English)

Read the English translation of the same text by Jabra (translated by Mohammad Shaheen, pages 26–27).

Tasks:

- Work in teams to discuss the same text features that you applied on the Arabic version (sentence structures, word choices, idiomatic/figurative expressions, etc.)
- Delineate items that constitute SIMILARITIES and/or DIFFERENCES for each category
- Discuss the extent to which those SIMILARITIES/DIFFERENCES constitute a change in meaning from the original Arabic text. Give examples on items that change the meaning, and other examples on items that do not change the original meaning.

Homework Assignment:

- Write an analysis paper of approximately 500 words on how the activity (in all its stages) was useful to you. You may reflect on linguistic, stylistic and/or thematic aspects. Refer to your team notes on negotiating choices to provide supportive examples.

11 Developing Translingual Dispositions to Negotiate Gatekeeping in the Graduate Writing Center

Sarah Summers
Rose-Hulman Institute of Technology

Writing programs must respond to the unmet—and mostly unstudied—needs of multilingual graduate writers. Consequently, programs are pulled between the pressure to help these students navigate academic writing and the desire to help them challenge linguistic norms. Using transcripts of graduate writing center (GWC) tutorials with multilingual graduate writers, I analyze how tutors enact translingual pedagogies that honor writers' linguistic backgrounds and acknowledge academic gatekeeping norms. Specifically, I examine tutorials that focus on building confidence, making language use transparent, and rethinking higher- and lower-order concerns. These strategies, I argue, help multilingual writers identify as scholars who can both fulfill and challenge academic writing expectations.

Keywords: graduate writing, writing centers, translingual tutoring, international students

During an interview in Liberty University's graduate writing center (GWC), Kwan explained that for international graduate students like him, "writing is the most important. I can just keep a silence in the classroom. But I cannot keep the silence in my paper." In other words, writing requires him to demonstrate a voice. Drawing on transcripts of GWC tutorials, I demonstrate how translingual dispositions observed between tutors and writers help international multilingual graduate students cultivate this voice. This chapter helps to define the needs and priorities of international graduate students writing in English—a population not yet comprehensively studied by translingual scholars—as they relate to, and sometimes challenge, translingual scholarship. This chapter also situates these needs within the context of writing programs and larger institutional goals. This connection between scholarship, writers'

DOI: https://doi.org/10.37514/INT-B.2020.0438.2.11

and tutors' experiences, and institutional context is particularly important in making these findings applicable to writing programs, both international and national, that employ English-medium instruction. By understanding how these theoretical and practical factors influence one another in this example case, writing programs can determine how to best leverage ongoing translanguaging conversations and pedagogies within their own contexts. For example, as reflected in both U.S. writing center scholarship and the content of the European Writing Centers Association Conference (2016), writing centers, like Liberty's GWC, are often at the heart of the struggle between helping students navigate academic gatekeeping norms and the desire to be sites of progressive language policy.

Despite the breadth of work on multilingual writers in writing centers— and general agreement that multilingual graduate students can benefit from more focused writing center and writing program efforts (Brooks & Swain, 2008; Ferris & Thaiss, 2011; Jordan & Kedrowicz, 2011)—very little attention has been given to multilingual graduate students specifically. Multilingual graduate writers have unique needs and those needs, on the surface, seem to run counter to progressive attitudes toward language, including translanguaging. For example, multilingual writers in GWCs often ask for help with sentence-level writing, grammar, and error correction (Phillips, 2013; Zhang, 2011). As the introduction to this collection establishes, one of the frameworks for understanding a translingual disposition is acknowledging the limited visibility of translingual processes in final writing products. This chapter shows how a translingual disposition can lead to a seemingly "standardized" product. This tension is particularly important to capture for multilingual graduate students whose professional careers depend on their ability to create standard academic writing, even as we acknowledge that those norms are beginning to change (Canagarajah, 2002; Lillis & Curry, 2004, 2006; Tardy, 2003; Thaiss & Zawacki, 2006).

In this chapter, I argue that the flexible and open habits of mind that characterize translingual pedagogies allow Liberty's tutors to inhabit a middle space between these two poles of linguistic gatekeeping and resistance to linguistic norms. Moreover, I demonstrate how multilingual graduate writer's priorities and requests necessitate the kind of negotiations that set the stage for the translingual dispositions that I observed. As both Canagarajah's (2013) definition of translingual communication as orientation and this collection's framework emphasize, the negotiation of meaning is at the heart of translanguaging. That spirit of negotiation extends to the practices of setting goals and expectations for tutoring sessions. As this study demonstrates, when both tutors and writers are willing to negotiate—both in terms of textual meaning and the meaning (or purpose) of the tutorial, translingual dispositions emerge.

The ability to write technically correct prose not only determines international graduate students' ability to succeed professionally, but also influences their confidence as writers and scholars. Beyond external barriers, Elizabeth Erichsen and Doris Bolliger (2011) also found that language differences contribute to internal barriers to success, including anxiety, stress, and a loss of confidence among international graduate students that create a sense of social and academic isolation. In these contexts, style, grammar, and word choice are no longer lower-order concerns, but instead represent ways to help students gain a particular kind of institutional power that allows them to pass through academic and professional gates. That these gates remain, in part, controlled by markers of linguistic difference is no doubt problematic, but, however much writing centers wish to strive for a translingual disposition, they cannot do so at the expense of the needs of graduate writers in the present. Thus, GWCs offer spaces to reconsider not only how different populations of students prioritize writing problems—and therefore necessitate a reprioritization of writing center practices—but also how to integrate a focus on those problems with discussions about students' scholarly identity and the mutual respect and inquiry that characterize a "translingual approach" (Horner et al., 2011).

Throughout this chapter, I rely on Bruce Horner, Min-Zhan Lu, Jacqueline Jones Royster, and John Trimbur's (2011) definition of a translingual approach as one that "encourages reading with patience, respect for perceived differences within and across languages, and an attitude of deliberative inquiry" (p. 304). The tutors I observed for this chapter all exhibit these traits in their consultations, despite the fact they had not received explicit training in translingual dispositions toward writing.[1] The value of these transcripts is that they demonstrate how translingual principles—"patience," "respect," and "inquiry"—can help tutors navigate a graduate writing culture that is obsessed with error, correctness, and standards. The language of error, then, is not absent from these transcripts, and I never witnessed tutors encouraging writers to create linguistically heterogeneous documents. Though Horner et

---

[1]   At the time of this study, Liberty's GWC tutors received no explicit training about translingual pedagogies. To prepare them to work with multilingual students, they read "Helping ESL Writers Grow" (Green, 1998) and "Reading an ESL Writer's Text" (Matsuda & Cox, 2011), discussed Ferris' (2002) concept of treatable errors, and viewed *Writing Across Borders*. Most of their training happened on-the-job and through informal conversations during staff meetings.

al. (2011) argue that the concept of "Standard Written English" is "bankrupt" (p. 305), I demonstrate throughout the chapter its very real consequences for graduate writers—consequences felt by the GWC. This chapter examines how what I have identified as translingual dispositions—though sometimes imperfect or incomplete—can grow organically from relationships between tutors and multilingual writers that are built on a foundation of respect. These dispositions—perhaps especially because they arise naturally from relationships with peers, rather than being imposed from theory—also help tutors honor linguistic diversity within a larger discourse that reifies standard academic writing.

In the sections that follow, I first provide context both for Liberty University's GWC and for my role and methods as a researcher. I then describe and analyze the practices I observed between GWC tutors and multilingual writers that allow tutors to address the expressed needs of clients within the larger pedagogical goals of the writing center, and I connect these practices to translingual pedagogies. I conclude by considering the broader applications of these practices, and the ways writing programs might foster more translingual dispositions across their campuses.

Institutional Context

Liberty University's GWC began as a response to a Southern Association of Colleges and Schools (SACS) accreditation requirement. According to the "Quality Enhancement Plan" (QEP) (Runion, 2006), which outlines Liberty's response to SACS, a university-wide assessment found that "on average, Liberty's first year residential graduate students needed writing skills training in areas including (but not limited to) organization structure, clarity of content, and grammatical or mechanical errors" (p. 5). Moreover, a survey distributed to graduate faculty found that the majority of faculty members "were unsatisfied with respect to the scholarly and discipline-specific syntactical writing skills of their students" (Runion, 2006, p. 7). With these problems in mind, the university outlined a five-year plan for improving graduate writing, which included required graduate-level writing courses, professional development for graduate faculty, and a graduate writing center. The GWC, which opened in 2006, offers free, hour-long appointments to students from across Liberty's residential master's and doctoral programs.

Liberty's focus on conservative ministry and counseling degrees contributes to the international student population at the university and, thus, at the writing center. Over two-thirds of the GWC's returning clients are international students. Many of these students are from South Korea, which has "linguistic and rhetorical traditions markedly different than those of the U.S." (Jordan & Kedrowicz, 2011, n.p.). Kwan, the doctoral student in counseling from South Korea, whom I quoted at the beginning of the chapter, explains that many South Korean students come to Liberty to study theology or seminary because of the large American missionary presence in South Korea:

> The first American missionaries had a very conservative theology, and there was so many Koreans who want to study conservative theology. Liberty is one of the most conservative universities in America. That's the reason why many Korean students want to come here.

Recognizing the needs of this large group of students, Liberty's GWC employs Kwan as a liaison who translates for Korean students during appointments and helps both clients and tutors become more attuned to differing norms between American and Korean academic cultures. The GWC also employs two international students as tutors, including Michael, who is a Master's of Divinity student from South Korea. Many of the tutors—international and native to the US—see themselves as cultural informants who help initiate international students to American academic and social customs.

For international students, the typical needs for graduate students—to learn new genres and become part of new discourse communities—are layered with new cultural norms and differing levels of familiarity with Standard Written English. As a result, GWC tutors spend many of their consultations helping students with academic literacy, such as research strategies, and language issues, such as grammar and word choice. The GWC's tutors have grown to see meeting these needs as an integral part of their work in helping graduate students become confident, independent writers and scholars—a goal that I address more specifically in later sections of this chapter. The perception outside the GWC, however, as reflected both in institutional documents and in faculty attitudes reported by the GWC director, is that these consultations and workshops are meant to remediate weak writers. This perception reflects what Harry Denny (2010) refers to as the "othering" of second-language writers. He defines othering as a practice "either explicit or lurking just under the surface. *They* are a problem that requires solving, an irritant and frustration that resists resolution" (2010, p. 119). Thus, Liberty's GWC has the complex challenge of meeting the needs of international students without "othering" them.

The QEP itself, while integral in establishing a resource for graduate writers, is not blameless in the remedial perception of the center or in the othering of multilingual writers. Both in terms of language and execution, the plan contributes to an institutional view of what it terms "developmental writers" as others who need to be remediated and establishes the GWC as the frontline for that remediation. For example, the QEP describes the GWC as a site that can "bear some of the burden the QEP imposes on faculty members' time" (Runion, 2006, p. 35). The burden, as the paragraph explains, arises from the obligation to "diagnose," "ferret out," and "fix" student errors and problems (Runion, 2006, p. 35). Thus, the QEP represents a struggle between the importance of "creating a culture of professional writing" for graduate students that is supported through a variety of resources, and the perceived need to "fix" students who do not meet the assumed standards of professional writing. Liberty's GWC is at the heart of this struggle.

Methods

I came to study multilingual writing pedagogies because I was familiar with the type of struggle Liberty's GWC faces. As the graduate student coordinator of Penn State University's GWC, I collaborated with many international graduate writers who felt anxious about their academic writing ability and, in turn, their potential as graduate students and scholars. Writing center scholarship suggests a range of best practices for supporting multilingual students (Bruce & Rafoth, 2009; Harris, 1997; Harris & Silva, 1993; Myers, 2003; Severino, 2009; Thonus, 2004), with very little written about multilingual graduate students. Thus, I selected Liberty as a case study site because the GWC director indicated, in response to an initial survey, that over 60 per cent of their recurring clients are multilingual students and that they employ multilingual students as consultants. As such, Liberty is a data-rich site for investigating the role of linguistic differences and the resulting pedagogies in GWC consultations. Moreover, Liberty is a small, private institution with a religious affiliation and thus provides a unique institutional perspective that extends the current picture of graduate writing beyond the traditional, high-profile research institution.

Over three days in February 2013, I visited Liberty's GWC and conducted interviews with three administrators, five tutors, and two clients. I observed and audio recorded four consultations, two with international students. Table 11.1 provides information about the participants included in this chapter, all of whom have been assigned pseudonyms with the exception of the director. During those three days, I also attended two workshops hosted by the GWC and one meeting of the semester-long required writing course for graduate students, and participated in informal conversations with administrators and tutors. The case study was part of a larger,

IRB-approved study. I approached my data using grounded theory, which begins with themes in the data, rather than an external theory, and allows researchers to see data collection, analysis, and theory building as a recursive, open-ended process.[2] Thus, rather than beginning with translingualism and trying to fit tutors' practices into that theory, translingualism entered at the end of the process as one potential lens for locating the practices I observed in a larger scholarly conversation.

Table 11.1. Liberty University case study participants.

Name/Pseudonym	Role
Tess Stockslager	GWC Director
Jim	GWC Tutor Graduate Writing Course Instructor
Eric	GWC Tutor M.A. Student, English
Brittany	GWC Tutor M.A. Student, Counseling
Michael	GWC Tutor International Student, Seminary
Kwan	Korean Liaison to the GWC International Ph.D. Student, Counseling
Marlena	GWC Client International M.A. Student, Counseling
Sun	GWC Client International M.A. Student, Counseling

Using Translingual Pedagogies to Reach Beyond the Remedial

In the sections that follow, I analyze the ways that Liberty tutors attempt

---

2   Although I used Dedoose, a software program that allows users to visualize the frequency of codes, I did not arrive to my conclusions by counting codes. I share the rationale for not counting codes that Creswell (2007) provides in *Qualitative Inquiry and Research Design*. As he explains, "counting conveys a quantitative orientation of magnitude and frequency contrary to qualitative research. In addition, a count conveys that all codes should be given equal emphasis and it disregards that the passages coded may actually represent contradictory views" (p. 152). Thus, this chapter represents the richest and most relevant examples from my research.

to meet the needs of their clients while moving beyond merely "fixing" their work or "remediating" them. While tutors' goals do not come from an explicit focus on translingual pedagogy, their training materials reflect many of the attitudes that invite a translingual disposition, including identifying one's own biases and assumptions and emphasizing respect and understanding. Prior to their first consultations, tutors read a document called "GWC Tutor Guide to Working with International and ESL Students." Rather than provide specific tasks or strategies to students (those are discussed in relationship to readings and reflection on tutorials), the document focuses on assumptions and attitudes. For example, the document reminds tutors that "Many of our students have previous graduate degrees and may have excellent writing and/or speaking proficiency in their native languages; they may be accomplished preachers or published authors." In other words, the document reminds tutors that multilingual graduate students are experts in their fields and in their native languages, which sets the tone for a mutual exchange between peers who both have something to offer in the tutorial. The document also reminds them that there's "no single correct way" to conduct a tutoring session, thus positioning both the tutor and the writer as individuals who must negotiate the trajectory of their session together. This document, while it never references translingualism, still encourages the habits of mind and communication that help tutors and writers together build relationships that reflect a translingual disposition of mutual respect and negotiation.

There are three ways that the practice and foundational attitudes of Liberty's GWC encourage translingual dispositions (even if they ultimately result in conventional products). First, Liberty's GWC blends writing center practice and the values of their campus environment, which privileges fields like ministry and counseling, as a way to build writers' confidence. Many tutors mentioned confidence building as a primary goal in their consultations, and they see it as a way to make "better writers" while still improving students' writing. Second, I argue that Liberty's GWC rethinks the traditional categories of higher-order concerns (HOCs) and lower-order concerns (LOCs) based on the expressed needs and wishes of their multilingual clients. They recognize that, for example, word choice might represent a HOC for an international student, and they have developed strategies for addressing these concerns that move beyond merely correcting an error. Finally, I argue that Liberty tutors use both of these strategies—confidence building and rethinking HOCs and LOCs—to attempt to help clients see themselves as scholars and write in a way that reflects their place in the scholarly community, perhaps a concern of the highest order for graduate students.

Building Writers' Confidence

All of the tutors I interviewed mentioned building writers' confidence as a primary part of their role in the GWC. As Brittany put it, "I think it's just making people feel more confident in their ability to write a paper without someone else's help." Confidence building, then, becomes a version of "make better writers, not better writing"—a common writing center mantra—by focusing on helping the writer feel able to complete writing tasks—something with which international students often struggle. Similarly, international students often feel insecure about their language proficiency and the ability for their speaking and writing to fit in with their native-speaking peers. This anxiety reveals itself even during writing center consultations, as it did in this appointment between Brittany and international student Marlena:

> **Marlena:** It seems that the author did not do any experiment, any metho- . . . how do you call that?
>
> **Brittany:** Method section.
>
> **Marlena:** Method. He just did research about how Christianity is . . . how do I say this? Sorry.
>
> **Brittany:** That's okay.

Marlena apologized several times during the consultations when she paused to think of or ask for words, suggesting that even with Brittany she felt self-conscious about her language skills. Michael confirmed that this lack of confidence in speaking with peers is often a problem for international students at Liberty. He finds that the students he consults with in Korean are often much less nervous than students who cannot conduct their consultations in their native language, despite what Michael describes as their "substantial ability to actually say what they want." Despite this ability, he explains, international students often have "this intense nervousness to explain their idea in English, because they feel like they just can't talk." Thus, building confidence is important in helping students overcome nervousness or anxiety with tutors and for helping students overcome barriers—like writer's block and writing anxiety—outside the classroom that may hinder their academic success.

At the most surface level, the tutors in the GWC build students' confidence by verbally reassuring them throughout appointments. Often praise is as simple as Jim telling a writer, "I think that's a great idea," when she comes up with a new way to focus her topic, or Eric reassuring a writer that her sentence structure is "actually very good." Tutors also praise good writing habits, like students bringing a draft in well before the due date, or giving themselves plenty of time to do research. To allay writers' anxieties, tutors often also draw on their roles as peers to reassure writers that the difficulties they experience are normal. As Romy Clark and Roz Ivanic (1997) argue, "it is important to share insights about the process and practices of writing with learner writers as soon as possible and to let them voice their worries about them" (p. 233). In Liberty's GWC, writers can express their anxiety about writing and be met with reassurance about the difficulty of managing the writing process. In fact, tutors' willingness to put themselves in the position of "peer" and relate to the difficulties of writing in graduate school is one reason that Stockslager believes GWCs are places that build confidence: "It's just this [writing center] environment; I think it builds confidence for a lot of people."

The most common strategy employed by tutors to build writers' confidence is listening. As Brittany, who is working toward a graduate degree in crisis counseling explains,

> Through my experience in practicing counseling sessions and really just reflecting back to people, if they ask me a question, I'll be like, "Well, what do you really think about that? What is it that you noticed?" rather than just telling them [what to think or notice].

In other words, Brittany and others use genuine listening to help students discover their own ideas or reflect ideas back to students. Recent rhetorical scholarship has recovered the practice of listening as not just one-sided reception but as an active, engaged rhetorical practice. For example, feminist rhetorician Krista Ratcliffe (2005) describes what she terms "rhetorical listening" as "a trope for interpretive invention" (p. 17). For Ratcliffe, listening is not just receptive; it can be generative and lead to moments of rhetorical production. Cheryl Glenn, feminist historiographer and rhetorician, similarly redefines silence as productive in *Unspoken: A Rhetoric of Silence* (2004). She argues that a "rhetorical silence of careful listening" (p. 153) changes the goal of rhetorical interaction from one of persuasion to one of understanding that can "readjust relations of power" (p. 156). When tutors listen, then, they give writers the power to express their ideas or their anxieties about writing in an atmosphere that encourages understanding and invention. Indeed, one of the central goals of Horner et al. (2011) translingual approach is "honoring the power of all language users to shape language to specific ends" (p. 305). Rhetorical listening, then, is one way to demonstrate to writers that they have linguistic power because it removes the perceived barriers created by linguistic difference and creates a mutual context for communication—an essential feature to enable translingual dispositions.

Rethinking HOCs and LOCs

Students' feelings about writing are not the only issue that Liberty's GWC reframes as a higher order concern. My observations reveal that Liberty's tutors are, like many writing center tutors, highly attuned to the distinctions between Higher Order Concerns (HOCs), such as argument, structure, and evidence and Lower Order Concerns (LOCs), such as word choice, grammar, and formatting, as well as the benefits and pitfalls of "fixing" grammar. For example, Michael explained that he tries to leave grammar to the end of a session, particularly if he notices larger structural problems with a student's argument. This approach is consistent with the traditional writing center philosophy to address HOCs over LOCs. However, the tutors also realize that what seem like LOCs in general writing center scholarship may, in fact, be HOCs in practice. As I suggest in my introduction, sentence-level concerns are often a priority for international students. The stakes are too high for graduate writers, as Phillips (2013) suggests, for graduate students to adopt policies that merely resist standards or refuse to help students correct their work: "Sentence-level problems—even those that tutors might judge to be minor or moderate—may have serious implications for [multilingual graduate writers'] professional advancement" (n.p.).

Translingual dispositions provide yet another way of understanding the value of attention to style. Horner et al. (2011) call for "*more*, not less, conscious and critical attention to how writers deploy diction, syntax, and style" but not in order to force students' work to conform to a standard (p. 304). Instead, this focus on style creates a rhetorical opportunity to consider audience, purpose, and the potential effects of language (Horner et al., 2011). In order to best navigate institutional demands, pedagogical goals, and student needs, GWC tutors may have to embrace multiple approaches. That is, they can help students identify a standard while modeling the rhetorical engagement that demonstrates the power of language. This section reveals the strategies that Liberty's tutors use to treat word choice and citation style as HOCs worthy of engaged collaboration between tutor and writer. As the following consultation between Eric and Sun shows, this collaboration ranges from more directive correcting to less directive conversations about choices the writer has.

As Eric explains in an interview, he does sometimes correct students' work: "Yes, I correct. I read it [aloud], usually I read it incorrectly, and then I tell them or I show them . . . I give them a demonstration of what needs to be changed and usually explain why." I observed Eric using this technique in his appointment with Sun. Sometimes—most often with missing articles— he just offered corrections without any explanation. Articles, for example, are incredibly difficult for non-native English speakers to master and explaining the complicated rules regarding articles would likely not have a lasting effect (Ferris, 2002; Myers, 2003). In most other cases, however, Eric would point out the error, explain how to fix it, and explain the rule, so that the student might be able to better understand the mistake. Thus, Eric did not merely edit the papers; he tried to also offer a way for Sun to understand a mistake and potentially correct it herself in the future. For example, in her text, Sun had written, "The actions people might chose to do might harm themselves." Eric explained that chose is the past tense of the verb, and that "choose" would make the most sense in the sentence: "The actions people choose to do might harm themselves," and that keeps us in the present tense, because you're talking theoretically." Eric, in other words, provides a correction and then an explanation that the writer might be able to recall the next time she uses the verb "to choose." Sun responded that she understood, and they continued with the document. A purely translingual approach would not have treated Sun's document this way. Horner et al. (2011) argue that "the possibility of writer error is reserved as an interpretation of last resort" (p. 304). Thus, Eric's calls upon a range of approaches, some—like the former—more corrective and others, like the following example, more deliberative.

Other kinds of difference, particularly those related to syntax or idiomatic speech, inspired much more collaborative, engaged discussions between Eric and Sun—the kind of "deliberative inquiry" called for in a "translingual approach" (Horner et al., 2011, p. 304). For instance, when Sun arrived, she specifically requested help with word choice, explaining, "I just don't know what are the words that can be used . . . So maybe I will keep using the same words, or I will like to try more variety of words." With this request in mind, Eric addressed word choice specifically throughout the appointment. Rather than merely correct poor word choice, however, he engaged in conversations with Sun about her choices, as he does in the following example. In a sentence about counselors using rational thinking as opposed to Biblical examples, Sun had used the verb "alternate," which confused Eric.

> Eric: Well, let's see. Okay. So you're saying that, I mean, basically that when people are getting counseled, they should alternate rational thinking with Biblical truth? They should use both?

> Sun: For a counseling session which is not Biblically based, they don't need to use the Bible. But if it is for a Christian counselor, they would use Bible truth because that's what they believe.

Eric: Okay, so . . . are you saying "alternate" as in "use both one and the other," you know, use them like, you know, you alternate between going to class one day and going to a difference class on a different day?

Sun: Oh, no. No. Alternate with negative with the positive.

Eric: Okay, yeah. I think that's what we were getting confused on. I think you mean "alternate," which is the same word, same spelling, just, basically, used differently. So you're saying the Biblical thinking should be the alternative to purely rational thinking?

Sun: Should be substituted. The negative thoughts should be substituted with the Biblical thinking.

Eric: Okay, say that one more time.

Sun: The negative thoughts, which are stated here, should be substituted with the Biblical truth.

Eric: Okay, okay. I get it. Okay. So not "alternate" as in "switch back and forth" but as "substitute." So that's probably the word you want to use there. "Substitute."

In this exchange, Eric does not simply correct what he perceives to be a mistake in word choice. Doing so would, in part, assume meaning on the part of the writer—meaning that he seems to be unsure about. Instead, he adopts a more collaborative stance and engages the writer in a conversation about her meaning. Throughout the conversation, he employs several strategies. For example, he provides a definition of the word "alternate" and then gives an accessible example about alternating between classes. Immediately, the student realizes that her intended meaning does not match the meaning as Eric understands it. Eventually, the student comes up with her own word—substitute—as a way to replace the confusing "alternate," which could be a verb or an adjective.

By treating word choice as a higher order concern—one that deserves engaged collaboration—as opposed to a lower order concern to be left to the end of the appointment, Eric accomplishes a number of goals, all of which address Sun's stated need to improve her word choice. First, he models the rhetorical effects of word choice by discussing his evolving understanding of the meaning of the passage. This modeling is Canagarajah's (2013) definition of "translingual literacy" in action; it demonstrates shifting meanings and the importance of mutual influence on both composing and understanding texts.

Second, he explains the possible range of meanings and parts of speech of the word alternate. Finally, he helps Sun perform the process of making decisions between possible word choices by asking her to rephrase her original meaning. This leads Sun to come up with a new—and clearer—word choice on her own. Thus, Eric does not just correct Sun's passage, but gives her a more focused understanding of the word in question and collaborates with her to give her strategies for addressing word choice in the future.

Word choice might seem remedial, particularly in the larger contexts of graduate writing, which includes publishing articles and drafting dissertations. However, Liberty's tutors realize that style and mechanics represent real concerns for students. Working with multilingual dissertators has created opportunities for Liberty tutors to rethink HOCs and LOCs so that appointments meet the needs of the student population that use the GWC. And rather than treat these students as remedial or merely "fix" errors, as the observations described above demonstrate, Liberty's tutors use these appointments as opportunities to model the processes that academic writers use, from considering the rhetorical effects of word choice to matching a citation question to the answer in a style manual.

Moving from Style to Scholarship

By building writers' confidence and paying attention to the issues of grammar and style that often serve gate-keeping functions in the academy, Liberty's GWC tutors are not just remediating students or proofreading their work. Within these conversations about style, Liberty's tutors also use strategies to attempt to help initiate writers into a scholarly community, and allow anxious and sometimes underprepared writers to see themselves as scholars. Because international and returning adult students may feel isolated (Erichsen & Bolliger, 2011), helping these students see themselves as scholars and represent that scholarly identity in their writing is an invaluable role for the GWC. Moreover, this role allows the GWC to have a more holistic goal in mind while still addressing LOCs. I observed tutors making this move from addressing style to addressing issues of scholarship in two ways. First, they provide academic vocabulary to writers. Second, they give writers strategies for developing a distinct scholarly voice.

Although international students may be unfamiliar with academic jargon, Liberty's tutors do not talk down to their clients or omit this jargon from their appointments. Instead, they give students access to these terms that are often markers of belonging to an academic community. In fact, helping graduate students develop a distinctive scholarly voice also often requires sharing particular language with them. Myers (2003) suggests, for example, that international students "may require macro-organizing language . . . or other language to signal sequencing of information across a text, provide background for contrast, or announce the dimensions in which the topic will be presented (e.g., whether the writer is going to evaluate, analyze, report, or critique). The language and the writing are inseparable" (Myers, 2003, p. 52). While this macro language is important across undergraduate and graduate writing, it is especially crucial to graduate students, whose careers hinge on their ability to make original arguments while aligning with and distinguishing themselves from other scholars. In other words, graduate writers are expected not only to articulate the scholarly conversation but also to articulate their position within that conversation. Brittany described it as moving writers to "the next level of paper writing," and accomplished this by modeling ways for Marlena to distinguish her scholarly voice from others during their appointment.

One of the strategies Brittany used was to give Marlena specific vocabulary for indicating the source of each of her arguments. For example, after reading a passage that left her unclear about whether Marlena was explaining another author's work or her own interpretation, Brittany said, "I think what the big thing is, is just making sure that whoever is reading it understands that this is the author's point, not your point. So, saying things like 'the author found' or 'the author researched.'" Later in the appointment, Brittany repeats these phrases for Marlena, "Even just saying, like, 'the author stated,' or 'the author found,' those sorts of [phrases]." Pointing to very specific passages in Marlena's work, Brittany is providing the kind of macro-level signaling language that is typical of academic writing but perhaps unfamiliar to Marlena.

Beyond providing sign-posting language, Brittany also encourages Marlena to more clearly develop her own voice throughout the paper. The assignment, a critical review of an article, asks for the writer's analysis of and interaction with the main ideas of the article. Marlena, however, feels uncomfortable moving beyond summary: "I was just cautious on not to push myself on saying so much." Brittany encourages her to think about her own response to the article:

> **Brittany:** Your interaction would be a combination between the two [your ideas and the article]. It would be how you understood the article, like the lessons learned, and how you understand love differently.

> **Marlena:** It doesn't have to be . . . like I have to research, cite it, and all that?

> **Brittany:** Not necessarily. It would depend on if you pulled the statement from the article saying, like, 'This is what he says, and I believe that this . . .'"

Again, Brittany models a way for Marlena to use scholarly patterns of language that mark the difference between the author's voice and her own opinion. Simultaneously, she reassures Marlena that her opinion is a valuable source of critique in a review and does not necessarily have to depend on research. During the appointment, Marlena expresses clear opinions about the theme of Biblical love, but she does not use conventional academic markers to signal those opinions in her work. Brittany helps Marlena to develop a more distinct scholarly voice by modeling for her how to separate her own ideas from those she is analyzing.

Brittany often seems to focus on smaller, sentence-level concerns. However, she is able to translate these concerns to larger issues of the kind of voice markers that are expected in academic writing, particularly graduate-level academic writing. Thus, even as she seems to be focusing on word choice or transition phrases, those phrases actually model for inexperienced graduate writers how to write their way into academic discourse.

Together, these strategies—confidence-building, rethinking lower- and higher-order concerns, and recognizing style as a way to address scholarly identity—help Liberty's GWC meet the expressed needs of clients while also providing strategies to enhance their academic and professional writing style more holistically. As Phillips (2013) argues, GWCs "need to explore ways of providing support for writers' whole texts—from the first word to the complete paper in all of its disciplinary situatedness—and for the whole writing process, from research design to editing" (p. 5). By combining sentence-level concerns with larger issues of scholarly discourse and a sense of academic belonging, Liberty's GWC tutors move toward this holistic approach to attempt to meet the range of scholarly needs for their populations of graduate students.

Applications

Tutor training presents the most direct applications of reframing the goals of writing center sessions to include LOCs, issues of style, and affective dimensions like building writers' confidence. The tutors in my study had no specific exposure to translingualism; instead, they cultivated these strategies through intensive experience with multilingual graduate writers. Tutors would no doubt benefit, however, from reading work on translingualism and discussing how it might influence their practices as tutors. Using transcripts of tutorials (with consent) and analyzing them for translingual moments might also help tutors see that the dispositions cultivated in a translingual approach are already very much a part of the collaborative spirit of a writing center. Those discussions should also include reflections on the limitations of translingualism and, returning to the exchange between Eric and Sun, considerations of when "error" is an appropriate construct for graduate writers.

A second and equally important application of this chapter is a reconsideration of the (often unwritten) rules and policies of writing centers, particularly at the graduate level. A blanket policy not to edit work, for example, or training tutors to exclusively address HOCs and leave LOCs for the final five minutes of a session might not best meet the needs of multilingual graduate writers. A "respect for perceived differences within and across languages" (Horner et al. 2011, p. 304) also means a respect for perceived differences in priorities. Part of the deliberation and collaboration inherent in a tutorial should be exploring priorities, making those priorities and their rationales transparent, and negotiating how tutors can best help writers respond to issues of style and syntax.

Conclusion

Writing centers, particularly those that serve graduate students, are often pulled between wanting to be sites of progressive language policy and needing to acknowledge the standards of their institutions and of professional and academic writing that have real stakes for writers. Bringing a translingual disposition to writing center work, particularly as tutors help writers build confidence and cultivate a scholarly voice, can help tutors better navigate these tensions. While translingual theory certainly has a place in tutor training, as this chapter demonstrates, emphasizing respect and the truly mutual capacity of tutors and writers to make meaning can create the conditions for translingual dispositions to develop organically. One potential strategy would be to allow these dispositions to develop and then to introduce them to tutors, allowing them to name and more consciously develop their translingual dispositions. Bringing attention to translingual dispositions in tutoring can enhance writing center praxis in at least three ways:

- Revealing new areas of scholarship, including applied linguistics, and rhetorical studies of listening and silence, that can complement and inform writing center practice and scholarship.
- Challenging default dichotomies, like directive or indirective tutoring or HOCs and LOCs, by providing suggested practices that value

flexibility and a range of practices to meet the needs of individual writers.

- Encouraging tutors and writing center administrators to identify and articulate norms in academic writing, which may make them more aware of generic conventions and how and when those conventions can be subverted.

Writing centers and writing programs more broadly can also benefit from the active promotion of translingual dispositions. Often writing centers, particularly those that serve a large population of international students, carry a remedial stigma that causes other writers and faculty to resist writing center services (Isaacs, 2011). One way Liberty has tried to address this problem is to expand their services as cultural ambassadors. As Kwan explains, "I sometimes make PowerPoint for faculty members [about] how they can understand Korean [students]." These kinds of projects, which translate what the writing center knows about its clients to faculty who teach these students, can recast the writing center as a resource for helping writing programs and institutions better understand the linguistic backgrounds and resources that their students bring to the classroom. The GWC, then, becomes a site of research and produces knowledge that aids both writers and the university.

Localized research projects might also help change the campus perception of international students as remedial. As Paul Matsuda (2010) explains, despite a perception that students acculturated in academic writing should be the norm, in reality, "the presence of language differences is the default." Thus, academic writing could—perhaps should—represent a larger variation of language use and scholarly voices. Min-Zhan Lu (1994) advocates a "way of teaching which neither overlooks the students' potential lack of knowledge and experience in reproducing the dominant codes of academic discourses *nor* dismisses the writer's potential social, political, and linguistic interest in modifying these codes" (p. 449). This approach toward the teaching of writing, she argues, encourages innovative language use and a broader range of rhetorical options for writers. The GWC could play a leading role in shaping institutional attitudes toward language difference and in determining what standards best capture the range of linguistic and academic diversity among an institution's students. A shift in perception—of both the GWC and the students it serves—ultimately would allow the writing center to embrace the hybrid space between institutional standards and a wholesale rejection of those standards by helping students work within established standards while leading the way in reshaping and rethinking them—a truly translingual goal.

References

Brooks, L. & Swain, M. (2008). Languaging in collaborative writing: Creation of and response to expertise. In A. Mackey & C. Polio (Eds.), *Multiple perspectives on interaction: Second language research* (pp. 58–85). Routledge.

Bruce, S. & Rafoth, B. (Eds.). (2009). *ESL writers: A guide for writing center tutors.* Boynton/Cook.

Canagarajah, A. S. (2002). *A geopolitics of academic writing.* University of Pittsburgh Press.

Canagarajah, S. A. (2013). *Translingual practices: Lingua Franca English and global citizenship.* Routledge.

Clark, R. & Ivanic, R. (1997). *The politics of writing.* Routledge.

Creswell, J. W. (2006). *Qualitative inquiry & research design: Choosing among five approaches* (2nd ed.). Sage Publications.

Denny, H. C. (2010). *Facing the center: Toward an identity politics of one-to-one mentoring.* Utah State University Press.

Erichsen, E. & Bolliger, D. (2011). Towards understanding international graduate student isolation in traditional and online environments. *Educational Technology Research and Development, 59*, 309–326.

Ferris, D. (2002). *Treatment of error in second language student writing.* University of Michigan Press.

Ferris, D. & Thaiss, C. (2011). Writing at UC Davis: Addressing the needs of second language writers. *Across the disciplines, 8*(4). https://wac.colostate.edu/docs/atd/ell/ferris-thaiss.pdf.

Glenn, C. (2004). *Unspoken: A rhetoric of silence.* Southern Illinois University Press.

Harris, M. (1997). Cultural conflicts in the writing center: Expectations and assumptions of ESL students. In C. Severino, J. Guerra & J. Butler (Eds.), *Writing in multicultural settings* (pp. 220–233). Modern Language Association.

Harris, M. & Silva, T. (1993). Tutoring ESL students: Issues and options. *College Composition and Communication, 44*(4), 525–537.

Horner, B., Lu, M., Royster, J. J. & Trimbur, J. (2011). Opinion: Language difference in writing: Toward a translingual approach. *College English, 73*(3), 303–321.

Isaacs, E. (2011). The emergence of centers for writing excellence. In N. Mauriello, W. J. Macauley & T. Koch (Eds.). *Before and after the tutorial: Writing centers and institutional relationships* (pp. 131–149). Hampton Press.

Jordan, J. & Kedrowicz, A. (2011). Attitudes about graduate L2 writing in engineering: Possibilities for more integrated instruction. *Across the Disciplines, 8*(4). https://wac.colostate.edu/docs/atd/ell/lancaster.pdf.

Lillis, T. & Curry, M. J. (2004). Multilingual scholars and the imperative to publish in English: Negotiating interests, demands, and rewards. *TESOL Quarterly, 38*(4), 663–688.

Lillis, T. & Curry, M. J. (2006). Professional academic writing by multilingual students: Interactions with literacy brokers in the production of English-medium texts. *Written Communication, 23*(1), 3–35.

Lu, M. (2004). Professing multiculturalism: The politics of style in the contact zone. *College Composition and Communication, 45*(4), 442–458.

Matsuda, P. K. (2010). The myth of linguistic homogeneity in U.S. college composition. In B. Horner, M. Lu & P. K. Matsuda (Eds.), *Cross-language relations in composition* (pp. 81–91). Southern Illinois University Press.

Matsuda, P. K. & Cox, M. (2011). Reading an ESL writer's text. *Studies in Self-Access Learning Journal, 2*(1), 4–14.

Myers, S. (2003). Reassessing the "proofreading trap": ESL tutoring and writing instruction. *Writing Center Journal, 24*(1), 51–70.

Phillips, T. (2013). Tutor training and services for multilingual graduate writers: A reconsideration. *Praxis: A Writing Center Journal, 10*(2).

Ratcliffe, K. (2005). *Rhetorical listening: Identification, gender, whiteness.* Southern Illinois University Press.

Runion, G. (2006). *Response report to the visiting committee: Quality enhancement plan, Revised.* Liberty University. https://www.liberty.edu/media/1136/QEP%20%20Final%20Revised%208-10-06.pdf.

Severino, C. (2009). Avoiding appropriation. In S. Bruce & B. Rafoth, (Eds.), *ESL writers: A guide for writing center tutors* (pp. 48–59). Boynton/Cook.

Tardy, C. (2003). A genre system view of the funding of academic research. *Written Communication, 20*(1), 7–36.

Thaiss, C. & Zawacki, T. M. (2006). *Engaged writers, dynamic disciplines: Research on the academic writing life.* Boynton/Cook.

Thonus, T. (2004). What are the differences?: Tutor interactions with first- and second-language writers. *Journal of Second Language Writing, 13*(3), 227–242.

Zhang, Z. (2011). A nested model of academic writing approaches: Chinese international graduate students' views of English academic writing. *Language and Literacy, 31*(1), 39–60.

12 Enacting Linguistic Justice: Transnational Scholars as Advocates for Pedagogical Change

Ligia A. Mihut
BARRY UNIVERSITY

This chapter examines the politics of language difference performed in the public texts of nine multilingual/ transnational writing scholars and the proposed pedagogical practices included in these scholars' texts. While much attention has been devoted to the translingual and transnational approach—in particular to theoretical underpinnings, the student body, and the changing of the U.S. writing classroom—little notice has been paid to the influences and pedagogical approaches of multilingual, transnational scholars in the US and abroad. Drawing on the analyzed pedagogical suggestions of transnational scholars, this chapter shows how these scholars employ public texts to enact a politics of difference and interconnect personal, professional, and public spheres. Based on these findings, this chapter proposes a *linguistic justice* approach as a frame for pedagogies of language pluralism, a model that simultaneously and necessarily incorporates two moves: on the one hand, it exposes monolingual standards and on the other hand, it actively integrates cross-cultural rhetorics and translingual writing in the classroom. In a linguistic justice frame, both actions—*critique* of monolingualism and *integration* of plurilingual practices and theories—are essential to centering and valorizing linguistically-rich practices.

Keywords: transnational writing; linguistic justice; language difference; transnational scholars

While much attention has been devoted to the transnational turn and more recently, to the translingual approach—in particular to theoretical underpinnings, student demographics, and the changing of the U.S. writing classroom (e.g., Donahue, 2009; Martins, 2015; Tardy, 2015)—we need to hear more directly from multilingual, transnational writing scholars on their approaches

DOI: https://doi.org/10.37514/INT-B.2020.0438.2.12

to writing pedagogy in the US and abroad.[1] Their experiences across diverse academic contexts and through different roles both expose the limitations of classroom practices and suggest new approaches. In this chapter, I examine a series of pedagogical suggestions proposed by transnational writing scholars for the ways in which these pedagogies *reorient* and *attune* students' discursive practices to language difference, global geopolitical and social contingencies, and cross-cultural rhetorics. I call this *orientation* of writing instruction a *linguistic justice approach*. Linguistic justice implicates an enactment of the politics of difference defined not only in U.S. terms but rather developed across rhetorical traditions and writing cultures. In a linguistic justice frame, both actions—*critique* of monolingualism and *integration* of plurilingual practices and theories—are essential to centering and valorizing linguistically-rich practices. Ultimately, pedagogies grounded in linguistic justice offer scholars practical suggestions on how to develop and enact plurilingual discursive frames and critical knowledge in the classroom and beyond.

Author's Background

I identify as a multilingual, transnational scholar. The "transnational" descriptor is particularly significant as an identifier of my personal and professional work since I view *nation* as a term that needs to be both acknowledged and contested in multiple ways. Nation-states manage identities and literacies in ways that must be continuously interrogated and deconstructed. Originally from Romania, over the course of years, I have developed a broad linguistic repertoire—English, Romanian, French, and Latin—either through exposure or practice. As I mention later in this chapter, listing my language proficiency in a linear progression, L1, L2, or L3 would misrepresent how languages operate in my experience and in my students' lives. I ground my work on the premise that languages are dynamic, tied to spaces of affinity and experience: Romanian, for instance, is the language of my home and family; English is the language of written expression and academic professionalization; Latin

---

1   The viability of the translingual approach was formally acknowledged with the publication of "Language Difference in Writing: Toward a Translingual Approach" (2011). I say *formally* because evidently cross-cultural, global, or international initiatives developed earlier than 2011. The translingual approach gained momentum in rhetoric and composition with the publication of the aforementioned article, the significance of which was reinforced by the appended undersigning of approximately 50 teacher-scholars. Criticism of this approach has been multifold. In his *PMLA* article (2014), Paul Kei Matsuda offers a more extensive assessment of the term and its various roots in applied linguistics.

is the language of my ancestors, one associated with formalist grammar, and with Romanian linguists' efforts of legitimation as they sought to demonstrate the Romanian language's ties to Latin, and thereby, to reclaim a certain prestige as a Romance language; French is my foreign language—one that I studied assiduously through quizzes and drills in high school and college; it remained foreign to me, far from my heart and experience as I rarely interacted with its active users. This, however, is changing due to new encounters with Creole-speaking users in the Miami area. As I grew up in a border zone in Western Romania, I was also exposed to several border languages: Hungarian, German, Serbian, and Czech. These are languages of trespassing and contact zones since they throve in shifting territories, wars, and occupations.

Prior to my move to the US, I worked as an English teacher at a public high school in Romania, a school specifically intended for German, Hungarian, and Roma minorities. Currently, I am Associate Professor of English at Barry University and a multilingual writing pedagogy consultant. From exposure to my students' linguistic repertoires, I have learned to expand my own views of languages and to consider additional variations such as Cuban Spanish, Mexican Spanish, Jamaican patois, French, German, Italian, Puerto Rican Spanish, Creole, American English, British English, Arabic, and several others. Many of my students went through the process of acquiring one language, losing another, and occasionally, recommitting to relearning a lost home language. Many carry with them histories of reading and writing that cannot be squeezed into English-only academic contexts. In South Florida, Spanish, Portuguese, Creole, Russian, and even Romanian permeate our social worlds—stores, local neighborhoods, radio programs, or homes. In light of this linguistic pluralism, it is my responsibility as a teacher-scholar to explore practices that valorize my students' linguistic repertoires and educate them to communicate effectively and ethically in a globalized world. For me, multilingualism has always been the norm. In my research and pedagogy, I practice and advocate for multilingualism and transnational orientation as the norm, an orientation that in this chapter I call *linguistic justice*.

Trends in Transnational and Translingual Scholarship

In the introduction of the edited collection *Transnational Writing Program Administration*, David S. Martins (2015) directs readers' attention to the changing face of higher education and the exigency to reframe the common responsibilities of a writing program administrator (WPA), including curricula design, assessment, and faculty training, in light of dynamic global shifts that impact academia. Introducing various definitions of transnationality and the set of relationships established between various entities, Martins (2015) also points to the unequal partnerships established in transnational exchanges. He gives the example of transnational educational programs set-up between "a delivery institution" and recipients, namely campuses located internationally. Other scholars (e.g., Donahue, 2009; Tardy, 2015) have critiqued U.S. composition's tendency to practice export-based models of internationalization. While Martins (2015) acknowledges critical power relationships between globally positioned institutions, one element is omitted—the fact that local or "delivery institutions" may have already experienced a diversification of faculty. International mobility does not implicate only students, but faculty as well. Recent trends show that upon graduation, former international students in rhetoric and composition increasingly secure employment at U.S. institutions. This leads to the possibility that "delivery institutions" are becoming more transnationalized from the inside out, through the changing of the teaching staff. What are the implications of this trend? How do these transnational scholars approach the politics of language difference? What impact does their transnationality and border-crossing experience have on the pedagogies that they profess?

Representing a slice of the internationalization of our field, the transnational lives of multilingual,[2] transnational scholars have been explored but only limitedly. Comparing U.S. scholars with expertise in transnational work and international scholars with similar scholarly interests, Santosh Khadka (2013) illuminates a few methodological distinctions between these two groups. Specifically, Khadka explains that the multilingual, international scholars tend to use more prominently self-reflexivity, Bhabha's "double vision,"[3] literacy narratives, and other anecdotal evidence in addition to more established methodologies. A few other transnational scholars have referred to their personal literate trajectories in terms of the digital divide (Pandey, 2006), the path toward purposeful publication as a graduate student (Matsuda, 2003), and more recently, Ghanashyam Sharma's (2015) reflection on his

---

2   I acknowledge and problematize the term "multilingual" for its erroneous treatment of languages as two or more separate, non-interfering systems. Yet, I prefer to use it as an adjective knowing that these scholars have deployed their language repertoires in a dialogic manner, across and within multiple contexts. I will employ the term translingual to refer to the approach and the method of acknowledging and cultivating language difference practices.

3   Double vision is a term introduced by postcolonial critical theorist Homi J. Bhabha that captures one's dual affinity or membership to different linguistic, cultural, or national communities. The term captures the notion of hybridity, which was further taken up by Canagarajah through the "shuttling" metaphor.

own literacy narrative and this genre's role in the context of transnationalism and global mobility. While additional studies pay attention to international scholars' experiences (e.g., Lillis & Curry, 2006; Sharma, 2013), the focal subjects in the process of internationalization remain multilingual students (see Berry et al., 2012; Canagarajah, 2016; Lorimer Leonard, 2013).

In this chapter, I shift the lens onto multilingual, transnational scholars for their critical role in shaping pedagogies of language pluralism in mono- or multilingual writing classrooms. Specifically, I examine the public texts of nine multilingual scholars, and the ways in which their pedagogical suggestions advance a politics of language difference in the classroom. Drawing on my analysis of these scholars' pedagogical propositions, I argue that, collectively, this work advances a linguistic justice agenda and the manifestation of this "justice" is largely geographical/ socio-politically dependent. While these texts promote a dynamic view of language and writing that crosses cultural and geo-political borders, much of their practices and beliefs is shaped by local and or national ideologies. In my subsequent discussion of these scholars' texts, I will make a necessary distinction between multilingual, transnational scholars at U.S. institutions and transnational scholars in international settings since their approach to the teaching of writing differs in scale. While both of these groups of scholars approach writing pedagogy with attention to language pluralism, the U.S.-based transnational scholars discuss pedagogy with closer attention to classroom activities, pedagogies, and belief systems, whereas scholars from international contexts are more attuned to larger national, global, and institutional contexts that shape writing instruction. An important characteristic of U.S.-based transnational scholars is the accumulation of experiences as students in their home countries, former international students in the US, and as current faculty at U.S. institutions. Thus, their predispositions to language pluralism and cross-cultural writing have been configured through personal and professional histories with language across multiple national and educational contexts. Taken together, these scholars' consideration of pedagogies of language pluralism responds pertinently to a pedagogical gap noted by Dana Ferris' (2014) review essay "'English Only' and Multilingualism in Composition Studies" where she rightly notes a tendency to underscore a "philosophical rather than pedagogical" approach to multilingual matters (p. 80).

In this chapter my interest lies in what these multilingual, transnational scholars *do* with their accumulated language and rhetorical experiences across borders. Collectively, the different pedagogical approaches proposed by these scholars—suggestions that address course themes, readings, assignments, belief systems, and other concrete practices promoting linguistic pluralism—may be culled together under a coherent instructional frame. I call this frame a *linguistic*

justice approach, a pedagogical construct built through integration of these scholars' personal stories, accumulated experiences, and agility in various rhetorical
traditions. Offering both a *critique* of monolingual practices and *actions* that
promote language rights, a linguistic justice approach is constituted through
a series of activities that function on two levels: on the one hand, they decon-
struct rigid, one-dimensional models of writing, and on the other hand, they
introduce varied discursive practices as the norm, practices that some might call
alternative. In adopting the term linguistic justice I was influenced by Philippe
Van Parijs' discussion of linguistic justice in Europe (2002). However, I depart
from his development of the term that resorts to an economic exchange model
to explain "asymmetric bilingualism." Rather, I envision linguistic justice within
a social justice frame, calling for specific attention to language and discourse.
A linguistic justice model is exigent since for decades, we have affirmed that
students should have the right to their own languages; we have stated language
relations expressed in writing are *shaped* by socio-economic and political factors.
But, we need to act more directly on these beliefs. A language justice model
calls for such action. Premised on the fact that languages and discourses have
unequal power in their deployment in social fields, language justice is a concept
that invites concrete yet heterogeneous actions. Drawing on an analysis of pedagogies centered on language pluralism and cross-cultural rhetorics proposed
by transnational scholars located both in the US and abroad, I suggest a linguistic justice frame wherein pedagogical practices *challenge* standards, wherein
we *adapt* to different and multiple discursive contexts, and wherein we *integrate*
more directly cross-cultural rhetorical traditions in the writing classroom.

Literature Review: Three Models of Language Difference

I have found it generative in my own scholarship and analysis, particularly in
terms of the linguistic justice approach I am proposing here, to consider translingual and transnational conversations in terms of the following three models.
This is not intended as a comprehensive overview of scholarship on language
difference. Rather, the purpose is to ground our understanding in particular
frames useful for the latter part of the chapter where I discuss pedagogies of
language difference proposed by transnational scholars.

The first set of scholarship—the sovereignty model—approaches language
pluralism with an eye to ideologies of domination and subordination associated with monolingualism and multilingualism, respectively. In "Translingual
Literacy, Language Difference, and Matters of Agency," Min-Zhan Lu and
Bruce Horner (2013) challenge ideologies that feed negative attributions and
attitudes toward language difference—the ideology of monolingualism. Lu

and Horner (2013) expand on the view that monolingualism imposed itself as an elitist, mainstream ideology; monolingualism is an ideology of the center cast against "subordinate social groups" (p. 583) where the latter are identified with multi/pluri or translingualism. In presenting this sovereignty paradigm, Lu and Horner (2013) aim to dislodge underlying ideologies associating mainstream with acceptable, standardized practice and language plurality with the subordinate or minority groups. Ultimately, their goal is to advocate for the translingual approach as the "norm" not as a deviation from the mainstream (Lu & Horner, 2013). Framed as a relationship of dominance-subordination, monolingual ideology holds sovereign power over the subordinate pluri-lingual subject. This frame of linguistic conquest connotes the United States' expansionist ideology throughout history. It comes as no surprise, then, when in a linguistic justice pedagogical model, significant action in the classroom is directed toward critiquing monolingual, U.S.-based ideologies and standardized forms of writing and instruction.

Another category of scholarship concerned with language difference takes an expansive approach—moving from the local to the internationalization of our discipline. Specifically, Christiane Donahue (2009) identifies three major areas: 1) the teaching of writing, 2) scholarship focused on writing, and 3) consulting about writing or language-related programs/ initiatives/ curricula, etc. These forms of internationalization, Donahue (2009) argues, reinforce a model where the US remains the center of expertise. Donahue's (2009) pertinent critique exposes a misunderstood trend of internationalization—the U.S.-export model where U.S. scholars transport their knowledge to other parts of the world. In this polarized construct, we find the US at the center, and the world, as a unified other, at the margins. Essentially a business model, the exchanges may allow benefits on both sides of a transaction, or at least, result in some fringe profits to additional stakeholders, but the US remains the center of expertise, knowledge, and delivery to other parts of the globe. It should be noted that the business model that Donahue (2009) critiques is not metaphorical. In comprehensive analysis of the websites of twenty-eight U.S. institutions, Christine Tardy (2015) offers a clear description of the public discourse on the internationalization of these campuses. Tardy (2015) explains two dominant trends: one where the international is represented through global markets, which aligns with Donahue's export model (2009); and one where the international is represented via a global community, generally expressed as global citizenship, which is more prevalent at privileged, liberal arts colleges. Both of these trends are present in the pedagogical approaches in my data. In this current study, Monique Yoder, a Lithuanian scholar, exemplified in her blog post the import model of the U.S. education presented earlier as she referenced the university where she has been teaching as a liberal arts college "founded by North Americans . . . in 1991."

A third model reflecting language/cultural/ discourse difference—the center-periphery dichotomy model—is similar to the business model except that it employs a spatial parlance. Spatial metaphors seem to be particularly valued in our field. In *Geographies of Writing*, Nedra Reynolds (2004) explains extensively the multiple ways in which spatial metaphors have flourished in the field of rhetoric and composition. Reynolds (2004) notes that most recently, in the postmodern frame, binary metaphors are quite widespread: "metaphors of inside and outside, margin and center, boundaries and zones" (p. 28). Of these, one of the most acknowledged, Reynolds shows, is *borderlands* (Gloria Anzaldua). While *borderlands* would more adequately capture translanguaging—the mixing of languages and cultures—the center-periphery binary has been used to show the power relationship established between academic culture of the West and the "minor" academic scholars situated at the margins. This center-periphery conception has been more extensively discussed in Canagarajah's *A Geopolitics of Academic Writing* with reference to the academic publishing sphere. Since knowledge-making and writing conventions are dictated by the center, a hierarchical structure is preserved in terms of U.S. English and Standard Written English (SWE) as principles representing the center's ideology. The rest of the languages, including varieties of English, are relegated to the periphery. In my analysis, this center-periphery model defined in terms of geopolitical spatiality is the most pervasive in the case of transnational scholars situated in international settings. In this chapter, scholars coming from Eastern Europe, a fairly heterogeneous region, made numerous references to their positionality relative to Western Europe. In certain blog posts, Eastern Europe is perceived as going through a development delay in writing instruction compared to Western Europe, thus following the center-periphery model discussed in the literature review where Western Europe represents the advanced rod stick against which countries from the former Eastern bloc are measured.

To sum up, these three models attending to the internationalization of writing studies, and specifically, to language difference, reveal frames based on sovereignty, business and economic realities, and geopolitical mapping. Each one of these frames has value in revealing power relations governing discourses, and by extension, language users. While the import-export model accentuates the economics of language difference, the center-periphery frame introduces more forcibly the perspective of the marginalized. Yet, these models have deeper roots than is often acknowledged. In his 2014 PMLA article, Paul Kei Matsuda explains that many of the newly proposed directions in translingual writing have been discussed for some time in applied linguistics. He gives the examples of Braj B. Kachru work's on World Englishes and Robert Phillipson's discussion of linguistic imperialism as early as the 1980s. Although elsewhere Matsuda (2013) expresses more enthusiasm (albeit reserved) with regard to a language pluralism turn in writing studies, in his *PMLA* article, he questions a bandwagon mentality of writing scholars, as well as a tendency to readily adopt new positions and practices without much interrogation. Many scholars, Matsuda suggests, join in this new intellectual wave for fear of being on the wrong side of the current.

While I value Matsuda's critique especially the connections established to applied linguistics, I propose another alternative for why transnational and translingual approaches to writing have gained popularity. For many scholars, particularly for scholars with multilingual and transnational backgrounds or situated in international contexts, the translingual/ transnational approach[4] has been *the norm*. Thus, this turn becomes the long-awaited moment to claim and advocate the translingual/transnational movement that has guided many scholars' orientation prior to its development into a coherent, explicit manifestation in the US. Many of these scholars have long, often unacknowledged in U.S. histories with language difference and cross-cultural rhetorics. In the following section, I center my analysis on nine accounts written by such scholars, precisely because their understanding of language difference has originated in global sites, and many of them negotiated multiple transitions into the U.S. educational system, first as international students and then, as teachers/ scholars of rhetoric and composition. These scholars' public texts function as advocacy platforms for multilingual pedagogies; they also index contexts where translingual and transnational language practices have been "the norm." As they become advocates for *the value* of writing across languages, cultures, and across difference, they also seek to *legitimize* linguistic pluralism.[5]

Methodological Choices in Studying the Public Texts of Multilingual, International Scholars

As a data set, I selected nine, pedagogy-focused, public blog posts of multilingual and/ or transnational scholars published on the blog platform of

---

4   Clarifying the relationship between two terms, Kilfoil (2016) eloquently establishes a clear distinction between "translingual" and "transnational." A basic clarification comes from understanding that "languages and nations are very different things."

5   For a discussion of valorizing and legitimizing language practices, see Whyte, 2013.

the Transnational Composition Special Interest Group (SIG). The *Transnational Composition SIG* achieved standing group status in April 2015 as part of the U.S.-based professional organization, College Conference on Composition and Communication. Prior to and following this date, a team of scholars with interests in transnational issues collaborated actively in building the group's social media presence on Facebook, Twitter, and a WordPress blog. Several of these scholars—Santosh Khadka, Shyam Sharma, and Moushumi Biswas—volunteered to jumpstart the transnational composition blog with entries on their own choice of topics. Others—Ivan Eubanks, Brooke Ricker Schreiber, Natalia Smirnova, and Monique Yoder—responded to an open call—a call that I launched to foreground work and scholars from Eastern Europe. Circulated on the European Association for the Teaching of Academic Writing (EATAW) listserv, the call attracted the interest of established scholars whose work in Eastern Europe is widely known—Otto Kruse and John Harbord—and emerging scholars who responded to the initial message (Eubanks, Schreiber, Smirnova, and Yoder). Since the topic of our interactions and their blogs were concerned with the teaching of writing in Eastern Europe, their blog entries, including my contribution as a facilitator and curator of these posts were incorporated in this study. Since the publication of the first blog entries, this scholarly network has grown in recognition and membership (871 members in the FB group as of May 20, 2019).

Since weblogs offers a means of examining writing for public, rather than solely academic, audiences, I center my analysis on blog entries on language difference and cross-cultural writing instruction. According to Miller and Shepard (2010), a blog is "a complex rhetorical hybrid with genetic imprints from prior genres, such as the diary, clipping services, broadsides, commonplace books, and even ship's logs" (cited in Bawarshi & Reiff, 2010, p. 164). Building on Miller and Shepherd's view on the blog as both personal and public, Kathryn Grafton and Elizabeth Maurer (2007), examining blogs that take on social issues such as homelessness and community events, remarked on bloggers' performance of "mediated selves," as they engaged public issues. In the blog entries examined in this chapter, some authors mixed the personal and public while others used digital space as a way to foreground the work of scholars from regions that have been traditionally neglected such as Eastern Europe. Similar to Bazerman's (2002) remarks on the proliferation of political websites as public genres and the Internet's power to change civic participation, I note the impact of the Internet on the ways in which scholars have begun to take advantage of digital affordances including web blogs, social media networks, and digital communication. Particularly in our globalized world, blogs as public genres provide discursive spaces where knowledge is more fluid and open to transnational interactions irrespective of physical geographical boundaries. It is also a space where academic conventions, standards, and discourses can be more easily challenged.

Once I identified the blogs as the data set for my analysis of public texts of multilingual, transnational scholars, I adopted critical discourse analysis (CDA) as a tool for analysis. Jan Blommaert (2005) defines CDA as having "lively interest in *theories of power and ideology*" (emphasis in original, p. 27). Positioned at the juncture between agency and social structures, CDA is often used to examine public and macrodiscourses such as political discourse, advertising, gender, education, etc. (Blommaert, 2005). Theoretically, CDA is a "dynamic model" in that language and discursive practices are understood as simultaneously being shaped by and constitutive of social structures and ideologies. Given the frame and purpose of this study—to examine conversations about pedagogies that center on language difference—I focused on nine (of a possible eighteen by September 2016) blog posts that addressed directly this topic. A comprehensive list with the authors, titles of the blog entries, foci, and date of publication can be found in the Appendix.

Using Fairclough's (1992) *discourse-as-text* analytical tool, I marked patterns of lexicon, grammatical structures, and repeated textual markers indexing linguistic pluralism and writing pedagogies. First, I coded all the instances in the nine posts (including my own) when an aspect of pedagogy was mentioned and in what form. For instance, I coded for all references to student writing: transition essays, argument-based essays, essays focused on a universal concept, etc. Then, I grouped all these under the subcategory of "composition assignments." I also marked the use of or references to linguistic pluralism such as "cross-cultural," "transcultural," "global issues," "translingual skills," "cross-border," "intercultural," etc. Based on the codes and subcategories, I developed the following four broad categories:

1. beliefs about language standards and writing such as language ideologies and views on writing;

2. methods of writing instruction and assignments (e.g., discussion-based seminar, lecture, multimedia instruction, teaching grammar rhetorically, argument-based papers, etc.;

3. cross-cultural, globally-oriented curriculum including integration of cross-cultural themes and readings (e.g., readings on global citizenship and transnational socio-political issues, transcultural knowledge, classical texts from China, writing style in Japan, etc.); and

4. cross-linguistic approaches of transnational scholars in international settings: rhetorical traditions, national, and global reforms.

Although personal experience especially of transnational writing scholars located in the US was marked as a significant code, it turned out that it represented an angle from where a scholar advanced a particular pedagogical insight. Thus, I did not consider it as a separate category. For instance, for some, the experience of being a former international student in the US (Khadka) motivated the writing of the blog post; personal experience also functioned as a tool for establishing one's ethos in the teaching of writing as cross-cultural experience (Khadka). For others, personal experience represented a springboard for foregrounding the experience of translingual and/or international students (Biswas).

Analysis of the Public Texts of Multilingual, International Scholars

Beliefs about Language Standards and Writing

To a certain extent, each blog entry published by the transnational writing scholars in the US carries an underlying critique of U.S. writing instruction's monolingual, English-only approach. This critique is enacted in how assignments are structured to accommodate linguistic pluralism, cultural adaptations, and global perspectives. Challenging U.S.-centric standards is a recurrent theme operationalized in a need to reassess methods of instruction such as the discussion-based seminar and the unchallenged use of SWE as the sole acceptable norm of communication. Several scholars ask that instructors adopt a more "expansive notion of writing with the students" that recognizes the "situated nature of writing" (Khadka), that we acknowledge various rhetorical traditions and writing across cultures and contexts (Sharma), that we valorize students' linguistic repertoires (Biswas), and that we understand the role of the writing classroom as a gateway to critical thinking and global orientation (Nezami).

Challenging Standards, Advancing a Translingual Approach

With this frame in mind, I will discuss more explicitly Moushumi Biswas', a doctoral candidate at University of Texas at El Paso, proposal to challenge such standards. Biswas draws from her experience as a student in India and the US when she proposes a reconceptualization of first-year writing (FYW). While Biswas proposes a three-pronged pedagogy of change—language pluralism, attention to writing education prior to college, and grammar as a rhetorical tool—her commitment to challenging beliefs about language and writing instruction through the English-only lens is central to her agenda. Biswas starts her blog post with this statement:

Even as we speak for the cause of the many Englishes, I realize that those of us who are from other countries have tried to conform to the so-called standards of American English as we strove to succeed in the academy. (italics mine)

The three main themes combined together—speaking for the advancement of linguistic pluralism ("many Englishes"), personal experience of foreign internationals ("those of us who are from other countries"), and the challenge of discourses of power ("so-called standards of American English" and "in the academy") formulate an agenda for a linguistic justice approach to writing instruction. Biswas' strategy here is marked by a call to dismantle conformism and singular, U.S. models of writing. In each of her pedagogical proposals, Biswas questions the "conformity" to the standards of U.S. writing. Juxtaposing her experience as a multilingual learner against standard-driven U.S. composition, with each of her points, Biswas breaks free from the bondage of uniformity. First, she identifies FYW's historical connection to the "need to *standardize* college-level academic writing" (italics mine). She further confesses her own choice of adhering to the "so-called *standards* of American English" as a strategy to avoid miscommunication and to attain good grades (italics mine). In her second move, she advises on the repurposing of the FYW classroom as a space of writing instruction that would accommodate diverse language repertoires, border students, and their rich literacy histories. It is in this critical space where we can "help students gain their right to their own languages while using the language differences as resources," explains Biswas.

I expound on Biswas' challenge of ideologies about writing and language standards here because without this move to critique and question conformist practices, it is rather futile to incorporate global and cross-cultural perspectives in our curriculum. A linguistic justice approach to teaching would inevitably implicate a discussion of language and writing standards. Although Biswas' focus is solely on the FYW programs, other scholars suggest a more expansive integration of multilingual and global perspectives in other courses such as literature (Nezami), or special topics seminars, such as the one proposed by Shyam Sharma on global citizenship.

Methods of Writing Instruction and Assignments

In addition to challenging beliefs and ideologies of language, several transnational scholars from U.S. institutions discussed and often contested established writing instruction methods in traditional U.S. writing classrooms. Some critiqued the discussion-based seminar (Khadka), the teaching of grammar as a set of rules of U.S. standard English (Biswas), or argument-driven assignments that fail to consider alternatives (Khadka; Sharma). In the following section, I examine in more detail Khadka's critique of the discussion-based seminar and argument essay promoted in many U.S. writing classrooms, and Biswas' proposition to teach grammar rhetorically.

Discussion-based Seminar and the Argument Paper

In terms of pedagogy, Khadka challenges two pedagogical practices in the U.S. classroom: the discussion-based seminar and argument-driven writing. As an international multilingual student, Khadka recounts his difficulty with open style, conversation-based seminars that served as a springboard for diverse opinions. Affirming that silence in the classroom is wrongly associated with being deficient, Khadka shows that in home cultures like his, power relationships between student and teachers are clearly hierarchical and should be respected. The voicing of alternative views to that of the teacher are often a mark of interference and disrespect. Although indirectly expressed, Khadka found speaking openly an ineffective teaching strategy in the classroom. As an international student, with lack of knowledge of local practices, it seemed unwarranted to advance and make public informed opinion while still holding the position of a novice.

A second pedagogical critique shows the international student's difficulty with writing argument or thesis-driven models of writing. Khadka's position is not against this form of writing, yet he wants to acknowledge other approaches and the time needed to learn new genres. Juxtaposing his past writing experiences in Nepal against the argument-driven, source-based U.S. discourse, he notes two things: 1) there are writing practices in other countries that differ from U.S. argument essays; 2) the notion of time: to learn new writing strategies one needs to practice a process that Khadka calls, "trial and error." These observations ask instructors to acknowledge and familiarize themselves with the presence of other discursive traditions, and, with this knowledge, to build a foundation for new writing practices such as argument-based writing.

In critiquing the two methods of instruction—discussion-based seminar and the argument-driven essay— Khadka draws attention to the deficit labels often affixed to international students. But he simultaneously proposes new ways of acting and adapting to U.S. academic genres. Khadka's actions toward linguistic pluralism are deployed through a rhetoric of negotiation, or in Khadka's exact words, "adaptations." *Multiplicity and adaptations* are the emergent discursive strategies, and there is clear connection between the two. In naming his diverse background a series of "*inter*cultural," "*inter*-linguistic," and "*inter*-academic adaptations" the repetition of the prefix *inter*- indexes pluralism and interactions among cultures, languages, and academic as well as non-academic experiences. Thusly, Khadka proposes a pedagogy of change that acknowledges relationships between cultures and languages. Embedded in these relationships is a sense of inequality invoked in the very fact that adjustments and changes are necessary. Different from Biswas' earlier proposition that challenged beliefs about language, Khadka's approach calls for adaptability of old and new knowledge depending on one's context and purpose.

Rhetorical Grammar and the Nuances of Languages

Linking her experience to recommended pedagogical practices, Biswas regards as valuable what has been largely marginalized or ignored in the U.S. college composition: 1) the teaching of grammar, 2) multilingualism, and 3) writing education prior to college. Understanding the U.S. attitudes toward the teaching of grammar in a writing class, Biswas includes an extended explanation on the teaching of grammar not as a set of rules, but serving rhetorical ends. When learned and taught rhetorically, grammar can change a student's relationship to language, Biswas explains, since language becomes alive and a support for learning other languages as well. Her attention to grammar instruction is an expression of calling into question strict obedience to rules as she proposes a *rhetorical approach* to grammar. Biswas' goal in teaching grammar rhetorically is to introduce her students to "nuances of language." Drawing on her language pluralism repertoire (English, Bengali, and Hindi), Biswas further discusses nuances in language in light of India's postcolonial past,

> I remember the times I got funny looks in class for pronouncing "niche" as "neesh" and "pastiche" as "pasteesh," which are the French ways of pronouncing them as I had "learnt" (not "learned") in India.

This discussion of conformity to one standard of acceptable grammar and rules has deeper implications than initially noticed. Citing Victor Villanueva's (1993) *Bootstraps*, Biswas continues, "I become "raceless" through "consensus" when subjected to "acculturative and assimilationist forces" (113). Such impositions of language, grammar, and white English as lingua franca controls and regulates not only communicative practices but identities that become reduced to one size fits all.

The undoing of rules of grammar, or of the monolingual, standardized writing practices she has called out, are all part of her desire to advance a pedagogy of change. Her account of her multi-literate experience in India is for the sake of language pluralism, that is to advance linguistic justice not just for herself, but for her students studying at an institution bordering Mexico. In the last segment of her blog entry, Biswas proposes a specific pedagogical activity that breaks the rules of standard grammar—code-meshing. She introduces the TED talk of Jamila Lyiscott, "Tri-tongued Orator," a multimodal tool that advances linguistic justice. The multiple codes that facilitate an intimate connection to friends, academy, and parents reveal Lyiscott's purposeful use of so-called "broken English." Lyiscott's advocacy message: "Yes, I have decided to treat all three of my languages as equal," calls for a reassessment of rules and correct grammar.

"Grammar ceases to be lifeless," Biswas explains when the rules become compliant to the rhetor's intentions rather than the other way around. However, the challenge for many instructors is to identify and familiarize themselves with the students' intentions and varieties of English and codes. Biswas explains that many writing instructors in the US may lack awareness of the "student's tone, style, organization, or in other words, manner of expression" which leads to what Canagarajah describes as an "[instinctive] turn to the first language (L1) or "native" culture (C1)" as the default standard for that context.

Cross-Cultural, Globally-Oriented Curriculum, Global Citizenship

Two transnational scholars from U.S. institutions, Shyam Sharma and Rita Nezami, concentrated their pedagogical suggestions on cross-cultural reconceptualization of the curriculum. Unlike previous discussions of methods of instruction and assignments, these texts propose a comprehensive, cross-cultural approach to writing instruction. In other words, Sharma and Nezami offer pedagogical suggestions and cross-cultural activities in a series of courses rather than one single class. When proposing a reorientation of monolingual practices, a linguistic justice approach may call for a revision of an entire curriculum. As the examples below show, adopting a global and cross-cultural approach is no longer limited to one assignment or one pedagogical approach. Rather, it encompasses and reframes the curriculum within and across disciplines.

Cross-Cultural Approaches of Transnational Scholars in the US

Sharma begins by discussing the activities and assignments in a special top-ics seminar, "Global Citizenship," in the Department of Global Studies and Human Development, then discusses "Intermediate Writing Workshop," a First-Year Writing general education course. In his "Global Citizenship" course, Sharma covers class activities such as image-search for a "universal" idea and the description of three assignments (essay on a "seemingly univer-sal idea," multimodal collaborative presentation on communicative/rhetorical practices, and reading responses to various rhetorical traditions). In offering this comprehensive list of activities and types of assignments for students to engage with, he proposes a curricular approach to cross-cultural knowledge and writing. In the second course, the "Intermediate Writing Workshop," Sharma gives examples of activities that focus on "untranslatable" words as well as research projects and peer review that incorporates multiple perspec-tives. In these activities, Sharma asks students to think, write, and respond "across language, cultural, and epistemological borders/ barriers." The focus of this curricular approach is demonstrated in repeated words and phrases, such as cross-cultural, diverse, transcultural, translingual, diverse audiences, global citizenship, perspectives, knowledges, and communities.

Rita Nezami takes a similar approach to Sharma as she integrates global citizenship themes in both her intermediate writing course and upper-division course, "International Literature." From class discussions focused on current, international events such as the Arab Spring, the use of technologies and visual rhetoric, to reading texts and doing research on global issues,[6] Nezami encourages her students to break away from their "customized digital cocoons that keep the world out." In taking this approach, Nezami shifts her entire curriculum toward global issues and as students discuss, research, or respond to these issues, they have opportunities to expand their rhetorical repertoires.

Thus far, in the previous sections, the focus has been on decentering, cri-tiquing, and dismantling old ideologies and practices of monolingualism. However, a language justice approach also needs to build and advocate for new practices in which plurilingual, transnational orientations reconfigure the curriculum. This restructuring of the curriculum does not limit itself to isolated changes—modify an assignment here or there, introduce one or two

---

6   Some of the global issues covered in Nezami's course include: immigrant experience (Chimamanda Ngozi Adichie, Nigeria); the Arab Spring and dictator-ship (Tahar Ben Jelloun, Morocco); post 9/11 discrimination/racism toward Muslims (Mohsin Hamid, Pakistan); immigrant workers/cheap labor (Elaine Chiew, Malay-sia); Taliban terror, fundamentalism, human repression (Yasmina Khadra, Algeria).

global readings, etc. Instead, it asks instructors to fundamentally change and to plan an entire course with an orientation toward cross-cultural and global discourses.

Cross-Linguistic Approaches of Transnational Scholars in International Settings

In this section, I treat the work of transnational scholars located in international contexts as a distinct category due to their emphasis on geopolitical contexts and macrodiscourses, which I find to be fundamentally different from U.S.-based scholars' attention to micro-level classroom practices. In response to a call I launched as mentioned earlier, the blog entries studied here come from a series of connected posts focused on Eastern Europe, titled "Writing Perspectives from Eastern Europe." The authors, academics from Lithuania, Russia, Serbia, and indirectly from Switzerland and Hungary (one blog post reported on an email exchange I had with the respective scholars), bring forth cross-cultural perspectives in the teaching of writing in international contexts. Rather than classroom practices, this group of scholars approach pedagogy as shaped by larger institutional, national, and global contingencies. In doing so, they engage with larger discourses of power that impact the teaching of writing in their classroom.

Rhetorical Traditions, National, and Global Reforms

In the introductory blog post that I facilitated and authored, I sought to engage with two established scholars teaching writing in Europe, Otto Kruse (Switzerland) and John Harbord (Hungary) who were asked to address the question, "Can we talk about an Eastern European rhetoric?"

In the blog post (Mihut, 2015), I report and synthesize the conversation between these scholars, and their remarks on the presence (or absence) of an Eastern European rhetoric. At first, Kruse cast doubt on identifying a "homogeneous writing culture" in the region, yet he later notes a "transformation lag" in writing in Eastern European countries compared to Western Europe, thus pointing to the familiar center-periphery model presented earlier (as quoted in Mihut, 2015). Moving away from defining the writing culture in this region in terms of advancement, regression, or stagnation, Harbord explains this culture in terms of values and affiliation with various writing traditions: the German, French, and Anglo-Saxon. He identifies the influence of the German Humboldtian university and in doing so, describes a writing/rhetoric from this region that celebrates "complexity of phrase, wide vocabulary, virtuosity of language mastery" adopting a reader responsible approach (as quoted in

Mihut, 2015). He offers further details on the preferred genres in the German tradition compared to the Anglo-Saxon with the former showing preference for "the seminar writing and thesis writing genres which rely heavily on the sources" while the latter is dominated by the argument-driven approach (as quoted in Mihut, 2015).

In a subsequent blog entry, I reiterate a similar line of argument, taking Romania as a specific case and its affiliation with the French intellectual tradition. With each tradition, different aspects and purposes are emphasized: "to advance a theory, to engage in dialog, and display for eloquence," which correspond to the German, Anglo-Saxon, French traditions, respectively. This identification with historical writing traditions in Europe—the German, French, and Anglo-Saxon—all ultimately located in Western Europe, is balanced with an attempt to establish a particular identity. Harbord (2010) mentions, for instance, anecdotal evidence about writing the "Russian way" and the emergence of "Serbian rhetoric." From an email exchange with a Georgian scholar, he learned that

> Georgian doesn't have its own culture of academic scholarship. The way we have written until now is the Russian way, which was imposed upon us as part of the Russian empire in the 19th century and the Soviet emprise in the 20th. (as cited in Harbord, 2010)

From the conversation with Kruse and Harbord as well as from other posts (see for instance, Natalia Smirnova's "Personal Reflections on Writing Instruction in Russia," 2015), awareness of various writing and intellectual traditions and writing in multiple languages are dominant in writing instruction in Eastern Europe. The teaching and research of writing is situated across geopolitical contexts and, often, across disciplines. Smirnova, for instance, explains that L1 writing appears "fragmented and localized" and this distributed approach to writing is taken up in a number of disciplines that address the teaching of writing: literary studies, linguistics, teaching foreign languages, education, and pedagogy (2015). Although attention to L1, L2, and writing in the various language-related disciplines is an asset in this region, much of the national and global reforms such as the Bologna process are challenging the teaching of writing toward a more universal model which often entails the adoption of and adaption to Western writing traditions. Pressures from national and global forces have also shaped the teaching of writing largely as a means to an end—"to produce (essays, research articles, theses)"—rather than as a process (Smirnova, 2015). In Russia, recent educational reforms ask faculty to produce scholarship and publish in English so as to make their work more visible on a global scale, and by extension to increase their universities' global recognition (Eubanks).

The pedagogies professed by scholars in international settings remain attuned to larger reforms at the national and global level. These pedagogies, thus, engage discourses of power, pressures of and resistance to various forms of standardization often couched in beneficial global rewards. Pedagogies grounded in a linguistic justice model would necessarily be equally responsive to macrodiscourses and global pressures. For instance, knowledge of rhetorical traditions of Anglo-Saxon, German, or French origin would facilitate an understanding of how scholars in Eastern Europe borrow, resist, and adapt pedagogical practices from these established discourses. Less concerned with individual classroom practices, these scholars look at how top decision agents establish educational pathways that impact their own in the classroom. This connectivity between local, institutional, national, and global forces is necessary in a linguistic justice approach as it situates our practice in concrete socio- and geopolitical realities.

Conclusion

Given this overview of pedagogical practices and approaches to language pluralism and cross-cultural rhetorics, rather than advocate for one single model especially in light of local and translocal contingencies, I propose the linguistic justice approach that comprises elements from all of the pedagogical models advanced by the transnational scholars discussed herein. A linguistic justice approach implicates, on the one hand, the undoing of monolingual thinking and practices, and on the other, actions that would advocate for a plurality of languages, writing, and pedagogies. To situate the transnational/translingual approach within a linguistic justice frame is essential. First, linguistic justice, an enactment of the politics of difference, underscores the contingent nature of difference, exposing the reality of language power relationships and identities. Certainly, the models discussed earlier—the business model, the geopolitical, and the sovereignty frame—are extremely useful in exposing unequal relationships as well. They reveal the intricate connections between language/writing and economies of mobility, languages of the center vs. languages of the margins, and geopolitical contexts. Yet, as noted in a Biswas' blog post, in the constant tug between Western and Eastern rhetoric, there is a need to directly call out the inequality between discourses and languages and formulate ways to remedy such disparities which is what a linguistic justice approach does. In "Theorizing and Enacting Translanguaging for Social Justice," Garcia and Leiva (2014) explain that "it is not enough to claim that languaging consists of social practices and actions; it is important to question and change these when they reproduce inequalities" (p. 203). Garcia and Leiva (2014) define languaging or translanguaging as "the flexible use of linguistic resources by bilinguals in order to make sense of their worlds" and they deploy the term mostly in classroom settings for its "potential in liberating the voices of language minoritized students" (p. 200). A language justice approach, then, demands a critique and action toward change. And that is what many of these blog entries reveal—a call to dismantle oppressive discursive standards and strategies to build more equitable practices.

Specifically, in these public texts linguistic justice exposes monolithic pedagogies and promotes pedagogies of difference. Notably, pedagogies of difference do not come packaged in one shape. They are intrinsically heterogeneous. Each blog post exposed and proposed a pedagogy of difference contingent on one's personal, professional, institutional, or global experiences and contexts. While all writers affirm language and cultural differences in the writing classroom, each does so in a different manner. Biswas questions *standards* of writing communication, Khadka advocates for pluri-pedagogies as *adaptations* to a diverse student body, Sharma and Nezami implement cross-cultural rhetorics in the curriculum, and Mihut centers the work of Eastern European scholars as a way to allow different writing cultures, such as the Russian or Serbian way of writing, to become visible. The action items emerging from these public texts include challenging standards and embracing adaptations and cross-cultural approaches across the curriculum. In the writing classroom, we may acknowledge, discuss, and encourage the writing of *linguistically diverse texts*, global Englishes and texts that employ varieties of English. These might include literacy memoirs and texts that unveil ideologies and unequal relationships between languages and registers (e.g., Geneva Smitherman's (1974) "Soul 'n Style"), as well as multimodal and multilingual texts such as the one shared by Biswas. We may also introduce argument-based writing along with *other non-argument-based genres of writing*. We may include multiple rhetorical traditions, Chinese, Serbian, Russian, German, French, etc. We may also create spaces for our students' public texts to circulate and engage with larger discourses, as seen in the series of blog entries from Eastern Europe that feature scholars from this region. However, we also have to explicitly discuss standards and strategies for adapting to different rhetorical contexts. Writing cannot be fully socially situated unless we dynamically expose and address structural aspects of language difference and power.

To close, I will briefly address the role of personal experience in prompting linguistic justice. In several of these public texts, personal experience served as a catalyst for change—it was the glue that connected the self to others, and then, to pedagogies of language difference. Three of the transnational scholars in the US referred to their personal experience directly (Moushumi Biswas, Santosh Khadka, and Rita Nezami), and I did so indirectly as facilitator of the conversation about Eastern European writing culture when I used my transnational experience to challenge stereotypes about Eastern Europe's value being measured against the Western standard. Personal experience manifests in one's identity as an international student, in one's formal citizenship based on country of origin, in one's identity as a multilingual speaker and writer, and all these identities bring valuable knowledge. In an exposition on autoethnography as a research tool in multilingual writing, Canagarajah (2012) explains that personal experience facilitates a depiction of writing and writing pedagogy as contextually-based and distinctive. It also facilitates "cross-cultural understanding" (Canagarajah, 2012, p. 117). While the personal may come in conflict with the academia's values of objectivity and rational discourse, these transnational scholars' personal experiences and geopolitical positionalities are less concerned with when and to what extent a scholar should reveal personal details. Rather personal or pedagogical experiences aim to unveil socio-economic and political structures that shape identities, languages, and cultures—and, implicitly, individual life trajectories. In calling for focused attention to economic, political, and social structures and their impact on language and discourse, transnational scholars and their texts enact linguistic justice at their local institutions and across geographical contexts.

References

Bawarshi, A. S. & Reiff, M. (2010). *Genre: An introduction to history, theory, research, and pedagogy*. Parlor Press; The WAC Clearinghouse. https://wac.colostate.edu /books/referenceguides/bawarshi-reiff/.

Bazerman, C. (2002). Genre and identity: Citizenship in the age of the Internet and the age of global capitalism. In R. M. Coe, L. Lingard & T. Teslenko (Eds), *The rhetoric and ideology of genre: Strategies for stability and change* (pp. 13–35). Hampton Press.

Berry, P. W., Hawisher, G. E. & Selfe, C. L. (2012). *Transnational literate lives in digital times*. Computers and Composition Digital Press. http://ccdigitalpress .org/transnational.

Biswas, M. (2015, March 20). Transnational writing [Blog post.] *Transnational Writing*. https://transnationalwriting.wordpress.com/2015/03/10/transnational -writing-blog-post/.

Blommaert, J. (2005). *Discourse: key topics in sociolinguistics*. Cambridge University Press.

Brandt, D., Cushman, E., Gere, A. R., Herrington, A., Miller, R. E., Villanueva, V. & Kirsch, G. (2001). The politics of the personal: Storying our lives against the grain. Symposium collective. *College English, 64*(1), 41–62.

Canagarajah, S. A (2002). *A Geopolitics of academic writing.* University of Pittsburgh Press.

Canagarajah, S. A. (2006). Toward a writing pedagogy of shuttling between languages: Learning from multilingual writers. *College English, 68*(6), 589–604.

Canagarajah, S. A. (2012). Autoethnography in the study of multilingual writers. In L. Nickoson & M. P. Sheridan (Eds.), *Writing studies research in practice: Methods and Methodologies* (pp. 113–124). Southern Illinois University Press.

Canagarajah, S. A. (2015). *Clarifying the relationship between translingual practice and L2 writing: Addressing learner identities.* [Pre-publication manuscript]. https:// transnationalwriting.files.wordpress.com/2015/09/transnational-writing-file.pdf.

Donahue, C. (2009). "Internationalization" and composition studies: Reorienting the discourse. *College Composition and Communication, 61*(2), 212–243.

Eubanks, I. (2015, April 11). Writing perspectives from Eastern Europe: Blog three *Transnational Writing.* https://transnationalwriting.wordpress.com/2015/04/11 /writing-perspectives-from-eastern-europe-blog-three/.

Fairclough, N. (1992). *Discourse and social change.* Polity Press.

Ferris, D. R. (2014). Review: "English Only" and multilingualism in composition studies: Policies, philosophy, and practice. *College English, 77*(1), 73–83.

Garcia, O. & Leiva, C. (2014). Theorizing and enacting translanguaging for social justice. In A. Blackledge & A. Creese (Eds.), *Heteroglossia as practice and pedagogy* (pp. 199–216). Springer.

Grafton, K. & Mauer, E. (2007). Engaging with and arranging for publics in blog genres. *Linguistics and the Human Sciences, 3*(1), 47–66.

Harbord, J. (2010). Writing in Central and Eastern Europe: Stakeholders and directions in initiating change. *Across the Disciplines, 7.* https://wac.colostate.edu/docs /atd/articles/harbord2010.pdf.

Horner, B., Lu, M., Royster, J. J & Trimbur, J. (2011). Opinion: Language difference in writing: Toward a translingual approach. *College English, 73*(3), 303–321.

Khadka, S. (2015, January 26). Navigating the U.S. academy [Blog post]. *Transnational Writing.* https://transnationalwriting.wordpress.com/2015/01/26/navigating -us-academy/.

Khadka, S. (2013). In/variability in research methods/ methodologies of trans/ national compositionists. *Journal of Global Literacies, Technologies, and Emerging Pedagogies, 1*(2), 71–88.

Lillis, T. & M. Curry. (2006). Professional academic writing by multilingual scholars: Interactions with literacy brokers in the production of English-medium texts. *Written Communication, 23*(1), 3–35.

Lorimer Leonard, R. (2013). Travelling literacies: Multilingual writing on the move. *Research in the Teaching of English, 48*(1), 13–39.

Lu, M. & Horner, B. (2013). Translingual literacy, language difference, and matters of agency. *College English, 75*(6), 582–607.

Martins, D. (Ed.). (2015). *Transnational writing programs*. Utah State University Press.

Matsuda, P. K. (2014). The lure of translingual writing. *PMLA, 129*(3), 478–483.

Matsuda, P. K. (2013). It's the wild west out there: A new linguistic frontier in U.S. college composition. In A. S. Canagarajah (Ed.), *Literacy as translingual practice: Between communities and classrooms* (pp. 128–138). Routledge.

Matsuda, P. K. (2003). Coming to voice: Publishing as a graduate student. In C. P. Casanave & S. Vandrick (Eds.), *Writing for publication: Behind the scenes in language education* (pp. 39–51). Lawrence Erlbaum Associates.

Mihut, L. (2015, March 27). Writing perspectives from Eastern Europe: Blog one [Blog post]. *Transnational Writing*. https://transnationalwriting.wordpress.com /2015/03/27/writing-perspectives-from-eastern-europe/.

Miller, C. R. & Shepherd, D. (2004). Blogging as social action: A genre analysis of the weblog. In L. J. Gurak, S. Antonijevic, L. Johnson, C. Ratliff & J. Reyman (Eds.), *Into the blogosphere: Rhetoric, community and culture of weblogs*. Digital Conservancy. http://hdl.handle.net/11299/172840.

Milson-Whyte, V. (2013). Pedagogical and socio-political implications of code-meshing in classrooms: Some considerations for a translingual orientation to writing. In A. S. Canagarajah (Ed.), *Literacy as translingual practice* (pp. 115–127). Routledge.

Nezami, R. S. (2015, June 26). Bringing global issues into the writing class. *Transnational Writing*. https://transnationalwriting.wordpress.com/2015/06/26/bringing -global-issues-into-the-writing-class/.

Pandey, I. P. (2006). Literate lives across the digital divide. *Computers and Composition, 23*, 246–257.

Reynolds, N. (2004). *Geographies of writing: Inhabiting places and encountering difference*. Southern Illinois Press.

Sharma, G. (2013). Third eye: An exhibit of literacy narratives from Nepal. A multimodal book chapter. In H. L. Ulman, S. L. DeWitt & C. Selfe (Eds.), *Stories that speak to us: Exhibits from the digital archive of literacy narratives*. Computers and Composition Digital Press. https://ccdigitalpress.org/book/stories/sharma.html.

Sharma, G. (2015). Cultural schemas and pedagogical uses of literacy narratives: A reflection on my own journey with reading and writing. *College Composition and Communication, 67*(1), 104–110.

Sharma, G. (2015, February 26). Part I: Translingual, transcultural, transnational— From buzzwords to teaching strategies [Blog post]. *Transnational Writing*. https://transnationalwriting.wordpress.com/2015/02/26/part-i-translingual -transcultural-transnational-from-buzzwords-to-teaching-strategies/.

Sharma, G. (2015, February 26). Part II: Translingual, transcultural, transnational— From buzzwords to teaching strategies. *Transnational Writing*. https://trans nationalwriting.wordpress.com/2015/02/26/part-ii-translingual-transcultural -transnational-from-buzzwords-to-teaching-strategies/.

Smirnova, N. V. (2015, April 11). Writing perspectives from Eastern Europe: Blog three. *Transnational Writing*. https://transnationalwriting.wordpress.com /2015/04/11/writing-perspectives-from-eastern-europe-blog-three/.

Tardy, C. (2015). Discourses of internationalization and diversity in U.S. universities and programs In Martins, D. (Ed.), *Transnational writing program* (pp. 243–264). Utah State University Press.

Van Parijs, P. (2002). Linguistic justice. *Politics, Philosophy, and Economics, 1*(1), 59–74.

Appendix

The table comprises a list of the authors, the title, focus, and data of publication of the blog posts analyzed in this chapter. The posts addressing pedagogy are marked in a shade of gray.

Author	Title of blog post	Focus	Publication Date
Santosh Khadka	"Navigating the US Academy"	Pedagogy	January 26, 2015
Shyam Sharma	"Translingual, Transcultural, Transnational-From Buzzwords to Teaching Strategies" (2 posts)	Pedagogy	February 26, 2015
Shyam Sharma	"Transnational Presenters and Sessions at 4Cs15" (2 posts)	Announcement/ Dissemination	March 10, 2015
Moushumi Biswas	"Transnational Writing Blog Post"	Pedagogy	March 10, 2015
Ligia Mihut (facilitator and author) Monique Yoder Brooke Ricker Schreiber Ligia Mihut Natalia V. Smirnova Ivan Eubanks	"Writing Perspectives from Eastern Europe" blog series (3 posts) "The Importance of Writing Instruction: A Lithuanian Perspective" "EFL Writing Instruction in Serbia: One Perspective on Emerging Trends" "Perspectives on Writing from Romania" "Personal Reflections on Writing Instruction in Russia" "Academic Writing in Russia: A Writing Center Perspective"	Pedagogy/ Writing Traditions	March 27, 2015 April 11, 2015 April 11, 2015 April 11, 2015 April 11, 2015 April 11, 2015
Rita S. Nezami	"Bringing Global Issues into the Writing Class"	Pedagogy	June 26, 2015

Author	Title of blog post	Focus	Publication Date
Suresh Canagarajah/ Sara Alvarez Interview by Shakil Rabbi	Suresh Canagarajah on Translingualism: A (a four-part interview)	Theory	August 4, 2015; August 11, 2015; September 25, 2015
Suresh Canagarajah	Canagarajah's Discussion on Translingualism Extended: Predraft on Forthcoming Publication	Theory	September 20, 2015
Bruce Horner	"Moving Slowly: Transnational Composition"	History	April 2, 2016
Xiaoye You	"Taking Risks in Cross-Border Scholarship"	Theory and Research	April 22, 2016
Carrie Kilfoil	"What's the Difference Between "Translingual" and "Transnational" Composition?: Clarifying the Relationship between two Terms"	Theory	September 9, 2016

Afterword. Postmonolingual Projections: Translating Translinguality

Bruce Horner

UNIVERSITY OF LOUISVILLE

> Coexisting with these [language] practices there are representations—
> what people think about languages and the way they are spoken—rep-
> resentations that act on practices and are one of the factors of change.
>
> —*Calvet, 2006, p. 241*

This collection is part of a growing body of work attempting to forge a more productive approach to difference in language. Such work evinces, above all, the difficulties of breaking from the conceptual categories we have inherited for understanding difference in language—*representations*. I say inherited in the sense that these categories permeate the conditions of our thinking, present in the very language we use to think about language, and in the institutional categories and practices constituting our daily work with and on language as teachers, scholars, and public citizens. They are what we have to work with, and what we have to work on, and thereby, they shape and even define what we do and what we think about what we do. We can call these representations the language ideology of monolingualism.

Such attempts at change are not futile, however difficult they may seem. Instead, any sense of futility is itself an effect of that ideology, which (like all ideologies) presents itself as operating on material social history—time and space—from a position outside history, and (hence) as universal, unlimited in or by either time or space, simply the way things are and must be. The very attempts to forge something different index the ideological character of what is inherited, and, therefore, its vulnerability to revision, even refutation, through material social practice, to which ideology is by definition inadequate. Thus, as Calvet observes, we may, through language, re-represent language, language difference, and language relations, to ourselves and others, and thereby change language.

One feature of the language ideology of monolingualism is its identification of difference in language strictly in terms of form—glossodiversity. This is of a piece with its treatment of languages as outside material social practices, as indeed entities against which practices are to be measured (and usually found wanting). For the removal of language from practice renders language a matter of timeless, immaterial forms (abstracted from the full ecology of communicative practice). It is the treatment of languages as immaterial forms that renders sameness in language the norm, since that sameness depends on the evacuation of the crucial elements of time and space from communicative practice—all that inheres in the notion of "utterance." By contrast, we can see difference even in the reiteration of inherited language by virtue of the different spatio-temporal location of the reiteration from that which is reiterated.

It is at the point of utterance that translinguality enters as an insurgent view of language positing difference in language as itself the norm rather than a deviation from the norm. But this is at odds with monolingualist accounts of difference (and sameness) in language. The challenge of breaking with monolingualist accounts is that it requires refusing not only monolingualism's insistence on sameness, a.k.a. adherence to a chimerical set of language "standards," but also the alternative that monolingualist ideology offers to such sameness—what it proclaims as "different."

The challenge of breaking with monolingualist accounts of difference in language is exacerbated by the fact that the conditions making evident the inadequacies of monolingualist ideology as an account of language practice—signaled most clearly by the increasingly undeniable presence of heterogeneity in language practices attributed commonly to recent changes in the pace and directions of global migration and in global communication technologies—align with monolingualist ideology's definition of difference. There is more mixing, in f2f and global communication practices, of "different" people speaking and writing "different" languages. Such mixing makes increasingly evident the mythical character of the linguistic homogeneity posited by monolingualist ideology as the norm for either post (or pre-post) secondary classrooms, faculty, and nations (see Matsuda, 2006). But without discounting the reality of that mixing, and the challenge it poses to claims of monolingualism as the norm, acknowledgment of that reality need not in itself lead to any radical challenge to monolingualism's account of languages and language relations. Instead, what obtains most immediately as a consequence of that acknowledgment are pleas for tolerance of a pluralized version of monolingualism—multilingualism, a.k.a. linguistic diversity, both as a more accurate account of the reality on the ground and as an ideal to be pursued. We may characterize this as a shift from an assimilationist model (exemplified by "subtractive" language education policy) to an accommodationist model (exemplified by "bilingual" language education policy).

The strategy taken by the editors of this collection and their contributors to forge an alternative to either an assimilationist or accommodationist model is to focus on the "trans"—the crossing from and to, and the space of that crossing. Hence contributors address possibilities of not only trans-linguality (defined in various ways) but also trans-lating, trans-languaging, trans-nationality, and even (ideally) trans-formation. Such a strategy promises both to highlight the fluid movement between and within ostensibly discrete and stable languages and, as the editors argue, the shift from a monolingualist to a translingual "intellectual orientation," abjuring the more tempting, and hence prevalent, shift from mono- to multi-lingualism (monolingualism pluralized) that entails no shift in the conceptualization of language relations. But it is also the case that, as in instances of translanguaging, the state and act of movement carries with it both residues of the place of origin as well as of what is projected about the point of destination. For we find ourselves not in a condition of translinguality, any more than we find ourselves in a condition of monolinguality, but, rather, as Yasemin Yildiz (2012) has argued, in a "post-monolingual condition."

Perhaps the clearest evidence of our post-monolingual condition is the persistent association, if not conflation, of translinguality with transnationality and translanguaging, in contributions to this collection as well as in similar work, to the seeming neglect, if not exclusion, of translinguality among ostensible U.S. English monolinguals or their linguistic and civic equivalents elsewhere. For example, chapters in this collection do not focus on the exercise of translinguality among writers identified or who self-identify as U.S. English monolinguals except insofar as such persons encounter those marked as linguistic others: Hungarians (Palmer), Puerto Ricans (Khadka), Japanese video game characters (Roozen). Instead, the focus is either on sites where recognizable linguistic difference is institutionalized as the norm—e.g., Lebanon (Baalbaki et al.; Bou Ayash), or where encounters with such difference are orchestrated, as in Palmer's deployment of a Globally Networked Learning Environment to bring Hungarian and American students into conversation, or Khadka's involvement of English monolinguals with their "multilingual" others, or ESL courses and tutoring sessions (Campbell et al., Gramm), or graduate (and faculty) training of (primarily) non-English monolinguals in producing English academic writing (Lavelle and Ågren, and Summers).

Insofar as the increasingly undeniable presence of language difference introduced by the increasingly undeniable presence of a growing number of "transnationals" has served as catalyst for questioning monolingualism, this seems entirely justifiable. For, while the presence of these is neither necessary nor sufficient in itself for such questioning (language theorists having for some time now challenged key tenets of monolingualist ideology, (e.g., Firth & Wagner, 1997; Haugen, 1966; Paikeday, 1985) without recourse to the presence of transnational multilinguals, and adherence to monolingualist ideology continuing to persist despite their presence), it is an historical fact that the (call for the) development of orientations deemed "translingual" arose in response to that presence and the movement and intermixing of languages (see for example Horner, et al., 2010; Khubchandani, 1998; Kramsch, 1998; Liu, 1995; Modern Language Association, 2007; Singh, 1998; and cf. Bernabé et al., 1989, on *diversalité/créolité*).

There is, of course, a danger in focusing exclusively on sites where those whom monolingualism designates as deviant others—non-English speaking "multilinguals"—prevail, reinforcing monolingualism's definition of language difference as deviation from a norm of sameness in linguistic form. Translinguality, then, risks being understood merely as a distinctive and distinguishing feature of the language practices of "multilinguals," and hence something that "mainstream" (a.k.a. English monolingual) teachers, students, and, well, people can dismiss as irrelevant to normal life—at best a curious, exotic feature of "others": transnationals, multilinguals, *non*-native English speakers. In short, it can contribute to monolingualism's domestication of translinguality through its exoticization.

But this is the problematic of the post-monolingual condition. We cannot wish away monolingualism and its ongoing effects merely by invoking the specter of translingualism as the apparition of what is to come, like the inevitable revolution we can relax and wait for the arrival of. Instead, in the long meanwhile, language will very likely, in practice, largely remain a "countable," as will likewise the identities of language users, as inadequate as such representations may be as representations of language and language users. After all, long post/past Copernicus, we spinning on earth are still drawn to see the sun appear to "rise" and "set." Further, as Ligia Mihut cogently argues in her chapter, it is those whom monolingualism has designated its deviant others—again, the transnationals, multilinguals, *non*-native English speakers—who have the most immediately at stake in combating monolingualism and advancing a translingual orientation. It is no wonder, then, that those pursuing the latter orientation must engage the very terms against which that orientation is poised. Propulsion toward translingual orientations requires pushing against monolingualist tenets: friction is both necessary to and an inevitable product of movement.

Propitiously, the heat of such friction may well generate transformation of the dispositions and orientations of all those inhabiting the site of resistance, including those imagining themselves to be its "natives." And so, it is possible to discern destinations for us all in the trajectories of those propelled by the injustices wrought on them by monolingualism, and signposts by which we might work toward such destinations. That is to say, however much the attempts presented here may have originated in and aim quite justifiably to address the experiences of monolingualism's "others," these attempts are more broadly consequential in the ways forward they project for both those othered by monolingualism and those putatively favored by monolingualism—the ostensible "native English speakers" whom monolingualism privileges as the norm. This, then, may be what taking "globalized" approaches to the teaching of writing affords.

To illustrate, I will consider two chapters whose pedagogies might initially appear to be so directly tied to the "globalized"—a.k.a. non-U.S. based—settings in which they have developed as to seem largely inapplicable to other settings, and in particular, to the situation of those U.S. English monolinguals privileged as representatives of the cultural norm of monolingualism: Baalbaki et al.'s chapter discussing the use of Arabic as a home language in teaching English writing, and Lavelle and Ågren's chapter discussing the inculcation of translingual dispositions among "academically accomplished" multilingual professional and pre-professional scholars in Sweden working on the production of professional academic writing. Clearly there is no possibility of directly transferring the pedagogies discussed to other settings. Baalbaki et al., for example, base their pedagogy largely on the assumption that for most of their students, English will be a second or third language, with vernacular Arabic the L1 for the majority. And as Lavelle and Ågren caution, in their teaching they worked with "groups of writers with relatively high degrees of intrinsic motivation" and faced "none of the institutional impediments reported for other translingual innovations, where to varying degrees institutional architecture of various kinds impedes pedagogical initiatives" (this collection). Moreover, they note, they could "leverage" the fact that "all [their] participants use English as a lingua franca, both in the academy and in other endeavors," guaranteeing "a familiarity with multilingual interlocutors and with well-documented lingua-franca dispositions and communication strategies" (this collection) obviating the need for a pedagogy aimed at *developing* such dispositions and strategies.

That said, we might nonetheless translate the approaches they describe, keeping in mind the inevitable transformation of what is translated through the very act of translation (as Baalbaki et al. report their students observing). For example, we might well glean for other pedagogies the commitments and features that Lavelle and Ågren identify as characterizing their pedagogy—commitments to a "de-essentialized conception of language and languages," accepting the ideological operation of performative representations of language, acknowledging "language users' strong individual agency in carrying out this performance"; and strategies of "collaborative inquiry," leveraging students' "lingua-franca dispositions," and deploying "learning objects that focus . . . writers' prior knowledge and that help organize the conceptual space in which they exercise agency." Taking a mobilities perspective on dispositions, we can recognize that while the writers Lavelle and Ågren worked with were more inclined to adopt "lingua-franca" dispositions, those dispositions are themselves performative, positionings that writers adopt toward language use rather than ingrained characteristics, which accounts for what Lavelle and Ågren observe as the intrusion of "essentialist linguistic ideology" into conditions otherwise favorable to adopting translingual orientations. Dispositions and orientations toward language, then, are continually reworked as part of the work of courses, by students and teachers. Consequently, teachers, in collaboration with their students, must be prepared to re-present de-essentialized conceptions of language and the agency of writers in reproducing and revising language through their writing and reading. The commitments and strategies they outline are useful signposts for taking up such work.

Likewise, the course Baalbaki et al. describe brings out the strategic value of translation as a means of reworking notions of language and meaning production toward more translingual orientations. As they state, they use the "problematics of translation in teaching writing" to build on, rather than eradicate, "realities of [language] difference." One effect of their pedagogy is to increase sensitivity to the ostensible affordances of Arabic and English: as one student is quoted as observing, "'When we are working with several languages . . . we are capable of saying and expressing ourselves in a more enriched and elegant way because each language can have characteristics that another one doesn't have." But another effect is to engage students in the differences within either language produced by the act of utterance. For example, as one student reported discovering, "the English language is rich of words that are synonyms but can have different meanings," hence "[e]quating one language with one discourse is terribly limited" (quoting Canagarajah, 2006, p. 601). This arises as a result of engaging students in *multiple* and *collaborative* attempts at and comparisons of translations, which makes evident not only the difference arising from translating between one language and another but also the inevitable difference not merely of translation but among various such translations, and hence the agentive role of translators in producing meaning through translation both between and within languages. While the language ecology of the American University of Beirut necessarily differs from that obtaining at other colleges and universities (as shown by the other chapters), this simply means that any attempt at "transferring" the pedagogy Baalbaki et al. describe to other settings will itself entail the problematics of translation (see Horner & Tetreault, 2016). But, contrary to what monolingualist ideology would have us believe, this is normal, and translation inevitable, even within the "same" setting at different times, once the temporal location of any act (of speech, writing, teaching, learning) is recognized.

Engaging the problematics of such translation entails recognizing the ways in which, under the condition of post-monolinguality, monolingualist language ideology is part of the mix of representations acting on our, and our students', language practices. There is, then, no possibility of achieving a translingual orientation purified of residual monolingualist habits, dispositions, and beliefs, any more than it is possible, under the condition of post-monolinguality, of maintaining a monolingualist orientation purified of alternative possibilities, translinguality included. Global approaches may "afford," as current argot has it, the emergence of translingual dispositions, but they do not, cannot, produce them: globalization, after all, and lingua franca dispositions, have been with humanity for a long time (since, well, forever), yet these have not precluded the emergence and domination of monolingualist ideology and dispositions. In the space of movement through the act of translation, we bring with us elements of where we began, which are nonetheless transformed as they are transferred to new spatio-temporal settings, just as they then transform the setting into which they are brought by their presence.

So, for example, it is impossible to molt monolingualist conceptions of language—signaled, for example, by the invocation "language"—in discussions of, well, language and language difference. Instead, reverberations of those conceptions continue in dissonant relation to alternative conceptions introduced—what Bou Ayash productively terms a "tug-of-war between these coexisting yet competing ideological orientations and representations of language and language relations in literacy education." As Bou Ayash cautions, a "monolingual mindset . . . persists" "alongside a growing translingual-affiliated movement in language- and literacy-related scholarship," and it persists "*despite* its emergence from the context of eighteenth-century European-based thinking about language . . . and its failure to attend to drastic changes in the sociocultural realities and linguistic constellations of the twenty-first century" (emphasis added).

We can see such dissonance in chapters of this collection itself, as when, for example, transinguality is used to identify a particular kind of writer or form of writing—conflating transinguality with translanguaging and those who translanguage (e.g., Campbell et al., Mina & Cimasko), or when, in the pursuit of multiliteracies, students are asked to serve as emissaries of single, uniform "home" cultures (e.g., Khadka) and their languages. Such notions appear alongside the treatment of translinguality as an orientation not tied to any particular linguistic forms. It may be, however, that the identification of translinguality with the production of specific linguistic forms—what monolingualism defines as difference in language—is one of the *negative* affordances of globalized approaches. That is to say, such approaches, in their concern with those marked by monolingualism as "other" on the basis of recognizable difference in forms of language, are likely to draw attention precisely to an acceptance of the identification of difference in language in terms only of differences in form. Similarly, they are likely to identify agency strictly with the production of such differences—deviations from the standard—and to neglect the difference produced in reiterations of what is (formally) the same, and thereby invisible as difference, and as the exercise of agency, at least within the terms monolingualism offers. But such dissonance is the inevitable accompaniment to another "trans" term: transition. It is both a sign of change and a sign of the friction necessarily accompanying such change. Like dissonance in Western tonal music, it is a sign of, productive of, and necessary to tension (as in musical "suspension") and movement. A translingual disposition attuned to that dissonance is what globalized approaches to the teaching of writing may require, and afford.

References

Bernabé, J., Chamoiseau, P. & Confiant, R. (1989). *Éloge de la créolité.* Gallimard.

Calvet, L-J. (2006). *Towards an ecology of world languages.* (A. Brown, Trans.) Polity. (Original work, *Pour une écologie des langues du monde,* published 1999)

Canagarajah, S. (2006). Toward a writing pedagogy of shuttling between languages: Learning from multilingual writers. *College English, 68*(6), 589–604.

Firth, A. & Wagner, J. (1997). On discourse, communication, and (some) fundamental concepts in SLA research. *Modern Language Journal, 81*(3), 285–300.

Haugen, E. (1966). Dialect, language, nation. *American Anthropologist, 68*(4), 922–935.

Horner, B., Lu, M. & Matsuda, P. K. (2010). *Cross-language relations in composition.* Southern Illinois University Press.

Horner, B. & Tetreault, L. (2016). Translation as (global) writing. *Composition Studies, 44*(1), 13–30.

Khubchandani, L. (1998). A plurilingual ethos: A peep into the sociology of language. *Indian Journal of Applied Linguistics, 24,* 5–37.

Kramsch, C. (1998). The privilege of the intercultural speaker. In M. Byram & M. Fleming (Eds.), *Language learning in intercultural perspective: Approaches through drama and ethnography* (pp. 15–31). Cambridge University Press.

Liu, L. H. (1995). *Translingual practice: Literature, national culture, and translated modernity—China, 1900–1937*. Stanford University Press.

Matsuda, P. K. (2006). The myth of linguistic homogeneity in U.S. college composition. *College English, 68*, 637- 651.

Modern Language Association Ad Hoc Committee on Foreign Languages. (2007). Foreign languages and higher education: New structures for a changed world. Modern Language Association. https://www.mla.org/Resources/Research/Surveys-Reports-and-Other-Documents/Teaching-Enrollments-and-Programs/Foreign-Languages-and-Higher-Education-New-Structures-for-a-Changed-World.

Paikeday, T. (1985/2003). *The native speaker is dead!* Lexicography.

Singh, R. (Ed.) (1998). *The native speaker: Multilingual perspectives*. Sage.

Yildiz, Y. (2012). *Beyond the mother tongue: The postmonolingual condition*. Fordham University Press.

∫ Contributors

Maria Ågren is Professor of History at Uppsala University, where she is Director of Studies for the Ph.D. program in history. Her most recent books are *The State as Master: Gender, State Formation and Commercialisation in Urban Sweden, 1650–1780* (Manchester University Press, 2017) and *Making a Living, Making a Difference: Gender and Work in Early Modern European Society* (Ed.) (Oxford University Press, 2017). Her work has also appeared in journals such as *Past and Present*, *Urban History*, and *Continuity and Change*. In addition to early modern history, her research interests include the digital humanities (especially research infrastructure) and the academic writing of multilingual scholars.

Rula Baalbaki is an instructor of literary translation courses at the Department of English at the American University of Beirut. Among her published translations are: Said Akl's *If Lebanon Were to Speak*, Amin Rihani's *Rihanniyyat Essays*, Ussaima Darwiche's *The Smoke Tree*, Yahya Bal-Qassem's poems in *After Images*, as well as classical and contemporary Arabic and English poems. Having taught writing courses for 10 years, she tries to establish that literary translation is a re-writing occupation which employs cultural, historical and stylistic elements in the L1 (Arabic) to render into L2 (English) linguistically specific equivalents. Her current endeavor is to collate in a publication the highlights of the poems and lyrics which have been translated by her students and celebrated in academic/artistic musical performances at AUB.

Suzanne Blum Malley is Provost at Methodist University. Her scholarly interests include multilingual and digital/multimodal literacies and globally networked learning environments. She served as a founding executive committee member of the Rhetoric, Composition, and Writing Studies (RCWS) Literacy Studies Forum of the Modern Language Association (2015–2019, chair 2018, secretary 2017). Her recent publications include "Ludic is the New Phatic: Making Connections in Global, Internet-mediated Learning Environments" in *Thinking Globally, Composing Locally*.

Nancy Bou Ayash is Associate Professor of Language and Rhetoric at the University of Washington. Her work focuses on language ideologies, language politics in the study and teaching of writing, and translingual literacies. She has published in *College English*, *Writing Program Administration Journal* and several edited collections. She is the author of *Toward Translingual Realities in Composition: (Re)Working Local Language Representations and Practices* (Utah State University Press, 2019).

Shireen Campbell is Professor of English and Director of the Writing Center at Davidson College. Shireen's research interests include writing center theory and practice, second language writing, digital writing, and information fluency. Recent publications range from creative nonfiction to pedagogic scholarship on classroom/library partnerships to enhance student information fluency. Currently, she is collaborating with colleagues on a longitudinal project examining various aspects of the rhetorical and linguistic development of advanced multilingual writers.

Tony Cimasko is the ESL Composition coordinator in the Department of English at Miami University in Oxford, Ohio, teaching graduate courses on L2 writing theory and pedagogy as well as undergraduate and graduate second language writing courses. His ongoing research interests include multimodal composition, genre analysis and learning, professional and pedagogical genres, and feedback practices. His work has been published in the *Journal of Second Language Writing, Computers and Composition, English for Specific Purposes,* and *Written Communication,* and elsewhere. He was the co-editor of *Foreign Language Writing Instruction: Principles and Practices.*

Juheina Fakhreddine graduated from the Lebanese University with a teaching diploma in English in 1974 and worked for many years in secondary schools around Lebanon before going on to pursue her MA in education with an emphasis on teaching English as a second language from LAU in 2004. Her research focused on innovative methods and strategies for teaching the English language. She passed away in October 2018.

Rebeca Fernandez is Multilingual Writing Coordinator and Associate Professor of Writing and Educational Studies at Davidson College. Her research focuses on bilingualism, literacy, and writing development among international and domestic multilingual students. Recent scholarship includes a co-edited volume *Preparing Adult English Learners to Write for College and the Workplace* and longitudinal research of Chinese L2 writers with Shireen Campbell and Kyo Koo.

Alanna Frost is Associate Professor in the English Department at the University of Alabama Huntsville. Her work is invested in the intersections of students' communicative realities, English-education practice, and English language policy. She served as a founding executive committee member of the Rhetoric, Composition, and Writing Studies (RCWS) Literacy Studies Forum of the Modern Language Association (2015–2020, chair 2019, secretary 2018).

Marylou Gramm is a Senior Lecturer in the Department of English and the coordinator of ESL writing at the University of Pittsburgh, and prior to that she directed the writing center at Barnard College. Her Ph.D. dissertation in comparative literature from New York University focused on collaborative writing practices in early eighteenth-century London and Paris, and she has published essays on the novels of George Sand and about teaching literature and writing to international students from China.

Bruce Horner is Endowed Chair in Rhetoric and Composition, where he teaches courses in composition, composition theory and pedagogy, and literacy studies. His recent books include *Crossing Divides: Exploring Translingual Writing Pedagogies and Programs*, co-edited with Laura Tetreault, *Economies of Writing*, co-edited with Brice Nordquist and Susan Ryan, and *Rewriting Composition: Terms of Exchange*.

Yu-Kyung Kang is Assistant Professor in the English Department at Gonzaga University. She researches and publishes on transnational literacy, multilingual writing, and writing center practice and theory. As an international and ESL student with a background in Teaching English as a Second Language (M.A.) and Writing Studies (Ph.D.), in various teaching (ESL and first-year composition courses) and administrative capacities, she has been devoted to improving literacy support for the international and multilingual student population. Her current work now includes multilingual literacy practices of international/transnational scholars and teachers in U.S. higher education.

Santosh Khadka is Associate Professor of English at California State University, Northridge. He earned his Ph.D. in composition and cultural rhetoric from Syracuse University. He has authored a monograph and scores of articles and also co-edited three books. His monograph, *Multiliteracies, Emerging Media, and College Writing Instruction*, recently came out from Routledge. He has co-edited two books on multimodality—*Bridging the Multimodal Gap: From Theory to Practice* (Utah State University Press), and *Designing and Implementing Multimodal Curricula and Programs* (Routledge). His third co-edited book, *Narratives of Marginalized Identities in Higher Education: Inside and Outside the Academy*, was released earlier in 2018 from Routledge. He now teaches graduate and undergraduate courses in writing, rhetoric, digital media, and professional and business communication.

Malaki Khoury is Instructor in the Department of English at American University of Beirut, where she has been a member of the faculty since 1987. Her research interests include ethical writing and the teaching of writing. She has published articles in conference proceedings and chapters in edited collections, including *Emerging Writing Research from the Middle East-North Africa Region* (2017) and *Twentieth-century Arabic writers* (2014) and served as editor, with others, of *Ra'if Khuri: Al Kaatibu l Tanweeryy* (*Raif Khuri: The Enlightened Writer*).

Julia Kiernan is Assistant Professor at Lawrence Technological University. Her scholarly interests include pedagogical and curricular design across the digital humanities, translingual and transnational writing, science communication, and STEAM education.

Kyosung Koo is Director of Educational Technology in the College of Business at the University of Texas at San Antonio where he provides leadership in the development of strategic approaches for the integration of technology. He holds a Ph.D. in second language acquisition, and his research efforts have focused on corpus linguistics and technology-assisted language learning.

Thomas Lavelle directs the Center for Modern Languages at the Stockholm School of Economics. His current research projects address topics at the interface of language and learning in higher education. Beyond translingualism and the challenges to translingual pedagogy, these topics include lingua francas as media of instruction, materiality in the forms of written feedback, and the interplay of speech and writing in undergraduates' academic communication. He currently chairs the CCC Group on Transnational Composition.

Ligia A. Mihut is Associate Professor of English at Barry University where she teaches first-year composition, techniques of research, and professional writing courses. Her areas of research include immigrant literacies/rhetorics, writing for social justice, and transnationalism. Drawing on two years of ethnographic research, Ligia is currently working on a book, *Immigrants, Brokers, and Literacy as Affinity* exploring literacy's entanglement in networks of economic and political frames. As the recipient of the 2015–2016 CCCC Research Initiative Award (with Alvarez, Khadka, and Sharma), she is also involved in a comparative study of writing practices in four different countries, Romania, Nepal, India, and Colombia. Her work has published in *Literacy in Composition Studies, Reflections,* and a few edited collections.

Lilian Mina is Assistant Professor and the Director of Composition at Auburn University at Montgomery. She researches digital rhetoric with focus on multimodal composing and writing teachers' use of digital technologies. Her research in multilingual composition is centered around multilingual writers' use of digital technologies and examining their (digital) writing experiences. She is also interested in WPA scholarship, especially (technology) professional development of writing teachers, program assessment, and curriculum development. Her work has appeared in multiple journals and edited collections.

Zsuzsanna Bacsa Palmer is Assistant Professor in the Writing Department at Grand Valley State University where she teaches courses in professional writing, business communication, and document design. Because she believes that intercultural communication skills are crucial, she frequently involves her students in online projects where they collaborate with students in various countries to create documents and digital interfaces. Her research interests include intercultural communication, online writing pedagogy, visual rhetoric, website accessibility, and translingual writing. Her research has been published in edited collections, in the *Journal of Technical Writing and Communication,* and in *Business and Professional Communication Quarterly.*

Souha Riman teaches writing courses at the department of English at the American University of Beirut, and has previously taught several linguistics courses. Tutoring in the riting Center, she gained insight into students' writing needs and struggles which informed her teaching practices. Her current research examines how students' home language acts as a resource in an English writing course, and her graduate research explored how dialectal variation in Lebanese Arabic reflects religious affiliation.

Kevin Roozen is Professor of Writing and Rhetoric at the University of Central Florida. Kevin's research examines the development of literate identities and practices along the expansive histories that reach across and weave together people's multiple textual engagements. Co-authored with Joe Erickson, Kevin's recent book *Expanding Literate Landscapes: Persons, Practices, and Sociohistoric Perspectives of Disciplinary Development* (CC Digital Press/Utah State University Press, 2017) argues for increased attention to the histories that people and their textual practices trace through their lifespans and lifeworlds. Kevin's work has appeared in journals including *Written Communication, Research in the Teaching of English, College Composition and Communication,* and in a number of edited collections as well.

Sarah Summers is Associate Professor of English at Rose-Hulman Institute of Technology. Her scholarly work focuses on graduate writing and using design thinking to teach writing. She teaches advanced writing courses including grant writing and digital writing as well as courses in disability studies and visual rhetoric.